School Desegregation in the 21st Century

School Desegregation
in the
21st Century

Edited by
Christine H. Rossell
David J. Armor
Herbert J. Walberg

Westport, Connecticut
London

Library of Congress Cataloging-in-Publication Data

School desegregation in the 21st century / edited by Christine H. Rossell,
David J. Armor, and Herbert J. Walberg.
p. cm.
Includes bibliographical references and index.
ISBN 0-275-97769-2 (alk. paper)
1. School integration—United States. I. Rossell, Christine H. II. Armor,
David J. III. Walberg, Herbert J., 1937–
LC214.2 S353 2002
379.2'63'0973—dc21 2002025303

British Library Cataloguing in Publication Data is available.

Library of Congress Catalog Card Number: 2002025303
ISBN: 0-275-97769-2

First published in 2002

Praeger Publishers, 88 Post Road West, Westport, CT 06881
An imprint of Greenwood Publishing Group, Inc.
www.praeger.com

Printed in the United States of America

The paper used in this book complies with the
Permanent Paper Standard issued by the National
Information Standards Organization (Z39.48-1984).

10 9 8 7 6 5 4 3 2 1

Contents

Chapter 1

Introduction: Assessing the Promise of *Brown*

Christine H. Rossell, David J. Armor, and Herbert J. Walberg

School desegregation, in particular the court ordered "forced busing" that began in the 1970s, has been one of the most controversial issues in public education in this century. Although it no longer receives the national headlines that it did in the 1970s, hundreds of school systems, particularly larger ones, maintain desegregation policies, and many are still under court orders that originated decades ago. Nearly three-fourths of the 150 largest school districts in the United States had a desegregation plan in 1991 or earlier, as did four-fifths of those larger than 5,000 students. Local controversies continue to erupt over such issues as unitary status (ending existing court orders), busing to foster "economic" balance, and even new lawsuits to compel metropolitan desegregation. Recent unitary hearings and decisions have occurred in such diverse districts as Tampa, Florida; New Castle County, Delaware; Cleveland, Ohio; Prince George's County, Maryland; and Woodland Hills, Pennsylvania. Local board initiatives to bus for economic balance have occurred in La Crosse and Wausau, Wisconsin. Metropoliton desegregation litigation or controversy has occured in Hartford, Connecticut; Minneapolis and St. Paul, Minnesota; and Englewood/Tenafly, New Jersey.

Some people are surprised to learn that new desegregation plans have been ordered by federal courts during the 1990s and that they are still in place. For example, a "controlled choice" busing plan was ordered by a federal court for the Rockford, Illinois, school system in fall 1997. A second example is East Baton Rouge, Louisiana, where a voluntary plan with magnet schools was ordered by a federal court in the fall of 1996. Another example is Lafayette, Louisiana, where a federal court ordered a new desegregation to be implemented in 2000 after decades of litigation. After almost fifty years of controversy, why is school desegregation still a burning issue in so many communities as we move into the 21st century?

As we have noted elsewhere, the answer is not simple because it involves many different institutions, ideas, and players. It involves the courts and the complicated and changing case law on civil rights. It involves decades of social science theory and research, much of it incorporated into court decisions. It involves educators, school boards, and educational theories. Above all, it involves strongly held views by advocacy groups about the rights of individual students, the culpability of institutions for observed inequality, and the obligation of these same institutions to correct inequalities (Armor 1995: 4).

These strongly held views are driven, in large part, by the moral force of the civil rights movement and *Brown v. Board of Education.* No single court decision has had more moral force than *Brown,* and no other struggle has been as morally significant as the struggle for racial integration of American life. Nor has any other social policy been as strongly supported or idealized by social scientists. Social scientists provided the research evidence for the *Brown* decision and they were the primary support for racial balance plans in the 1970s and 1980s.

SOCIAL SCIENCE RESEARCH
AND SCHOOL DESEGREGATION LAW

School desegregation more than any other educational or social policy is driven by court decisions. Over the last fifty years, the parties involved in school desegregation litigation have used social science studies and expert testimony to support various claims and counterclaims during various stages of the litigation. These litigation stages can be broken down into liability, remedy, and unitary determinations, and different kinds of social science studies are appropriate for each stage. The chapters in this book review most of the social science research issues raised in school desegregation litigation, as well as offer a historical perspective (chapter 2) and a discussion of the major legal issues (chapter 3).

As chapters 2 and 3 indicate, the first stage of litigation culminates in a violation hearing where the court determines if the school district is guilty of de jure, or official, acts of segregation. At this stage, the court hears evidence on the extent to which school racial imbalance or other racial disparities are a result of racial discrimination on the part of the school district. During the early years of desegregation litigation, and mostly in southern school districts, evidence and testimony focused mainly on the existence of one-race schools and the failure of school district officials to change the student assignment process to eliminate one-race schools.

Later, in northern school districts, this evidence included not only the actions of school district officials, but survey research and demographic evidence on the behavior of residents in their choice of where to live and the process by which these choices create one-race neighborhoods and then one-race schools. A major legal debate, which has been paralleled in social science research, is the extent to which housing segregation (and the associated school segregation caused by neighborhood schools) is caused by government action and hence is unconstitutional, or by the private decisions of individuals and hence is legal (chapter 5).

If a school district is found guilty of intentional discrimination, the court must determine an appropriate remedy, which in almost all cases involves a new student assignment plan (chapter 3). The relevant social science evidence at this stage of the remedy includes the projected levels of desegregation for alternative plans, projected enrollment and enrollment losses caused by the plan, and the behavioral intentions of parents if the remedy is enacted (chapter 4). The latter includes evidence from public opinion surveys on the percentage of parents who will withdraw their child from the public schools if a particular plan is implemented and the intentions of parents to voluntarily transfer their child to an opposite-race school in a different neighborhood. Evidence on the outcomes of prior plans is also introduced. The remedy typically focuses on racial quotas in the schools, but it occasionally includes racial quotas in classrooms, changes in disciplinary methods, and the imposition of specific educational programs designed to produce racial equity if racial discrimination or violations were found in these areas.

Some years after the plan has been implemented, a school district can petition the court for unitary status, that is, to be freed from court supervision (chapters 2 and 3). The term "unitary status" comes from the notion that since the original violation was having a dual school system—one for black students and one for white students—the school district will have fulfilled its constitutional obligation when it has a single set of schools for all children without regard to their race, that is, a "unitary" school system.

Attaining unitary status involves demonstrating not only that there is a single set of integrated schools, but that the school district has achieved nondiscrimination and equity in all aspects of the school system. In a sense, unitary hearings are similar to violation hearings because the issue at this stage is whether the school district is still in violation, and whether it has eliminated all "vestiges" of the prior segregated system to the extent practicable. In order for a court to grant unitary status and dismiss the lawsuit, it must find that the school system has eliminated discrimination and established equity in six areas, often called *Green* factors (*Green v. County School Board of New Kent County*, 391 U.S. 430 [1968]). These factors are student assignment, faculty assignment, staff assignment, facilities, transportation, and extracurricular activities. There are also some additional, or "extra-*Green*," factors that are often assessed in a unitary hearing, including academic achievement, classroom integration, program equity, special education, and disciplinary procedures. Chapters 2 and 3 deal with the unitary status process. Chapters 4 to 9 deal with the most contentious of the unitary issues—student assignment, vestiges of segregation, student achievement, classroom desegregation, and disciplinary actions.

THE ORIGINS OF SCHOOL DESEGREGATION

This book begins with the history and legal background of school desegregation from the 19th century to the present (chapters 2 and 3). The seeds of school desegregation were planted in 1868 when the Fourteenth Amendment failed to provide equal education for blacks in the South. By 1885, all of the former Confederate states had passed laws segregating Negroes from whites in every walk of life and this was not successfully challenged until more than a half-century later. The most important of these decisions, of course, was *Brown v. Board of Education,* which began the dismantling of state-imposed segregation. At 12:52 P.M. on 17 May 1954, Chief Justice Warren read the eleven-page opinion to a hushed courtroom: "We unanimously conclude that in the field of public education the doctrine of separate but equal' has no place."

The principles established in *Brown* may be surprising in light of the modern conception of school desegregation. Oliver Brown testified that he wanted his eight-year-old daughter, Linda, to be able to go to her neighborhood school. Under de jure segregation, she was required to cross a railroad yard to catch a bus that brought her twenty-one blocks to a school which often did not open for another half hour. Her father, Oliver Brown, testified that she should have been able to attend her neighborhood school five blocks from their home. As a mother, Linda Brown later said:

I don't want my kids bused. I know what that's like. One of the reasons I went to court back in the 1950s was to escape busing and all the hassle it causes. Kids like me were taken out of our neighborhoods and bused across town. I still feel kids should be able to attend schools in their own neighborhoods. (Wolters 1984: 270)

The Supreme Court agreed with the Browns on this issue. Neighborhood schools were considered a legitimate desegregation tool by the Supreme Court in *Brown II* (349 U.S. 294, 300–301 [1955]) when it opined that a permissible remedy would be the "revision of school districts and attendance areas into *compact units* (emphasis added) to achieve a system of determining admission to the public schools on a nonracial basis." A year later, the federal district court approved a desegregation plan in which ". . . hereafter, except in exceptional circumstances, school children irrespective of race or color shall be required to attend the school in the district in which they reside and that color or race is no element warranting a deviation from this basic principle" (*Brown v. Board of Education of Topeka*, 139 F.Supp. 468–469 [1955]). The district court went on to elaborate that although one of the schools in Topeka was "inhabited entirely by colored students, no violation of any constitutional right results because they are compelled to attend the school in the district in which they live" (139 F.Supp. 468–470 [1955])."

In the same year, in *Briggs v. Elliott* (1955), Circuit Court Judge John J. Parker further expounded on the non-discrimination principle established in *Brown*:

Nothing in the Constitution or in the decision of the Supreme Court takes away from the people the freedom to choose the schools they attend. The Constitution, in other words, does not require integration. It merely forbids discrimination. (*Briggs v. Elliott*, 132 F.Supp. 776–777 [1955])

But, after fourteen years of little actual desegregation, the Supreme Court established in *Green v. County School Board* (1968) that it was not enough for school districts to stop discriminating. School districts were required to develop a plan that promised realistically to convert promptly to a system without a "white" school and a "Negro" school, but just schools. In short, the Constitution did require integration after all.

THE HARM OF SEGREGATION AND THE BENEFIT OF DESEGREGATION

This change in legal doctrine from the principle of nondiscrimination to the principle of affirmative action was motivated, at least in part, by a belief in the harm and benefit thesis. The harm and benefit thesis (chapter 5) states that if schools, staff, and programs are thoroughly integrated and resources allocated equitably, the psychological and educational harm of segregation would be eliminated, and African American children would be able to compete with whites on an even footing not only in school, but in their adult lives.

The harm and benefit thesis appeared prominently in the research of Professor Kenneth B. Clark of City College of New York. In his testimony in *Brown*, he described an experiment conducted in segregated schools in Georgia in which he had asked black children questions about the relative attractiveness of a black doll and a white doll. A majority of black children in segregated schools preferred to play with the white doll, indicated it was a "nice color," and said the black doll looked "bad." About one-third of the children said the white doll looked like them (Bartz and Maehr 1984: 144–46). From these results, Professor Clark concluded that de jure segregated schools had a detrimental effect on the self-esteem of black children:

> I think it is the desire of the Negro to be a human being and to be treated as a human being without regard to skin color. He can only have pride in race—and a healthy and mature pride in race—when his own government does not constantly and continuously tell him, 'Have no pride in race,' by constantly segregating him. (Kluger 1976: 498)

Clark's research, and that of other social scientists, is cited in footnote 11 of *Brown* as evidence of the harm of segregation (Brameld 1949; Chein 1949; Clark 1950; Deutscher and Chein 1948; Frazier 1949; Myrdal 1944; Witmer and Kotinsky 1952). This notion that school desegregation is beneficial to black children, independent of the effect of simply eliminating racial discrimination, gained support from the 1966 Coleman Report and the 1967 U.S. Commission on Civil Rights report which found that black children who went to school with whites had higher achievement.

But there were some important qualifications to the benefit that could be obtained from school desegregation, particularly with regard to interracial friendships and positive racial attitudes. The social scientists who filed an amicus curiae brief in the *Brown* case offered the following qualifications:

> Under certain circumstances desegregation . . . has been observed to lead to the emergence of more favorable attitudes and friendlier relations between the races . . . There is less likelihood of unfriendly relations when change is simultaneously introduced into all units of a social institution . . . The available evidence also suggests the importance of consistent and firm enforcement of the new policy by those in authority. It indicates also the importance of such factors as the absence of competition . . . the possibility of contacts which permit individuals to learn about one another as individuals, and the possibility of equivalence of positions and functions among the participants. (Allport and 35 cosigners 1953: 437–38)

Thus, from the beginning there were at least some social scientists who admitted that school desegregation might accomplish positive race relations and interracial friendships only under ideal conditions not likely to be found in the average school. However, this caveat, like many caveats, was largely ignored. The school districts that implemented school desegregation were preoccupied with complying with their court orders, which, after 1968, generally meant racially balancing the schools. The plaintiffs' attorneys who monitored school desegregation typically maintained that attaining racial quotas in every aspect of school life would produce racial equity and positive outcomes. If it did not, it was because the school districts were still discriminating.

We are not saying here that a belief in psychological harm was the major basis of the *Brown* decision; the Court clearly stated that separate schools were "inherently unequal," a doctrine that may not depend on social science evidence. But the harm thesis played a major role in many lower-court decisions during the 1960s, and it also provided a justification for some of the educational remedies that became popular starting in the 1970s.

ASSUMPTIONS ABOUT
SCHOOL DESEGREGATION OUTCOMES

In its simplest form, the harm and benefit thesis offers a simple model of school desegregation that has guided most of the litigation of the last half-century. Segregation has stigmatized black children, causing lower self-esteem and leading to lower achievement, lack of participation in advanced courses, lower graduation rates, higher suspension rates, and, ultimately, lower educational and occupational attainments in their adult lives. School desegregation would eliminate this stigma, thereby raising both self-esteem and achievement of black children so that the achievement gap would be eliminated. It would also provide the opportunity for interracial friendships, reduce prejudicial behavior of whites, and ultimately equalize all other student outcomes such as graduation rates, suspension rates, and enrollment in advanced courses. It should be noted, as well, that this simple model does not recognize any costs that might accrue to desegregation plans, such as monetary costs, the costs of white flight by parents who object to busing, or the costs of lost community support such as an inability to pass construction bonds.

This model of the benefits of school desegregation probably motivated the racial balance plans of the 1970s and 1980s. The abandonment of the non-discrimination principle in *Brown* and the adoption of affirmative action principles of mandatory racial balance quotas and crosstown busing makes sense only if one believes that inequity is caused by racially isolated schools, not discrimination.

This model is also the standard used by plaintiffs when assessing whether school districts are unitary. According to plaintiffs, although the school district may have complied with the court order's racial quotas, any differences in achievement, course enrollment, graduation rates, suspensions, and other student activities are vestiges of the dual school system.

The social scientists writing in this book subscribe to a more complex model of school desegregation. The complexity stems from considering a wide range of factors and conditions that are ignored by the simple model. These include demographic forces that affect the degree of desegregation that can be attained, the type of desegregation plan adopted that impacts on the effectiveness of a plan, the variety and scope of school programs that are available to students in the desegregated district such as cooperative learning and multicultural learning, and last but not least, the socioeconomic characteristics of families and neighborhoods which have independent effects on such student outcomes as achievement, dropout rates, and self-esteem. These additional causal variables must be taken into account before one can determine if school desegregation is going to be effective and whether differences in student outcomes are a function of racial discrimination in the schools rather than of factors outside the control of the school system.

In the complex model, an evaluation of school desegregation must also include cost factors. These include phenomena like white flight (from busing), protest demonstrations, protest voting (such as voting down school bonds), public perceptions of low school quality, and the dissatisfaction of both black and white parents over their lack of school choice and neighborhood schools. One of these costs, white flight, has a direct effect on the extent to which the schools are effectively desegregated. Because it affects the amount of desegregation achieved, by the mid-1970s the courts were taking white flight into account in choosing among alternative plans. In addition, school white flight and residential change have been considered by the courts in determining whether districts were unitary. The courts are tolerant of school racial imbalance if it was caused by demographic white losses from the school system, rather than from the school district's failure to implement part of a desegregation order.

SCHOOL RACIAL BALANCE

The first critical task of a school district under a desegregation order is to devise a plan so that black and white children are actually going to school together. According to the harm and benefit theory, everything else is dependent on that. But how do we measure school desegregation? The definition of desegregation was neither self-evident nor constant during the early years of remedy. The permissible remedies have also varied over time as new evidence on the effectiveness and efficiency of different types of desegregation plans in achieving desegregated schools was published. Voluntary desegregation plans and neighborhood schools were permissible from 1954 to 1968 until evidence mounted that in many, if not most, school districts, this did not desegregate black schools. The Supreme Court responded to this evidence by ruling in *Swann* that racial balance, defined as each school's racial composition approximating the racial composition of the school district, had to be achieved in all the schools even if it meant long-distance busing.

The effectiveness of the racial balance strategies—school pairings, changes in attendance boundaries, magnet schools, and majority to minority (M to M) transfers—can be measured simply by the number of schools that achieved numerical balances similar to the overall percentages in the district as a whole. This is typically the court's approach.

Another measure—interracial exposure—has been used in research to assess the effectiveness of desegregation plans, and, in a number of school desegregation cases, to choose from among alternative desegregation plans. Interracial exposure—the percentage white in the average black child's school—measures not just whether whites are evenly distributed across schools, but the absolute level of contact between the races. Because interracial exposure goes up with desegregation transfers, but down with white flight, it measures the net benefit of different strategies for achieving school desegregation.

Interracial exposure, racial imbalance, and white enrollment trends are assessed in chapter 4 with data from a national random sample of 600 school districts from 1968 to 1991. These outcomes vary according to the kind of school desegregation plan—that is, whether it is voluntary, mandatory, or controlled choice. The prevalence of each type of plan as of 1991 is also presented. The mandatory reassignment plans were still the most prevalent plan in 1991.

With so many school districts attaining unitary status in the 1980s and 1990s, it might be expected that school desegregation would decline precipitously. The conventional wisdom is that it is only the court orders that keep the schools racially balanced. But chapter 4 presents some surprising results on this issue. Indeed, one of the great successes of the civil rights movement has apparently been to convince school districts that racial diversity is a desirable goal.

THE RACIAL COMPOSITION OF CITIES AND THEIR SCHOOL DISTRICTS

Although school racial balance has been maintained during the 1980s and 1990s, interracial exposure has not. The percentage white in the average black child's school has declined along with the percentage white in the medium and large school districts of the United States, particularly those under a court-ordered school desegregation plan. The United States is becoming less white, and school districts that are or were under court order are becoming less white at an even faster pace than the rest of the country.

Chapter 5 uses census data to explore these and other demographic issues in liability, remedy, and unitary hearings in Boston, Denver, Charlotte (Mecklenburg County), Kansas City, St. Louis, Tampa (Hillsborough County), and Prince George's County, Maryland. The first use of demographic analysis was in liability hearings. But, as previously noted, demographic issues were more important in determining liability in districts that had never had dual school systems—that is, the northern districts. In these districts, the courts examined the role of school siting, optional attendance zones, student transfer policies, and individual consumer preferences to determine how much of the school racial imbalance was due to the actions of the school board and how much to the behavior of individuals in choosing where to live.

Demographic information has also been used in remedy hearings to inform the court's decision on proposed modifications to a plan. Most importantly for the courts' purposes is the change in the resident school age population of each race. Many courts have decided, on the basis of demographic information, to limit the number of schools required to be racially balanced or to order a voluntary, rather than a mandatory, reassignment plan.

At the time of a unitary hearing, the court will want to know whether deviation from the court order in the schools that are desegregated is caused by demographic change or school board actions. Beginning with *Swann* in 1971, the courts have concluded that although neither neighborhood schools nor one-race schools offends the constitution, a school board that has already been found liable has the burden of showing that one-race schools are not vestiges of the prior dual school system.

Regardless of their cause, these desegregation outcomes constrain how much integration can be achieved. Racial balance is increasingly irrelevant in the many school systems that are now overwhelmingly minority.

EQUAL ACHIEVEMENT

School districts must not only eliminate one-race schools to the extent practicable and achieve some semblance of racial balance, but they are frequently expected to achieve equity in educational outcomes. In many cases, the simple model of school desegregation envisioned by some social scientists serves as the standard by which school districts are deemed to be unitary (that is, desegregated schools should produce equal outcomes), and so in one sense a unitary hearing becomes a hearing on the veracity of a social science theory. As chapter 6 will show, however, studies of desegregated school districts have failed to support the simple model.

The first, and probably most prominent, benefit of desegregated schools envisioned by some social scientists is that the academic achievement of black students would come to equal the academic achievement of their white counterparts. Indeed, as far as most African-American parents are concerned, this is the raison d'être of school desegregation; it trumps all other outcomes.

Chapter 6 answers the following questions about school desegregation and achievement. First, what is the state of empirical evidence on the relationship between school desegregation and achievement? Can one fairly conclude that desegregation has or has not improved minority achievement or closed the achievement gap to a significant degree? These questions are answered with evidence from several important historical studies and the more recent National Assessment of Educational Progress.

It is sometimes claimed that attaining true school integration means not only racially balancing the schools, but also implementing one or more of the following additional treatments: (1) assigning faculty to balance the staff

by experience or education, as well as by race; (2) providing greater resources (e.g., smaller classes or after-school tutorials) to minority children
than what they would receive under a simple "equity" rule; (3) eliminating
ability grouping, (4) imposing racial quotas for gifted and talented programs, and (5) eliminating prerequisites for honors or advanced placement
courses. From this perspective, school racial balance is not enough. From
another perspective, school racial balance isn't even necessary, since all of
these treatments could be achieved, technically, in segregated schools.

The most important evidence on the extent to which school desegregation closes the racial achievement gap comes from case studies of the Dallas, Wilmington, Kansas City, and Charlotte-Mecklenburg school districts.
Long-term data on achievement trends, the nature and scope of desegregation plans, and individual student characteristics such as achievement, race,
poverty (free or reduced lunch), school, grade, and residence were analyzed
in order to isolate the portion of the achievement gap between the races that
is due to schools and the portion due to family characteristics.

For some analysts, however, this is not enough. They agree that the socioeconomic characteristics of minority families explain much of the achievement gap, but argue that socioeconomic characteristics are simply an effect
of segregation two generations removed. This "intergenerational" version of
the harm and benefit thesis contends that parents of contemporary black
schoolchildren attended segregated schools during the 1950s or 1960s, and
this school segregation caused the black parents to have lower socioeconomic
status. Thus, even if family socioeconomic differences explain most of the
current achievement gap, school segregation is still the cause, but through
the segregation of the parents rather than the children. In other words, the
causal process simply takes place over two (or possibly more) generations.
The validity of the intergenerational argument was tested first by analyzing
the relationship between a child's test score and the racial composition of the
parent's school, and second, the relationship between the racial composition
of the parent's school and the parent's socioeconomic status.

The analyses presented in chapter 6 thus reflect the complicated nature
of the desegregated school. Children come to school with different characteristics, and these characteristics must be taken into account, to "level the
playing field" so to speak, before one can determine the effect of segregated
or desegregated schools on children.

ACHIEVING EQUITY IN CLASSROOM, COURSE, AND PROGRAM ENROLLMENT

One of the occasional demands of the plaintiffs in a school desegregation court case is to have racially balanced classrooms, that is, classrooms
whose racial composition is the same as the school's racial composition. At

the secondary level, this means racially balanced courses, including the most advanced courses. Sometimes the demand for racially balanced classrooms is made in a motion for further relief and in a few cases it has been incorporated into the court order to desegregate the schools. Sometimes the issue is brought up for the first time in response to a motion for unitary status as a reason the school district should not attain unitary status.

Surprisingly, classroom racial balance has not been a major issue in school desegregation cases. Most desegregated elementary schools have racially balanced classrooms. Classroom racial imbalance is more of a problem at the secondary level because students typically choose which courses they will enroll in. The higher-achieving students, who are disproportionately white, are more likely to take the more difficult courses than the lower-achieving students, who are disproportionately minority. This phenomenon is often called tracking and ability grouping even if there is student choice. Although tracking and ability grouping are controversial educational policies, it is a constitutional issue only when it results in racial isolation within schools. Of course, school districts under court order have the burden of proof—that is they are presumed guilty until they prove their innocence—if there is a complaint about racially imbalanced classrooms.

Chapter 7 analyzes this issue by first assessing the extent of classroom racial balance that exists in the United States, as well as in specific school districts under court order. To calculate classroom racial balance indices, classroom enrollment by race was obtained from the Office for Civil Rights and from individual schools that have applied for unitary status: San Jose, California; Brandywine, Christina, Colonial, and Red Clay, Delaware; Prince George's County, Maryland; Woodland Hills, Pennsylvania; and Rockford, Illinois.

Like school desegregation, classroom desegregation is motivated by the same harm and benefit thesis. Racially imbalanced classrooms, it is alleged, are bad because they harm black children educationally. Black children are disproportionately low-achieving, so a predominantly black classroom is a predominantly low-achieving class. Teachers teach at a slower pace in low-achieving classes and thus further lower the achievement of their low-achieving (black) students. Finally, the thesis argues that remedying this harm by assigning children to academically heterogeneous classes will benefit the low achievers without harming the high achievers.

Several federal district courts have responded to this argument by ordering school districts to attain classroom racial balance quotas and/or to eliminate course differentiation. Three of them—San Jose, Woodland Hills, and Rockford—are analyzed in chapter 7. As with school desegregation, the orders and their implementation are complicated and the districts invest a considerable amount of resources in determining and reporting compliance.

None of the school districts analyzed in chapter 7, however, achieved high school course enrollments that were racially balanced to the satisfaction of the plaintiffs. Where there is racial disparity in enrollment in courses that differ in difficulty, it is possible to control for achievement to determine if the disparity is due to racial discrimination or to differences in achievement. Interestingly, although the racial achievement gap is alleged to be a vestige of the dual school system, its use as a control variable to explain racial disproportionality seems to be accepted by the plaintiffs, their experts (see Oakes 1994, 2000), and the courts.

ACHIEVING EQUAL STUDENT SUSPENSIONS

Student discipline is another racial equity issue that can arise as a demand for further relief during the remedy phase or be raised for the first time at a unitary hearing as a reason the school district is not unitary. According to the simple model, school desegregation should bring about racial equity in suspensions unless school administrators are discriminating. In the complex model, student characteristics that are known to be related to student suspensions must be controlled for. Chapter 8 takes this approach and analyzes individual student data from several school districts—Woodland Hills, Pennsylvania; Brandywine, Christina, Colonial, and Red Clay, Delaware—and the United States. The purpose of the analysis is to determine if black students are suspended more because they are being discriminated against or because they commit more acts that would get any student suspended. In this approach, racial disparities in school suspensions are compared to disparities in other categories: age, academic standing, and gender, in order to determine whether school suspensions should be expected to be random within groups in a category. In addition, racial disparities in school suspensions are compared to racial disparities in out-of-school arrests. The race of the school administrator is also analyzed to see if white administrators suspend black students more than black administrators do. Finally, data is analyzed to see if racial disparities increase when there is more administrative discretion.

These analyses indicate that the desegregated school is a place where students differ considerably not only by race, but by gender, socioeconomic status, academic standing, and age, all of which affect whether a student commits a suspendable offense. Examining the outcomes for these other causal variables enables us to assess whether the school administration is discriminating against black students.

ACHIEVING POSITIVE RACE RELATIONS

As noted above, the social scientists who signed the amicus curiae brief in *Brown* believed that desegregation would provide the opportunity for blacks and whites to like and respect each other. Chapter 9 assesses whether this occurred by answering two questions. First, did desegregation in the schools change relations between the races? The research reviewed was conducted from 1978 to 1999 in individual school districts and includes both short-term studies of students in desegregated schools and long-term studies of what happens to these students when they become adults.

The second question addressed is what else can be done in the schools to improve relations between the races? The answer to this question comes from research on programs implemented in individual school districts to create equal status contact. These programs include cooperative learning, multicultural education, intergroup dialogues, moral development training programs, conflict resolution, and intercultural training programs. All programs require pre-training of teachers and the strong support of administrators to be successful. Cooperative learning requires even more than that—changing the American classroom from competitive to cooperative—which is no easy task.

Thus, the tools are available to improve race relations in desegregated school. The major obstacle at this point is that additional resources must be marshaled to improve relations between black and white students in desegregated schools, resources that schools have in limited supply. Moreover, these resources would be directed away from a goal which the public feels is the central task of schools—academic achievement—and towards a goal the public feels is less important—student race relations.

COMMUNITY ATTITUDES

When *Brown* was decided, most whites, and virtually all southern whites, believed that white and black students should go to separate schools. Today, only the lunatic fringe believes in racial separation. Chapter 10 presents evidence on these attitude gains from fifty years of public opinion surveys and research on adult attitudes and behavior, including national studies by the Gallup Poll, the Institute for Social Science Research, and the National Opinion Research Center from 1942 to 1993, as well as surveys of parents in sixteen school districts over a twenty-year period. These districts comprise a diverse group, including Los Angeles, California; Chicago, Illinois; Yonkers, New York; Savannah-Chatham County, Georgia; Natchez-Adams, Mississippi; Worcester, Massachusetts; DeKalb, Georgia; Topeka, Kansas; Stockton, California; Knox County, Tennessee; the Hartford Metropolitan Area, Connecticut; East Baton Rouge Parish, Louisiana; Rockford, Illinois; Hattiesburg, Mississippi; and the St. Paul/Minneapolis Metropolitan Area, Minnesota. The first survey was taken in 1977 and the last in 1998.

The evidence indicates a remarkable change in the opinions of whites towards blacks, school integration, and the racial composition of their schools. What hasn't changed, however, is opposition to mandatory assignment to schools to achieve racial balance (i.e., busing). The question addressed in this chapter is whether opposition to busing is caused by racism or self-interest. This is answered by comparing white attitudes to black attitudes on these issues and by comparing white attitudes on one issue to white attitudes on another issue. The evidence suggests that the civil rights movement has had considerable success in capturing the hearts and minds of white America on most issues having to do with race and school integration.

EFFICIENCY AND EFFECTIVENESS IN ACHIEVING RACIAL EQUITY

The research presented in this book represents our assessment of how far we have come since 1954 in achieving racial equity and how we can most efficiently and effectively achieve the promise of *Brown*. Although social scientists once thought, and many still believe, that school desegregation alone can equalize academic achievement and attainment, eliminate high dropout rates, reduce school discipline problems, and improve racial harmony, our experience and studies indicate that these goals are influenced by many variables, not just school desegregation. By examining these additional variables, we believe we are able to more accurately assess what school desegregation has and has not accomplished, what its costs and benefits have been, and which plans and programs have been more or less effective. We end this book with recommendations that we believe are most likely to achieve racial equity in the 21st century.

REFERENCES

Allport, Gordon and 35 cosigners. 1953. Social Science Statement. Amicus curiae brief in *Brown v. Bd of Educ.*

Armor, David J. 1995. *Forced Justice: School Desegregation and the Law.* Oxford UP.

Maehr, Martin L., and David E Bartz. Eds. 1984. *The Effects of School Desegregation on Motivation and Achievement.* Greenwich, CT: JAI Press, Inc.

Brameld, Theodore. 1949. Educational costs. In *Discrimination and National Welfare: A Series of Addresses and Discussion,* edited by Robert M. MacIver. Institute for Religious and Social Studies.

Chein, Isodor. 1949. What are the psychological effects of segregation under conditions of equal facilities? *International Journal of Opinion and Attitude Research* 3: 229–34.

Clark, Kenneth B. 1950. *Effect of Prejudice and Discrimination on Personality Development.* Midcentury White House Conference on Children and Youth.

Deutscher, Max, and Isodor Chein. 1948. The psychological effects of enforced segregation: A survey of social science opinion. *Journal of Psychology* 26: 259–87.

Frazier, Edward Franklin. 1949. *The Negro in the United States.* Longman.

Kluger, Richard. 1975. *Simple Justice: The History of* Brown v. Board of Education *and Black America's Struggle for Equality*. Knopf.

Myrdal, Gunnar. 1944. *An American Dilemma: The Negro Problem and Modern Democracy*. Harper and Row.

Oakes, Jeannie. 1994. Ability grouping, tracking and within-school segregation in New Castle Count [*sic*] schools. Report to the U.S. District Court for the District [sic] of Delaware: *Coalition to Save Our Children v. State Board of Education et al*. 9 December.

————. 2000. Within-school integration, grouping practices, and educational quality in Rockford schools. Report with *People Who Care et al. v. Rockford Board of Education et al*. Revised February.

Witmer, Helen and Ruth Kotinsky. 1952. *Personality in the making: The fact-finding report of the Midcentury White House Conference on Children and Youth*. Harper.

Wolters, John. 1984. *The Burden of* Brown: *Thirty Years of School Desegregation*. U of Tennessee P.

Chapter 2

History of
School Desegregation

Jeffrey A. Raffel

The history of school desegregation is complex, marked by landmark U.S. Supreme Court decisions and shifting legal standards, interwoven with significant events in the nation's history, and affecting and reflecting changing values and public opinion. This chapter summarizes this history by describing eight stages of school desegregation over the nation's history (see appendix 2.1).[1] For each historical stage I have tried to capture in the figure the time period, key legal decision(s), most significant legal standard set and the criterion used by the federal courts to judge the constitutionality of state action, the overall status of school desegregation, key historical events related to school desegregation and race relations, and the most significant social science research of the period; the entry in appendix 2.1 for the last epoch, the post-2000 period, is yet to be completed.

DE JURE SEGREGATION

From Compulsory Illiteracy to Schools for Negroes

In 1860 there were almost 4.5 million Negroes[2] in the nation but less than 500,000 were free. The South had more than 4 million Negroes of whom slightly more than one-quarter million were free (Kujovich 1992). Bondage meant compulsory illiteracy: slaves were not allowed to learn to read. Thus, for the vast majority of Negroes, the possibility of education did not exist until the Civil War was won by the North.

Schooling for Negroes started in 1865, with the establishment of the federal Freedmen's Bureau. Working with religious organizations such as the American Missionary Association, the Bureau provided organizational and financial support and shielded schools and teachers from violent attacks and intimidation from hostile whites (Kujovich 1992). The Bureau created over 4,000 schools and hired over 9,000 teachers to serve almost one-quarter of a million children. The Bureau, with the later assist of the Morrill Acts, helped to establish institutions to train Negro teachers.

The most important school desegregation action taken during the post–Civil War era was the passage of the Fourteenth Amendment to the Constitution in 1868. Republicans in Congress had insisted on the passage of this amendment to ensure the civil rights of Negroes when the Confederate states were reincorporated into the Union. The Equal Protection Clause stated that "No State shall make or enforce any law which shall abridge the privileges or immunities of citizens of the United States; nor shall any State deprive any person of life, liberty, of property, without due process of the law; nor deny to any person within its jurisdiction the equal protection of the laws." While the wording was broad, the clause's immediate substantive effect in public education was nil.

Segregation: "Separate but Equal"

Reconstruction led to resentment and bitterness in the southern states. Racial prejudice grew as uneducated Negroes played significant roles in state governments. By 1885, all of the former Confederate states had passed laws segregating Negroes from whites. These Jim Crow laws ensured that whites would not have to share water fountains, seats on the same floor in movie theaters and baseball parks, swimming facilities and beaches, barbershops, libraries, restrooms, ticket windows, buses, taxis, streetcars, and state colleges and classes in universities with colored people. State-imposed segregation was challenged in the landmark *Plessy v. Ferguson* (163 U.S. 537 [1896]) decision involving the state of Louisiana.

In 1890, the state legislature of Louisiana passed a bill to segregate passenger trains. The bill required all railway companies to provide "separate but equal accommodations for the white, and colored races." The law also called for penalties for passengers who did not go to their assigned car. A deliberate challenge to the law was planned by an aptly named organization of Negroes and Creoles, the Citizens' Committee to Test the Constitutionality of the Separate Car Law. On 7 June 1892, Homer Adolf Plessy, who appeared to be white but was seven-eighths Caucasian and one-eighth Negro, refused to follow a conductor's direction to sit in a "colored" railroad car on the East Louisiana Railroad. He deliberately sat in a "white" car as part of this prearranged test case. He was arrested for violating Louisiana law, convicted, and imprisoned. Plessy's appeal reached the U.S. Supreme Court and resulted in the 1896 *Plessy v. Ferguson* decision.

Eight of the Supreme Court's justices agreed with the majority opinion written by Justice Henry Billings Brown. According to Brown, even though the law called for separating colored from whites on railroad cars, it was not aimed at stigmatizing Negroes. According to the Court, "the underlying fallacy of the plaintiff's argument . . . [lies] in the assumption that enforced separation of the two races stamps the colored race with a badge of inferiority. If this be so, it is not by reason of anything found in this act, but solely because the colored race chooses to put that construction upon it." Separating those with different racial backgrounds was permissible as long as the principle of separate but equal was not violated. While the decision referred to railroad cars, the Court commented that valid laws existed requiring racial separation in public schools, thereby broadening the scope of their decision. It must be noted that one justice was ahead of his time. In his lone dissent, Justice John Marshall Harlan wryly noted that, "Everyone knows that the statute in question had its origin in the purpose, not so much to exclude white persons from railroad cars occupied by blacks, as to exclude colored people from coaches occupied or assigned to whites." But at least eight men didn't know, or didn't care, and it would be over fifty years before Harlan's grandson would have the chance to build a Supreme Court decision on the elder Justice Harlan's argument that "our Constitution is colorblind and neither knows nor tolerates classes among citizens."

The *Plessy* decision affirmed the legality of Jim Crow and segregation in all areas of public and private life, and southern legislatures walked, if not ran, through the open gate. By 1905, Negro leaders, upset with segregation and the inadequate education of their children, met in Niagara Falls, Ontario, where facilities were open to Negroes, to discuss what might be done to achieve "Negro freedom and growth." Led by W.E.B. DuBois, the Niagara Movement continued to meet annually at historic sites to develop a new organization that would lead their race from unequal schools to better education. Following race riots and lynchings in Springfield, Illinois, the National Association for the Advancement of Colored People (NAACP) was officially formed on the 100th anniversary of Abraham Lincoln's birthday, 12 February 1909, in his hometown of Springfield. Several whites, including millionaire southern social reformer William English Walling, grandson of abolitionist William Lloyd Garrison, joined with the Niagara Movement to create the NAACP. The goal from its inception was to abolish enforced segregation and establish equal educational opportunities for Negro children.

By 1930, it was clear that the *Plessy* decision stood as a major obstacle to achieving better schools for Negroes. While the Court had propounded a principle of separate but equal, the emphasis was on separate, not on equal. For example, in South Carolina, per-pupil expenditures for white students were ten times that for colored students and in Florida, Georgia, Mississippi, and Alabama, the ratio was five to one. Dual systems had become the rule in the South. School boards were running two sets of schools, one for colored children and one for white. (In Delaware, even this was not good enough; the state also had a system for Moors and a system for Indians.) The colored systems were under-funded, under-maintained, and under-performing. To develop a legal strategy to get past the *Plessy* brick wall, or perhaps to knock it down, the NAACP enlisted the help of lawyer Nathan Margold.

Margold and the NAACP faced a conflict that had confronted Negro leaders in the nineteenth century and would perplex them in the twentieth century. The leaders had to decide whether they should challenge segregation and *Plessy* by demanding that separate but equal be actually achieved—that is, that schools and other segregated institutions be given the resources to achieve equality—or to challenge the concept that segregation could ever be equal. For decades, two Negro leaders had been debating these positions, with Booker T. Washington taking the position that integration into American society was the goal and W.E.B. DuBois arguing that the development of Negro institutions was necessary for his people to achieve their potential in America.

Challenging Segregation

Margold's advice was to challenge the inequality that existed under separation, and force southern states to increase expenditures for Negro students, which would greatly increase the cost of maintaining the segregated educational system. In 1939, the NAACP created a new arm, the NAACP Legal Defense and Educational Fund (LDF), to implement the Margold Report. The LDF modified the Margold strategy somewhat, by attacking segregation not in elementary and secondary schools but in professional schools. Their reasoning was that inequality would be easier to prove at the higher level, since in many states no facilities for Negro professional education existed, and the threat to states would be less, since the cost of any remedy would not be as great as at the elementary and secondary levels. In addition, the threat of violence would be minimal if higher education were to be the battlefield.

Under the leadership of Charles Hamilton Houston (appointed as the NAACP's first legal counsel in 1935) and Thurgood Marshall, the NAACP and LDF's strategy was successful. *Missouri ex rel. Gaines v. Canada* (305 U.S. 337 [1938]) was the first challenge to *Plessy* at the Supreme Court level. The court accepted the argument that a scholarship program to send Negroes wishing to attend law school to another state was not consistent with the separate but equal principle because no law school existed within the state. The decision led to the establishment of "overnight law schools," quickly established at Negro colleges and universities to forestall the threat of desegregating state law or professional schools. Following World War II, the Supreme Court decided *Sipuel v. Oklahoma Board of Regents* (332 U.S. 631 [1948]). In this case, Thurgood Marshall of the LDF argued that establishing a separate law school for Negroes to meet the requirements of the separate but equal principle was not sufficient, because separate education, at least for law students, was inherently unequal. The U.S. Supreme Court accepted the argument that Negro students had to be treated equally with white students but it refused to decide that an ad hoc Negro law school with a faculty of three provided Ms. Sipuel with an unequal education. Subsequent to this decision, the university did admit her on a desegregated basis.

In 1950, the LDF had two important Supreme Court triumphs—*Sweatt v. Painter* (339 U.S. 629 [1950]) and *McLaurin v. Oklahoma State Regents for Higher Education* (339 U.S. 637 [1950]). *Sweatt* established the principle that intangibles such as the quality of the alumni, faculty reputation, and the experience of the administration play a role in comparing separate law schools and determining their equality. Marshall and James Nabrit of the LDF argued that rejecting Herman Sweatt at the nationally renowned University of Texas Law School and providing a legal education at the new Texas State Law School for Negroes, quickly set up in a basement of a petroleum company in four rooms with a leased toilet and a part-time faculty, did not meet the separate but equal standard. While the Court did not address the question of whether separate was inherently unequal, it did conclude that in this case the Negro law schools were unequal and Sweatt must be admitted to the University of Texas. *McLaurin v. Oklahoma State Regents* extended the principle of quality established in *Sweatt* to professional schools and recognized the role that intangible factors play in comparing professional schools. These higher education cases laid the legal foundation, as in the NAACP-revised Margold strategy, for the challenge to *Plessy* at the elementary and secondary level.

Events beyond judicial conflicts in the nation's capital were also helping to build the challenges to state segregation. The successful participation and bravery of Negro soldiers in World War II, albeit in segregated units, led to a questioning of segregation. In 1946, President Truman appointed a group of distinguished Negro and white citizens to the President's Committee on Civil Rights. The committee was chaired by Charles E. Wilson, president of the General Electric Company. Their October 1947 report, *To Secure These Rights,* called for extensive government action. To ensure equal rights, they called for an end to segregation in all areas including public schools, the military, public accommodations, and employment. The report had been based on a previous study funded by the Carnegie Foundation and directed by Swedish economist Gunnar Myrdal, which resulted in the classic book, *An American Dilemma.* This massive study (over 1,400 pages), published in

1944, had documented the condition of the Negro in American society across a broad array of areas including schools, housing, jobs, and justice. Myrdal had concluded that the status of the Negro in America violated the American ideal and was the American dilemma:

the ever-raging conflict between, on the one hand, the valuations preserved on the general plane which we shall call the "American Creed," where the American thinks, talks, and acts under the influence of high national and Christian precepts, and, on the other hand, the valuations on specific planes of individual and group living, where personal and local interests; economic, social, and sexual jealousies; considerations of community prestige and conformity; group prejudice against particular persons or types of persons or types of people; and all sorts of miscellaneous wants, impulses, and habits dominate his outlook. (Myrdal 1944: xii)

Addressing the American dilemma head-on, President Truman began his campaign for equal rights. In June 1947, the President addressed 10,000 people assembled for the NAACP national convention on the steps of the Lincoln Memorial and called for ending "insult, intimidation, violence, prejudice, and intolerance" and making the "federal government a friendly, vigilant defender of the rights and equalities of all Americans." On 26 July 1948, he ordered the desegregation of the armed forces through an executive order. His Department of Justice supported Negroes in civil rights cases. He established a Fair Employment Board to ensure that federal jobs were awarded on a nondiscriminatory manner. At the 1948 Democratic convention, he supported a civil rights plank that called for equal opportunity in employment, angering the southern wing of the party and leading to the third-party candidacy of Governor Strom Thurmond of South Carolina. Truman's actions both reflected the changing mood of the nation and helped to lead it. But the nation (and the Democratic Party) was still divided. Thurmond carried Alabama, Georgia, Mississippi, and South Carolina on the State's Rights ticket.

Ending State Segregation

While the LDF had established the legal foundation for ending state-imposed segregation, and President Truman had helped to create a public mood to support such a change, there was no consensus on the Court or in the nation that segregation should end. President Dwight D. Eisenhower's nomination of Governor Earl Warren of California as the Chief Justice of the Supreme Court, confirmed by the Senate on 1 March 1954, was critical in the process of ending the doctrine of separate but equal. As Chief Justice, Warren used his political skills to forge a consensus on the Court to outlaw school segregation and reject the separate but equal principle established by the *Plessy* decision (Kluger 1975). To minimize opposition to a unanimous ruling rejecting this principle, Warren gave special attention to the three justices from states with segregated school systems and decoupled the question of segregation from the anticipated problems in the implementation of the ruling. At 12:52 P.M. on 17 May 1954, Chief Justice Warren read the eleven-page opinion on *Brown v. Board of Education* (347 U.S. 483 [1954]) to the hushed courtroom. "We unanimously conclude that in the field of public education the doctrine of 'separate but equal' has no place."

There remains much debate over the legal reasoning of the Court and the role that social science research, cited in footnote 11 of *Brown*, may have played in their deliberations. The more immediate issue, however, concerned the question of remedy; that is, how *Brown* would be implemented. It was not until a year later that the Court made its implementation decision known as *Brown II* (349 U.S. 294 [1955]), and this decision left termination of dual systems to the discretion of federal district courts, which had better knowledge of local conditions. The Court gave local school district authorities and state officials the responsibility for implementation and called for the district courts to monitor their progress. The decision showed an understanding of the issues that would face the implementers, including the physical conditions of the school plants, the school transportation system, and the need to redraw school attendance boundaries. The Court specified that district courts should "enter such orders and decrees consistent with this opinion as are necessary and proper to admit to public schools on a racially nondiscriminatory basis with all deliberate speed the parties to these cases." As Wasby, D'Amato, and Metrailer (1977) note, the Court, however, did not state guidelines for such actions and did not set a specific date for plans to be submitted or desegregation to occur. The Court had established a framework for state and local officials to implement their decision but had left much to the discretion of southern officials and southern judges who faced their own mixed feelings and strong public pressure to resist any measures that would substantially alter the schools.

A decade of massive resistance followed from 1955 to 1964. The eleven states of the Old Confederacy tried to avoid the impact of the *Brown* decisions through an array of tactics. State laws were passed to delay or stop desegregation. Pupil placement laws made sure that Negro students who tried to attend the local white school, formally available under freedom-of-choice plans, would not meet the multitudinous psychological and educational criteria for admission. Local authorities were given permission to close their public schools if desegregation was the only alternative. In Prince Edward County, Virginia, public schools remained closed for five years while six "private academies" for white students were funded with public funds. Politicians fanned the flames of their constituents' anger. On 12 March 1956, one hundred and one southern congressmen signed the Southern Manifesto, denouncing the *Brown* decisions as a "clear abuse of judicial power [that] climaxes a trend in the federal judiciary undertaking to legislate in derogation of the authority of Congress and to encroach upon the reserved rights of the states and people." The signers, who included all southern senators except Majority Leader Lyndon Baines Johnson of Texas and Albert Gore and Estes Kefauver of Tennessee, and all but twenty-four southern representatives, vowed to use all legal means to maintain segregation and resist desegregation. State legislatures passed resolutions of interposition and nullification reaffirming states rights and questioning the supremacy of the Supreme Court. White citizens councils, the middle class equivalent to the Ku Klux Klan, were formed in many southern states. In contrast to the KKK, the councils forswore violence, but they harassed the NAACP and those individuals who challenged segregation, and used propaganda to fight the end of segregation.

The most publicly visible defiance of the Supreme Court's decision occurred in Little Rock, Arkansas. Three days after the 1954 *Brown* decision, the city's board of education declared that it would comply. A year later the board approved a school desegregation plan to begin in the fall of 1957. Seventeen Negro students were selected by the school board to enter all-white Central High School. Nine students stuck to their plans despite ads placed in local newspapers by the white citizens councils citing the evils of school desegregation in graphic terms. Governor Orval Faubus, elected as a moderate, appeared on television the night before the nine students were to enter Central and announced that he had called in the National Guard to avoid bloodshed. This, of course, ensured the opposite by focusing the attention of angry whites on the school. A white mob greeted the Negro students with taunts as they arrived at the school and Faubus' National Guard turned the students away. Despite a meeting with President Eisenhower at the President's vacation office in Newport, Rhode Island, Faubus remained defiant. Nine days later the students were again turned back by a mob. President Eisenhower nationalized 10,000 members of Arkansas National Guard and sent 1,000 combat-ready paratroopers of the 101st Airborne Division, veterans of the Korean War, to ensure that the students could enter the high school. On 24 September 1957, the President explained his actions to the nation on television and radio. Eisenhower made clear that "a final order of a Federal Court . . . must be obeyed by State authorities and all citizens of the land . . ." After some legal losses (*Cooper v. Aaron*, 358 U.S. 1 [1958]), the Governor closed all three Little Rock high schools to avoid school desegregation. But violence, including some bombings on Labor Day, led to a retreat by the more avid opponents to desegregation and the schools were finally opened on a desegregated basis.

While border states were more compliant and some local officials more responsive, by a decade after *Brown I* only two percent of the Negro children in the Old Confederacy were attending desegregated schools. Progress in federal courts was slow and, without their own police or enforcement mechanism, the federal courts were making little progress in implementing *Brown*. The principle of nondiscrimination had been established, dual systems had been declared unconstitutional and the principle of equity had been affirmed, but few Negro children in the South were attending schools with whites.

Achieving Racially Balanced Schools

The turning point for the end of state segregation and the beginning of the desegregation era was clearly the *Green* decision in 1968, but the foundation for the impact of *Green* lay in the Civil Rights Act of 1964 and the Elementary and Secondary Education Act of 1965. As President, John F. Kennedy had placed civil rights on the back burner. Stern (1992) has called JFK "an intimidated president," who was concerned that he needed to build his relationship with Congress before he could propose controversial legislation. His selection of Texan Lyndon Baines Johnson had brought the Democratic Party together, but action on civil rights would split the party, which JFK could ill afford since he won by only a few thousand votes. Yet President Kennedy was drawn into the civil rights struggle by events. He was forced to send troops to ensure that James Meredith could enroll at the University of Mississippi in 1962, and his deputy attorney general, Nicholas Katzenbach, forced Governor George Wallace of Alabama to allow two students to enter the state's university under federal court order. As a result of the violence aimed at civil rights advocates in Birmingham, Alabama in May 1963, coupled with the March on Washington that same month, and the increasing northern anger about southern treatment of Negroes, the once reluctant President on 11 June 1963 told the nation, "If an American, because his skin is dark, cannot eat in a restaurant open to the public, if he cannot send his children to the best public school available, if he cannot vote for the public officials who represent him, if, in short, he cannot enjoy the full and free life which all of us want, then who among us would be content to have the color of his skin changed to stand in his place?" Kennedy not only called for each American to "examine his conscience" about segregation, he proposed a comprehensive civil rights bill to right these wrongs; he was killed before the bill would be passed by Congress.

In the period of national mourning following JFK's assassination on 22 November 1963, southerner Lyndon Baines Johnson maneuvered the bill through Congress despite a southern filibuster. The bill, signed on 2 July 1964, guaranteed equal access to public accommodations such as hotels, motels, restaurants, and places of amusement, and prohibited a number of means that the South had used to limit voting. While Title II, the public accommodations component, had drawn the most controversy, Title VI proved to be the most influential. Under Title VI, the federal government was allowed to cut off federal funds where discrimination was shown. The Office for Civil Rights was given the responsibility for collecting data and investigating charges of school segregation, and the Attorney General was given the authority to bring suits against segregated school districts or institutions of higher learning. The bill also required the U.S. Office of Education to provide technical assistance to school districts developing school desegregation plans through desegregation assistance centers and increased the authority of the U.S. Commission on Civil Rights. The Commission would "put the facts on the table" as President Eisenhower had stated when he signed the Civil Rights Act of 1957 authorizing the commission. By holding hearings, for example in Louisville, Denver, Los Angeles, and Boston in 1975–76, and writing reports such as *Racial Isolation in the Public Schools* (1967), the Commission played an active role in describing and investigating the problems of school segregation. The Commission focused the public's attention on segregated schools.

The threat of cutting federal funds increased greatly after passage of the Elementary and Secondary Education Act of 1965 (ESEA) on 11 April 1965. This was the first general aid to education bill to pass Congress. Title I of ESEA granted over $1.5 billion for local school district expenditures on disadvantaged children. With the carrot of substantial federal aid now available, the removal of federal aid could now serve as a stick to force compliance. But what would be the nature of such compliance? The *Green* decision provided a new answer.

Formally called *Green v. County School Board of New Kent County* (391 U.S. 430 [1968]), the case involved a small, rural school district in eastern Virginia with two schools, one serving whites from elementary to high school (New Kent School) and the other similarly serving Negroes (Watkins School). The county was not residentially segregated. The threat of losing funds under enforcement through the 1964 Civil Rights Act led the county school district to finally respond to the 1954 *Brown* decision by adopting a freedom-of-choice plan. The plan called for students to select one of the two schools in first and eighth grade; in other grades students could select a school or, if they did not, were assigned to their previous school. In reality, no whites had applied to the Negro school, although 115 black children, 16 percent of the black student population, had applied to the white school. Not only did the schools remain racially identifiable, the Court concluded that "every facet of school operations—faculty, staff, transportation, extracurricular activities and facilities" were also racially identifiable. The Court decided that this plan had no promise of desegregating the schools and a plan was required that "promises realistically to convert promptly to a system without a 'white' school and a 'Negro' school, but just schools." The district had the "affirmative duty to take whatever steps might be necessary to convert to a unitary system in which racial discrimination would be eliminated root and branch."

The *Green* decision suggested that the Supreme Court had lost its patience with southern school districts that had adopted freedom-of-choice plans; these plans were nondiscriminatory on their face but allowed schools to maintain their identifiability. With the *Green* decision, the new criterion was based on results: that is, were Negro and white children attending the same schools? Racial balance had replaced nondiscrimination as the legal standard.

Three years later, a second court decision, *Swann v. Charlotte-Mecklenburg Board of Education* (402 U.S. 1 [1971]), went even further by setting numerical targets for racial balance. It also affirmed the use of busing, the mandatory transportation of students out of their neighborhood attendance area or previously assigned school, as a permissible means to achieve such racial balance. In the rural South, residential areas generally were limited to smaller defined areas and busing was used to avoid school-based attendance areas. In metropolitan areas like Charlotte-Mecklenburg County, 550 square miles in size and serving over 80,000 pupils, residential segregation, "vanilla suburbs surrounding chocolate cities," meant that racial balance would require transferring students out of their immediate neighborhoods (Farley et al. 1978). According to the Court,

All things being equal, with no history of discrimination, it might well be desirable to assign pupils to the school nearest their homes. But all things are not equal in a system that has been deliberately constructed and maintained to enforce school segregation. The remedy for such segregation may be administratively awkward, inconvenient, and even bizarre in some situations and may impose burdens on some; but all awkwardness and inconvenience cannot be avoided in the interim period when remedial adjustments are being made to eliminate the dual school systems. (*Swann v. Charlotte-Mecklenburg*, 402 U.S. 1, 28 [1971])

Within months, over forty plans throughout the South were based on the principles of *Swann*.

The assassinations of Mississippi NAACP field secretary Medgar Evers in 1963, Malcolm X in 1965 and Martin Luther King and Bobby Kennedy in 1968, the riots in cities such as Cleveland, Newark, Detroit, New York City, Chicago, and Atlanta in 1967, and the rise of Black Power served as the backdrop for the battle in the federal courts over school desegregation. In 1968, the Kerner Commission concluded that America was headed toward two nations, "one white, one black, separate and unequal." School desegregation looked like a moderate response compared to those arguing that the civil rights movement had not led to the promised land and therefore what was needed was black power and black control.

While there were still many bumps on the path to desegregation, the dual forces of federal legislation and federal court decisions, which demanded "just schools," rather than nondiscrimination, led to the desegregation of southern schools. The Office of Education (OE) and the Justice Department worked with federal courts to seek acceptable desegregation plans. In April 1965, OE distributed specific guidelines for desegregation, and then issued tougher plans in March, 1966. In the decades following this act, the Justice Department initiated over 500 school desegregation suits and the Department of Health, Education, and Welfare (HEW) initiated 600 actions. The results were startling. Orfield, Monfort, and Aaron (1989) report the percentage of black students in predominantly minority schools dropping from 76.6% in 1968 to 63.6% in 1972 and the percentage in intensely segregated schools (more than nine-tenths minority) dropping from 64.3% to 38.7% over the same period. Similarly, Rossell and Armor (1996) report an increase in the average black student's percentage of white students in their school (interracial exposure) from 30% to 43% from 1968 to 1972 in the nation's largest school districts (districts with more than 27,750 pupils).

Some communities were willing to voluntarily enact desegregation alternatives. In the Boston and Springfield, Massachusetts metropolitan areas, a voluntary city-to-suburbs busing program (METCO) provided opportunities for city minority students to voluntarily attend suburban public schools. In the Boston, area 220 students from the inner city were transported voluntarily to a number of suburban school districts in 1966 that had voluntarily agreed to accept them. The number of students increased to over 3,000 annually. (The state of Massachusetts had also passed the Massachusetts Racial Imbalance Act in 1965, the first state action that required racial balance in its schools.) Project Concern was begun in the Hartford metropolitan area in September 1967 with 267 Hartford elementary students voluntarily traveling to five suburban communities, reaching a peak of over 1,000 students attending schools in thirteen suburban districts in 1978. A few individual districts such as Berkeley, California and Seattle, Washington voluntarily implemented mandatory reassignment plans that racially balanced their schools. Others voluntarily implemented intra-district voluntary transfer plans called M to M plans (majority to minority plans).

Perhaps the greatest symbolic act during this era of school desegregation was President Johnson's appointment and the U.S. Senate's confirmation of Thurgood Marshall to the U.S. Supreme Court in 1967. The man who had led the NAACP Legal and Educational Defense Fund to fight legal segregation in the federal courts would now be one of the nine top judges in the nation, the first black to serve on the Supreme Court.

DE FACTO SEGREGATION

Limiting Desegregation Remedies

Physicists have instructed us that "for every action there is a reaction," and such was true in the school desegregation arena. Resentment in the South of "forced integration" and fear in the North about the threat of school desegregation and busing led to actions to curtail desegregation in the 1970s. These actions not only took place in the courts with the issue shifting from de jure to de facto segregation, but also in the political, executive, research, and legislative arenas.

OE's attempt to extend its influence to the North, where there had been no state laws segregating the schools, that is, where there was de facto rather than state-mandated de jure segregation, was not as successful. In Chicago, OE went after Superintendent Benjamin Willis and the Chicago school board, which had maintained segregated schools by the manipulation of school attendance areas in the decade after *Brown*. During this time period, "Willis wagons," portable schools, were used to keep black students in black schools and away from whites. Democratic Mayor Richard Daley fought federal intrusion, and OE, which was inexperienced and unprepared to attack this type of segregation, was forced to give way when Daley confronted President Johnson at the signing of the new immigration bill at the Statue of Liberty on 3 October 1965. Heads rolled in OE, and Chicago's segregated schools were left intact.

A critical post-*Swann* question was how this decision would impact the North. In the 1973 *Keyes* (413 U.S. 189 [1973]) decision in Denver, the Supreme Court had concluded that desegregation could be ordered in districts that may not have been under state laws to remain segregated but that had taken explicit action to segregate at least a portion of their school district. As a result, a number of northern cities, including Cleveland, Cincinnati, and Buffalo, faced desegregation orders.

The next frontier was the boundary separating city schools from suburban school districts. The Supreme Court had been split 4–4 on whether Richmond needed to adopt a school desegregation plan that would extend beyond its city boundaries and involve the white suburban schools districts; by its split vote, it left a Court of Appeals decision limiting a remedy to the city intact (*Bradley v. Richmond* 412 U.S. 92 [1973]). (Justice Lewis Powell, who had been involved as a city and later state school board member in the Richmond case, had to recuse himself from the case.) In the South, many school districts, including those in Florida and North Carolina, were county or metropolitan districts, so busing plans did not need to flow over school district lines. But the North was different—multiple, small suburban school districts were protected from desegregation orders as long as their borders were inviolate. The battleground to resolve this issue took place in Detroit.

It would be hard to find a city more northern than Detroit, and it would have been harder to find a situation where more suburban school districts would be impacted by a court decision on a metropolitan busing plan. Federal Judge Stephen Roth had ordered a desegregation plan involving Detroit and fifty-three suburban school districts. With the city's schools having few white students, only a plan including suburban students could desegregate the city's schools. In 1974, however, the U.S. Supreme Court, in a 5–4 decision, ruled that the suburban districts did not have to be included in the plan because they had not themselves been guilty of collusion with city seg-regation. Nor had the state of Michigan played a significant role in increas-ing the segregation of the city's schools. In addition, the *Milliken v. Bradley* (418 U.S. 717 [1974]) decision stated that the "cost" of merging all these districts—destroying the locally controlled suburban school districts, send-ing children on long rides across city lines, having the federal courts in-volved in educational and governance issues—was too great. While the federal courts later found special circumstances to warrant a metropolitan, interdistrict court order in a few sites such as Wilmington, Delaware and Louisville, Kentucky, *Milliken* essentially shut the door on interdistrict, met-ropolitan school desegregation.

In 1968, Governor George Wallace of Alabama had run for president on the American Independent party ticket and by winning forty-six electoral votes had shown that opposition to federal judges, desegregation and bus-ing could gather southern or even northern votes. Wallace had received na-tional fame or notoriety by declaring "segregation now . . . segregation tomorrow . . . segregation forever" in his January 1963 inauguration speech and later that year "standing in the schoolhouse door" to try to block the desegregation of the University of Alabama. His success in the North and the South did indicate that a "charismatic demagogue" (Wilhoit 1978) could appeal to a significant number of northern voters. Republican can-didate and former Vice President Richard Nixon, although never accused of being charismatic, was accused of adopting a "southern strategy" to pull the South from the Democratic column and add these states to traditional Republican states in the West while winning swing states with appeals on racial issues to suburban voters. When the southern strategy proved to be a winning strategy, President Nixon raised questions about civil rights poli-cies and directed his executive branch appointees to go slow on forcing desegregation. Civil rights advocates brought suit, and the *Adams v. Richardson* (480 F.2d 1159 [1973]) decision forced the administration to retreat from its slowdown. The election for president in 1972 featured Wal-lace again, this time seeking the Democratic Party nomination. Although halted by a would-be assassin's bullet, Wallace was scoring points in the North with his attacks on busing. In March 1972, President Nixon called for a national moratorium on busing.

Boston, once the home to abolitionists, became the site of a violent con-frontation between the federal courts and angry whites. In 1974, U.S. Dis-trict Court Judge W. Arthur Garrity found the Boston School District guilty of intentional school segregation and on 21 June 1974, ordered the state plan for school desegregation that limited busing to two miles. He also or-dered the Boston School Committee (BSC) to begin developing a citywide desegregation plan that would conform to federal decisions requiring racial balance across the district. The BSC refused to comply, and Judge Garrity, despite vehement-working class resistance, appointed four masters and two experts to develop a comprehensive plan to enforce his order. Council-woman Louise Day Hicks continued to lead the opposition to busing, which had actually begun before the 1974 federal district court decision, in opposition to state pressure to force compliance with the Massachusetts Racial Imbalance Act. In her district of South Boston, where a strong Irish Catholic community lived, opposition was the most vehement and violent. Black students brought into white areas of the city were confronted by angry mobs; extra police were needed to keep the peace. The scene was ugly, and the American public was confronted with an image of massive resistance in the North, racial hatred, and federal judges who wanted (or needed, as one's view might be) to run local schools.

While social science research had been used to buttress the arguments for school desegregation in the *Brown* case and to increase public support for desegregation by documenting the degree and effects of segregation, in this phase, social scientists raised questions about the efficacy of busing and school desegregation as remedies. In 1972, David Armor presented "The Evidence on Busing," an analysis of desegregation plans with busing, with the focus on METCO. Armor concluded that busing did not result in achievement gains for blacks or positive improvements in race relations. Researchers focused on "white flight," the loss of white student enrollment in school districts undergoing mandatory school desegregation (Coleman, Kelley, and Moore 1975; Pettigrew and Green 1976; Rossell 1975–76). Whatever the merits of research, it was clear that the support of social science had shifted from documenting the plight of Negro school children in segregated schools to debating the merits of school desegregation, at least by means of busing.

Congress also had continued to debate the issues of school desegregation and busing. Some southerners sought to draw in northern school districts so that their northern colleagues would realize the problems with forced busing and racial balance. A few southern Congressmen viewed school desegregation as the leading edge of a transformation of the South from antebellum to modern. Northern liberals demanded that southern schools follow the dictates of the federal courts to desegregate. Some northern legislators were now being driven to oppose federal action on school desegregation by constituents drawn into what was once a southern problem. Symbolic gestures might please the home folks but many recognized that the federal judiciary still had the last say on the meaning of the U.S. Constitution. In addition, many of their constituents continued to support the principle of school desegregation while opposing busing as a means to achieve it. Given this backdrop, it is not surprising that the actions of Congress were confusing and contradictory.

There were four different antibusing approaches (Keynes and Miller 1989). First, some in Congress tried to limit HEW's role in forcing school districts to bus students with the threat of withholding federal funds. While early efforts passed Congress but were interpreted by HEW as not really limiting their authority when a constitutional violation was involved, the Eagleton–Biden Amendment to the Labor–HEW Appropriations Act of 1978 did place limits on the department's power to force busing. Bills to prohibit the Department of Justice from joining or leading suits to force busing were passed in the House but fell victim to conference committees and the presidential veto of Jimmy Carter. Bills to restrict the federal courts' authority to order busing did lead to passage of the Esch Amendment to the Equal Opportunities Act of 1974, but this bill also affirmed the federal courts' authority to fully enforce the Fifth and Fourteenth Amendments to the Constitution. The desire to stop busing once again ran up against those who favored the righting of constitutional wrongs and those who sought to avoid constitutional crises' pitting one branch against another. Finally, antibusing resolutions were introduced but none passed Congress.

Even the U.S. Commission on Civil Rights, a group with little authority, has been a focus of attack. The activist stance of the Commission for busing and affirmative action was incompatible with President Reagan's more conservative position on civil rights. Arguments over the commission led to a reduction in its budget from $11.8 to $7.5 million and almost a halving of its staff. By 1996, the Commission was targeted by Congress for phasing out in two years. It nevertheless survived.

African Americans, divided since the era of W.E.B. DuBois and Booker T. Washington over the wisdom of desegregation as the primary strategy for racial progress, again rethought the wisdom of school desegregation. The original efforts of the NAACP and its legal arm, the LDF, were inspired by the goal of improving the education of black students. In the 1990s, there was increased questioning in the black community, however, about whether school desegregation should be the leading edge of this longstanding goal (Days 1998). African American leaders in Detroit, Cleveland, Atlanta, Kansas City, Milwaukee, Oakland, and Washington, D.C. advocated schools serving only African American students or even only male African American students to ensure sensitivity to the unique concerns of this group. Others have abandoned the goal of desegregating school districts and instead called for tuition vouchers that would allow African American students to select from private, religious, and public schools for their education. Public opinion surveys have indicated a lack of passion for integration among African American parents, the vast majority of whom in a Public Agenda survey placed their priority on achievement rather than racial diversity and integration (Rossell 1995; Armor 1995; Bradley 1998). There have even been stirrings in the NAACP questioning the efficacy of school desegregation.

Federal courts have clearly read the signs of resistance and concern about "forced busing." Only one school assignment plan with a mandatory student assignment component has been ordered by a federal court since the

1989 Natchez, Mississippi plan. (The Rockford, Illinois plan is a controlled choice plan with a mandatory backup.) Not only have the federal courts backed off of mandatory school assignment plans, they have defined what school districts need to achieve to be released from implementing previously imposed mandatory plans.

Achieving Unitary Status

In the 1990s, the federal courts have worked on defining the legal definition of the successful achievement of school desegregation, that is, the standard by which to judge the transformation of a dual system into a unitary system. In January of 1991, the Supreme Court decided *Board of Education of Oklahoma City v. Dowell* (498 U.S. 237 [1991]), making it clear that federal court orders to desegregate dual school systems were "not intended to operate in perpetuity." School districts that complied in good faith with their court orders for several years and successfully addressed the *Green* factors—student assignments, faculty, staff, transportation, extracurricular activities, and facilities—could achieve unitary status. This decision also established the right to return to neighborhood schools once a school district was declared unitary. A little over a year later, the Court issued a decision in *Freeman v. Pitts* (503 U.S. 467 [1992]), reaffirming the temporary nature of school desegregation court orders and indicating that court control could be lifted for some or all of the *Green* factors, depending on district compliance. Furthermore, the court made it clear that while racial balance must be achieved when a constitutional violation was its cause, demographic changes, even in a district under court order, did not necessitate constant plan modifications. In *Missouri v. Jenkins* (515 U.S. 70 [1995]), the court rejected the argument that any black–white achievement gap, regardless of cause, must be eliminated before a school district could be declared unitary.

The result of these decisions has been a steady stream of school districts declared unitary and therefore no longer under a federal court order. In the Wilmington, Delaware metropolitan case, U.S. District Court Judge Sue Robinson rejected the argument that the achievement test score gap between black and white students was due to a failure to implement the court's school desegregation order, and she declared the four pie-slice-shaped school districts born of the interdistrict metropolitan court case unitary. Austin, Texas; Broward County, Florida; Denver; Norfolk, Virginia; and Oklahoma City have returned to some version of neighborhood schools after their court orders were lifted (Hendrie 1998b). Other school districts terminating or dramatically altering their school desegregation plans in the 1990s included Cleveland, Ohio; Buffalo, New York; Clark County (Las Vegas); Nashville–Davidson County, Tennessee; Duval

County (Jacksonville), Florida; Mobile, Alabama; San Jose, California; Seattle, Washington; and Boston, Massachusetts (Orfield and Yun 1999).

The only movement in the other direction was in state court. In Connecticut, the *Sheff v. O'Neill* (678 A.2d 1267 [Conn. 1996]) decision by the State Supreme Court, based on the State not the U.S. Constitution, indicated that Connecticut was guilty of failing to desegregate the Hartford schools, even though this could only have been done by involving the suburban districts. The State Court gave the job of designing a remedy to the state legislature. The state legislature rejected interdistrict consolidation and mandatory reassignment and instead authorized funding for a system of interdistrict magnet schools and voluntary interdistrict transfer programs. The plaintiffs objected to the slow pace of interdistrict desegregation and two years after the Supreme Court ruling, filed suit. After a trial, the superior court judge ruled in 1998 that the voluntary plan had not been given enough time to work and that the state could continue with its interdistrict magnets and the interdistrict transfer program.

A number of events in the 1990s besides school segregation or desegregation focused the nation's attention on race relations. The beating of African American Rodney King (1991) in Los Angeles and subsequent acquittal of his alleged white attackers (1992), and the 1995 murder trial of O.J. Simpson and reaction to his acquittal highlighted major problems and lack of understanding of African American/white relations. But the September 1998 report of President Clinton's advisory commission on race relations, chaired by African American historian John Hope Franklin, failed to ignite the public, Congress, or even the President. By the year 2000, only the presidential candidacy of former Senator Bill Bradley promised any chance of focusing the nation's attention on figuring out, as had been asked years ago, "why can't we just get along." While school desegregation was not totally ignored by social scientists, no work in the decade of the 1990s seemed to stir the passions of academics or the general public the way *An American Dilemma* and "The Evidence on Busing" had done. Gary Orfield, a long-standing supporter of school desegregation and busing to achieve racial balance, documented the "resegregation" of schools in his book *Dismantling Desegregation* and reports (e.g., Orfield and Yun 1999). David Armor (1995) analyzed the changing federal court view of busing and the research literature on the lack of positive effects from school desegregation in *Forced Justice*. But neither work seemed to influence policy.

Pursuing Diversity

Predicting the future, especially where politics, federal courts, and human emotion play a huge role, is not an easy task. But a number of trends that began in the 1990s are likely to survive the year 2000 change.

The Kerner Commission had warned Americans that we were heading toward two nations in 1968. Over thirty years later, however, we find less racial polarization and a much greater recognition and emphasis on diversity in the nation. The student group that is growing rapidly in the country is Latinos, not blacks or whites. In their 1999 report, Orfield and Yun conclude that the changes in restrictive immigration laws in 1965 and low white and high Latino birth rates have led to a tripling of the percentage of Latinos in public schools from 2 million in 1968 to over 6 million (as compared to 7.7 million blacks) in 1996. From 1940 to 1960, non-white students comprised 11 to 12 percent of total enrollment; in 1996 the percentage of non-whites was 36 percent and their proportion is predicted to grow to 58 percent by 2050. Five states—California, Texas, Mississippi, New Mexico, and Hawaii—had a majority of minority students before the year 2000.

While busing and even desegregation are now viewed skeptically by many, diversity efforts are viewed as legitimate and even productive for a society where Latinos, Asian immigrants, and women are playing an increasingly important role. Policies that focus on only African Americans as a minority are increasingly discredited. The legal framework for school desegregation was built upon the court challenges of African Americans; it was not until the *Keyes* decision in 1973 that issues concerning Latinos were addressed. Subsequent decisions addressing questions of Latino segregation did not have the legal impact of black–white desegregation decisions. The increasing enrollment of Latinos, as well as Asian students, is a further reason for the focus shifting from desegregation to diversity.

Changes in the governance of education have led to different challenges in the arena of pupil assignment and race. The increasing role of magnet and charter schools has led to new suits over the admission of non-African Americans to these schools of choice. As Hendrie (1998a) reports, "magnet schools . . . are proving to be nearly as adept at attracting discrimination lawsuits as they are luring students." Whites and Asian-Americans are suing (e.g., Boston and San Francisco) to gain places in magnet schools after failing to gain entrance and blaming racial quotas as the reason. The majority of the Supreme Court has been applying a standard of "strict scrutiny" to governmental action, including school district student assignment plans that are the basis for magnet schools. Under this doctrine (e.g., *Wygant v. Jackson Board of Education*, 476 U.S. 267 [1986]), race-conscious legal remedies must be based on an explicit finding of racial discrimination and must be narrowly tailored to the violation. The court has reasoned that to do more would violate the Fourteenth Amendment. To maintain racial balance at a magnet school, school districts generally have developed affirmative action plans which set different admission standards for students. Black students may find it easier to be admitted to selective magnets or assigned to a regular magnet school or program, thus opening the school district to charges of discrimination against whites. Under the "strict scrutiny" standard, the burden is on the school officials to prove that unlawful racial discrimination can only be reduced by such an assignment plan. This a difficult burden, for more than societal discrimination must be proven and magnet assignment plans have been ruled unconstitutional by federal courts in Boston in 1998 in the *Wessman v. Gittens* (160 F.3d 790) case over admissions policy to Boston Latin School, and federal court rulings resulted in the abandoning of racial-balance limits for schools in San Francisco. By 1999, Houston and Buffalo had rejected long-standing race-based admission policies and similar policies were under attack in Charlotte-Mecklenburg, Arlington, Virginia, and Montgomery County, Virginia. The lack of legal certainty in this realm, however, is likely to lead to more court challenges in the decade ahead.

The legal battle over school desegregation was fought in the federal courts while the battle over school finance, because of the limiting *San Antonio Independent School District v. Rodriquez* (411 U.S. 1 [1973]) decision of the U.S. Supreme Court, has been fought in state courts. With the conservative U.S. Supreme Court declaring districts unitary and applying the "strict scrutiny" standard, and with even the most supportive state court in Connecticut accepting a voluntary plan, desegregation victories are unlikely to be achieved in the courts. The federal courts are now moving toward certifying unitary school districts rather than demanding dual systems become desegregated.

The politics of school desegregation are clear. The public rejection of de jure segregation, at least by the public in the North and progressive areas of the South, has not developed into a political force for racial balance. The political will to challenge demographic forces and suburban enclaves is simply not there. The federal courts now reflect the lack of political support. The public is focused on school choice and vouchers, standards and accountability, and educational technology. If school integration is again to be a national goal, new forces will have to emerge in the new century.

ENDNOTES

1. These stages are derived, in part, from Myers (1989) and Wilkinson (1979) as well as from my book, *Historical Dictionary of School Segregation and Desegregation* (Raffel, 1998). The *Dictionary* includes over 260 entries of terms and concepts, people, organizations, court decisions, desegregation plans, reports, and legislation. In addition, a chronology and bibliographic essay should also interest readers of this chapter. The *Dictionary* was the main source for this chapter.

2. I find it awkward not to use the term "Negroes" when discussing 19th-century history and court cases. I therefore shift my terms from Negro to Black to African American as the historical context demands.

Stages of School Segregation/Desegregation

Stage	Time	Legal Marker	Legal Standard	Evaluation Criterion	Desegregation Status	Key Historical Events	Major Social Science Work
From Compulsory Illiteracy to Negro Schools	Pre 1896	Fourteenth Amendment	Segregation allowed		Schools for Negroes allowed	Civil War; Reconstruction	No research
Segregation: "Separate but Equal"	1896-1935	*Plessy*	Separate and unequal	Inequity	Dual systems allowed	End of Reconstruction	*Souls of Black Folk*
Challenging Segregation	1935-1954	*Gaines*	Separate but equal (higher education)	Equity in higher education	Dual systems unconstitutional	World War II	*An American Dilemma*
Ending State Segregation	1954-1964	*Brown*	Nondiscrimination	Equity	Dual systems unconstitutional	Assassination of JFK	Footnote 11
Achieving Racially Balanced Schools	1964-1974	*Green; Swann; Keyes*	Racial balance	Equity	Desegregation to be achieved in dual systems	Civil Rights Act of 1964; Assassinations of M.L. King and Robt. Kennedy	*Racial Isolation in the Schools*
Limiting Desegregation Remedies	1974-1990	*Milliken*	Remedy fit violation	Efficiency	Desegregation limited by district boundaries	Nixon's election by Southern Strategy; Reagan Administration	White Flight Debate
Achieving Unitary Status	1990-2000	*Dowell; Freeman v. Pitts; Missouri v. Jenkins*	Effort; *Green* factors	Effectiveness	Achievement of desegregation in unitary districts	Rodney King beating; O.J. trial; Columbine H.S. shooting	*Forced Justice v. Dismantling Desegregation*
Pursuing Diversity	Post 2000			Fairness	Post-desegregation		

REFERENCES

Armor, David J. 1972. The evidence on busing. *Public Interest* (Summer): 90–126.

———. 1995. *Forced Justice: School Desegregation and the Law*. New York: Oxford UP.

Bradley, Anne. 1998. Black parents want focus on academics: Survey finds lack of passion for integration. *Education Week* 17.43 (5 August): 1.

Coleman, James S., Sara D. Kelly, and John A. Moore. 1975. *Trends in School Desegregation, 1968–73*. Washington, D.C.: Urban Institute.

Days, Drew. 1998. Brown blues: Rethinking the integrative ideal. In *Redefining Equality*, edited by Neal Devins and Davison M. Douglas. New York: Oxford UP.

Farley, Reynolds, Howard Schumann, Susanne Bianchi, Diane Colasanto, and Shirley Hatchett. 1978. Chocolate city, vanilla suburbs: Will the trend toward racially separate communities continue? *Social Science Research* 7: 319–44.

Hendrie, Caroline. 1998a. New magnet school policies sidestep an old issue: Race. *Education Week* 17.39 (10 June): 10.

———. 1998b. Pressure for community schools grows as court oversight wanes. *Education Week* 17.40 (17 June): 23.

Keynes, Edward, with Randolph K. Miller. 1989. *The Courts vs. Congress: Prayer, Busing and Abortion*. Durham: Duke UP.

Kluger, Richard. 1975. *Simple Justice: The History of* Brown v. Board of Education *and Black America's Struggle for Equality*. New York: Vintage.

Kujovich, Gil. 1992. Equal opportunity in higher education and the black public college: The era of separate but equal. In *Race, Law, and American History, 1700–1990: The African–American Experience*, edited by Paul Finkelman, 217–360. Vol. 7, Part II. *The Struggle for Equal Education*. New York: Garland.

Myers, Samuel. 1989. *Desegregation in Higher Education*. Lanham: NAFEO Research Institute, University Press of America.

Myrdal, Gunnar. 1944. *An American Dilemma: The Negro Problem and Modern Democracy*. New York: Harper and Row.

Orfield, Gary, Susan Eaton, and The Harvard Project on School Desegregation. 1996. *Dismantling Desegregation: The Quiet Reversal of* Brown v. Board of Education. New York: New Press.

Orfield, Gary, Franklin Monfort, and Melissa Aaron. 1989. *Status for School Desegregation: 1968–1986*. Report of the Council of Urban Boards of Education and the National School Desegregation Research Project. U of Chicago.

Orfield, Gary, and John T. Yun. 1999. *Resegregation in American Schools*. Cambridge, Mass.: Civil Rights Project, Harvard University.

Pettigrew, Thomas F., and Robert L. Green. 1976. School desegregation in large cities: A critique of the Coleman white flight thesis. *Harvard Educational Review* 46.1 (February): 1–53.

President's Committee on Civil Rights. 1947. *To Secure These Rights*. New York: Simon and Schuster.

Raffel, Jeffrey A. 1998. *Historical Dictionary of School Segregation and Desegregation*. Westport: Greenwood Press.

Rossell, Christine H. 1975–76. School desegregation and white flight. *Political Science Quarterly* 92 (Winter): 675–96.

———. 1995. The convergence of black and white attitudes of school desegregation issues during the four decade evolution of the plans. *The William and Mary Law Review* 36.2 (January): 613–63.

Rossell, Christine H., and David J. Armor. 1996. The effectiveness of school desegregation plans, 1968–1991. *American Politics Quarterly* 24.3 (July): 267–302.

Stern, Mark. 1992. *Calculating Visions: Kennedy, Johnson, and Civil Rights*. New Brunswick, N.J.: Rutgers UP.

U.S. Commission on Civil Rights. 1967. *Racial Isolation in the Public Schools*. Washington, D.C.: U.S. Government Printing Office.

Wasby, Stephen L., Anthony A. D'Amato, and Rosemary Metrailer. 1977. *Desegregation from Brown to Alexander: An Exploration of Supreme Court Strategies*. Carbondale, Ill.: Southern Illinois U.

Wilkinson, J. Harvie, III. 1979. From *Brown to Bakke: The Supreme Court and School Integration: 1954–1978*. Oxford UP.

Wilhoit, Francis M. 1973. *The Politics of Massive Resistance*. New York: George Braziller.

Chapter 3

Legal Issues Related to School Funding/Desegregation

∞

Alfred A. Lindseth

INTRODUCTION

Desegregation lawsuits in the 21st century? You can't be serious! *Brown v. Board of Education* outlawed school segregation in 1954, almost a half-century ago.[1] Since then, there have been hundreds of court cases and decisions spelling out the rules when it comes to the desegregation of schools. One would think that all significant legal issues related to school desegregation had already been litigated and decided. What more can there possibly be to say about the subject? The answer, surprisingly, is "quite a lot."

It is true that the primary goal of *Brown*—to end state-mandated separate schools for black and white children—has been realized. Deliberate segregation of school children by race is rarely even alleged any longer, much less proven. Despite these successes, however, legal issues relating to school desegregation and related issues of minority student achievement and school funding are likely to remain with us well into the 21st century. Many despair that the promises of *Brown* have not yet been fully realized. Numerous school districts remain under active federal court supervision. Large numbers of schools, especially those located in our central cities, are attended largely by poor and minority students, having been abandoned by much of the white, as well as black, middle class. Even more important, decades of expensive and often disruptive desegregation plans have failed to close or even appreciably narrow the achievement gap between black and white students. Therefore, as the demographics in many of our urban centers render further racial integration of their schools impractical, and substandard achievement by disproportionately large numbers of minority students continues to plague the nation, the focus of desegregation efforts has shifted from racial balance measures to programs designed to increase educational opportunities for minority students in schools that are overwhelmingly minority.[2] Even given this relatively recent emphasis on quality of education rather than racial balance, it is clear that federal court supervision of our nation's schools is waning and will probably become a thing of the past within the next decade as school districts still under federal court supervision are released.

However, as federal court supervision over the desegregation of school districts formerly segregated by governmental policy or practice is being phased out, a whole new generation of legal actions are being filed, mostly in state courts. These actions allege state constitutional violations as a basis for the judiciary to order additional education dollars for schools in predominately poor and minority urban areas that cannot be obtained through normal political processes. Some of these lawsuits also attempt to require desegregation on a cross-district basis that plaintiffs have been unable to attain in federal court. These state law claims do not require proof of intentional racial discrimination, one of the major obstacles inherent in establishing a right to relief in a traditional desegregation action under the Fourteenth Amendment. Instead, they rely on state constitutional provisions which have been interpreted in many states to require the state government to ensure an "adequate" or particular standard of educational opportunity for all children in the state. The plaintiffs bringing such "adequacy suits," as they are commonly referred to, are both local school districts and civil rights or other advocacy groups, often working together as they seek a common goal—more dollars, usually from the state, for education.

At the same time these legal challenges are being asserted against state officials and entities, many local school districts that have succeeded in desegregating their schools and have been released from federal court supervision now find themselves back in court if they try to voluntarily continue the very desegregation steps they were required to take while under court order. Several courts have ruled that student assignment or transfer plans that continue to take race into account after the school district has been declared unitary are in violation of the Equal Protection Clause of the Fourteenth Amendment. In school districts operating under court supervision, transfer and magnet school plans customarily utilize racial guidelines to ensure that the student enrollment of the schools remains integrated. When a school system becomes unitary, by definition, it has remedied all prior constitutional violations, and there is no longer any necessity for remedial measures. Since such plans no longer serve a remedial purpose, the continued use of racial criteria to ensure racial diversity in a unitary school system has been repeatedly, although not always, struck down by the courts as a violation of the Equal Protection Clause.[3] Until the Supreme Court issues a definitive ruling on this issue, local school boards will continue to struggle with the question of how much, if at all, they may consider race in assigning children to schools for the purpose of maintaining diversity.

In this chapter, I discuss the evolution of school desegregation law from the *Brown* decision to the present time. I then address the major legal issues likely to face state and local educational authorities as they enter the next millennium. These issues are (1) school desegregation and the closing of the black–white achievement gap, (2) more state education dollars for predominately poor and minority urban school districts, and (3) whether school authorities can use racial criteria in student assignment and transfer plans to promote diversity in school districts that, by judicial declaration, have already remedied the discrimination of the past. These are the major desegregation related issues that we believe will face local and state leaders and educators in the next century.[4]

SCHOOL DESEGREGATION LAW: A SHORT HISTORY

Prior to 1954, schools in states of the Deep South, as well as in many border states and the District of Columbia, were segregated under state law and the "separate but equal" doctrine approved by the Supreme Court in 1896.[5] However, in 1954, the Supreme Court decided the famous case of *Brown vs. Board of Education*, ruling that state-sponsored segregation of schools violated the Equal Protection Clause of the Fourteenth Amendment of the federal constitution.[6] In *Brown II*, decided a year later, school districts were ordered to dismantle state-mandated dual school systems "with all deliberate speed."[7] The *Brown* ruling was extremely controversial in that it mandated fundamental changes in the social fabric of the South (and eventually in other areas of the country as desegregation efforts moved north and west). However, it is doubtful that the federal judiciary or anyone else could have predicted the course of events following the *Brown* decision.

That the legal issues related to desegregation are likely to be different in the next decade or century should not surprise anyone familiar with the subject. There have been several significantly different stages in the desegregation of the nation's schools and they roughly correspond to the decades which have passed since *Brown* was decided. The 1950s was characterized by massive resistance by most of the southern states to the *Brown* decree. The 1960s was largely a decade of accommodation, as courts approved "freedom-of-choice" plans that resulted in token integration of some formerly white schools, but virtually no integration of black schools. The 1970s was the decade of controversial forced busing plans, as the courts grew weary of resistance to court orders and took strong, affirmative steps to forcibly integrate not only schools in the South, but in the rest of the country. In the 1980s, as the weaknesses of mandatory busing plans became more apparent, the courts began to rely more and more on voluntary de-segregation plans utilizing magnet schools and other incentives designed to attract to schools on a voluntary basis a racially diverse student population. These plans were expensive, and so it was also in the 1980s that plaintiffs began to shift their attention to establishing state liability as a means of obtaining necessary funding for the more expensive remedies, that is, magnet schools and measures designed to address low student achievement. Finally, the 1990s have been characterized by the efforts of school districts and states to win release from court supervision.

The 1950s: Massive Resistance

Southern states, by and large, reacted to the *Brown* decision with massive resistance to desegregation of their schools. State governors and legislatures led the opposition and enacted various forms of "segregation" laws designed to maintain segregated schools, including, among other things, state statutes which withheld funding from school districts that integrated any of their schools.[8] Some states, for example, Virginia, went so far as to close their public schools rather than integrate them.[9] Some states anticipated the ruling in *Brown,* and began to take steps even prior to the Court's decision to ensure that their schools would remain segregated even if *Brown* struck down their school segregation laws. For example, in 1951, South Carolina passed a "penny sales tax" and used the proceeds to embark upon a massive school building program in the early 1950s. The schools were purposely built in racially "homogeneous" neighborhoods so that geographic practicalities would keep the schools largely of one race or the other even if a court ruled that government-enforced school segregation was unconstitutional.[10] As a result, with few notable exceptions, southern public schools remained completely segregated throughout the rest of the 1950s and into the early 1960s.[11]

The 1960s: A Short Period of Accommodation

Although a small number of black students attended predominately white schools during the 1960s, the schools remained largely one race or the other during most of that decade. The courts approved freedom of choice plans which allowed children and their parents to choose the schools they wanted to attend. These plans were relatively uncontroversial, but also ineffective in desegregating most schools (which is the main reason they were not very controversial). In actual practice, virtually no white children elected to attend black schools, and such schools remained 100 percent black. At the same time, only small numbers of black children chose to attend white schools; therefore, those schools, although nominally integrated, remained mostly white.

In 1964, Congress took an important step toward promoting school desegregation when it passed the Civil Rights Act of 1964.[12] This landmark legislation authorized the federal government to withhold funds from school districts that did not comply with the law. In those states which formerly required segregated schools, a school district could only qualify for federal funds if it adopted a desegregation plan approved by the Office for Civil Rights (OCR). Since court suits were an impractical way to desegregate thousands of school districts, this legislation did more to desegregate the South than any other single event, except, of course, for the *Brown* decision itself.

However, OCR, which was charged with enforcing the Civil Rights Act, took its lead from the courts and initially approved freedom of choice plans that, with few exceptions, resulted in only token integration. Therefore, even with the passage of the Civil Rights Act, most schools remained predominantly one race or the other until the end of the 1960s. Since the more controversial forms of school desegregation measures, such as forced busing, were still in the future, the 1960s was a relative period of calm before the storm that was just over the horizon.

The 1970s: Forced Busing and the Expansion of Desegregation to the North

In 1968, after several years of token desegregation, the Supreme Court decided *Green v. School Board of New Kent County*, a case which fundamentally changed the courts' approach to desegregation.[13] In *Green*, the Court held that desegregation plans which failed to produce effective desegregation of schools were no longer acceptable, thereby spelling the end to freedom of choice plans.[14] More important, it commanded school districts to take all affirmative steps necessary to eliminate "all vestiges" of the former dual school system in several key areas of school operations thereafter known as the *Green* factors—student assignment, faculty and staff assignment, facilities, extracurricular activities and transportation.[15] Taking its lead from the Court, OCR also began requiring plans that promised substantial, and not minimal, desegregation. The six *Green* factors have served ever since as guidelines for the courts in not only evaluating and approving desegregation plans, but in deciding when and if a school district has satisfied its affirmative obligation to desegregate and is entitled to unitary status and release from court supervision.[16]

Green was followed in 1971 by the Supreme Court's decision in *Swann v. Charlotte-Mecklenburg Board of Education*, which approved the use of mandatory student reassignments, or "forced busing" as it became known.[17] As a result of *Green* and *Swann*, school districts throughout the South were desegregated, sometimes literally overnight, through the mandatory reassignment of students. Mandatory busing took many forms, including the pairing of black and white schools, gerrymandering of attendance zones and the use of noncontiguous school attendance zones. The bottom line of all such plans was that they mandatorily reassigned substantial numbers of children from their neighborhood schools, normally predominately white or black, to an integrated school outside the child's neighborhood.

The era of relative calm during the 1960s ended with the advent of forced busing as white parents vigorously opposed busing plans with boycotts, instances of violence and, in the end, withdrawal of their children from public schools. For example, in Savannah–Chatham County, Georgia, over 40 percent of the white children assigned to formerly black schools in the first year of forced busing failed to enroll at their assigned school, suggesting they either moved out of the school district or otherwise withdrew their children from the public schools.[18] As a result, despite mandatory reassignments, many inner-city schools gradually lost their white enrollment and became predominately poor and minority.

The 1970s was also characterized by the expansion of school desegregation lawsuits in school districts outside the South. Indeed, the most controversial and often most violent reaction to forced busing occurred not in the South, but in northern and western school districts in cities like Boston and Pontiac. The 1970s also saw the advent of legal efforts in many metropolitan areas to obtain court-ordered busing across school district boundaries in order to integrate predominately minority inner city schools with the predominately white suburban schools.[19] However, with a few notable exceptions, this effort at interdistrict desegregation failed.

The 1980s: Voluntary Desegregation/State Funding

Despite widespread use, forced busing plans remained very unpopular among white parents. Such plans were often followed by massive white enrollment losses, especially in central city school systems. As middle-class white (and black) students abandoned inner-city schools for the suburbs or private schools, the enrollment of these schools became largely minority, as well as poor, making real integration even more difficult regardless of the type of plan used.[20] It was particularly difficult to integrate formerly all-black schools. Despite having significant white residential areas assigned to them, these schools often remained mostly black because of large numbers of white "no shows."

In the search for effective desegregation methods, school districts and courts began to turn to the use of so-called "voluntary" plans, which used incentives to persuade students to voluntarily transfer to racially integrated schools. The most common type of plan involved the use of magnet or theme schools, such as schools for the performing arts, math/science magnets, and honors magnets for high-performing students. The idea behind these schools was to entice children of different races to transfer to the magnet schools. The magnets would be subject to specified racial guidelines (e.g., 50% white and 50% black), so that the end result would be an integrated school. While such plans did not produce overnight racial balance, as forced busing plans could, studies showed that they were more effective at retaining middle-class students in the public schools and produced a longer-lasting, more stable level of desegregation.[21] At the same time courts began to order magnet plans, they also began to make much more use of so-called *Milliken II* educational enhancement remedies.

Despite their advantages, magnets and educational enhancement remedies had one serious drawback—they were expensive. Therefore, civil rights plaintiffs, as well as school districts, began to look to state governments as a source of additional funding. Desegregation cases were filed or expanded specifically for the purpose of joining states and their educational departments and officials in order to obtain court orders requiring states to pay for all or a significant portion of the increasingly expensive desegregation remedies. Perhaps the most significant of these state liability suits were against the state of Missouri in connection with the funding of extensive desegregation plans in St. Louis and Kansas City.[22] Between 1983 and 1997, the state of Missouri was ordered by the federal courts to spend over *three billion dollars* on desegregation measures in those two cities, raising per-pupil expenditures in both cities to unprecedented levels.[23]

The 1990s: The Ending of Court Supervision/Concurrent Emphasis on Quality of Education

Beginning in the late 1980s and continuing into the 1990s, many school districts began to seek an end to continued court supervision. Most had been under court supervision for a decade or more, and believed that they had successfully dismantled their prior segregated school systems. In most cases, the courts agreed. In a series of decisions, the Supreme Court made it clear that court supervision was not intended to be permanent and spelled out the requirements a school district had to meet in order to be released from court supervision. In 1991, the Court decided *Board of Education v. Dowell*, in which it made clear that school desegregation decrees "are not intended to operate in perpetuity," and that school districts are entitled to be released from court supervision once they proved that (1) they had complied in good faith with the desegregation decree and (2) eliminated all vestiges of past discrimination to the extent practicable.[24] A year later in *Freeman vs. Pitts*, a case involving the DeKalb County, Georgia, School

District, the Supreme Court further held that a school district could not be held responsible for segregated housing patterns that the school district did not cause, thereby making it clear that de facto segregation caused by housing patterns could not serve as a permanent bar to unitary status.[25] The third case decided by the Supreme Court was *Jenkins v. Missouri* (*"Jenkins III"*), which grew out of the extensive efforts to remedy segregation in the Kansas City, Missouri, School District. In *Jenkins III*, the Court severely scaled back an extensive remedy ordered by the lower courts and made it clear that desegregation remedies could not be ordered to enhance the quality of education unless the harm sought to be remedied was specifically caused by the prior de jure school system.[26]

As a consequence, school districts that had been under court order for decades began to seek unitary status and release from court supervision. During the late 1980s and 1990s, school districts in urban areas such as Cleveland; Dallas; DeKalb County, Georgia; Boston; Savannah; Jacksonville; Charlotte-Mecklenburg, North Carolina; Wilmington, Delaware; and a number of other urban areas were declared unitary. In other cases, settlements were negotiated and approved by the courts, which provided for a phasing out of court supervision over several years.[27]

So what is the current situation when it comes to school desegregation? Although a number of large school districts and states still remain under active federal court supervision,[28] school desegregation litigation as we have come to know it is likely to disappear early in this century. In the cases that remain, the main issues will not be whether the vestiges related to the six *Green* factors have been eliminated. Instead, courts will focus on the issue of whether the achievement gap or low minority test scores are traceable to the prior segregated school system, and, if so, what further measures are necessary and practicable to remedy such "educational vestiges," and how and by whom will they be funded. Because traditional federal court desegregation actions are becoming more and more difficult to maintain, state court actions are likely to become the main mechanism by which civil rights and other advocacy groups will seek to achieve their goals.

SCHOOL FUNDING LAWSUITS

With the shift in emphasis from racial balance to improvement of educational quality, legal strategies pursued by plaintiffs' groups have changed. The key elements of school desegregation remedies no longer address the so-called *Green* factors, but instead focus on "educational improvement plans" designed to improve student performance, especially among poor and minority students.[29] These plans include reduced class sizes, expanded professional development programs for teachers, increased pay intended to attract higher-quality teachers, before- and after-school programs, early childhood education programs, and special literacy and reform programs such as Success for All and Reading Recovery. Because some local school districts may not have the financial resources to fund these types of educational improvements, states have become the main targets in lawsuits designed to bring about increased funding for such reforms. Local school districts, which are the recipients of increased state funding, have themselves a strong financial interest in the success of such litigation and, therefore, are often a named plaintiff or a supportive participant with school advocacy groups in such lawsuits.

To date, such state funding lawsuits have taken the following forms:[30]

1. Traditional desegregation lawsuits brought in federal court based on the Fourteenth Amendment of the United States Constitution to require states to fund education programs which will eliminate educational vestiges.

2. Educational adequacy lawsuits brought in state courts to enforce state constitutional provisions requiring that an adequate or some other minimum standard of education be provided.

Fourteenth Amendment Claims

Until the Supreme Court's decision in *Freeman*, most court hearings to either approve or modify a desegregation plan or to determine if a school district had satisfied its constitutional obligations and was, therefore, entitled to unitary status, concentrated almost entirely on evidence as to whether all remaining vestiges of segregation related to the six *Green* factors had been eliminated to the extent practical. However, in 1992, the *Freeman* Court injected an additional factor into the equation when it held that "quality of education" could also be considered by a federal court in deciding whether a school district had attained unitary status.[31] While it is unclear exactly what the Court meant by its reference to "quality of education," subsequent to *Freeman*, civil rights plaintiffs have relied on *Freeman* to argue that desegregation plans must include measures designed to eliminate educational vestiges and that until these educational vestiges are eliminated, court supervision, together with a panoply of education programs designed to eliminate these vestiges, must be continued. A number of courts have agreed that quality of education should be considered in conjunction with motions for unitary status, and, therefore, the most important issue in unitary hearings in recent years has become whether or not education vestiges remain to be remedied.

As measured by standardized test scores, as well as other measures of student performance, minority student achievement lags significantly behind that of white students both nationally and in virtually every urban school district in the country with any appreciable minority school enrollment. It is this achievement gap, as well as other evidence of lower minority student performance, such as dropout and graduation rates, that plaintiffs most often cite in support of their arguments that court-ordered educational improvement plans remain necessary and that court supervision (and most important, the court-ordered state funding that accompanies it) should be continued as long as these achievement gaps persist.

In 1995, the Supreme Court decided *Jenkins III*, in which it directly addressed issues of educational vestiges.[32] *Jenkins III* involved the extensive desegregation measures ordered by the federal court in the Kansas City, Missouri, School District (KCMSD). In that case, the lower court had ordered a series of expensive measures, including teacher raises, in an effort to improve minority achievement in the KCMSD. It based its authority to order such educational enhancements on its prior finding that black children were performing below the national average on nationally normed standardized tests. Although the Court of Appeals for the Eighth Circuit had upheld the district court's order, the Supreme Court reversed, holding that the fact that black students did not test at the national average did not justify the extensive remedial programs ordered by the district court. Although it confirmed the holding of the *Freeman* court that quality of education could be considered in conjunction with a motion for unitary status, it limited the effect of the *Freeman* decision by holding that the trial court had to determine "the incremental effect that segregation has had on minority student achievement."[33] Reflecting its further distrust of test score evidence, the Court instructed the trial court on remand that it "should sharply limit, if not dispense, its reliance" on test scores.[34]

Despite the door left slightly open by *Freeman* and *Jenkins III*, plaintiffs face significant hurdles in securing additional state funding through a traditional desegregation suit. First, plaintiffs, whether school districts, individuals, or advocacy organizations, face a host of procedural and technical obstacles when attempting to join state entities in a desegregation suit or to assert new claims against them even if the state is already a party to the lawsuit. Thus, claims against states have been dismissed, among other things, because plaintiffs lack standing to sue or because the state enjoys Eleventh Amendment immunity.[35]

Second, if plaintiffs are successful in overcoming these initial hurdles, under *Jenkins III*, they must still prove that the particular deficiencies, for instance, low achievement test scores by minority students, are attributable to the prior dual school system, a very difficult undertaking. Several generations have passed through most school systems since state-sponsored segregation was declared illegal, and the effects of past discrimination, in the words of Supreme Court Justice Scalia, "cannot realistically be assumed to be a significant factor."[36] Almost fifty years have passed since the *Brown* decision. Most school districts have been operating under court-approved desegregation plans for fifteen to thirty years. During that period, one and sometimes two or three generations of students have passed through the schools. It is likely that in most schools, even parents (and perhaps even the grandparents) of current minority students did not attend a school segregated by law. Moreover, problems such as poverty, single-parent status, limited English-speaking ability, and lower levels of parental education, which are more prevalent among minority than white families, are known to adversely affect student achievement.[37] Therefore, the task of determining what portion of present-day reduced minority performance, if any, is due to the prior dual school system, and not to other societal problems, is a formidable, if not, an impossible, undertaking.

Because of this difficulty, the issue of which party has the burden of proof becomes very important. Desegregation law has long held that, in a school district segregated by law or official government action or policy, racial disparities in the areas of school district operations described by the *Green* factors[38] are presumed to be linked to prior de jure segregation. Therefore, once such racial disparities were proved, that is, a school was disproportionately minority, the burden of proof shifted to the defendant school district or state to prove that such disparities were not causally linked to past de jure segregation.[39] However, when it comes to educational vestiges, courts have not been nearly as willing to give plaintiffs the benefit of this presumption. Instead, the majority of courts have held that plaintiffs bear the burden to prove that any disparities in test scores, for example, the achievement gap, is causally linked to the prior de jure school system.[40]

There are only a few cases that directly discuss the requirements of *Jenkins III*. One of them is a subsequent opinion of the district court in the *Jenkins* case itself. Following the Supreme Court decision in *Jenkins III*, the case was remanded to the district court, which then held a hearing on whether unitary status had been attained. The state of Missouri, which was funding the lion's share of the remedial plan in the KCMSD, argued that the KCMSD had attained unitary status. The plaintiffs and the school district, which faced financial difficulties if it was declared unitary and court-ordered state and local funding abruptly ended, opposed unitary status principally on the grounds that educational vestiges traceable to the prior dual school system had not been eliminated. The district court, based largely on its own statistical analysis, found that 26 percent of the achievement gap was attributable to the prior dual school system and ruled that the school district had to eliminate that portion of the achievement gap before it would be entitled to unitary status.[41]

The district court's decision was affirmed, without comment, by the Court of Appeals for the Eighth Circuit.[42] Unfortunately, the district court's rationale was utterly incomprehensible, so much so that the plaintiffs and the school district did not even attempt to defend the analysis on appeal. Nor does the Court of Appeals' opinion provide any assistance because it merely accepted the court's rationale without any discussion or effort to address the criticisms of it. Thus, the opinion provides little guidance to school authorities, or legal practitioners, in how one determines what, if any, part of the achievement gap in school districts is attributable to prior de jure segregation.

Other federal appeals courts have been much more strict when it comes to the type of evidence that they will accept as a basis for finding that educational vestiges still exist. A number of recent federal Court of Appeals' decisions illustrate the court's reluctance to accept lower court findings of educational vestiges premised on subjective and often anecdotal evidence.

In a recent opinion from the Second Circuit Court of Appeals, the court reversed the trial court's findings of educational vestiges in the Yonkers, New York, school district. The Court held that a finding of educational vestiges could not be based on the evidence cited by the trial court, which included anecdotes of low expectations by teachers for their minority students.[43] In another recent opinion, the First Circuit Court of Appeals reversed a decision of the trial court in the Boston desegregation case which had upheld a race-based student assignment plan in part because of remaining educational vestiges. Again the court refused to accept vague, anecdotal evidence of low teacher expectations as a basis for a finding of educational vestiges.[44]

Finally, in the Rockford, Illinois, desegregation case, the Seventh Circuit Court of Appeals in 1997 reversed the decision of the trial court that 50 percent of the achievement gap between black and white students in Rockford was attributable to the prior de jure segregation. In a scathing opinion, Judge Richard Posner held that the evidence did not support the district court's finding.[45] Upon remand, the district court again found educational vestiges. On appeal, the Court of Appeals, obviously disgusted with the lower court's continued efforts to maintain its supervision over the school district, reversed and dismissed the case, holding that the district had attained unitary status.[46]

At the same time, defendants, even when they have the burden of proof, have been able to establish through statistical analysis that the current achievement gap is not traceable to the prior dual school system. Perhaps the best example of such proof is the evidence relied on by the district court in a recent decision declaring that the state of Pennsylvania had satisfied its burden in proving that the achievement gap in the Woodland Hills school district (Pittsburgh) was not causally linked to prior segregation.[47] In reaching its conclusion, the district court relied primarily upon expert studies which first showed that the achievement gap existed at the time children entered school. The district court reasoned that this portion of the gap could not be the result of school segregation practices since it arose before the children even entered the school system. Second, expert studies, relying on multiple regression analyses, showed that factors outside the control of the schools, including poverty, explained most of the difference between the test scores of minority and white children, resulting in the district court's conclusion that the prior dual school system was not a causal factor.[48]

In summary, while *Jenkins III* permits plaintiffs the opportunity to prove that educational vestiges traceable to the prior dual school system still exist, it will be difficult for plaintiffs to meet this burden. It will become even more difficult to establish a causal link with the policies and practices of the already distant past as time goes on. Therefore, it is doubtful that plaintiffs will continue to rely on traditional desegregation suits as a means of obtaining court-ordered state funding for educational improvements. Rather, plaintiffs are more likely to pursue the new causes of action discussed in the next section of this chapter, in which it is not necessary to establish a nexus with events of the distant past.

Adequacy Lawsuits Under State Constitutional Law

As the era of federal court desegregation remedies has been winding down, plaintiffs' groups have sought other means by which to increase funding available to school districts with significant poor and minority enrollments or to pursue desegregation objectives that seem not likely to be attained in the federal courts. At first, the use of the property tax as the primary means of funding K–12 education was challenged because of large disparities in funding between wealthy and poor districts in many states. These so-called "equity" cases failed in the federal courts with the decision in *San Antonio Independent Sch. Dist. v. Rodriquez*, which held that education was not a fundamental right under the United States Constitution and that spending disparities based on wealth were not actionable.[49] However, litigants found more success in the state courts.[50] As a result, most state school financing systems now incorporate some mechanism to reduce the disparities in funding between property-rich and property-poor school districts. Usually, this is in the form of state funding formulas which allocate less state aid to the wealthier districts and more state aid to the poorer districts.

While these funding formulas do have an equalizing effect, they may not increase state aid to the level deemed necessary or adequate by some school districts and advocacy groups. Therefore, in the last decade or so, a different type of lawsuit has emerged which is intended to enforce state constitutional provisions requiring states to provide an adequate or other minimum level of education. These are not the same as the equity cases. A school district may enjoy higher than average funding, that is, have equitable funding, but may still have a claim that the amount of funding is insufficient to enable it to provide the particular level of education required by the state constitution, especially given the special needs of a student population disadvantaged by poverty and other societal problems.[51]

Most state constitutions contain an education clause that requires the state to create a "system" of education meeting one or more requirements. The wording of these provisions is usually fairly broad, including requirements such as creating "a system of free common schools"[52] or a "thorough and efficient"[53] system of education. In most states, the state's highest court has construed these vague provisions to require the state to provide for all of its children the opportunity for an education meeting certain standards. For example, New York's highest court has interpreted a state constitutional provision requiring the state to establish a "system of free common schools" to mean that the state has a constitutional obligation to provide the opportunity for "a sound basic education," consisting of "basic literacy, calculating, and verbal skills necessary to enable children to eventually function productively as civic participants capable of voting and serving on a jury."[54]

As a result, adequacy lawsuits have been filed in many states. Typically, the objective of the lawsuits has been to aid large urban school districts with low-performing and predominately poor and minority student populations. The plaintiffs are either advocacy groups or the urban school districts themselves, which stand to benefit from increased state financial aid. Defendants normally include the state, its governor, the state commissioner of education, the state board of education and the state department of education or similar governmental bodies. The relief sought in such suits almost always includes requests for additional state monies for programs designed to enhance education, such as reduced class sizes, before- and after-school programs, professional development programs, increased teacher pay, special facilities and equipment, special literacy and other programs (e.g., Success For All, Reading Recovery). In addition to monetary relief, such lawsuits sometimes allege that concentrations of race and poverty in the school district at issue inherently prevents the delivery of an adequate education, and that therefore the remedy must also include measures designed to break up such concentrations—in other words, a desegregation remedy.[55]

To date, adequacy actions have been brought in over twenty states. Particularly notable is the New Jersey case. In 1998, plaintiffs were able to obtain a final court order (after twenty-eight years) that required spending in the state's lowest performing districts be increased to the level spent in the state's highest spending districts.[56] Similarly, in Wyoming, the State Supreme Court held that students were entitled to the "best" education available and ordered the state to provide the necessary funding to reach that level.[57] Plaintiffs have also been successful in many other states.[58]

The momentum in plaintiffs' favor is likely to increase as a result of several recent victories for plaintiffs at the trial court level. In 2001, after a very controversial and lengthy trial, a New York City judge held the state of New York liable, ruling that the education available to New York City's over one million public school students did not satisfy minimum adequacy requirements. The court held that state and local funding of approximately $10,000

per student (or about $240,000 for the average classroom) was not suffi-
cient to provide even a basic education.[59] Another trial court recently declared that the Arkansas system of public education did not comply with the
Arkansas Constitution. While the trial court referred the matter to the state
legislature for necessary remediation action, it clearly indicated that significant increases in state funding would be necessary. Moreover, in an order almost certain to encourage plaintiffs' groups who wish to pursue such suits,
the court awarded plaintiffs' attorneys over $9 million in attorney's fees.[60]
These decisions, if upheld, are likely to require huge tax increases to fund
the improvements deemed essential by the trial courts.

In North Carolina, a trial court also found that the state's system of education failed to deliver an adequate education to the state's poor and minority students. Although the court stopped short of ordering additional
state funding, it did find that state funding would have to be reallocated to
address the problem of at-risk students.[61]

Because the stakes are so huge, these types of cases are given extraordinary scrutiny by the appellate courts. Therefore, whether plaintiffs' recent
trial court victories will be upheld in the appellate courts remains to be seen.

Despite much success, plaintiffs face many hurdles in ultimately obtaining significant relief. In adequacy suits filed in Florida,[62] Illinois,[63] and
Rhode Island,[64] plaintiffs' cases were dismissed before trial on the ground
that they presented issues to the courts traditionally reserved under those
states' constitutions to the legislative and executive branches of government. Even where such suits have survived a motion to dismiss, the results
have sometimes been a mixed bag for plaintiffs. For example, in 1996, the
St. Paul school district sued the state of Minnesota, contending that it
needed more funding to provide an adequate education. However, after
two years of expensive litigation, the district dismissed its lawsuit with no
assurance of any further state financial assistance.[65] In another action involving the Minneapolis public schools brought in 1995, the NAACP dismissed its suit against the state of Minnesota in return for state cooperation
regarding an interdistrict transfer plan among several school districts in the
Minneapolis metropolitan area, but without any significant additional state
funding.[66] Even when plaintiffs ultimately win in courts, significant relief
may be difficult to get. In *Sheff v. O'Neill*, the trial court rejected the plaintiffs' claim that the education provided in Hartford, Connecticut schools
failed to meet state constitutional standards. However, the Connecticut
Supreme Court, relying on a provision of the state constitution that prohibited segregation, ruled that even de facto segregation of the schools was
unconstitutional and reversed the trial court decision.[67] Even though plaintiffs succeeded in their quest to establish state liability, the Connecticut
courts have thus far shown little inclination to require the legislature to
enact a remedy that is significantly different from what was already in
place.

Finally, and perhaps most disappointing, even where such suits have resulted in significantly increased state funding, there is little empirical evidence that student achievement has significantly improved.[68]

Nevertheless, one thing is clear: given the phasing out of federal desegregation remedies and the substantial successes plaintiffs have enjoyed in state court adequacy cases, it is inevitable that the number of such cases is likely to increase in the next decade.

The trials of such adequacy cases are enormously complex, as well as controversial. State education financing systems are among the most complicated statutory schemes found in most states; large urban school systems are equally complicated; and there is no consensus among experts or educators on most of the important educational issues likely to arise in such a trial. These issues include:

1. The appropriate definition of an adequate education or whatever the standard is under the particular state constitutional standard at issue;
2. What performance outcomes should apply;
3. Whether the funding available is or should be sufficient to provide the necessary resources or opportunity for such education;
4. The applicability of existing state standards adopted by the legislature or administrative agencies;
5. Whether low performance in the school districts is due to a lack of necessary resources and funding or to other factors for which the state may or may not be held responsible, for instance, improper or inefficient use of existing funds by local boards of education, or constraints imposed by locally negotiated collective bargaining agreements;
6. Whether the states should be held liable for societal problems not within the control of school authorities, such as poverty and its debilitating effect on student performance.

The answers to these important issues will vary from state to state, depending on a number of factors, including the provisions of the particular state constitution and how it has been interpreted, and, of course, the evidence at trial. While some such suits may be resolved through settlement, many are likely to go to trial, because of the fundamental education and separation of powers issues involved.[69]

RACE-BASED REMEDIES IN A POST-UNITARY WORLD

The discussion thus far has centered mostly on state liability, primarily because it is states (and their "deep pockets") which are the main targets of the expensive educational remedies sought by most plaintiffs' groups. The issues facing local boards of education are quite different. Although some local boards of education must still concern themselves with ensuring that they are in compliance with court-ordered desegregation plans, most have completed or are in the final phase of desegregating their school districts. It is a rare case today in which a federal court orders controversial faculty and student reassignments. Moreover, when it comes to educational improvement plans, most local school boards stand to benefit from the increased funding that often flows from such plans; therefore, they are much more likely to join with plaintiffs in seeking such plans than they are to insist that they are unitary as to educational vestiges.[70] For that reason, while local boards of education may assert such claims against states, they are unlikely to become a source of potential liability or controversy for local boards.

The issue most likely to concern local school districts for the foreseeable future, unless the Supreme Court clarifies the issue, is the extent to which school districts may use racial criteria, if at all, in conjunction with pupil assignment or transfer plans to promote racial diversity or integration in their schools. Several years ago, this was a nonissue. Most school districts were still under court order where such race-conscious plans were often required. Even if a school district obtained unitary status, it was generally believed that an abandonment of long-standing desegregation measures soon after having been declared unitary might signal a return to institutional segregation, and be used as evidence to reinstitute federal court supervision. Therefore, it was not uncommon in the 1980s for school board attorneys to counsel their school district clients to resist constituents who wanted to immediately dismantle controversial student assignment plans once unitary status had been attained.

However, the law began to change in the 1980s with decisions in *Adarand Constructors, Inc. v. Pena*[71] and *City of Richmond v. J.A. Croson Co.*,[72] which held that the government must justify any racial classifications subjecting a person to unequal treatment under the strictest judicial scrutiny. When a school district is declared unitary, it has obtained a judicial declaration that it has eliminated all racial discrimination. In other words, the court makes a judicial finding that the school authorities have remedied the constitutional violation that gave rise to liability and court supervision in the first place. Applying the *Adarand* and *Croson* decisions to schools, a strong argument can be made that, once a school district has been declared unitary, it is no longer legally permissible to operate pupil assignment and transfer programs which employ racial criteria. If racial criteria are utilized, the court is required to subject such racial classifications to strict scrutiny to determine whether such use of race violates the Equal Protection Clause of the Fourteenth Amendment. In order to survive strict scrutiny, under *Adarand* and *Croson*, the court must find that the racial classifications (1) serve a compelling government interest, and (2) are narrowly tailored to achieve that interest. This is very difficult to establish where race clearly plays a role in the school assignments of children.

As a consequence, in many school districts that have been declared unitary (and some that have not),[73] student assignment systems which seek to maintain racial diversity by utilizing racial criteria in approving student transfers and assignments have not only been challenged, but have almost uniformly been ruled invalid and enjoined by the courts.[74]

Such lawsuits are as likely to be brought by representatives of black students, as by representatives of white students. Most such lawsuits involve magnet school or transfer programs which have been carried over from the time the school district was under court supervision and was required to implement such programs. To maintain desegregated magnet schools, for example, school racial guidelines were employed which required all magnet programs to be a certain percentage of each race, for instance, 50 percent white and 50 percent black. Often magnet seats would go empty because a program could not attract its required quota of white children, but additional black children could not be assigned to the magnet school because that would cause it to exceed its fifty–fifty requirement. Therefore, in several cases, it has been black students who have challenged such admissions criteria because they kept black students, often from the very neighborhood in which the magnet school was located, from attending the school even though it had empty seats.[75] In other cases, the complainant might be a white child denied the right to an interdistrict transfer while black children had the right to freely transfer.[76]

This issue has been a particularly vexing problem for school districts who are anxious to maintain the racial diversity in their schools that it has taken years of desegregation efforts to attain. While very few courts have directly addressed the issue of whether the interest of maintaining or encouraging racial diversity in our public schools serves a compelling interest strong enough to survive the strict scrutiny of the courts, the court decisions thus far have almost uniformly enjoined assignment and transfer plans which have the potential of disqualifying a student based on his or her race. With few exceptions, plans that have been challenged in court have not satisfied the legal requirements that the racial classification not only serve a compelling governmental interest, but also be narrowly tailored to achieve that interest.[77]

Can race never be used by a school board to encourage diversity in its schools? While the lower court decisions thus far are not a source for optimism on this subject, only two courts have definitively ruled that diversity is not a compelling government interest.[78] Most lower courts have ducked this issue, striking such programs down instead on the ground that, even assuming, without deciding, a compelling government interest is being served, the programs are not narrowly tailored enough to survive strict scrutiny.[79] This suggests that there may be a way to structure such programs to survive a constitutional challenge. However, this is an issue which the Supreme Court has not yet tackled.[80] Therefore, until the Supreme Court addresses this issue, it cannot be said with certainty that all use of race is unconstitutional. However, it is fairly clear that, at least for the present, any plan under which a child's race can make a real difference between his or her getting admitted to a magnet or special school or being approved for a transfer, is most likely going to be enjoined if challenged in court. Therefore, a school district trying to maintain diversity in its schools would be well-advised to rely on nonracial criteria in its student assignment plans, for example, a student's socioeconomic background.[81]

CONCLUSIONS

The judiciary will undoubtedly continue to play a significant role in public elementary and secondary education as we enter the new millennium. First, as school districts strive to maintain ethnic diversity in their schools even though no longer required as a remedial matter, the Supreme Court will be called upon to decide what balance, if any, should be struck between the consideration of race in student assignments and transfers and the maintenance of ethnic diversity in our schools. Second, as federal desegregation suits wind down and are dismissed, state adequacy lawsuits are likely to increase as plaintiffs' groups, disillusioned with the normal legislative process, turn to the courts as salvation for the problems plaguing inner-city schools serving large numbers of poor and minority children.

The stakes in such lawsuits are huge. For students in affected districts, the plaintiffs' success may mean more resources for education of students disproportionately suffering from poverty and other disabling societal problems known to adversely affect performance. Whether students will benefit from such increased funding is not by any means guaranteed, however. There is no consensus among experts regarding whether increased spending leads to higher achievement.[82] Moreover, if by focusing on money and resources, more fundamental problems of inefficiency and waste in the local district are ignored, pupils in such districts may not benefit from such additional resources. For taxpayers, a decision for plaintiffs may mean significantly increased taxes, since the money to finance court-ordered reforms will have to come from someplace (it is unlikely that as a political matter the money can be taken from other school districts). For the legislative and executive branches, a decision in plaintiffs' favor might well mean loss of control over not only a significant part of the state budget, but the very process and content of educational reform. It may mean indefinite court supervision of the state's school systems and less control by not only state leaders, but also local boards of education and other local leaders. While this may appeal to some, court supervision of schools has not in the past, even with corresponding significant court-ordered increases in school district funding, been a panacea when it comes to increasing pupil achievement.[83]

ENDNOTES

1. *Brown v. Board of Education*, 347 U.S. 483 (1954).

2. Programs designed to address educational needs of minority children are sometimes referred to as "Milliken II" programs after the Detroit desegregation case in which such desegregation measures were first approved by the Supreme Court. *Milliken v. Bradley*, 433 U.S. 267 (1977).

3. *Equal Open Enrollment Association v. Board of Education of Akron*, 937 F.Supp. 700 (N.D. Ohio 1996) (open enrollment transfer plan limited to black students struck down); *Wessman v. Gittens*, 160 F.3d 790 (1st Cir. 1998) (admissions criteria to Boston Latin School which relied partly on race unconstitutional); *Brewer v. West Irondequoit Central School District*, 32 F.Supp. 2d 619 (W.D.N.Y., 1999) (interdistrict transfer plan utilizing racial guidelines unconstitutional); *Eisenberg v. Montgomery County Public Schools* 197 F.3d 123 (4th Cir. 1999) (transfer plan utilizing racial guidelines unconstitutional); *Tuttle v. Arlington County School Board*, 195 F.3d 698 (4th Cir. 1999) (admissions criteria for "alternative" public kindergarten which relied upon racial balancing unconstitutional). See also, *Capacchione v. Charlotte-Mecklenburg Schools*, 57 F.Supp. 2d 228 (W.D.N.C. 1999), *rev'd sub nom, Belk v. Charlotte-Mecklenburg Board of Education*, 233 F.3d 232 (4th Cir. 2000), *vacated and reh'g en banc granted* (4th Cir. 17 Jan. 2001), *rev'd in part and aff'd in part by en banc court* (4th Cir. 21 Sept. 2001[2001 U.S. App. LEXIS 20712]) (admissions process to magnet schools that utilized racial criteria unconstitutional).

4. "High stakes" tests, increased standards and their impact on poor and minority children are also likely to be important issues in the next decade. While discussion of these issues is beyond the scope of this chapter, the standards movement has been sweeping the country and as states move more toward the use of "high stakes" tests to enforce graduation and other standards, lawsuits will be brought to challenge the use of such tests. See, for example, *Alianza Dominican v. N.Y.S. Education Department*, Civ. no. 4175 (E.D. N.Y., filed 18 July 2000).

5. In *Plessy v. Ferguson*, 163 U.S. 537 (1896), the Supreme Court held that separate, but equal accommodations did not constitute a denial of equal protection under the Fourteenth Amendment. This "separate, but equal" doctrine remained the law of the land until the decision in *Brown v. Board of Education*.

6. *Brown*, 347 U.S. 483 (1954).

7. *Brown II*, 349 U.S. 294 300–301 (1955).

8. See, for example, 1955 Georgia Laws 174, No. 82 (no state or local funds could be appropriated or spent for public school purposes "except for schools in which white and colored races are separately educated").

9. *School Board of the City of Richmond v. Baliles*, 829 F.2d 1308 (4th Cir. 1987).

10. *Stanley v. Darlington County School District*, 879 F.Supp. 1341, 1398–1400 (D.S.C. 1995).

11. Not all states with school segregation laws actively resisted the mandate of *Brown*. For example, almost immediately after *Brown* was decided, the Attorney General of Missouri instructed all state and local school superintendents that Missouri's segregation statutes were no longer the law of the state, and that school segregation in Missouri was illegal. *Jenkins v. Missouri*, 593 F.Supp. 1485, 1504–1505 (W.D. Mo. 1984). Years later the state of Missouri was held liable for school segregation in St. Louis and Kansas City and ordered to pay what eventually amounted

to over $3 billion in remedial costs. With one exception (Arkansas), none of the other eleven states of the old Confederacy, which, unlike Missouri, actively resisted compliance with *Brown,* have provided any significant amounts for school desegregation. See testimony of Christine Rossell in *Liddell v. Board of Education of St. Louis,* Case No. 72-0100C(6), (E.D. Mo. 1996).

   12. 42 USC§ 2000d.

   13. *Green v. School Board of New Kent County,* 391 U.S. 430 (1968). Although not as well known as *Brown* and other desegregation cases, the *Green* case is, in the author's view, the most significant case decided after *Brown* in that it provided the tools for effective enforcement of the *Brown* decision.

   14. *Green,* 391 U.S. at 441.

   15. *Green,* 391 U.S. at 437–438.

   16. The term "unitary status" is generally used to describe a school system which has successfully desegregated its former "dual" school system, that is, one system for white students and a second system for black students, and has transformed itself into a single or "unitary" school system for all races with all "vestiges" or signs of the prior dual school system having been eliminated.

   17. *Swann v. Charlotte-Mecklenburg Board of Education,* 402 U.S. 1 (1971).

   18. *Stell v. Board of Education for the City of Savannah and County of Chatham,* 860 F.Supp. 1563, 1565 (S.D. Ga. 1994).

   19. See, for example, *Milliken v. Bradley,* 418 U.S. 717 (1974).

   20. Los Angeles; Prince George's County, Maryland; St. Louis; and Kansas City are examples of just some urban school districts that lost most of their white school enrollment.

   21. Christine H. Rossell, 1990, *The Carrot or the Stick* (Temple UP).

   22. *Liddell v. Board of Education,* 491 F.Supp. 351, 359 (E.D.Mo. 1980), *aff'd and remanded* 667 F.2d 643 (8th Cir. 1981), *cert. denied* 454 U.S. 1081 (1981); *Jenkins v. Missouri,* 639 F.Supp. 19, 23–24 (W.D.Mo. 1985), *aff'd as modified by,* 807 F.2d 657 (8th Cir. 1986), *cert. denied* 484 U.S. 816 (1987).

   23. For example, by 1991–92, per-pupil operating expenditures in Kansas City had reached $9,412 versus $2,854 to $5,956 per student in the surrounding suburban districts. Total per-pupil expenses in Kansas City, including capital expenditures, were $13,500. *Jenkins et al. v. Missouri,* 19 F.3d 393, 399 (8th Cir., 1994).

   24. *Board of Education of Oklahoma City v. Dowell,* 498 U.S. 237, 248–250 (1991).

   25. *Freeman v. Pitts,* 503 U.S. 467, 491 (1992). In removing one significant impediment to unitary status, *Freeman* created another one by holding that "quality of education" was an element that courts could consider in deciding whether a school district qualified for unitary status. *Freeman,* 503 U.S. at 483. As discussed, vestiges relating to "quality of education" (i.e., the existence of the black–white achievement gap) have been the primary means by which plaintiffs' groups have in recent years sought to maintain court supervision over school districts.

   26. *Missouri v. Jenkins,* 515 U.S. 70 (1995) (*"Jenkins III"*).

   27. For example, see order dated 31 August 1998, *Vaughns v. Board of Education of Prince George's County,* Civil no. PJM-72-325 (D.C.Md. 31 August 1998) (settlement approved phasing out busing plan over three-year period).

   28. There are hundreds of smaller school districts across the nation (mostly in rural areas) that are still technically under court order, but in which the courts have little or no impact on the operations of the school district. Since it is expensive, and

sometimes controversial, to file and pursue a motion for unitary status, it is simply not worth the trouble and expense of many of these school districts to move for unitary status. Therefore, they are likely to remain under court order until the courts themselves take action to close such cases.

29. A good example is the current desegregation remedy proposed by plaintiffs for the Yonkers, New York, school district. Educational Improvement Plan II, or EIP II, as it is called, despite a projected cost of hundreds of millions of dollars, does not address any of the *Green* factors.

30. In some states, plaintiffs have supplemented their "adequacy" claims with causes of action alleging that the allocation of state financial aid also violates the implementing regulations under Title VI of the Civil Rights Act of 1964 because the distribution of such funds adversely impacts minority students. See, *Campaign for Fiscal Equity v. New York ("CFE")*, 86 N.Y.2d 307 (1995); *Powell v. Ridge*, 189 F.3d 387 (3d Cir. 1999). Plaintiffs actually succeeded at trial in establishing their Title VI regulation claim in the *CFE* case. However, after the *CFE* trial court decision, the U.S. Supreme Court held that private parties did not have standing to bring such claims under the Title VI regulations; see *Sandoval v. Alexander*, 121 S.Ct. 1511 (2001). Therefore, the trial court's decision in *CFE* is likely to be reversed, and similar actions may be of little use to private litigants in the future.

31. *Freeman*, 503 U.S. at 483.

32. *Jenkins III*, 515 U.S. 70 (1995).

33. *Jenkins III*, 515 U.S. at 101.

34. *Id.*

35. *Kelly v. Metropolitan County Board of Education of Nashville and Davidson County*, 836 F.2d 986 (6th Cir. 1987); *Stanley v. Darlington County School District*, 84 F.3d 707 (4th Cir. 1996); *DeKalb County School District v. Shrenko*, 109 F.3d 680 (11th Cir. 1997), *cert. denied*, 522 U.S. 1015 (1997).

36. *Freeman*, 503 U.S. at 506.

37. See, for instance, *Wessman v. Gittens*, 160 F.3d 790, 803–804 (1st Cir. 1998).

38. Student assignments, faculty and staff assignments, transportation, facilities, and extracurricular activities.

39. For example, *Columbus Board of Education v. Penick*, 443 U.S. 449 (1979).

40. Most of the courts that have addressed the burden of proof issue have placed the burden on the plaintiffs. *Oliver v. Kalamazoo Board of Education*, 640 F.2d 782, 811 (6th Cir. 1980); *United States v. Yonkers*, 833 F.Supp. 214, 222 n.3 (S.D.N.Y. 1993); *Coalition to Save Our Children v. State Board of Education of Delaware*, 90 F.3d 752, 776–778 (3d Cir. 1996); *People Who Care v. Rockford Board of Education*, No. 89-C20168, 1996 WL 364802 (N.D.Ill. filed 7 June 1996). Only where the court has previously found that achievement disparities are linked to the former dual school system will it sometimes require the defendant to prove the negative, that is, that current low minority achievement is not attributable to the prior dual school system. See, for example, *Jenkins v. Missouri*, 122 F.3d 588, 594 (8th Cir. 1997).

41. *Missouri v. Jenkins*, 959 F.Supp. 1151, 1164–1165 (W.D.Mo. 1997).

42. *Jenkins v. Missouri*, 122 F.3d 588, 595 (8th Cir. 1997).

43. *United States v. Yonkers*, 197 F.3d 41 (2d Cir.1999).

44. *Wessman v. Gittens*, 160 F.3d 790, 803–807 (1st Cir. 1998).

45. *People Who Care v. Rockford Board of Education*, 111 F.3d 528, 537–538 (7th Cir. 1997).

46. *People Who Care v. Rockford Board of Education*, 246 F.3d 1073 (7th Cir. 2001).

47. *Hoots v. Commonwealth of Pennsylvania*, 118 F.Supp. 2d 577 (W.D.Pa. 2000).

48. *Hoots*, 118 F.Supp. at 602–603.

49. *San Antonio Independent School District v. Rodriguez*, 411 U.S. 1 (1973).

50. See, for example, *Serrano v. Priest*, 557 P.2d 929 (Cal. 1976).

51. In several of the school districts that have brought or been the beneficiary of adequacy lawsuits, per-pupil expenditures have been significantly above the statewide average. See evidence developed during discovery in Minnesota adequacy cases, notes 65–66.

52. N.Y. Const, Art XI, §1.

53. Minn. Const, Art XIII, §1.

54. *CFE*, 86 N.Y.2d at 316 (1995).

55. An important, but yet unresolved, legal issue, pertaining to such lawsuits is whether a state court remedy which takes a student's race into account in making pupil assignments, which would seem to be necessary in order to break up racially concentrated schools, would survive a challenge under the Fourteenth Amendment. Since the purpose of such remedies is not to remedy prior intentional discrimination, the traditional remedial basis for permitting race-based assignments would not be present. In effect, the court would have to decide whether the state's interest in requiring a certain level of education in its schools constituted a compelling enough interest to permit the use of racial criteria and to overcome the "strict scrutiny" test applied by the courts to racial classifications. Since under the *Rodriquez* decision, the Supreme Court has already decided that the right to an education is not a fundamental right under the United States Constitution, the fact that it is deemed a fundamental right under state law may not be enough to overcome the Fourteenth Amendment's strict scrutiny of racial classifications.

56. *Abbott v. Burke*, 710 A.2d 450 (N.J. 1998).

57. *Campbell County School District v. State*, 907 P.2d 1238 (Wyo. 1995).

58. See, for example, *Horton v. Meskill*, 376 A.2d 359 (Conn. 1977); *Pauley v. Kelley*, 255 S.E.2d 859 (W. Va. 1979); *Rose v. Council for Better Education*, 790 S.W. 2d 186 (Ky. 1989); *McDuffy v. Secretary, Executive Office of Education*, 615 N.E. 2d 516 (Mass. 1993); *Roosevelt Elementary School District v. Bishop*, 877 P.2d 806 (Ariz. 1994); *Brigham v. State*, 692 A.2d 384 (Vt. 1997); *Claremont School District v. Governor*, 703 A.2d 1353 (N.H. 1997).

59. *CFE*, Case No. 111070/93 (N.Y. Sup. Ct. 10 Jan. 2001).

60. Order entered in *Lake View School District No. 25 of Phillips County v. Mike Huckabee* (Ch. Ct., Pulaski Co., Ark. 25 May 2001, Case No. 1992-5318.

61. Order entered in *Hoke County Board of Education v. North Carolina* (Super. Ct. N.C. 26 Mar. 2001), Case No. 95-CVS-1158.

62. *Coalition for Adequacy and Fairness in School Funding. v. Chiles*, 680 So.2d 400 (Fla. 1996).

63. *Committee for Education Rights v. Edgar*, 672 N.E.2d 1178 (Ill. 1996).

64. *City of Pawtucket v. Sundlun*, 662 A.2d 40 (R.I. 1995).

65. Settlement Agreement entered into in *Independent School District No. 625, St. Paul, Minnesota v. Minnesota*, No. C2-96-9356 (Dist. Ct. Ramsay Co. 1999).

66. Settlement Agreement entered into in *NAACP v. Minnesota*, No. 95-14800 (Dist.Ct. Hennepin Co. 2000).

67. *Sheff v. O'Neill*, 678 A.2d 1267 (Conn. 1996).

68. For example, as a result of dramatic court-ordered spending increases in *Jenkins v. Missouri*, per-pupil expenditures in the Kansas City, Missouri, School District dramatically increased, yet student test scores declined. See Expert Report of Dr. John Murphy introduced during 2001 unitary hearing in *Berry v. School District of Benton Harbor*, Civil Action No. 4:67-CV-9 (W.D. Mich. 2001) (Dr. Murphy was the court-appointed monitor of the Kansas City, Missouri, School District from 1997 to 2000).

69. Because of the long-term impact such settlements can have on state education funding and policymaking, they can be very problematic for state leaders in the years following the settlement. For example, the state of Maryland is currently struggling with a settlement agreement regarding the adequacy of education in the Baltimore City schools that is costing the state much more than originally anticipated and which essentially takes the process of determining appropriate costs out of the hands of the lawmakers. Eric Siegel, 2000, "Judge seen backing city on school aid." *Baltimore Sun*, 29 June.

70. For example, in 1997, Prince George's County (PGC), which was the main funding source for the PGC schools, moved to have the county school district declared unitary. At trial, the local board of education joined with the county in arguing that it was unitary as to all of the *Green* factors, but took the plaintiffs' side on the issue of educational vestiges, arguing that such vestiges remained and that additional county funding would be necessary to eliminate such vestiges.

71. *Adarand Constructors v. Pena*, 515 U.S. 200, 224 (1995).

72. *City of Richmond v. J.A. Croson Co.*, 488 U.S. 469 (1989).

73. Such challenges are not limited to school districts in which the district has already sought and obtained a judicial declaration of unitariness. In several cases, parents' groups, perhaps tiring of the board of education's refusal to seek unitary status itself, have taken matters into their own hands by arguing that the school district has in fact remedied all prior discrimination. Therefore, they argue, its programs should be judged under the same legal standards as those school districts which have already obtained a judicial declaration that all prior discrimination has been eliminated. Thus, although the school board in Charlotte-Mecklenburg, North Carolina, had not sought, and indeed had argued it was not entitled to, unitary status, parents' groups were nevertheless successful in intervening and convincing the court that the district was, as a matter of fact, unitary and that therefore, race-based magnet school admissions criteria in the districts was unconstitutional. *Capacchione v. Charlotte-Mecklenburg School*, 57 F.Supp. 2d 228 (W.D.N.C. 1999), *rev'd sub nom, Belk v. Charlotte-Mecklenburg Board of Education*, 233 F.3d 232 (4th Cir. 2000), *vacated and reh'g en banc granted* (4th Cir. 17 Jan. 2001), *rev'd in part and aff'd in part by en banc court* (4th Cir. 21 Sept. 2001).

74. See endnote 3.

75. For instance, *Hampton v. Jefferson County Board of Education*, 102 F.Supp. 2d 358 (W.D. Ky. 2000).

76. *Equal Open Enrollment Ass'n. v. Bd. of Ed. of Akron*, 937 F.Supp. 700 (N.D. Ohio 1996).

77. One exception to this general trend is *Hunter v. Regents of the Univ. of California*, 190 F.3d 1061 (9th Cir. 1999). It should be noted that the school in *Hunter* was a unique school and its research-oriented mission may have influenced the court's decision. A similar policy for an ordinary school might not have passed court muster.

78. *Hopwood v. Texas*, 78 F.3d 932, 945 at n.27 (5th Cir. 1996). See also, *Lutheran Church–Missouri Synod v. Federal Communications Commission*, 141 F.3d 344, 354–356 (D.C. Cir. 1998).

79. For cases that suggest diversity might be a compelling interest if the racial classification is sufficiently narrow, see *Regents of the Univ. of California v. Bakke*, 438 U.S. 265, 314–315 (1978); *Wessman*, 160 F.3d at 796–798.

80. The same issue faces colleges and universities defending admission policies that consider student race. The courts are split on the issue, as illustrated by two federal circuit court decisions arising out of the admissions policies of the Universities of Texas and Michigan law schools. In *Hopwood v. Texas*, 78 F.3d 932 (5th Cir. 1996), the Fifth Circuit Court of Appeals held that the admissions policies of the University of Texas Law School violated the Fourteenth Amendment because they illegally considered student race. It rejected plaintiff's contention that racial diversity was a compelling enough state interest to survive a Fourteenth Amendment challenge. In 2002, in *Grutter v. Bollinger*, 2002 FED App. 0170P (6th Cir.), the Sixth Circuit Court of Appeals reached the opposite conclusion, holding that the University of Michigan Law School admission criteria, which also took into account student race, did serve a compelling state interest in promoting educational diversity and therefore met the strict scrutiny test of the Fourteenth Amendment. Because of the split in authority between the Fifth and Sixth Circuits, there is a strong likelihood that the Supreme Court will hear the Michigan case and decide what role, if any, student race may play in admission to institutions of higher learning. Such a decision will likely also provide guidance for those struggling with similar issues at the elementary and secondary school levels.

81. If the use of socioeconomic or other factors is found to be merely a pretext or proxy for the use of race, then such plans also are unlikely to survive a court challenge.

82. For example, Gary Bartless, ed. 1996. School Resources and Student Performance, *Does Money Matter? The Effect of School Resources on Student Achievement and Adult Success*, 43–73 (Washington, D.C.: Brookings Institution).

83. See endnote 68.

Chapter 4

The Effectiveness of Desegregation Plans

Christine H. Rossell

The purpose of this chapter is to analyze the effectiveness of different types of school desegregation remedies that have been implemented over the last four and a half decades since *Brown v. Board of Education*. In the first part of the chapter, I present a classification scheme for school desegregation remedies that helps us understand the characteristics of school segregation remedies and their effects. In the second part, I analyze empirical data from a national sample of 600 school districts and from one school district in particular.

THE EVOLUTION OF SCHOOL SEGREGATION REMEDIES

School desegregation plans have evolved gradually since 1954. To many observers, it seems we have come full circle from freedom of choice in the early 1950s and 1960s back to freedom of choice in the 1980s and 1990s. The plans of the 1980s and 1990s, however, are very different from the plans of the 1950s.

From 1954 to 1968, the criterion for finding a Fourteenth Amendment violation was the existence of government enforcement of segregation by law. The only remedy required was that states rescind their segregation laws and school districts desist in assigning children to schools on the basis of their race rather than their residence.

In the North, desegregation was often accomplished by political rather than legal demands, but its outcome was the same as in the South. Most school districts either did nothing or instituted a freedom-of-choice plan, called "majority-to-minority" transfer, in which any child could leave any school in which his or her race was in the majority to go to any school in which his or her race was in the minority. A few school districts instituted geographic assignment plans, but they varied in the degree to which desegregation was accomplished.

Desegregation in the South during this time period consisted of court-approved "choice" plans, some very similar in concept to the northern plans. Because only a small percentage of black students transferred to white schools, and no white students transferred to black schools, these plans were generally perceived to be ineffective. As a result, the Supreme Court decided in 1968 in *Green v. County Board of Education of New Kent County* (391 U.S. 430 [1968]) that eliminating racial discrimination was not enough and that school districts were required to produce racially mixed schools to a greater degree than would be obtained from merely ending discrimination. The court's conclusion was based on their empirical observation that forbidding discrimination and permitting voluntary transfer plans had not desegregated black schools. In addition, there was a growing belief on the part of social scientists and the courts that school desegregation—the actual enrollment of blacks and whites in the same schools—was beneficial and would solve many, if not most, of the existing racial problems.

Green thus marked the end of "nondiscrimination" remedies and the beginning of "affirmative action" remedies. The actual blueprint for how this was to be done was provided by the Supreme Court's 1970 decision in *Swann v. Charlotte-Mecklenburg*, where, for the first time, specific racial balance quotas and cross-district busing techniques were approved. After this pivotal decision, mandatory reassignments plans were implemented in school districts all over the United States in the 1970s. However, in 1975 and 1976, four years prior to the Reagan administration, three separate federal district courts approved plans in Houston (1975), Milwaukee (1976) and Buffalo (1976) that relied primarily on incentives in the form of magnet schools to motivate voluntary transfers. Although throughout the 1970s and 1980s the violation standard continued to be an affirmative action standard—that is, school districts with former dual school systems or other acts of intentional segregation were found guilty when they did not do something affirmative to integrate their schools—by the late 1970s, permissible remedies expanded to include voluntary plans with magnet schools. Thus began the period of court-approved voluntary magnet school plans.

By the 1980s, the courts had gone even further in abandoning mandatory reassignment. They began allowing school districts to dismantle mandatory plans and replace them with voluntary magnet school plans while still under court order.[1] Since 1981, there have been only two new court-ordered mandatory reassignment plans, one in Hattiesburg, Mississippi in 1986 and one in Natchez, Mississippi in 1989. All others have been voluntary or controlled choice. Nevertheless, many, if not most, of the mandatory reassignment plans that were implemented from 1954 through 1981 are still in existence today, even in school districts that have been declared unitary.

CLASSIFYING DESEGREGATION PLANS

Voluntary and Mandatory Plans

The school desegregation plans that have been created over the last four decades can be classified on a number of dimensions. The broadest classification of plans is voluntary versus mandatory, which refers to the extent of parental choice over school assignment, not to the source of the plan (that is, a court order or voluntary adoption by a school board). Although in the South all school desegregation plans were ultimately court-ordered, some of these court-ordered plans did and do allow parental choice. This is also true of the North. In addition, although most of the comprehensive, mandatory reassignment plans in the United States are court-ordered, there are a few northern school districts (most notably, Berkeley and Seattle) that have initiated such plans without having been ordered to do so by a court.

Thus, school desegregation plans can be classified by the source of the order to desegregate—court or board—and the extent of parental choice—voluntary, controlled choice, or mandatory—as shown in figure 4.1. There is no difference in the types of plans in the column labeled "Court/OCR" and the column labeled "Board." This is because both the courts and school boards have ordered all three of the basic types of desegregation plans—voluntary, mandatory, and controlled choice (the middle row of figure 4.1), which involves parental choice but a mandatory backup if not enough parents choose the right schools. Since some boards have adopted mandatory reassignment plans (e.g., Seattle and Berkeley) and many courts have approved voluntary plans, the custom of labeling a plan only by the source of the order can be misleading. The research indicates that the extent of white flight and protest is primarily a function of the extent to which parents are allowed to stay at their neighborhood school if they desire (the "Yes" row in figure 4.1) or are assigned across town to an opposite race school they did not choose (the "No" row in figure 4.1) not to the source of the order (Coleman, Kelly and Moore 1975a, 1975b; Rossell 1978, 1997; Smylie 1983; Rossell 1983a).

All of these plans can be either metropolitan or non-metropolitan in scope. A metropolitan plan includes a central city and its surrounding suburbs, whereas a non-metropolitan plan encompasses only the central city, thus leaving suburbs for whites to flee to. Although metropolitan mandatory

Figure 4.1
A Classification of Desegregation Plans

SOURCE OF ORDER TO IMPLEMENT

		COURT/OCR	BOARD
PARENTAL CHOICE WHETHER STUDENT REASSIGNED	YES	VOLUNTARY: Magnet-Voluntary Freedom of Choice M to M 1	VOLUNTARY: Magnet-Voluntary M to M 2
	SOME, (MANDATORY BACKUP)	CONTROLLED CHOICE 3	CONTROLLED CHOICE 4
	NO	MANDATORY REASSIGNMENT: Pairing and Clustering Rezoning 5	MANDATORY REASSIGNMENT: Pairing and Clustering Rezoning 6

Geographic Scope: Metropolitan Or Non-Metropolitan

reassignment plans produced less white flight and more interracial exposure than non-metropolitan mandatory reassignment plans with the same characteristics (Coleman, Kelly, and Moore 1975a, 1975b; Rossell 1978, 1997; Smylie 1983) and greater housing integration (Pearce 1980), the advantage is not as great as it is thought to be.

On the one hand, metropolitan plans eliminate some (but not all) of the suburbs that whites can flee to. But since only half of white flight is to the suburbs (Rossell and Ross 1979)—the rest being to private schools—this advantage is not quite as overpowering as it seems. On the other hand, metropolitan plans will have longer busing distances than non-metropolitan plans, all other things being equal, and this is the single greatest predictor of white flight (Armor 1988; Lord 1975; Rossell 1988c). These crosscutting factors may explain Rossell's (1990b; 1997) findings that metropolitan mandatory reassignment plans had white flight from desegregation that was only somewhat less than non-metropolitan mandatory reassignment plans. Moreover, the metropolitan mandatory reassignment plans did not achieve as much interracial exposure as a citywide voluntary plan.

Mandatory Reassignment Plans

Each of these plans—voluntary, controlled choice, and mandatory—can be further classified. Mandatory reassignment plans, implemented throughout the United States from 1970 through the early 1980s, can be classified according to whether there is a grade-structure change in individual schools and whether the new school attendance zones after desegregation are contiguous or noncontiguous. Plans that link two or more opposite-race schools and change the grade structure so that half the grades are in one school and half in the other are called pairing and/or clustering plans. When this linking of schools and grades occurs for more than two schools, it is called clustering.

The 1989 Natchez, Mississippi plan, still in existence as of fall 2001, is an example of pairing and clustering. One of each paired school was the historically black school and the other the historically white school. Students of both races in one portion of the school district attend the same school for pre-kindergarten through first grade and then the same students attend another school for second through sixth grade.

When school districts desegregate, school attendance zones are typically redrawn. Pairing and clustering plans can have noncontiguous school zones as is typically the case with medium and large school districts, or contiguous school zones as often occurs in small districts. A contiguous attendance zone is one in which a person could go to any part of the zone without having to cross another attendance zone. In a noncontiguous attendance zone, a person would have to cross another attendance zone in order to reach all parts of the same attendance zone.

To summarize, pairing or clustering mandatory plans are characterized by a grade-change in the schools so two or more schools share a grade span. If there is no grade-change, it is not pairing but either satellite zoning—if attendance zones are noncontiguous—or contiguous rezoning if they are not. The 1975 Boston school desegregation plan, which was replaced by controlled choice in 1989,[2] is an example of satellite zoning because the school system was divided into hundreds of geocodes assigned to schools in such a manner as to desegregate them, with all schools remaining K–5, 6–8, or 9–12—the grade configuration they were before desegregation.

Any of these mandatory reassignment plans can have magnet schools. The Boston satellite zoning plan, for example, had twenty-two of them, because it was thought that the inclusion of magnet schools would reduce white opposition and flight.

Voluntary Desegregation Plans

Voluntary plans can also be metropolitan or non-metropolitan. Unlike mandatory reassignment plans, however, the districts participating in a metropolitan voluntary plan retain their independent political identities. The more prominent of these voluntary metropolitan plans are METCO in Boston, VIDT in St. Louis, and Project Concern in Hartford. The largest of these is the St. Louis VIDT because a 1983 Consent Decree required each suburban school district to accept black transfer students up to a percentage black in their student population of 25 percent. At its peak in 1993, almost 13,000 black students from the city of St. Louis voluntarily took a bus ride each day to the suburbs. The number has declined since a 1999 settlement agreement, but it is still more than 11,000.

The smallest interdistrict plan is what was called Project Concern in the Hartford metropolitan area. The program is voluntary for both the students and the participating school districts although it is being monitored by a state court as part of a voluntary metropolitan remedy that has no racial quotas. As of the 2001–02 school year, 1,540 black students transferred out to the suburbs, although Project Concern is now part of the Interdistrict Cooperative Program and called Open Choice.

Voluntary plans can be further classified according to whether there are incentives for motivating opposite-race transfers (typically in the form of magnet schools) and whether attendance zones are redrawn. It is common for court-ordered, voluntary desegregation plans to include the redrawing of contiguous attendance zones in order to maximize integration. Obviously, there is some point at which this can be so extensive that it might more properly be called mandatory reassignment.

Voluntary desegregation plans began with the old freedom-of-choice plans in the South in the 1950s and 1960s and the "stand-alone" majority to minority (M to M) transfer programs (i.e., not part of a magnet–voluntary plan) in the North in the 1960s. The most recent innovations in voluntary desegregation plans, magnet–voluntary plans, are distinguished by the fact that every student receives an assignment to their neighborhood school and can remain in that school if they so choose, at least after the implementation year, when some contiguous rezoning occurs. Incentives for voluntary transfers are provided, such as free transportation and magnet schools with specialized curricula, reduced class size, and resource teachers.

Although there are options to transfer out of the neighborhood school, racial criteria are imposed on these transfers so that usually only those that have a desegregative impact on the receiving school (and often the sending school) are allowed. Typically, the options to transfer also include an M to M program where any student in the school district can transfer from any school in which his or her race is in the majority to any school in which his or her race is in the minority.[3] In general, only minority students participate in the M to M program since even today few whites will voluntarily transfer to schools in minority neighborhoods without an incentive in the form of a magnet program (Rossell 1990a, 1990b).

Controlled-Choice Plans

Controlled choice is the third of the three basic types of desegregation plans. These plans came into existence in the early 1980s as mandatory re-assignment plans became less popular with the courts, other policymakers, and minority parents. The academics and policymakers who embraced controlled choice (Alves and Willie 1987; Glenn 1991) were those who no longer supported simple mandatory reassignment plans because of the protest and white flight they produced, but who remained uneasy over the lack of control over student reassignment found in voluntary plans. Controlled choice thus represents a mixed desegregation remedy that is between purely mandatory reassignment plans that reassign everyone and completely voluntary plans that allow students to remain at their neighborhood school. It must be noted, however, that a controlled choice plan can have as much, or even more, mandatory reassignment as a purely mandatory plan, depending on how comprehensive the plan is and how strict the racial balance standard.

There are different kinds of controlled choice plans and they can be classified generally in terms of whether they have neighborhood attendance zones and whether they have magnet schools. There are controlled choice plans with and without neighborhood attendance zones, and any of them can have magnets. The basic foundation of all controlled choice desegregation plans is that at least some parents are *required* to rank-order a number of schools in the school system in order of preference. The school administration, while trying to give parents their first choice, reserves the right to assign students to any school they want them to go to (typically one where their attendance will satisfy racial balance requirements). Once enrolled, however, a student is usually allowed to stay at a school unless they request a transfer or graduate to a higher school level (i.e., from elementary to junior high to senior high).

In its pure form, a controlled choice plan has no school attendance zones and no magnets. Since no child has a neighborhood school, all parents who are new to the district or whose child is changing school are asked to choose a school from among those in the system. Although it is common to exempt (i.e., "grandfather") currently enrolled students, each successive cohort of kindergarten students is required to choose and rank-order four or five schools, as are all new students and those changing school, until finally the school system reaches the pure state: there are no students attending their former neighborhood school *solely* because of their residence, and all entering students have to "ballot."

Although many school systems with controlled choice plans claim that 90 percent or more of their parents receive their first choice school (in Boston, it is their first three choices), it is not clear how meaningful these figures are. First, they are rarely broken down by race and they are typically only of the initial registration period when the lottery is run. Armor (1998), however, has done an analysis of the Rockford controlled choice plan. He found that first-choice assignments increased with school level and that white students were more likely to be assigned to their first-choice school. First-choice assignments were made to 60 percent of black and 70 percent of white elementary students. In addition, 85 percent of black and 88 percent of white seventh graders were assigned to their first-choice school. Among ninth graders, 78 percent of black and 87 percent of white ninth graders were assigned to their first-choice school. Analyses conducted of San Jose also show higher first-choice assignments for whites because minorities are more likely to enter the school system after the initial lottery period when the most popular schools are chosen. Across the entire registration period, 87 percent of whites and 76 percent of minorities were assigned to their first choice (Rossell 1996).

Second, these statistics do not include parents who did not receive their first choice, but left the school system. Thus, the proper analysis—the calculation of the proportion of parents of each race who received their first choice among those who applied, not those who enrolled—has yet to be conducted. In addition, some unknown number of parents are counseled at Parent Information Centers to choose less-popular schools not among their most preferred to minimize the probability they will be reassigned to a school they really despise (Thernstrom 1991).

Magnets are not supposed to be included in the pure controlled choice plans because they are viewed as elitist (Alves and Willie 1987). Moreover, they are theoretically unnecessary because in a controlled choice plan, all schools are competing against each other and presumably developing their own reputations for excellence. There are many controlled choice plans, however, that include magnet schools but have no school attendance zones. One of these districts, Montclair, New Jersey, has made all the schools magnets with a special focus but it is able to do so, despite the expense, because there are only six elementary schools, two middle schools, and one high school in the district.

Many school districts that have implemented controlled choice plans with no school attendance zones previously had a mandatory reassignment plan so the loss of neighborhood school attendance zones was less onerous. This is the case with Boston, which adopted a "pure" controlled choice plan in 1989 to replace its mandatory reassignment plan of 1974.

San Jose and Yonkers both implemented a variation on pure controlled choice in 1986. The plan that was approved by the courts in each case was actually a neighborhood school plan with magnets that I had designed. In order to meet the racial balance requirements of their court orders however, both school districts changed their plans to controlled choice plans under the advice of David Bennett, the former Superintendent of the St. Paul Public Schools. He called the technique "enrollment capping." The difference between the plan I designed and the plan actually implemented in each district was that in my plan, no student could be denied the right to enroll in their neighborhood school. In the plans implemented, students would be allowed to enroll in their neighborhood school only up to the quota for their race (i.e., the enrollment cap for their race). While not as popular as a neighborhood school plan with magnets, this kind of controlled choice plan at least avoids the daunting logistical feat of eliminating neighborhood school zones and thus is presumably more popular than a pure controlled choice plan.

Although in theory controlled choice would seem to be an ideal compromise between voluntary and mandatory reassignment plans, parents of all races support controlled choice in only slightly greater (or in some cases even smaller) percentages than they do mandatory reassignment plans and up to one-third of white parents will definitely or probably withdraw their child from the school system if a controlled choice plan is adopted, with the withdrawal rate being higher in the school systems with no prior mandatory reassignment plan and lower in those having had one (Rossell 1995a). These opinion surveys are corroborated by longitudinal analyses of enrollment trends in the San Jose and Yonkers school systems (Rossell 1988a, 1991b) showing that both school systems have incurred more white flight than would be expected from a magnet–voluntary desegregation plan, but less than with a mandatory reassignment plan.

All of these plans can be arrayed on a parental choice continuum that almost exactly matches parental support among parents of all races. Voluntary plans are the most popular because they allow the most parental choice and mandatory plans are the least popular because they allow the least parent choice. Controlled choice is somewhere in between (Armor 1995; Rossell, 1995a, 1995b).

MEASURING SCHOOL DESEGREGATION

The Courts

In the post-*Swann* era, a typical court-ordered plan specified the schools that were paired with each other or the attendance zones that were assigned to each school and the expected racial composition of each school. Most, but not all, also specified a permissible deviation from racial balance because perfection is obviously not achievable in the real world. The most common deviation allowed by the courts in the 1970s was a plus-or-minus

15 percentage-point variance for each school from the school district's over-all racial proportions.[4] Although allowing some flexibility, this measure is somewhat crude in that a school district could make great strides in reducing racial imbalance, but if it only brought imbalanced schools to within 16 percentage points of the district's overall racial proportions, it would get no credit. A school district that had brought them to within 15 percentage points, however, would be considered racially balanced. Because of the greater white flight produced by stricter racial balance quotas, a plus-or-minus 20 percentage-point criterion became the most common permissible deviation beginning in the mid-1980s (*United States v. Yonkers*, 635 F.Supp. 1538 [1986]; *Stell and U.S. v. Board of Public Education for the City of Savannah and the County of Chatham et al.* 724 F.Supp. 1384 [1988]; *Diaz v. San Jose Unified School District*, 633 F.Supp. 808 [1985]).

Occasionally the courts established a specific absolute criterion, such as all schools must be within 40 to 55 percent black. With an absolute criterion, the school board had to go back to court every few years to get the specific percentages changed as the school system's racial composition changed. For example, if a school district's racial composition was 50 percent minority and the court order said all schools had to be between 35 and 65 percent minority, the school district would have to petition the court to have the range changed when its racial composition approached 65 percent minority. It is simply impossible, for example, for a school system which is 66 percent minority to have all schools racially balanced at 65 percent minority. Milwaukee, Charlotte, and Buffalo are three of the many school districts that had this problem.[5]

Social Science Measurement

The two most common school desegregation variables used by social scientists to measure school desegregation have been (1) change in racial balance, which technically is an outcome of a particular desegregation plan, not a policy instrument, and (2) a dichotomous variable—desegregated or not desegregated. Change in racial balance is typically used as the independent variable in comparative, statistical analyses of white flight and other measures of community impact (Coleman, Kelly, and Moore 1975a, 1975b; Farley, Wurdock, and Richards 1980; Frey 1977; Pearce 1980; Smylie 1983; Wilson 1985). This measure has the virtue of reflecting the extent of the plan. The dichotomous measure—desegregated or not—is used in studies of achievement, race relations, and career outcomes of students (Crain and Strauss 1985; Eyler, Cook, and Ward 1983; Mahard and Crain 1983; Schofield and Sagar 1983). These studies are limited by the fact that there is no assessment of how extensive the plan is or what type it is—that is, mandatory, voluntary, or controlled choice.

The measure of school desegregation most commonly used by social scientists is the index of dissimilarity. The formula is

$$Db = 1/2\Sigma \left| \frac{Wi}{W} - \frac{Bi}{B} \right|$$

where Wi is the number of whites in each school, Bi is the number of black students in each school, and W and B the numbers of whites and blacks in the school district as a whole. This calculation is then summed for all schools and divided by 2. The index of dissimilarity represents the proportion (or percentage if multiplied by 100) of black students who would have to be reassigned to white schools, if no whites were reassigned, in order to have the same proportion in each school as in the whole school district. The index ranges from zero (perfect racial balance—that is, no black students need to be reassigned) to 100 (perfect racial imbalance—that is, 100 percent of the black students need to be reassigned, if no whites are reassigned).[6] This measure can be used to compute the imbalance of any two racial groups, not just whites and blacks.

In the late 1970s, scientists began to use a third measure of school desegregation called interracial exposure. It is the proportion white in the average black child's school. Although the measure can be used for any two groups, for the purpose described here it is a racial minority group's exposure to whites.[7] The measure for black students' exposure to whites is calculated as follows:

$$Sbw = 1/B \; \Sigma \; BiPWi$$

where i stands for each individual school and thus Bi is the number of blacks in a particular school (i), PWi is the proportion white in the same school (i) and B is the total number of blacks in the district.[8] Hence, the number of blacks in each school is multiplied times the proportion white in the same school. This is summed for all schools and divided by the number of blacks in the school system (or school level) to produce a weighted average—the proportion white in the average black child's school. Since the proportion white in the average black child's school increases with racial balance reassignments, but declines as the white enrollment decreases, it yields the *net benefit* of desegregation reassignments. In other words, interracial exposure is a measure of the effectiveness of desegregation techniques in actually achieving desegregation.

I have written extensively on the superiority of interracial exposure as a measure of school desegregation (Rossell 1986c, 1990a, 1990b, 1995a; Rossell and Armor 1996). Interracial exposure is a function not only of racial balance, but of the proportions of whites and minorities in the school system. The level of interracial exposure for the average minority child can be no higher than the proportion white in the school system. Racial balance by contrast, ignores how many whites are coming into contact with minorities. The index of dissimilarity, or any other measure of racial balance, is thus less comprehensive than the index of interracial exposure because interracial exposure includes racial balance, but racial balance does not include interracial exposure. Racial balance can be achieved with very little interracial exposure, but interracial exposure cannot be achieved without significant racial balance. This is as true of the precise racial balance measures, such as the index of dissimilarity, as it is of the categorical racial balance standards used by the courts, such as the requirement that all schools be within plus-or-minus 15 or 20 percentage points of the district's racial proportions.

This becomes clearer if we consider a hypothetical segregated school system with six schools and the racial composition shown here.

	Minorities	Whites
School 1	100	0
School 2	100	0
School 3	100	0
School 4	0	100
School 5	0	100
School 6	0	100
TOTAL	**300**	**300**
%	50%	50%

Virtually all supporters of school desegregation would prefer a plan which produced outcome A (following) with considerable racial balance and 245 white students remaining to a plan which produced outcome B with perfect racial balance and six white students remaining.

	OUTCOME A			**OUTCOME B**	
	Minorities	Whites		Minorities	Whites
School 1	50	20	School 1	50	1
School 2	50	45	School 2	50	1
School 3	50	40	School 3	50	1
School 4	50	50	School 4	50	1
School 5	50	45	School 5	50	1
School 6	50	45	School 6	50	1
TOTAL	**300**	**245**	**TOTAL**	**300**	**6**
%	55%	45%	%	98%	2%

Although outcome B has only one white in each school, it has a racial imbalance score of 0, that is, perfect racial balance, and all schools within plus or minus 20 percentage points of the school district's proportions (98 percent minority and 2 percent white). If we multiply the number of minorities times the proportion white in each school, however, we find only two percent white in the average minority child's school. Outcome B thus has perfect racial balance, but very little interracial exposure.

Outcome A, by contrast, has an index of dissimilarity of 8.8—that is, it is more racially imbalanced than outcome B. It also has one school (17 percent of the total number of schools) racially imbalanced by the plus-or-minus 15 or 20 percentage-point criterion whereas outcome B had none racially imbalanced by that standard. If we multiply the number of minorities times the proportion white in each school, sum across schools, and divide by the number of minorities in the district (300), we find 44.2 percent white in the average minority child's school.

If we have racial balance as our goal, we are forced to choose the intuitively least desirable plan—Outcome B where there is only one white in each school. If we have interracial exposure as our goal, however, we will choose the intuitively most desirable plan—Outcome A where there is 44.2 percent white in the average minority child's school.

Racial balance measures do not accurately measure costs because they hold changing demographics constant and hence cannot distinguish between (1) a desegregation plan in which 99 percent of the whites have left but the remaining one percent are evenly distributed (producing an index of 0 and all schools within plus or minus 15 percentage points of the district's racial proportions); and (2) one in which none of the whites have left and each school is 50 percent white (producing an index of 0 and all schools within plus or minus 20 percentage points of the district's racial proportions). Since virtually no one trying to achieve school desegregation would prefer the former to the latter, and social scientists and the courts appear to believe that the goal of a school desegregation plan is the greatest possible contact between the races, interracial exposure is the best measure of school desegregation. On the other hand, when courts order a strict racial balance plan, with a narrow variance around the district percent black, the index of dissimilarity corresponds most closely to this particular definition of desegregation. For that reason, I frequently calculate both measures when evaluating the effectiveness of school desegregation plans.

I have used the index of interracial exposure in two ways over the last three decades. First, in school desegregation court cases, I have calculated the amount of interracial exposure that would be produced by each of the proposed desegregation plans, taking into account the expected white flight from each plan and the expected voluntary transfers to opposite race school. The white flight estimates and the number of whites who are expected to transfer to magnet schools in black neighborhoods and the number of blacks expected to transfer to regular schools in white neighborhoods either come from the results of a parent survey conducted prior to the trial or from research in other school districts. The number of magnets and their placement is then calculated as a function of the demand shown in the survey.

Then the interracial exposure for each plan is calculated for the first several years of the plan. This was done in desegregation cases in San Diego in 1979 (Rossell 1979a); in Port Arthur, Texas in 1980 (Rossell 1980); Marion County, Florida in 1983 (Rossell 1983b); Prince George's County, Maryland; San Jose; and Hattiesburg in 1985 (Rossell 1985a, 1985b, 1985c); Savannah and Yonkers in 1986 (Rossell 1986b, 1986c), Natchez in 1988 (Rossell 1988b), Stockton, California in 1991 (Rossell 1991a); the Robla School District, California in 1992 (Rossell 1992); and Rockford, Illinois in 1995 (Rossell 1995c).

David Armor and I have independently used interracial exposure as an outcome variable in our different research on the effects of school desegregation plans, adapting a measure that was originally created by James Coleman (Coleman, Kelly and Moore 1975a, 1975b). The first study I did using interracial exposure was published with a 113-school-district nationwide sample in 1978. David Armor's first study was an analysis of twenty-three comprehensive desegregation plans published in 1980 (Armor 1980).

In 1991, David Armor and I were co-principal investigators for a major national study of school desegregation and magnet schools.[9] The study drew a nationwide, stratified,[10] random probability sample of 600 school districts, drawn from a universe of about 6,400 school districts with more than one school for at least one grade level. Among other things, this study assessed the existence and type of desegregation plans in each district and long-term enrollment trends. This national study of school desegregation has resulted in three co-authored publications.[11]

The 600-district study included two types of data: enrollment data and questionnaire data. The questionnaires covered such areas as the number of magnet schools, the existence of a formal desegregation plan, the specific type of plan techniques used currently or previously, whether the district formerly had a desegregation plan, the year the plan started, and the source of the plan. The original study included enrollment data by school and by race from the 1968–69 school year through the 1991–92 school year. Subsequently I updated the enrollment data through the 1997–98 school year using the Common Core of Data (CCD) database maintained by the National Center for Educational Statistics (NCES). I use this updated database for the national trends discussed next.

NATIONAL TRENDS IN DESEGREGATION

Enrollment Trends

Figure 4.2 shows trends in the racial composition of the 600 school districts in our sample from fall 1968 through fall 1997.[12] The sample is broken down by size of district because the nature of desegregation plans, and

Figure 4.2
Trends in Percentage White by District Size in U.S., Fall 1968–Fall 1997

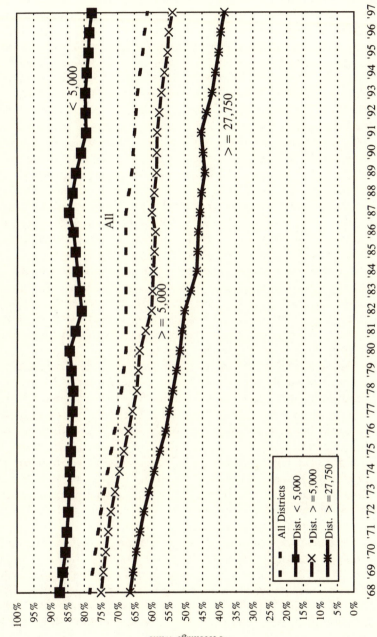

indeed even the need for them, are influenced heavily by the size of a district. In a smaller school district, for example, with only a single high school, two middle schools, and several elementary schools, desegregation of all the schools can often be accomplished by a relatively simple adjustment of school attendance zones. This would most likely be impossible in most large school districts. Thus, the analyses in figures 4.2 through 4.4 are carried out separately for four groupings of school districts by size—all districts, districts smaller than 5,000, districts at or above 5,000 and districts greater than 27,750. Overall, the percentage white in public school enrollment has been falling since the late 1960s, a trend that is especially marked in the very large school districts—those larger than 27,750—where most minority students reside. In these very large districts, approximately 64 percent of the enrollment was white in 1968, but by 1997–98 the percentage white had declined to 39 percent. This drop reflects not only a declining white student population, but an increasing black, Hispanic, and Asian population. During this time period, the percentage black increased from 28 to 33 percent, the percentage Hispanic increased from 7 to 21 percent, and the percentage Asian increased from 1 to 6 percent.

For all districts and districts with enrollments at or above 5,000, the percentage white has also fallen but not nearly as much as in very large districts. The small districts, those with enrollment fewer than 5,000, are still almost 80 percent white and have changed very little since 1968 when they were 87 percent white. It is the largest school districts that have diminishing potential for school integration.

Figure 4.3 shows trends in school desegregation as measured by the index of dissimilarity for black and white students. Figure 4.4 shows trends in the interracial exposure index for black students, that is, the percentage white in the average black child's school.[13] I present both of these measures because as noted previously, each gives a different picture of desegregation.

Figure 4.3 shows very substantial reductions in racial imbalance between 1968 and 1973, and smaller reductions until the early 1980s. Interestingly, although many school districts have been released from court supervision in the last decade, racial imbalance between blacks and whites has not worsened even in the largest districts.

Interracial exposure, the percentage white in the average black child's school, is shown in figure 4.4 for black students. For very large districts (>27,750), there are clearly two distinct phases to the trend. In 1968, black students were exposed to an average of only 30 percent white in their schools, which climbed to a high of almost 45 percent in 1972 after courts began implementing the *Green* and *Swann* decisions. But from 1974 onward, interracial exposure began to decline as the percentage white of the enrollment fell in these districts. By 1997, the exposure index had fallen to thirty-one, about where it was in 1968. Of course, the percentage white has

Figure 4.3

Trends in Black–White Racial Imbalance by District Size in U.S., Fall 1968–Fall 1997

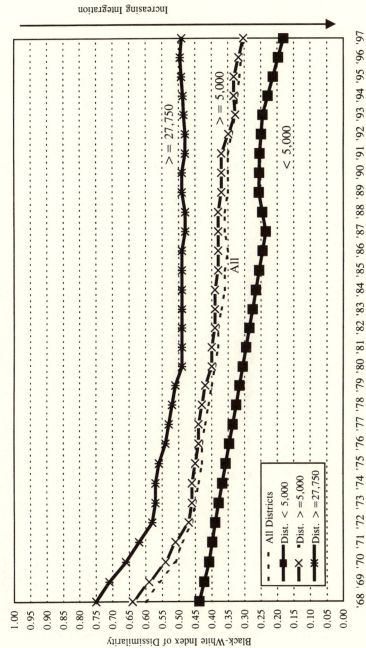

Figure 4.4
Trends in Interracial Exposure by District Size in U.S., Fall 1968–Fall 1997

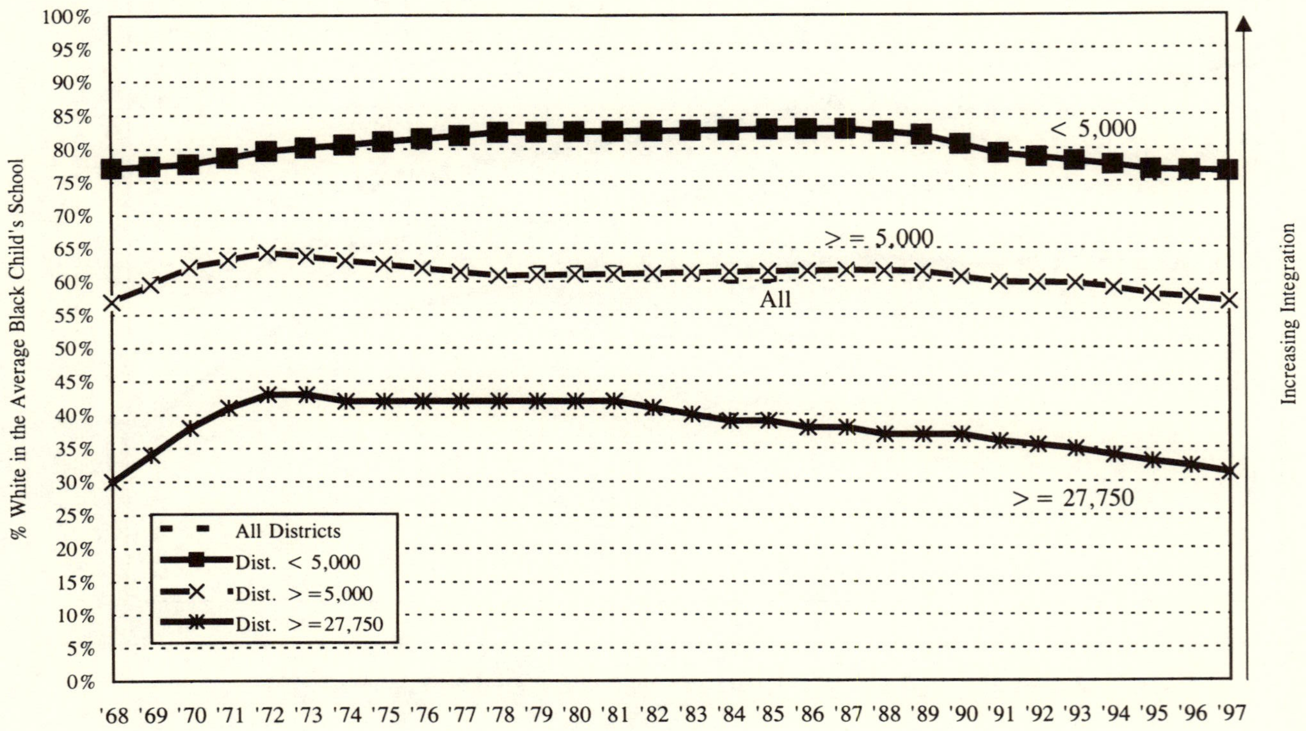

also declined, so that the degree of exposure relative to the available whites was much higher than it was in 1968. The same basic pattern is repeated for all school districts and districts at or above 5,000, although the trends are not as sharp.

The smallest school districts show much less movement in their index of interracial exposure. They had 77 percent white in the average black child's school in 1968, which peaked at 83 percent during the 1980s, and then declined slightly to 76 percent by 1997, lower than in 1968.

Trends by Desegregation Plan Status

The trends shown in figures 4.3 and 4.4 are undoubtedly influenced by the desegregation plans implemented in these districts during this time period. Across all districts, having a desegregation plan is fairly uncommon; only 12 percent of all districts had desegregation plans in 1991, which increases to 17 percent if we add to this group those who formerly had plans. The percentage is low because there is a large number of small school districts that never had a formal desegregation plan.

Among districts greater than 5,000, the percentage of districts that had a plan in 1991 is 29 percent and the percentage that had a plan, or formerly had a plan, is 40 percent. Almost 60 percent of the very large districts, those greater than 27,750, however, had desegregation plans in 1991 and more than 70 percent had one in 1991 or earlier. Because the universe of medium and larger districts in 1991 was about 1600, this means that over 450 medium or larger school districts in the United States had formal desegregation plans in 1991.

Figure 4.5 shows trends in interracial exposure and percentage white in the very large districts (>27,750) through fall 1997. To estimate the contribution of these desegregation plans to trends in interracial exposure, figure 4.5 compares districts that had a formal plan any time during this time period to those that never had one. I have selected these districts for further display because of their importance for desegregation—52 percent of all black students are in these districts and almost three-quarters of the districts had current or former plans in 1991.

The trends are further broken down by region. The trends in percentage white are added to the graphs to enable the reader to assess the extent to which interracial exposure is a function, not just of desegregation plans, but of the starting point in percentage white for districts with and without desegregation plans.

In both regions, districts without formal desegregation plans have more interracial exposure than those with formal plans throughout the twenty-seven-year time period. The most likely reason for this is that the districts without plans had a much higher percentage white and were more integrated

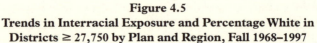

Figure 4.5
Trends in Interracial Exposure and Percentage White in
Districts ≥ 27,750 by Plan and Region, Fall 1968–1997

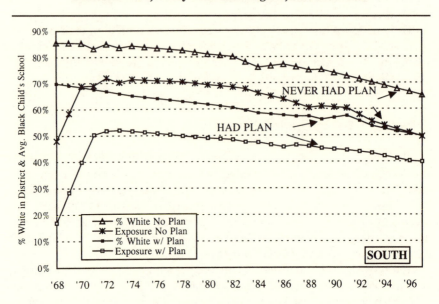

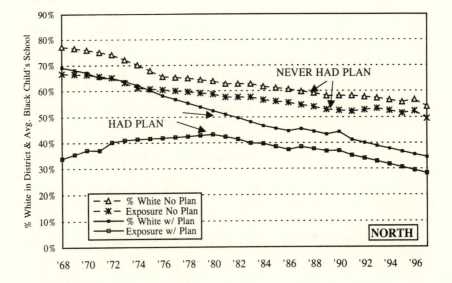

before the mandatory reassignment era began. In short, desegregation plans are characterized by a selection bias—the most segregated and highest percentage minority districts were ordered to implement them. The least segregated and lowest percentage minority districts were often left alone after *Brown* because neighborhood schools produced a reasonable level of integration in their school systems.

The southern districts with formal plans show the largest gains in exposure, increasing from less than 20 percent white in the average black child's school in 1968 to more than 50 percent by 1972. The white enrollment in these school districts started at nearly 70 percent, declined rapidly between 1968 and 1974, and then continued a steady decline to about 50 percent in 1997 with an interracial exposure of 40 percent.

There are only twelve very large districts in the South that never had formal desegregation plans, and they were an average 85 percent white in 1968. Desegregation was accomplished in 1969 or 1970 in these districts by adopting neighborhood attendance zones, in some cases closing all-black schools in the process. Nevertheless, dismantling the dual school system by adopting a single set of neighborhood attendance zones produced considerable improvement in black exposure to whites between 1968 and 1970, and a high level of exposure through 1997. In 1997, districts without formal plans still had ten points more exposure than districts with plans.

The northern districts with and without plans have different trends in exposure. Very large districts that never had formal plans show a gradual decline in exposure because of declining white enrollments. They do, however, show a modest closing of the gap between exposure and the percentage white, suggesting that racial balance has improved even without formal plans.

For very large districts with formal plans, however, black exposure to whites improved from about 34 percent in 1968 to a high of 42 percent in 1980, with a gradual decline after that because of falling white enrollments. The percentage white fell more sharply for districts with plans, so that by 1997 these districts had an index of 28 percent, less integration than existed in 1968.

Not surprisingly, most of the improvement in national desegregation trends is attributable to some sort of desegregation plan rather than to demographic changes and the greatest improvements were in the South where the dual school system was dismantled. This is especially true of the southern school districts that never had formal desegregation plans, that is, that were permitted to desegregate simply by adopting a unitary neighborhood school system.

The effect of desegregation plans in the North was not as impressive. Northern districts without plans did not show an increase in the exposure index at any time. But northern districts with plans achieved less interracial exposure than southern districts because of a rapidly declining percentage white, much steeper than any other group of districts. Implementing desegregation plans in northern districts that already had a considerable number of naturally integrated schools and a rapidly declining percentage white, seems to have accomplished little. Although the percentage white and the exposure index were aligned with each other by 1980, interracial exposure had increased by only ten points at that time. Then it began to decline precipitously.

Prevalence of Desegregation Techniques

The 1991 survey asked about the mandatory techniques of pairing and clustering, satellite zoning, and contiguous rezoning, and the voluntary techniques of M to M transfers and magnet schools. The questionnaire also asked about the use of controlled choice techniques.

Most desegregation plans used a combination of these techniques. Thus, David Armor and I developed a typology of desegregation plans that includes these techniques, but focuses on the basic thrust of the plan. The typology of plans, ordered by the extent of parental choice, is:

1. Voluntary M to M (Voluntary, no magnets; can have contiguous rezoning)
2. Magnet–Voluntary (Voluntary with magnets; can have contiguous rezoning)
3. Controlled choice with magnets[14]
4. Magnet–Mandatory (Mandatory with magnets)
5. Mandatory, no magnets

The prevalence of each type of plan in the districts that had desegregation plans as of the 1991–92 school year is presented in table 4.1 according to the size of the district. Voluntary M to M plans, which used only M to M and contiguous rezoning techniques, were found in only 8 percent of medium and larger districts and 5 percent of very large districts. Magnet–voluntary plans included magnet schools coupled either with contiguous rezoning or M to M or both. No pairing, clustering, or satellite zoning techniques were used. These plans were found in 21 percent of medium and larger districts and 29 percent of very large districts.

Across all size groups, mandatory plans were more common than voluntary plans. In the largest districts, however, mandatory reassignment plans typically included magnet schools (49 percent). Controlled choice plans were used by 4 to 6 percent of districts, depending on size (and all had magnet schools).

These plans were implemented at different times during the post-*Brown* time period. The median year for mandatory reassignment plans and for M to M plans was 1970, regardless of the size of the school district. The median year of the magnet–mandatory plans was 1973 to 1975. The me-

Table 4.1
**Prevalence of Types of Desegregation Plans
in Districts With Plans[a] in 1991**

	All Districts With Plans	Districts $\geq$ 5,000 With Plans	Districts $\geq$ 27,750 With Plans
Voluntary M to M	4%	8%	5%
Magnet-Voluntary	23%	21%	29%
Controlled Choice	4%	6%	5%
Magnet-Mandatory	17%	28%	49%
Mandatory--No Magnets	52%	37%	12%
Total	100%	100%	100%

[a] Twelve percent of all districts had plans; 29 percent of districts greater than
5,000 had plans, and 59 percent of districts greater than 27,500 had plans in 1991.

dian year for the magnet–voluntary plans was about four years later—
1977 to 1978. Controlled choice plans are the latest plans with a median
year ranging from 1977 to 1981, depending on size. Across all types of desegregation plans, the median desegregation year is 1976, regardless of
district size, with the mandatory plans coming first and the controlled
choice plans last.

"Forced busing" was still the most common desegregation technique in
1991, in spite of its controversy. Only about one-third of the very large districts had voluntary plans and two-thirds used mandatory techniques of
some sort, albeit supplemented with magnet schools in most cases. Moreover, although only two mandatory reassignment plans have been implemented since 1982, there are still thousands of students in dozens of
school districts across the country subject to mandatory reassignment
plans.

Desegregation Trends By Plan Type

Figure 4.6 compares desegregation trends in districts that never had formal plans to districts that had (1) a mandatory reassignment plan (magnet–
mandatory and mandatory, no magnets) at any time, (2) only voluntary
desegregation (voluntary M to M or Magnet–voluntary), or (3) only controlled choice plan.[15] Although I have enrollment data up through Fall

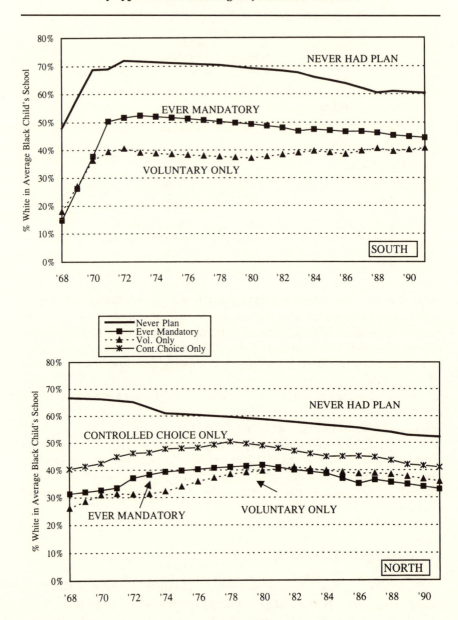

Figure 4.6
Trends in Interracial Exposure in Districts ≥ 27,750
by Type of Plan and Region, Fall 1968–Fall 1991

1997, the analyses of the impact of plan types ends with 1991 because this data was obtained from the 1991 survey of districts.

This typology is used rather than the plan types in table 4.1 because the effects of a mandatory desegregation plan appear to continue through subsequent plans. Districts that implemented voluntary plans and never implemented a mandatory reassignment plan or a controlled choice plan had very different outcomes from those that had ever implemented a mandatory reassignment or controlled choice plan.

Between 1970 and 1973, the Southern districts with mandatory plans achieved about 15 percentage points more interracial exposure than the voluntary plans. By 1991, however, the advantage of mandatory plans over voluntary plans had dwindled to less than five points.

In the North, the mandatory plans initially produced about ten percentage points more interracial exposure than the voluntary plans. By 1985, however, the voluntary plans had surpassed the mandatory plans. It would appear, then, that while mandatory plans are more effective in the short-run, in the long-run they are no more effective than voluntary plans. Unfortunately, neither type of plan seems to overcome the long-term demographic trend of declining white enrollment.

THE EFFECTIVENESS OF DESEGREGATION PLANS[16]

The trends shown above examine the impact of desegregation plans on interracial exposure controlling for size and region. In this section, I present a multiple regression analysis explaining three different desegregation outcomes, controlling for ten variables. The outcome variables are:

1. **white flight**, as measured by the percentage white enrollment change from 1968 to 1991;
2. **increase in interracial exposure**, as measured by the change in the proportion white in the average black child's school from 1968 to 1991;
3. **reduction in racial imbalance**, as measured by the change in the black-white dissimilarity index from 1968 to 1991.

Because of missing data, this analysis is not of annual change, but of change from 1968, the first year for which I have relatively complete data, to 1991, the year the survey of school districts was conducted. The independent variables include the following:

Desegregation Variables. The plan typology ever-mandatory, voluntary-only, and controlled-choice-only are used to explain all outcome variables and the five-plan typology (voluntary M to M, magnet–voluntary, controlled choice, magnet–mandatory, and mandatory, no magnets) are also used to explain change in interracial exposure.

Control Variables. These variables are included in the equations to disentangle the effects of current desegregation plans from other factors that also influenced desegregation outcomes.

1. **Former Desegregation Plan**

   Formerly having had a desegregation plan for those districts that currently have no plan

2. **Population and Enrollment Trend Characteristics**

Percent White 1968. Because interracial exposure—the percentage white in the average minority child's school—can be no higher than the percentage white in the school district, the pre-desegregation percentage white must be controlled for.

Region (South, Central, West, Northeast dummy variables). There are regional variations in state policies, court orders, and demographic trends that influence the desegregation outcomes.

County District (dummy variable). The argument is often made in the desegregation literature (see, for example, Orfield, 1988) that countywide districts, because they include the city and the suburbs, will have less white loss over time and thus less decline in interracial exposure, and more increase in racial imbalance.

Area (suburban, rural, urban dummy variables). Suburban and, in particular, rural districts are gaining whites, and urban districts, regardless of whether they adopt a desegregation plan, are losing them.

Percentage Change in Nonwhite Enrollment, 1968–91. Interracial exposure is heavily influenced by the percentage white in the district and the percentage white in turn is influenced by two factors: change in white enrollment and change in nonwhite enrollment.

Normal Percentage White Enrollment Change, 1968–91. This variable controls for the underlying demographic trend affecting school districts independent of any desegregation policy actions.[17]

Years Since Desegregation. Although desegregation plans have the greatest single annual negative effect on white enrollment and positive effect on interracial exposure and racial imbalance in the first few years following a desegregation plan (see Rossell, 1990a, 1990b, 1995), the greater the number of years since desegregation, the greater the white enrollment loss (see Armor, 1980; Coleman, Kelly, and Moore, 1975a, 1975b; Rossell, 1990a, 1990b, 1995a).[18]

Enrollment 1968 (log). The log of this variable is an estimate of busing distance and logistical difficulty in desegregating a school system as well as a measure of the underlying normal demographic trend. The greater the busing distance, the greater the white flight (Rossell, 1978, 1988c).

3. **Social Class Characteristics.** The effect of social-class characteristics varies depending on the outcome being studied. The higher the social class, the greater

the white flight with the implementation of a desegregation plan (Rossell 1978; Rossell 1990a, 1990b, 1995a). The social class variables are:

Percent Free/Reduced Lunch, 1991: this is a measure of the poverty of the public school children;

Median Family Income, 1980: census data aggregated up to school districts.

White Flight

Although the issue of white flight from mandatory desegregation plans has been hotly debated since Coleman, Kelly and Moore (1975a, 1975b) charged that mandatory desegregation plans were counterproductive, in only seven studies (Armor 1980; Orfield, 1988; Rossell 1990a, 1990b, 1995a; Smylie 1983; Welch and Light 1987; Wilson 1985) have voluntary and mandatory plans been compared specifically. With the exception of Wilson, mandatory plans were found to produce more white flight.[19]

White flight is assessed by calculating the percentage change in white enrollment from 1968 to 1991.[20] This differs from the percentage white shown in figures 4.2 and 4.5 because that variable is a measure of racial composition and is influenced by minority trends as well as by white enrollment trends. Increasing minority enrollment alone can produce a declining percentage white even if no whites have left the school system.

The average percentage white enrollment change for districts in this sample that never had desegregation plans is −3.0 percent over this time period. For districts that currently or formerly had desegregation plans, however, the loss is much higher, −25 percent.

Appendix 4.1 shows the effect of the major desegregation plan on the percentage white enrollment change from 1968 to 1991 in districts over 5,000 in enrollment, controlling for school characteristics. The first column is the b coefficient. The b coefficient tells us the change in the percentage white enrollment change from 1968 to 1991 for a one-unit change in the independent variable. A negative sign next to a b coefficient means that the greater the quantity of that variable or the presence of that factor (in the case of dummy variables), the greater the white enrollment decline (i.e., negative white enrollment change). The column to the right of the b coefficient is the t statistic. If it is at or above 1.98, the relationship between that variable and the outcome variable is statistically significant at .05 or better.

This regression shows the following relationships:

- Any desegregation plan implemented in a countywide school district will have 18 percent less white flight than the same plan implemented in a citywide school district;

- Having had a mandatory reassignment plan is associated with a white enrollment decline 33 percent greater than never having had a plan;
- Having had only a controlled choice desegregation plan is associated with a white enrollment decline 27 percent greater than never having had a plan;[21]
- Having had only a voluntary desegregation plan is associated with a white enrollment decline 2 percent greater than never having had a plan.

Racial Imbalance

Despite the fact that racial imbalance tells us little about how many whites are left in the school system and thus how much actual exposure there is, it has been the standard used by most academics. Therefore, it is important to know how effective different types of desegregation plans are in evenly distributing black and white students across the schools in a district. A negative sign next to a coefficient means that the greater the quantity of that variable or the presence of that factor (in the case of dummy variables), the greater the reduction in racial imbalance over this time period.[22]

Appendix 4.2 shows that from 1968 to 1991:

- virtually any type of formal desegregation plan, whether it is voluntary or mandatory significantly, reduces racial imbalance compared to districts with no plan at all;
- the magnitude of this reduction in racial imbalance is seven points for voluntary plans, thirteen points for controlled-choice plans, and fifteen points for mandatory reassignment plans.

Interracial Exposure

Interracial exposure, the percentage white in the average black child's school, measures the actual extent of contact between the races, not just how evenly distributed they are. Appendix 4.3 shows the change in interracial exposure from 1968 to 1991 produced by the major desegregation plan, controlling for prior plan and plan type, in districts with and without plans. A positive sign next to a variable means that the greater the variable or the presence of a factor (in the case of dummy variables), the greater the increase in interracial exposure over this time period. These data show that over this entire time period:

- Any plan implemented in a countywide school district will produce five points more interracial exposure than the same plan implemented in a city school district;

- Voluntary and mandatory desegregation plans produce significantly more interracial exposure over the twenty-three-year time period than no plan at all;
- Voluntary desegregation plans produce more interracial exposure than mandatory reassignment plans;
- Controlled choice does not produce significantly more interracial exposure than no plan at all;
- Formerly having had a plan produces four points more interracial exposure than never having had a plan.

Because of the fact that school districts that had formal plans tended to be more heavily minority and more segregated in 1968 and because of the importance of interracial exposure, I further controlled for this selection bias by examining change in interracial exposure only in school districts that had a plan. The results were basically the same, except that in the largest school districts ($\geq$ 27,750), the advantage of voluntary desegregation plans is even greater—it increases from six to fifteen points.

I also did an analysis of change in interracial exposure using the five-plan typology: voluntary M to M, magnet–voluntary, controlled choice, magnet–mandatory, and mandatory, no magnets in districts at or above 5,000 and those at or above 27,750. This analysis was repeated again just for the district that had desegregation plans. In both analyses, the voluntary M to M plans are the most successful, but in the very largest school districts they are about as successful as magnet–voluntary plans. In all analyses, the controlled choice plans do the worst, apparently achieving little or no increase in interracial exposure.

THE EFFECT OF MAGNET SCHOOLS

The equations shown in appendices 4.1 through 4.3 do not specifically look at the effect of having magnet schools in a desegregation plan. Unfortunately, magnets were not included in desegregation plans in any great numbers until after 1976, midway through our time period. Given the lateness of the magnet school innovation and their inclusion in comprehensive desegregation plans, it is possible that their true impact is swamped in equations that look at the entire period from 1968–91. Thus, further analyses were conducted of the 1978–91 time period in school districts that currently or formerly had formal desegregation plans to test the effect of magnets on desegregation outcomes.

The dummy variable, magnet schools, had no measurable positive effect on white flight and interracial exposure during this time period. But, as shown in Appendix 4.4, in equation 1, the percentage of schools that are magnets has a significant *negative* impact on white enrollment among school districts that had desegregation plans. This is true even when the extent of reduction in racial imbalance is controlled for. Equation 2 shows that this effect is greatest for the voluntary plans. The b coefficient for the interaction between a voluntary-only plan and the percentage of magnets is negative and statistically significant. The more magnets in a voluntary plan, the more white flight. The interaction between ever-mandatory and percentage of magnets is negative, but not statistically significant.

Appendix 4.5 shows the effect of magnet schools on change in interracial exposure in school districts that had a desegregation plan at any time during this time period. Equation 1 includes the percentage of schools that are magnets, equation 2 includes their interaction effects with plan type, and equation 3 contains the dummy variables for different percentages of magnets. Although the percentage of schools that are magnets is negatively related to change in interracial exposure in equation 1, the effect is not large. An increment of one percent in magnet schools is associated with a one-tenth-point reduction in interracial exposure over this entire time period.[23]

The negative effect is greatest for voluntary plans as shown in equation 2 where the coefficient is statistically significant for the interaction effect between voluntary plans and the percentage of schools that are magnets. The greater the percentage magnets in a voluntary plan, the less increase in interracial exposure. The relationship is also negative for mandatory plans, but not statistically significant.

The omitted magnet variable in equation 3 is no magnets. As shown, less than 5 percent magnets is the only group that is positively related to an increase in interracial exposures, but it is not statistically significant. The only magnet variable that has a statistically significant negative effect on interracial exposure, compared to districts with plans but no magnets, is more than 50 percent magnet schools. Here the effect is larger than with the percentage of schools that are magnets. If more than 50 percent of a district's schools are magnets, it will have three points less increase in interracial exposure over this time period than a plan with no magnets.

I also analyzed change in interracial exposure just for districts that adopted magnet schools as part of their desegregation plans. The results of this analysis are shown in appendix 4.6. Equation 1 shows that the percentage of schools that are magnets is still negatively associated with change in interracial exposure over this time period, and the effect is similarly small. An increase of one percentage point in magnets is associated with a one-tenth-point reduction in interracial exposure over this entire time period. Equation 2 indicates that this effect is statistically significant only for voluntary plans. Equation 3 shows that all groups of the percentage of schools that are magnets are negative compared to less than 5 percent magnets, but only greater than 50 percent is statistically significant.

In short, the more magnet schools added to a voluntary plan, the greater the white enrollment loss and the less the increase in interracial exposure. Moreover, there is no significant advantage to adding magnet schools to a mandatory plan. All groups of the percentage of schools that are magnets have a negative effect on interracial exposure compared to less than 5 percent magnets, but only greater than 50 percent magnets is statistically significant.

One of the reasons increasing the percentage of schools that are magnets may not have a positive effect on increasing interracial exposure is that magnet schools have to be tailored to the environment in which they are implemented. A fundamental principle all too often overlooked in creating magnet schools is that one must estimate white demand. Since one can only expect 10–20 percent of white students to transfer to magnets in minority neighborhoods (Rossell 1995a; Armor 1995), the number of magnets must be linked to the size of the white student population and the number of whites realistically expected to transfer in any given school district. Thus, an 80 percent minority school district with 5,000 whites may be able to support only three magnet programs in minority neighborhoods, whereas a 20 percent minority school district with 20,000 whites may be able to support a dozen magnets and completely desegregate the school system with them.

The federal government has not been helpful in this regard. It has been funding magnet schools since the mid–1980s through the Emergency School Assistance Act (ESAA), and beginning in 1984 through the Magnet School Assistance Program (MSAP). MSAP funding, unfortunately, is not only predisposed toward the high-percentage minority school districts where desegregation is most difficult to attain, but there seem to have been few limits placed initially on the number of magnets in these districts. Indeed, chapter 5 of Steel, Levine, Rossell, and Armor (1993) shows only minuscule changes in interracial exposure in MSAP-funded magnet schools with significant percentages having increased imbalance and reduced interracial exposure. It seems the additional goal that MSAP has of educational improvement in minority schools has often taken precedence over integration.

Magnet Program Structure

Demand is also a function of the specific characteristics of the magnet schools themselves, the most important of which are (1) their location within a school district, and (2) their structure. It is only in voluntary plans, however, that these issues are really important, since in a mandatory reassignment plan, demand is artificially generated by the threat of reassignment across town to a minority school not chosen by the parent.

With regard to location, there is strong political pressure to place magnets in both white and black neighborhoods. This is an inefficient use of the magnet school concept, however. Magnets should rarely be placed in white neighborhood schools because (a) they are not usually needed there—

blacks will transfer to white schools without any special incentive other than free transportation—and (b) magnets in white neighborhoods may be a disincentive for whites to transfer out. Nevertheless, school districts usually put magnets in both white and black neighborhoods and the greater the percentage of magnets in a school district, the more likely some of them will be placed in white neighborhoods.

Figure 4.7 shows a classification of magnet program structures. There are two important factors: (1) the scope of the program within the school and (2) whether a neighborhood population is assigned. This two-by-two classification produces three types of magnet structures: the whole-school attendance zone magnet shown in cell 1, the program within a school (PWS) magnet shown in cell 2, and the dedicated magnet shown in cell 3. With regard to the scope of the program, the dedicated and whole-school attendance zone magnets have programs that encompass the entire student body of a school. The PWS magnets encompass only a portion of the school. With regard to a neighborhood population, the whole-school attendance zone and PWS magnets have neighborhood attendance zones and resident students assigned to the school. The dedicated magnet has no neighborhood attendance zone and no students assigned to it because of their residence.

The most common magnet structures are the PWS and dedicated magnets. In a dedicated magnet, shown in cell 3, all students in the school are in the magnet program. There is no assigned resident attendance zone and all students have volunteered to attend. The biggest problem with a dedicated magnet is attracting enough students to fill a 500- to 2,000-student school to capacity. Thus high school dedicated magnets may have several different magnet programs that appeal to different audiences in order to increase the probability of filling the school.

The PWS magnet, shown in cell 2, has a neighborhood school population assigned to the school, but the only children in the magnet program are those who volunteered for it. Although resident students are typically given first priority for the magnet program, their admission must adhere to racial guidelines for the program. For schools in minority neighborhoods, the limiting factors are white transfers in and the physical capacity of the school.

The whole-school attendance zone magnet, shown in cell 1, has a neighborhood school population assigned to it but the program encompasses the entire school. Children of the opposite race of this neighborhood population are encouraged to transfer in from outside the attendance zone. Despite the fact that many of the resident children might not be interested in and did not choose the particular magnet theme of their school, they and all other children in the school are enrolled in the magnet program. In addition, rather than having the racial composition maintained at a point that might be attractive to opposite-race parents, the classroom racial composition is

Figure 4.7
A Classification of Magnet Program Structures

SCOPE OF PROGRAM

		ENTIRE SCHOOL	PORTION OF STUDENT BODY
ASSIGNED NEIGHBORHOOD STUDENTS	**YES**	Whole-School Attendance Zone Magnet 1	Program Within a School Magnet (PWS) 2
	NO	Dedicated Magnet 3	

whatever the school racial composition is. Whereas the PWS magnets in minority neighborhoods typically have classroom racial compositions close to 50 percent white and 50 percent minority, the whole-school attendance zone magnets in minority neighborhoods will have classroom compositions of 80–95 percent minority or even higher.

All other things being equal, the most attractive magnet structure to parents is the dedicated magnet because all students in the school choose it and the program. The PWS magnets and the whole-school magnets, by contrast, are less attractive particularly to white parents primarily because there is a nonmagnet neighborhood population of students. On the other hand, a problem with the dedicated magnet is that the school has to be emptied of students. In a magnet–voluntary plan, this typically can only be accomplished by redrawing attendance zones and reassigning students to nearby, generally same-race, schools resulting in that school becoming more segregated (assuming there is even room for them). This problem can be avoided by reassigning the resident students across town to opposite-race schools, but this is usually not politically acceptable because in a magnet–voluntary plan they would be the only ones being mandatorily reassigned. The few dedicated magnets that exist in a voluntary plan tend to be left over from a previous mandatory reassignment plan. Thus, type of magnet structure is related to type of desegregation plan with the dedicated magnet model found primarily in mandatory reassignment plans and the PWS and whole-school attendance zone magnets found primarily in magnet–voluntary and controlled-choice plans.

There are exceptions to this rule, however. The Milwaukee magnet–voluntary plan has a large number of dedicated magnets in black neighborhoods, and as a result has been criticized for putting the busing burden on black children because they were forced out of their neighborhood school (Harris 1983; Barndt, Janka, and Rose 1981). Charlotte-Mecklenburg implemented a magnet–voluntary plan with dedicated magnets in fall 1992 to replace their former mandatory reassignment plan. Because most of the dedicated magnets were placed in black neighborhoods, black students were similarly disproportionately forced out of their neighborhood schools.[24]

The next most attractive magnet structure, the PWS model, is primarily used in voluntary plans since it allows a neighborhood population to remain in their school. Although it has fewer implementation problems, the PWS magnet structure poses more operational problems than the dedicated magnet. There are interaction issues between the resident and the magnet students, including conflict over how many resident students will be allowed in the program given white preferences for 50–50 racial balance (Armor 1995; Rossell 1995a) and the extent to which resident students will be allowed to use the resources of the magnet program.

Because of the implementation problems of the dedicated magnets and the operational problems of the PWS magnets, some school districts with magnet–voluntary plans have adopted whole-school, attendance zone magnets. This occurred in San Diego after almost a decade of programs-within-schools when the plaintiffs convinced the court that PWS magnets were elitist. Unfortunately, the whole-school attendance zone magnets in minority neighborhoods in San Diego appear to have attracted few whites and the schools are virtually all minority.

This could have been predicted from the findings of parent surveys David Armor and I have conducted. These surveys show that the willingness of white parents to send their children to magnet schools in minority neighborhoods declines from 21 percent definitely willing when the program (i.e., classroom) within a school is 50 percent white and 50 percent minority to 13 percent definitely willing when the program (i.e., classroom) is three-quarters minority and one-quarter white. This further declines to about 5 percent willingness to transfer if the busing distance is forty-five minutes or longer (Armor 1995; Rossell 1995a).

I test this in figures 4.8 and 4.9, which is an analysis of the effect of magnet structure on school integration in Prince George's County, Maryland in 1996–97. Prince George's County is a large, 70 percent black countywide school district adjacent to Washington, D.C. that was under court order at that time.[25] The school system had all three kinds of magnet structures: (1) a dedicated magnet, (2) programs within schools, and (3) whole-school attendance zone magnets.

Figure 4.8
Effect* of Magnet Program Structure on School, Percent Black in Magnet Schools ≥ 70% Black, Prince George's County School District, 1996–1997

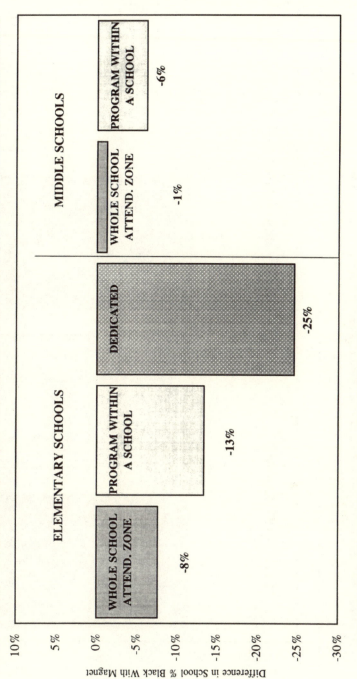

* Actual % black with the magnet transfers - % black without the magnet transfers.

Figure 4.9

Effect* of Magnet Program Structure on School, Percent Black in Magnet Schools < 70% Black, Prince George's County School District, 1996–1997

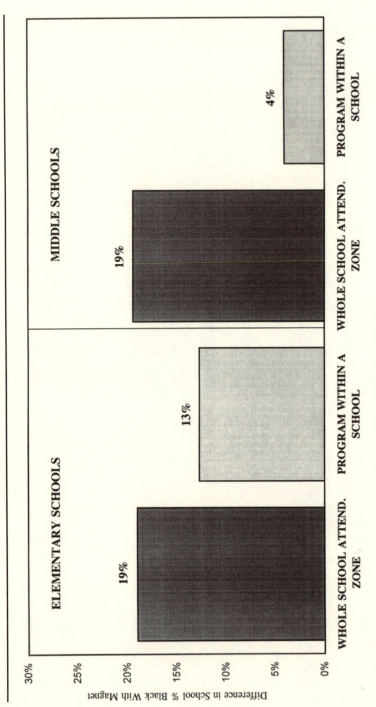

* Actual % black with the magnet transfers - % black without the magnet transfers.

The analysis was conducted by obtaining information on how many of the students of each race were in the school only because they had transferred in to enroll in the magnet program. I calculated the actual percentage black, and I compared this to the percentage black when these transfers were removed from the enrollment.

Figure 4.8 shows the effect of program structure in schools at or above 70 percent black. The whole-school attendance zone magnet programs in black schools are clearly the least effective in both elementary schools (on the left) and middle schools (on the right). The elementary schools were only an average eight points less black and the middle schools only one point less black because of the magnet transfers. In the programs within schools, by contrast, the elementary schools were an average 13 percent less black due to the magnet transfers and the middle schools 6 percent less black. The dedicated magnet program was the most successful. It was located in a mostly black neighborhood and if a contiguous attendance zone had been drawn around the school, it would have been 25 percent more black.

Figure 4.9 shows the same analysis for schools that had a lower percentage black than the districtwide percentage. In the whiter schools, the whole-school attendance zone magnets were the most successful. At both the elementary and middle school level, the schools were 19 percent more black as a result of the magnet program. The schools with programs within schools, however, were not so successful. The elementary schools were only 13 percent more black as a result of the magnet program. The middle schools were four percent more black as a result of the magnet program.

Thus, the success of a whole-school attendance zone magnet depends on the racial composition of the school it is in. These structures are the least successful when they are placed in predominantly black schools because they reduce the attractiveness of the program to white parents.

The whole-school attendance-zone magnets in white neighborhoods do not have this problem. What is unattractive to white parents—classrooms that reflect the racial composition of the neighborhood and no separation from the neighborhood population—is especially attractive to black parents because it is associated with a higher quality of education.

CONCLUSIONS

The civil rights movement achieved an extraordinary victory when it dismantled the dual school system in the South. But the research presented here suggests that if one's goal is the greatest interracial exposure, the civil rights movement and its government allies probably took a wrong turn in the late 1960s when they abandoned the principle of nondiscrimination and demanded racial balance in every school. Racial quotas, whether used in a mandatory reassignment plan or a voluntary plan with magnets, seem to have produced less interracial exposure than simply adopting a simple neighborhood (or geographic zone) school system.

We cannot know this for sure because there seems to have been a selection bias. The school districts that were ordered to implement comprehensive desegregation plans with racial balance quotas were the larger, more heavily minority, more segregated school districts. They may simply have been the school districts that could not desegregate their schools by closing a few black schools and adopting a single neighborhood school system.

Although racial balance was the guiding principle behind all plans ordered after 1968, the plans differed a great deal in how they achieved this. The mandatory reassignment plans of the 1970s ordered children to leave their neighborhood schools to go across town to an opposite-race school. These plans produced significant white flight, but also a large increase in interracial exposure. The controlled-choice plans of the 1980s allowed whites to choose a school, and then ordered some of them to leave their neighborhood school and/or their school of choice to go to another school in order to achieve racial balance. These plans produced less white flight than the mandatory reassignment plans, but also less of an increase in interracial exposure. Although neighborhood schools are associated with the highest level of interracial exposure, the greatest increase in interracial exposure is produced by voluntary desegregation plans, not neighborhood schools.

Although magnet schools have been warmly embraced by the courts, school districts, and state and federal governments as desegregation tools, their addition to a desegregation plan does not seem to reduce white flight or increase interracial exposure. On the other hand, they are one of only two techniques that can integrate black schools in a voluntary desegregation plan. The first is closing them and reassigning the students to adjoining white schools, and the second is putting magnet programs in them. The former stopped being politically feasible after *Swann*, which left only magnet schools to do the job.

If the civil rights movement had been willing to ignore all-black schools, they might have produced more interracial exposure by simply allowing a single neighborhood school system and M to M transfers, but that is a big "if." It is hard to imagine the civil rights movement tolerating black schools at a time when most school districts were predominantly white and school desegregation seemed feasible.

Although magnet schools are the only way to desegregate black schools in a voluntary desegregation plan, there is such a thing as too many magnet schools. Having a lot of magnet schools can be inefficient because the magnets compete against each other, dispersing the available whites among too many schools so that no school has enough whites to attract more whites. The average school district does not do a good enough job of estimating white demand and placing magnets in places where they are absolutely essential to desegregating the school.

In addition, some magnet structures are more attractive than others and their feasibility varies according to their desegregation context. Dedicated magnets are the most attractive type of magnet, but they are feasible primarily in a mandatory reassignment plan. The least attractive magnet structure is the whole-school attendance-zone magnet, but only when it is placed in a school in a minority neighborhood.

Although voluntary desegregation techniques seem to have achieved a greater increase in interracial exposure and produced less white flight than mandatory reassignment plans, all desegregation plans achieved considerable racial balance, which was, after all, their goal. This racial balance seems not to have declined with the dismantling of desegregation plans all over the United States as many school districts have attained unitary status. Thus, the real success of the civil rights movement may be that white school administrators believe in integrated schools and are willing to implement unobtrusive policies, such as building schools in more integratable sites, allowing voluntary transfers and choice, and refusing to adopt new discriminatory policies.

ENDNOTES

1. Although this actually started with the Houston Independent School District in 1975, it was almost a decade before the courts resumed ordering the replacement of mandatory with voluntary plans in any significant number.

2. As of fall 2000, race was not to be used as an assignment variable in the controlled choice plan.

3. Some school districts, particularly those that are predominantly of one race, use as their standard whether a student's race is above the district percentage. Similarly, the standard for the receiving school is whether a student's race is below the district percentage.

4. In California, the 15 percentage-point deviation was once part of the California Administrative Code for defining a segregated school.

5. Charlotte obtained unitary status in 2001 and Buffalo in 1994. Milwaukee has not petitioned for unitary status.

6. The measure originates with Duncan and Duncan (1955), but it has been most closely associated with Taeuber and Taeuber (1965). It has been used in numerous studies of school and residential racial imbalance since then. Some examples are Farley (1981); Farley, Wurdock, and Richards (1980); Smylie (1983); Van Valey, Roof, and Wilcox (1977). For very small school districts, Coulter (1989) argues the formula should be $D=ABS((Wi/W)-(Bi/B))/(2(1-minPW))$ where minPW is the smallest proportion white in any school in the district.

7. This measure has been used in several more recent studies of school desegregation to estimate the outcome of a plan. Some examples are Farley 1981; Orfield 1982; Orfield 1988; Orfield and Monfort 1986; Ross 1983; Rossell 1978, 1979a, 1986a, 1990a, 1990b.

8. Another way of expressing this is

$$IE_b = \frac{\sum\limits_k k\, N_{kb}\, P_{kw}}{\sum N_{kb}}$$

9. Laurie Steel and Roger Levine of American Institutes for Research were co-project directors.

10. The universe was stratified according to district size and racial composition. Sample sizes within strata were proportional to district size, and thus all 155 districts with very large enrollments (over 27,750) were sampled with certainty, while only 100 districts were sampled to represent approximately 4,800 small districts with enrollments of fewer than 5,000. Samples of 195 and 150 districts, respectively, represent large districts (10,000 to 27,750) and medium districts (5,000 to 9,999). In addition, at the request of the Department of Education, all school districts that had participated in the federal government Magnet School Assistance Program (MSAP) were also included with certainty.

11. The final report (Steel, Levine, Rossell, and Armor 1993) presents the initial findings of the research project. Armor and Rossell 2000; Rossell and Armor 1996; Steel and Eaton 1996; present additional analyses of the dataset. These analyses are very similar to those presented in this chapter.

12. In figures 4.2 through 4.4, districts are weighted to reflect the universe of students, so that the desegregation trends reflect the total population of students in the United States. In the remaining analyses of different types of district policies or plans, the districts are weighted to reflect the universe of districts.

13. The desegregation measures in this chapter are limited to blacks because over most of the 21-year period and in most of the districts, the demand for desegregation was made by blacks and the focus of the plans was integrating blacks with whites. Indeed, until recently, Hispanics in the South were classified as white in school enrollment statistics and desegregation plans. As a result, many of the school districts in our sample had no Hispanic students in the 1960s and 1970s. Hispanic desegregation trends can be found in Armor and Rossell (2000).

14. All of the controlled choice plans in this sample have magnet schools.

15. Districts that currently do not have a plan, but formerly had a plan were not queried as to the type of former plan that they had. For this plan typology, they are missing.

16. A similar analysis was first published in Rossell and Armor 1996 and Steel, Levine, Rossell, and Armor 1993.

17. Because, for most school districts, there is no pre-desegregation trend data and no information on metropolitan trends (Rossell, 1990a, 1990b, 1995b), our solution to estimating the "normal" demographic trend in white enrollment change was to compute a variable that measured the mean proportional white enrollment change from 1968 to 1991 among the districts that never had a desegregation plan for five different categories of 1968 percentage white crosstabulated by four different regions and further crosstabulated by size—above and below 27,750. This variable then became a control variable for the districts with desegregation plans in the same quintile of percentage white in 1968, the same region, and the same size cate-

gory. For the non-desegregating districts, the normal demographic trend was simply their actual white enrollment change during this period.

18. For districts that never had plans, years since desegregation was set to 1976, the average year of desegregation for those that had plans.

19. Since there were no control variables in the Orfield study, it can be disregarded.

20. This is calculated as 1991 white enrollment minus 1968 white enrollment and that sum divided by 1968 white enrollment and multiplied by 100. Thus, the measurement unit of the variable in the data file is percentages.

21. Because the controlled choice plans were implemented, on average, a decade after the mandatory reassignment plans, the control for the "normal" demographic trend may not be adequate. Nevertheless, the findings for controlled choice in this chapter are similar to the better controlled, pooled time series analysis of Rossell (1995a) with a much smaller sample.

22. The measurement unit of the variable in the data file is proportions: 00 to 1.0.

23. The measurement unit of the variable in the data file is proportions: 00 to 1.0.

24. A white parent whose child was denied admission to one of these magnets filed a lawsuit to have the school district declared unitary. The federal district court agreed Charlotte-Mecklenburg was unitary in *Cappacchione and Grant et al. v. Charlotte-Mecklenburg Schools et al.*, U.S. District Court, 3:97-CV-482P, 9 September 1999. An appeals court reversed this, but another appeals court agreed with the district court in 2001.

25. Prince George's County was in a transitional period toward unitary status from 1998 to 2002. They were to be declared unitary at the end of fiscal year 2002 if there were no outstanding lawsuits filed against it, and that in fact occurred on June 25, 2002.

Appendix 4.1

Relationship between Percentage White Enrollment Change, 1968–1991, and School District and Major Desegregation Plan Characteristics

SOCIAL, DEMOGRAPHIC, & GEOGRAPHIC VARIABLES	Districts ≥ 5,000	
	b	t
% White 1968	-.518 *	-5.530
South [vs. Central]	-27.072 *	-5.358
Northeast [vs. Central]	.780	.169
West [vs. Central]	-.101380	-.024
County District	18.307 *	5.007
Suburban [vs. Rural]	.034	.008
Urban [vs. Rural]	-1.144	-.254
% Nonwhite Enroll. Change '68-'91	9.92E-04	1.197
Normal % White Enroll. Change '68-91	.894 *	56.314
% Free/Reduced Lunch	-.425 *	-4.067
Income	2.01E-05	.055
Log of Enrollment 1968	-24.536 *	-5.177
Years Since Major Desegregation Plan	-1.127 *	-2.734
DESEGREGATION VARIABLES [a]		
Ever Had a Mandatory Plan	-32.829 *	-7.595
Voluntary Plan Only	-1.986	-.304
Controlled Choice Only	-26.890 *	-2.006
Formerly Had Plan (char. not known)	-20.687 *	-4.116
Constant	170.440 *	7.814
Adjusted r2	.862	
N (district weights)	1009	

* Significant at .05 level or better.

Note: E-04 or E-05 means move the decimal point 4 and 5 places to the left

[a] The omitted variable is never had a plan.

Appendix 4.2
Relationship between Racial Imbalance Change, 1968–1991, and
School District and Major Desegregation Plan Characteristics

SOCIAL, DEMOGRAPHIC, & GEOGRAPHIC VARIABLES	Districts ≥ 5,000	
	b	t
% White 1968	-6.202E-04	1.151
South [vs. Central]	.094 *	3.283
Northeast [vs. Central]	.169 *	6.598
West [vs. Central]	.062 *	2.629
County District	-.023	-1.122
Suburban [vs. Rural]	.090 *	3.780
Urban [vs. Rural]	.057 *	2.260
% Nonwhite Enroll. Change '68-'91	-2.02E-05 *	-4.370
Normal % White Enroll. Change '68-91	-2.96E-05	-.329
% Free/Reduced Lunch	1.01E-04	-.173
Income	-4.69E-06 *	-2.244
Log of Enrollment 1968	-.021	-.768
Years Since Major Desegregation Plan	-.008 *	-3.558
DESEGREGATION VARIABLES [a]		
Ever Had a Mandatory Plan	-.150 *	-6.046
Voluntary Plan Only	-.074 *	-2.048
Controlled Choice Only	-.131	-1.776
Formerly Had Plan (char. not known)	-.078 *	-2.811
Constant	-.093	-.746
Adjusted r2	.158	
N (district weights)	927	

* Significant at .05 or better.

Note: E-04 or E-05 means move the decimal point 4 and 5 places to the left respectively.

[a] The omitted variable is never had a plan.

Appendix 4.3
Relationship between Interracial Exposure Change, 1968–1991, and
School District and Major Desegregation Plan Characteristics

SOCIAL, DEMOGRAPHIC, & GEOGRAPHIC VARIABLES	Districts ≥ 5,000	
	b	t
% White 1968	-.304 *	-7.449
South [vs. Central]	7.871 *	3.643
Northeast [vs. Central]	-5.790 *	-2.972
West [vs. Central]	-12.533 *	-7.011
County District	5.306 *	3.396
Suburban [vs. Rural]	-8.362 *	-4.683
Urban [vs. Rural]	-9.194 *	-4.813
% Nonwhite Enroll. Change '68-'91	-8.95E-04 *	-2.550
Normal % White Enroll. Change '68-91	.046 *	6.796
% Free/Reduced Lunch	-.397 *	-8.978
Income	-.001 *	-7.547
Log of Enrollment 1968	5.090 *	2.536
Years Since Major Desegregation Plan	.732 *	4.240
DESEGREGATION VARIABLES [a]		
Ever Had a Mandatory Plan	11.173 *	6.134
Voluntary Plan Only	19.101 *	6.986
Controlled Choice Only	4.285	.764
Formerly Had Plan (char. not known)	4.463 *	2.110
Constant	32.566 *	3.505
Adjusted r2	.530	
N (district weights)	955	

* Significant at .05 level or better.

Note: E-04 or E-05 means move the decimal point 4 and 5 places to the left respectively.

[a] The omitted variable is never had a plan.

Appendix 4.4
Relationship between Percentage White Enrollment Change, 1978–1991, and the Percentage of Schools that are Magnets Controlling for School District and Plan Characteristics

	Districts > 5,000 with Plans			
	Equation 1		Equation 2	
SOCIAL, DEMOGRAPHIC, & GEOGRAPHIC VARIABLES	b	t	b	t
% White 1978	0.001	0.02	-0.005	-0.074
South [vs. Central]	-11.220 *	-2.89	-10.993 *	-2.825
Northeast [vs. Central]	-2.694	-0.79	-3.586	-1.040
West [vs. Central]	6.180	1.79	5.922	1.705
County district	17.719 *	5.70	17.942 *	5.811
Suburban [vs. Rural]	6.345	1.47	5.336	1.226
Urban [vs. Rural]	1.429	0.38	0.790	0.213
% Nonwhite Enroll. Change '78-'91	0.038 *	4.72	0.036 *	4.482
% White Enroll. Change '68-'78	26.241 *	8.19	26.531 *	8.333
% Free/Reduced Lunch	-0.116	-1.79	-0.123	-1.883
Income 1980	-0.001 *	-3.52	-0.001 *	-3.517
Log of Enrollment 1978	-9.890 *	-3.25	-9.869 *	-3.268
Years Since Major Plan	-0.090	-0.43	-0.082	-0.392
DESEGREGATION VARIABLES[a]				
Ever had a mandatory plan	9.854 *	3.74	10.691 *	3.791
Voluntary plan only	12.516 *	3.54	17.081 *	4.284
RACIAL IMBALANCE VARIABLES[b]				
Change 1968-78	-21.609 *	-4.21	-20.008 *	-3.873
Change 1978-91	8.677	1.10	11.890	1.480
MAGNET VARIABLES				
% of Schools that are Magnets	-0.1814 *	-3.3784	-0.003	-0.028
% Magnets X Voluntary Plan Only			-0.359 *	-2.407
% Magnets X Mandatory Plan Only			-0.152	-1.169
(Constant)	37.651 *	2.35	38.313 *	2.403
Adjusted R^2	0.58		0.59	
N (district weights)	300		300	

* Significant at .05 or better.

[a] The omitted variable is controlled choice only.

[b] Black-white index of dissimilariy.

**Relationship between Change in Interracial Exposure, 1978–1991,
and the Percentage of Schools that are Magnets Controlling for
School District and Plan Characteristics**

	Districts > 5,000 With Plans					
	Equation 1		Equation 2		Equation 3	
SOCIAL, DEMOGRAPHIC, & GEOGRAPHIC VARIABLES	b	t	b	t	b	t
% White 1978	-0.0002	-0.52	-0.0002	-0.64	-0.0006 *	-2.48
South [vs. Central]	-0.0878 *	-5.19	-0.0889 *	-5.26	-0.0870 *	-6.44
Northeast [vs. Central]	-0.0791 *	-5.19	-0.0837 *	-5.44	-0.0608 *	-5.02
West [vs. Central]	-0.0855 *	-5.57	-0.0874 *	-5.69	-0.0622 *	-5.15
County district	0.0246	1.80	0.0268 *	1.97	0.0628 *	5.81
Suburban [vs. Rural]	-0.0433 *	-2.37	-0.0432 *	-2.36	0.0019	0.12
Urban [vs. Rural]	-0.0743 *	-4.69	-0.0743 *	-4.72	-0.0124	-0.95
% Nonwhite Enroll. Change '78-'91	-0.0002 *	-4.69	-0.0002 *	-4.92	-0.0002 *	-7.53
% White Enroll. Change '68-'78	-0.0112	-0.78	-0.0093	-0.66	-0.0068	-0.61
Percentage free/reduced lunch	-0.0009 *	-3.16	-0.0009 *	-3.19	-0.0012 *	-5.32
Income 1980	0.0000 *	-4.08	0.0000 *	-4.14	0.0000 *	-4.26
Log of Enrollment 1978	0.0025	0.18	0.0025	0.18	-0.0101	-0.91
Years since major plan	-0.0033 *	-3.62	-0.0033 *	-3.61	-0.0013	-1.71
DESEGREGATION VARIABLES[a]						
Ever had a mandatory plan	0.0371 *	3.21	0.0424 *	3.48	0.0351 *	2.95
Voluntary plan only	0.0409 *	2.57	0.0583 *	3.26	0.0391 *	2.37
MAGNET VARIABLES[b]						
% of schools that are magnets	-0.0008 *	-3.13	0.0002	0.39		
% Magnets X Voluntary Plan Only			-0.0016 *	-2.39		
% Magnets X Ever Mandatory Plan			-0.0010	-1.68		
< 5 % of schools are magnets					0.0096	0.58
5-10% of schools are magnets					-0.0094	-0.60
10-50% of schools are magnets					-0.0112	-0.78
>50% of schools are magnets					-0.0467 *	-2.08
(Constant)	0.2481 *	3.43	0.2477 *	3.45	0.2628 *	3.39
Adjusted R^2	0.36		0.36		0.34	
N (district weights)	300		300		300	

* Significant at .05 or better.

[a] The omitted variable is controlled choice only.

[b] The omitted variable for equation 3 is no magnet schools.

Relationship between Change in Interracial Exposure, 1978–1991, and the Percentage of Schools that are Magnets Controlling for School District and Plan Characteristics

	Districts with Magnet Schools					
	Equation 1		Equation 2		Equation 3	
SOCIAL, DEMOGRAPHIC, & GEOGRAPHIC VARIABLES	b	t	b	t	b	t
Percentage White 1978	0.0005	0.84	0.0004	0.68	0.0004	0.75
South	-0.0865 *	-3.24	-0.0914 *	-3.49	-0.0923 *	-3.29
Northeast	-0.0593 *	-2.81	-0.0606 *	-2.90	-0.0642 *	-2.83
West	-0.0546 *	-2.28	-0.0468 *	-1.98	-0.0584 *	-2.38
County district	0.0054	0.21	0.0118	0.46	0.0085	0.32
Suburban	-0.1455 *	-2.69	-0.1495 *	-2.82	-0.1396 *	-2.51
Urban	-0.1942 *	-3.89	-0.1868 *	-3.81	-0.1939 *	-3.77
% Nonwhite Enroll. Change '78-'91	-0.0009 *	-4.01	-0.0009 *	-4.08	-0.0009 *	-3.99
% White Enroll. Change '68-'78	0.0525	1.35	0.0600	1.54	0.0583	1.40
Percentage free/reduced lunch	-0.0012	-1.94	-0.0016 *	-2.59	-0.0010	-1.67
Income 1980	0.0000 *	-2.90	0.0000 *	-3.57	0.0000 *	-2.79
Log of Enrollment 1978	0.0496 *	2.38	0.0482 *	2.35	0.0509 *	2.36
Years since major plan	-0.0036 *	-2.88	-0.0035 *	-2.86	-0.0033 *	-2.59
DESEGREGATION VARIABLES[a]						
Ever had a mandatory plan	0.0031	0.13	0.0224	0.74	-0.0068	-0.27
Voluntary plan only	0.0211	0.77	0.0854 *	2.27	0.0130	0.46
MAGNET VARIABLES[b]						
% of schools that are magnets	-0.0008 *	-2.87	0.0000	0.01		
% Magnets X Voluntary Plan Only			-0.0021 *	-2.34		
% Magnets X Ever Mandatory Plan			-0.0005	-0.62		
5-10% of schools are magnets					-0.0204	-0.95
10-50% of schools are magnets					-0.0192	-0.92
>50% of schools are magnets			*		-0.0627 *	-2.29
(Constant)	0.2409	1.77	0.2833 *	2.10	0.2416	1.72
Adjusted R^2	0.47		0.50		0.37	
N (district weights)	135		135		135	

* Significant at .05 or better.

[a] The omitted variable is controlled choice only.

[b] The omitted variable for equation 3 is less than 5% magnets

REFERENCES

Alves, Michael J., and Charles V. Willie. 1987. Controlled-choice assignments: A new and more effective approach to school desegregation. *The Urban Review* 19: 67–88.

Armor, David J. 1980. White flight and the future of school desegregation. In *School Desegregation: Past, Present and Future*, edited by Walter G. Stephan and Joseph R. Feagan. Plenum Press.

———. 1988. School busing: A time for change. In *Eliminating Racism*, edited by P.A. Katz and D.A. Taylor. Plenum Press.

———. 1995. *Forced Justice: School Desegregation And The Law*. Oxford UP.

———. 1998. Evaluation of the Rockford controlled choice plan. Rockford: Rockford Board of Education. 20 April.

Armor, David J. and Christine H. Rossell. 2002. Desegregation and resegregation in the public schools. In *Beyond Victimization*, edited by Stephen Thernstrom and Abigal Thernstrom. Hoover Institution Press.

Barndt, Michael, Rick Janka, and Harold Rose. 1981. The West and Midwest, Milwaukee, Wisconsin; Mobilization for school and community cooperation. In *Community Politics and Educational Change: Ten School Systems Under Court Order*, edited by Charles V. Willie and Susan L. Greenblatt. Longman.

Coleman, James S., Sara D. Kelly, and John A. Moore. 1975a. Recent trends in school integration. Paper presented at the Annual Meeting of the American Educational Research Association. Washington, D.C.

———. 1975b. *Trends in Segregation, 1968–1973*. Washington, D.C.: Urban Institute.

Coulter, Philip B. 1989. *Measuring Inequality*. Westview Press.

Crain, Robert, and Christine H. Rossell. 1989. Catholic Schools and Racial Segregation. In *Public Values, Private Schools*, edited by Neal Devins, 184–214. Falmer Press.

Crain, Robert, and Jack Strauss. 1985. School desegregation and black occupational attainments: Results from a long-term experiment. Baltimore: Johns Hopkins University, Center for Social Organization of Schools.

Duncan, Otis D. and Beverly Duncan. 1955. A methodological analysis of segregation indexes. *American Social Review* 20: 210–17.

Estabrook, Leigh S. 1980. *The Effect of Desegregation of Parents' Evaluations of Schools*. Ph.D. Dissertation. Boston University.

Eyler, Janet, Valerie J. Cook, and Leslie E. Ward. 1983. "Resegregation: Segregation within desegregated schools. In *The Consequences of School Desegregation*, edited by Christine H. Rossell and Willis D. Hawley. Temple UP.

Farley, Reynolds. 1981. Final report, Nie Grant #G-79-0151. Ann Arbor: University of Michigan, Population Studies Center.

Farley, Reynolds, Clarence Wurdock, and Toni Richards. 1980. School desegregation and white flight: An investigation of competing models and their discrepant findings. *Sociology of Education* 53: 123–39.

Frey, William H. 1977. Central city white flight: Racial and nonracial causes. Paper presented at the Annual Meeting of the American Sociological Association. Chicago.

Glenn, Charles. 1991. Controlled choice in Massachusetts public schools. *The Public Interest* 103 (Spring): 88–105.

Harris, Ian M. 1983. The inequalities of Milwaukee's plan. *Integrated Education* 21(1–6): 173–77.

Lord, Dennis J. 1975. School busing and white abandonment of public schools. *Southeastern Geographer* 15: 81–92.

Mahard, Rita, and Robert L. Crain. 1983. Research on minority achievement in desegregated schools. In *The Consequences of School Desegregation*, edited by Christine H. Rossell and Willis D. Hawley. Temple UP.

McConahay, John B. and Willis D. Hawley. 1976. Attitude of Louisville and Jefferson County public school students toward busing for school desegregation: Preliminary results. Durham: Duke University, Institute of Policy Sciences and Public Affairs.

———. 1978. Reactions to busing in Louisville: Summary of adult opinions in 1976 and 1977. Durham: Duke University, Institute of Policy Sciences and Public Affairs.

Orfield, Gary. 1982. Desegregation of black and Hispanic students from 1968 to 1980. Washington, D.C.: Joint Center for Political Studies.

———. 1988. School desegregation in the 1980s. *Equity and Choice* 4 (February): 25–8.

Orfield, Gary and F. Monfort. 1986. Are American schools resegregating in the Reagan era? A statistical analysis of segregation levels from 1980 to 1984. University of Chicago, National School Desegregation Project.

Pearce, Diana. 1980. Breaking down barriers: New evidence on the impact of metropolitan school desegregation on housing pattern. Washington, D.C.: National Institute of Education.

Pride, Richard A., and J. David Woodward. 1985. The Burden of busing: The politics of desegregation in Nashville. Nashville: Vanderbilt University.

Reagan, Michael D. 1987. *Regulation: The Politics of Policy*. Little, Brown and Co.

Ross, J. Michael. 1977. Does school desegregation work? A quasi-experimental analysis of parental attitudes toward the effect of desegregation on student achievement. Paper presented at the Annual Meeting of the Society for the Study of Social Problems. Chicago.

———. 1983. The effectiveness of alternative desegregation strategies: The issue of voluntary versus mandatory policies in Los Angeles. Boston: Boston University.

Rossell, Christine H. 1978. Assessing the unintended impacts of public policy: School desegregation and resegregation. Report to the National Institute of Education. Boston: Boston University.

———. 1979a. Declaration of Christine H. Rossell. *Carlin v. San Diego Unified School District*, California Superior Court. San Diego, California.

———. 1979b. Magnet schools as a desegregation tool: The importance of contextual factors in explaining their success. *Urban Education* 20 (October): 303–20.

———. 1980. Government Exhibit 67. *U.S. v. Texas Education Agency*, U.S. District Court. Port Arthur, Texas.

———. 1983a. Applied social science research: What does it say about the effectiveness of school desegregation plans? *Journal of Legal Studies* 12: 69–107.

———. 1983b. Options for desegregating Howard and Madison Street elementary schools, Marion County, Florida. *U.S. v. Marion County*, U.S. District Court. Middle District of Florida, Jacksonville, Florida. 5 Nov.

————. 1985a. The effectiveness of alternative desegregation plans for Hattiesburg, Mississippi. *U.S. and Pittman v. Mississippi and Hattiesburg Municipal School District,* U.S. Department of Justice. 21 March.

————. 1985b. The effectiveness of alternative desegregation plans for Prince George's County, Maryland. Report for Laurel Amici, *Vaughns et al. v. Prince George's County Board of Education et al.*

————. 1985c. Estimating the desegregation effectiveness of the San Jose unified school district's plan and "The Cambridge Plan." Report. U.S. District Court, 11 December.

————. 1986a. Estimating the effectiveness of a magnet school desegregation plan for the Savannah-Chatham county school district. *Stell and U.S. v. Board of Public Education for the City of Savannah and the County of Chatham,* U.S. District Court.

————. 1986b. Estimating the effectiveness of a magnet school desegregation plan for the Yonkers school district. Report. *U.S. and NAACP v. Yonkers Board of Education et al.,* U.S. District Court, 17 March.

————. 1986c. Estimating the net benefit of school desegregation reassignments. *Educational Evaluation and Policy Analysis* 7: 217–27.

————. 1988a. An analysis of enrollment trends in the Yonkers school district. Report to the superintendent of schools, Donald M. Batista. Yonkers Public Schools. 29 December.

————. 1988b. Defendant's exhibit. *U.S. and Nichols v. Natchez Special Municipal Separate School District,* U.S. District Court. Natchez, Mississippi.

————. 1988c. Is it the busing or the blacks? *Urban Affairs Quarterly* 24:138–48.

————. 1990a. The carrot or the stick for school desegregation policy. *Urban Affairs Quarterly* 25: 474–99.

————. 1990b. *The Carrot or the stick for School Desegregation Policy: Magnet Schools or Forced Busing.* Temple UP.

————. 1991a. Estimating the effectiveness of a voluntary magnet school desegregation plan for the Stockton Unified school district. *Hernandez v. Stockton Unified School District,* Cal. Superior Court. 19 September.

————. 1991b. White flight and elementary classroom segregation. Report on the desegregation of the San Jose Unified District, U.S. District Court. 30 April.

————. 1992. An analysis of the segregation of alternative proposals for the reorganization of the Grant Union High school district and its feeder elementary schools. Report to the Robla school district, Sacramento County, Ca. 3 Aug.

————. 1995a. Controlled choice desegregation plans: Not enough choice, too much control? *Urban Affairs Review* (formerly *Urban Affairs Quarterly*) 31(1): 43–76.

————. 1995b. The convergence of black and white attitudes on school desegregation issues during the four decade evolution of the plans." *The William and Mary Law Review* 36(2): 613–63.

————. 1995c. School desegregation in the Rockford public schools. Report. *People Who Care et al. v. Rockford Board of Education, School District #205,* U.S. District Court. 29 November.

————. 1996. An analysis of the San Jose unified school district's compliance with its remedial orders on student assignment and transportation. Report. *Vasquez et al. v. San Jose Unified School District et al.,* U.S. District Court. 14 June.

————. 1997. An analysis of the court decisions in *Sheff v. O'Neill* and possible remedies for racial isolation. *Connecticut Law Review* 29(3): 1187–1233.

Rossell, Christine H. and David J. Armor. 1996. The effectiveness of school desegregation plans, 1968–1991. *American Politics Quarterly* 24(3): 267–302.

Rossell, Christine H. and J. Michael Ross. 1979. The long term effect of court-ordered desegregation on student enrollment on Central City public school systems: The case of Boston, 1974–1979. Report for Boston School Department.

Schofield, Janet W. and Andrew H. Sagar. 1983. Desegregation, school practice, and student race relations. In *The Consequences of School Desegregation*, edited by Christine H. Rossell and Willis D. Hawley. Temple UP.

Serow, Robert C. and Daniel Solomon. 1979. Parents' attitudes toward desegregation: The proximity hypothesis. *Phi Delta Kappa* 60: 752–53

Smylie, Mark A. 1983. Reducing racial isolation in large school districts: The comparative effectiveness of mandatory and voluntary desegregation strategies. *Urban Education* 17: 477–502.

Steel, Lauri, and Eaton Marian. 1996. Reducing, eliminating, and preventing minority isolation in American schools: The impact of magnet schools assistance programs. Report for Undersecretary, U.S. Department of Education.

Steel, Lauri, Roger E. Levine, Christine H. Rossell, and David J. Armor. 1993. Magnet schools and desegregation, quality, and choice. Final report to U.S. Department of Education. 28 May.

Taeuber, Karl and Alma Taeuber. 1965. *Negroes in Cities*. Aldine.

Taeuber, Karl and David James. 1982. Racial segregation among public and private schools. *Sociology of Education* 55: 133–43.

Thernstrom, Abigail. 1991. School Choice in Massachusetts. Boston: Pioneer Institute.

Van Valey, Thomas L., Wade C. Roof, and Jerome E. Wilcox. 1977. Trends in residential segregation: 1960–1970. *American Journal of Sociology* 82: 827–44.

Welch, Finis and Audrey Light. 1987. New evidence on school desegregation. Washington, D.C.: U.S. Commission on Civil Rights.

Wilson, Franklin D. 1985. The impact of school desegregation programs on white public school enrollment, 1968–1976. *Sociology of Education* 58: 137–53.

Winship, Christopher. 1977. A revaluation of indexes of residential segregation. *Social Forces* 55: 1058–66.

Chapter 5

School Desegregation and Demographic Change

William A.V. Clark

Demography has changed the playing field on which courts make the decisions about desegregation and unitary status.[1] The United States in the late twentieth century is no longer black and white, it is a multicultural hue of races and ethnicities, and school desegregation decisions about blacks and whites will be less and less relevant in this changing demographic context. Not only are there fewer whites in inner cities in general, the biggest changes are in the very large metropolitan areas where immigrant minorities are rapidly becoming the "majority" population. In the inner cities where the majority population is African American or increasingly a mix of minorities, desegregating black and white schools, the focus of policy debates in the 1970s and 1980s, is no longer the core issue. But the courts are recognizing, only slowly, these demographic changes. Moreover, evaluations of levels of segregation sometimes combine blacks and other minorities, or in some cases whites and nonblack minorities, to assess levels of racial imbalance in the school systems, and thus obfuscate the nature of demographic change in central city school systems. Finally, racial balance is increasingly irrelevant in systems that are now majority minority or are made up of new immigrants.

The demographic changes in U.S. metropolitan areas are at the heart of determining liability in school desegregation issues, assigning levels of remedy when liability has been found, and in determining unitary status. In designing a remedy for past school board actions, or inactions, the court must be aware of the white and minority responses to intervention in the school system—especially white flight. In assigning unitary status, the court is forced to ask whether there are still vestiges of the past patterns of school segregation and at the same time ask what further remedies, if any, are available to the school system. The chapter will discuss demographic issues in liability, remedy and unitary status, but because almost all the legal and demographic issues now revolve around remedy and unitary status, the chapter will focus more heavily on those issues.

The research reported in this chapter examines the issues of liability, remedy and unitary status in the context of recent court cases in a variety of cities including Boston, Denver, Charlotte (Mecklenburg County), Kansas City, St. Louis, Tampa (Hillsborough County), and Prince George's County, Maryland. Boston, Denver, Kansas City, and St. Louis are older cities and school districts, surrounded by extensive suburban development and have had substantial white flight. Charlotte-Mecklenburg, Prince George's County and Tampa are countywide school districts. Charlotte-Mecklenburg now has a relatively stable white enrollment, although there was considerable white loss in the 1970s. Prince George's County is a wealthy suburban county adjacent to Washington D.C. that has changed fundamentally in the last twenty-five years, from a white to black majority population. Hillsborough County has an increasing Hispanic population as the county absorbs large numbers of new immigrants from Cuba and Mexico. Each of these cases will be used to illustrate the demographic shifts that are changing the composition of large city school districts. The chapter explores the implications of these demographic changes for court decisions about unitary status.

The argument of the chapter, which is supported with an analysis of the demographic changes at aggregate and local levels, is that court desegregation decisions are increasingly constrained by the nature and level of demographic changes in the large metropolitan areas. The research extends an earlier paper which also focused on issues of demographic constraints in school desegregation decisions (Clark 1995).

DEMOGRAPHY AND URBAN CHANGE

The discussion of the changing population composition of large school districts must be set within the changes that have occurred in all U.S. urban areas in the last four decades of the twentieth century. Beginning after the Second World War, but accelerating in the 1960s, the United States witnessed an unprecedented spatial suburbanization of the metropolitan population. In 1960, less than 50 percent of the U.S. metropolitan population lived in the suburbs of the urban areas but by 1990, three decades later, that proportion had reached 70 percent (Frey 1995). The issue of school desegregation and racial integration came into focus just at the time that the urban areas were undergoing substantial, and far-reaching, changes. The construction of freeways around and into the center of metropolitan areas made much more land, and thus residential development, accessible to the expanding urban populations. At the same time, increasing wealth made suburban home ownership available to larger and larger numbers of households. White out-migration, especially for middle-income white households, was inevitable (Long 1988).

In the decades after World War II, suburban growth was largely white. Even in 1990, the census showed that the suburbs were largely white numerically and proportionately (82%). However, beginning in the 1980s, the suburbs had very large percentage increases of African Americans (34%), Hispanics (69%) and Asians (6%). The changes in the central cities that began in the 1960s, continued as white populations migrated to the suburbs, and first blacks, and then Hispanics and Asians replaced the white losses. While the minority populations are rapidly approaching majority status in the central cities, and are already a majority of many central city school-age populations, they are beginning also to be an important part of the changes in the suburbs. As of 1990, the suburbs were 82.4 percent non-Hispanic white, 6.7 percent non-Hispanic black, 7.5 percent Hispanic, and 3.4 percent non-Hispanic Asians. That process will have important implications for the future of school integration in the suburbs.

DEMOGRAPHIC ISSUES IN LIABILITY

Early court hearings were concerned with whether or not school boards had acted in such a manner as to cause, or continue, patterns of segregated schools. The focus in the court hearings was to determine whether the school board was "liable" and hence if a remedy should be imposed. These "liability hearings" examined the so-called "Green factors," the measures of student and faculty assignment, staff assignment, school facilities, transportation and extra-curricular activities.

In the early 1970s many school districts, including the cities and metropolitan areas analyzed in this chapter, were found to be "segregated," and they were ordered to institute a plan of attendance-area boundary changes, including student busing, to eliminate racial segregation and create racial balance in school enrollment. From the legal standpoint, demography was largely irrelevant in these cases. In cases where there had been de jure segregation and schools were still segregated, courts routinely ordered busing and attendance-area changes.

Demographic issues have been more central in determining liability in districts that were never dual school systems, but had substantial segregation, and because of geographic zoning, substantial school segregation. In these districts, issues of school construction and school closing, and the structure of attendance zones, have been at the heart of determining the extent of school board liability.

In early findings in Pasadena and in San Francisco, the court reasoned that the school board had approved racially motivated boundary changes and school construction, and as a result contributed to the racial imbalance in the school systems (Armor and Clark 1995). The debates about determining liability culminated in the hearings in the Dayton and Columbus cases where the court examined the role of school siting, optional attendance zones and student transfer policies. In the Dayton case, the court focused on "how much" of the segregation was due to the actions of the school board and how the pattern of segregation in the system would have been different if there had been no violations. This 1979 decision opened the way for detailed demographic analysis in the light of violations and attempts to measure the evolution of the patterns of separation in the residential areas (Clark 1986; Galster and Keeney 1988; Massey and Denton 1987). Simulations of the development of the residential patterns were compared with the actual residential pattern as a method of estimating the effects of school board violations (Clark 1980). The research shows that the patterns of separation are generated by a complex interplay of the different incomes of black and white households, different preferences for neighborhood residential composition (Clark 1991; Schelling 1971), and the varying nature of the urban structure. Of course, private discrimination by landlords and real estate agents, though illegal, also played a role in the continuing separation of the races (Armor 1995; Clark 1986; Galster 1988; Yinger 1995).

In the last several years the same issues of school board actions and their impact on attendance zones and school construction have reemerged as an issue within unitary hearings as the Court has considered whether the school board "has done everything possible" to eliminate past segregation in the school systems. I return to this issue when I discuss demographic issues in unitary status hearings.

DEMOGRAPHIC ISSUES IN REMEDY

De jure school desegregation cases initiated in the late 1960s and early 1970s focused almost entirely on dismantling the previous system of segregated schools. For example, in 1969 a federal district court ordered transfers and rezoning for the Denver School District (*Keyes v. School District No. 1* 303 F.Supp. 279 [1969]). Similar orders were imposed on all the districts discussed in this chapter. They occurred in varying years during the early 1970s, and involved boundary changes and student busing to eliminate racial segregation and create racial balance. In some cases, the court orders were preceded by independent action by the school boards themselves. In many cases, the initial intervention was followed by almost yearly court orders and changes in the attendance-area assignments. In Charlotte-Mecklenburg following the rezoning order of 1969, there were Court orders

in 1970,1971, 1974 and 1978 (Welch and Light 1986). These Court decisions intervened in city school districts just at the time of the increasing dis-
enchantment with central cities and the increasing preference for suburban
living. White households that were already concerned about safety and de-
teriorating neighborhoods moved out, and other white households chose
not to move in (Rossell 1987, 1988).

White Losses

The impact of court intervention in school districts accelerated changes
in the composition of the school systems. Of course, not all the white enrollment loss in the school systems undergoing a remedy was generated by
court intervention. However, as Armor (1980) has pointed out, the white
enrollment loss was three to five times more than would have occurred from
demographic change alone. The combination of ongoing demographic
change and intervention served to fundamentally shift the composition of
many large school districts. Large inner-city school districts changed from
majority white districts to majority African American, while others changed
from majority white to a rainbow mix of different races and ethnicities.

In all of the examples in figure 5.1, there was substantial white loss in the
years following the court-ordered student reassignments. Black enrollment
was stable or increasing. In Charlotte-Mecklenburg, the losses were less pre-
cipitous and stabilized in the 1980s. The largest white enrollment decline
was in Prince George's County: almost 42,000 students in a six-year period.
Unfortunately, the demographic transformation of school districts was occurring just as the courts were attempting to balance schools by transfer
policies and changes in school-attendance zones. In the period of the most
intensive court activity, between 1970 and 1976, three of the four districts
had school enrollment declines of between 30 and 50 percent and the other
had a decline of 17 percent.

The changes in total school enrollment were accompanied by significant
shifts in the school enrollment composition. In every case, the school systems have become more minority. Boston, Denver and Prince George's
County were majority white systems in 1970 (Boston and Denver a little
above 60% and Prince George's almost 80%) and these three districts are
now majority minority districts. In two of them (Boston and Prince
George's), the white student composition is under 20 percent. Charlotte-
Mecklenburg was still a majority white district in 1990 but even in a large
county-wide district with a vibrant economy, there is a declining proportion
of whites (slightly more than 50%) in the school system.

Although these remedies certainly affected the demography of many
school districts, it varied by context and timing. The Supreme Court recognized that there was a legitimate fear that white students would leave the

Figure 5.1
Enrollment Trends in Two Inner-City and Two County School Districts

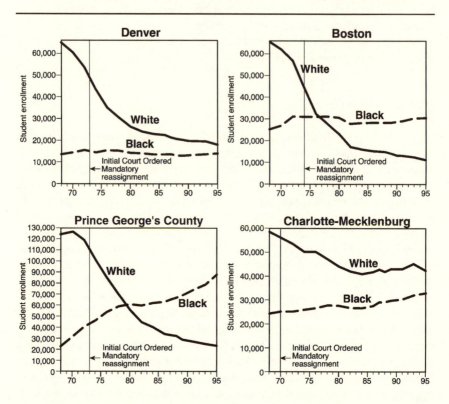

public school system during the difficult period of desegregation, but such fears could not justify any delay in the process of dismantling dual school systems (*United States v. Scotland Neck City School Board*, 407 U.S. 484 1972). At the same time, it is not clear that the courts had any real concept of either the extent to which the ongoing demographic changes were impacting inner city school systems, or the extent to which white households would opt to leave systems with large-scale, court-ordered busing. Nor did the courts seem to recognize that districts with large-scale, mandatory busing were unattractive to new residents. Indeed, the next section illustrates how the changes in enrollment are linked to changes in migration patterns.

Migration and Changing School District Composition

White enrollment losses occur in several ways, including shifts to private school systems within a school district, out-migration to surrounding suburban counties, and lower rates of in-migration. St. Louis and Prince George's County provide excellent case studies of the effects of inter- and intracounty population shifts in association with school desegregation. The relocation behavior of family households who move out, and others who fail to move in create the population composition changes we have already observed. Older cities like St. Louis have been losing population since the first decade after World War II. This suburbanization process accelerated in the late 1950s and 1960s, and in the St. Louis case, the city lost almost sixty thousand whites to the neighboring St. Louis County between 1965 and 1970.

Even greater changes occurred in the 1970s and 1980s. Between 1975 and 1980, the city lost more than 53,000 whites and gained fewer than 10,000 whites (figure 5.2). It is this differential that, of course, eventually changes the composition of the central city population. By the late 1980s, the losses were even greater. The city lost almost 50,000 whites to suburban St. Louis County and another 61,549 to other cities and states. In a five-year period, the city lost more than 100,000 whites, while gaining only 35,000 whites. In addition, the in-flows of households with children were almost nonexistent. Fewer than twelve hundred white households with children moved into St. Louis in the last half decade of the 1980s. Some black households were moving into St. Louis City, but in general it is the differential out-migration of whites that has determined the school enrollment composition of St. Louis.

The migration patterns in Prince George's County tell a similar story of significant population composition changes. In Prince George's County, the changes are closely tied to those in the inner city—Washington D.C. The minority population in the core communities of Washington D.C. has increased and as it has done so, those families with higher incomes, African American and white alike, have opted to move to the surrounding suburbs, including Prince George's County. Between 1975 and 1980, the African American population flow from Washington D.C. was about eighteen times that of the white population—26,040 compared to only 1,420 whites—although the flow from other states was disproportionately white—14,320 African American compared to 32,040 white households. Overall, the population flow into Prince George's County was about 48 percent African American and 44 percent white. At the same time, the population leaving Prince George's County was 86 percent white—84,760 whites and 13,600 African Americans. That differential—a majority African American inflow and a majority white outflow—explains the changes in the population composition of the County.

The inflows of the next decade in Prince George's County were again heavily African American—almost 55 percent. Between 1985 and 1990, the African American inflows were larger than in the earlier five-year period, both from Washington D.C.—39,168—and from other states—42,346. But there were also large white inflows—64,442—from other parts

Figure 5.2
St. Louis City and County Migration Flow

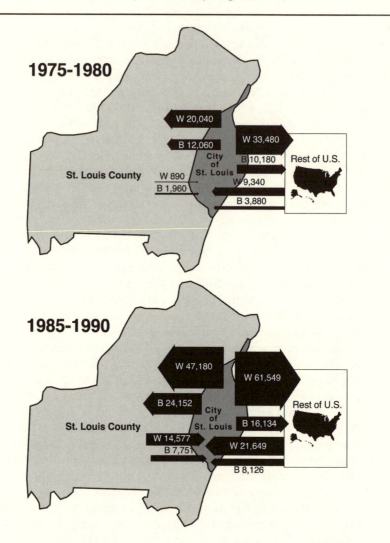

of the metropolitan region, and from Virginia, Maryland and other states, compared to only 2,735 from Washington D.C. However, the white growth was modest since the county was losing many more white persons than it was gaining. Even though the county had a continuing white inflow—about 67,000 white persons—it lost almost 111,000 white persons. Thus, the white population continued to decline despite the substantial inflows.

School-Age Population Change

Earlier sections of the chapter have emphasized the changes in the student enrollment in the inner-city school districts of U.S. metropolitan areas. These losses, as they bear on the possibility of further desegregation, are at the heart of questions about the demography of remedy and unitary status.

White flight and differential migration flows have generated some of the most wrenching changes in inner-city populations in this century. These changes have altered the composition of the school-age population and will continue to impact the changes in the coming decades. For example, the white school-age population was declining rapidly just as the courts began to intervene in the Kansas City school system. Between 1970 and 1980, Kansas City lost half of its white school age population (figure 5.3). Similarly, in St. Louis (figure 5.3), while there were nearly 150,000 children aged five to seventeen in 1970 in the city, there were only 64,000 in 1990. The city has changed from one that was almost equally black and white in school-age population to a two-thirds black majority and has declined in total enrollment at the same time.

The most dramatic changes in resident school-age population occurred in Prince George's County with the white losses we have already noted. The impact of demographic growth, especially from migration, changed the county fundamentally. The county went through an almost complete reversal from an 82 percent white school-age population in 1970 to 82 percent African American school-age population in 1996. This occurred as the school-age population declined from 245,532 in 1970 to just under 200,000 in 1996. The school-age population reached a low of 177,945 in 1990 but has increased by more than 20,000 since then. The impacts are obvious. There are no longer sufficient white school-age children to allow the school district to engage in any form of meaningful racial balance and racial balance is no longer a goal of the school system. By 1997, the school board had entered into a court-approved memo of understanding to return to a combination of neighborhood schools and magnet centers.

Even in metropolitan areas like Tampa (Hillsborough County), where the total and school-age population has continued to grow, there were substantial changes in the composition of the school-age population. In the almost thirty years from 1970 to 1997, the metropolitan population of Hillsborough County has more than doubled, from under one-half million to almost a million persons. The total white and black populations both increased at about the same rate, although the total white growth was greater. At the same time, the black school-age population increased by about 42 percent while the white school-age population had a small absolute decrease. The growth of the Hispanic population in the last seventeen years has been nearly 130 percent. It is the growth of this new ethnic population that will change the nature of school enrollment in Tampa and in other metropolitan

Figure 5.3
Changing Resident School Age (5–17) Population, 1970–1995

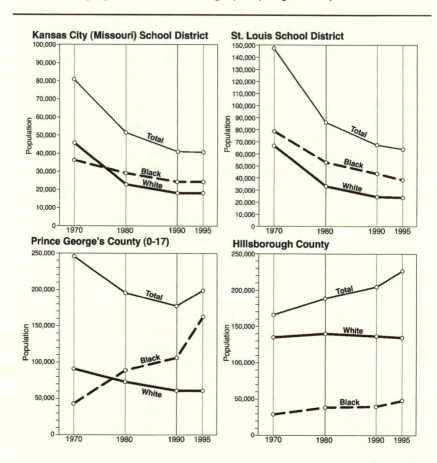

areas that are the gateway cities for the new immigrants. These changes will further weaken decisions which are based solely on balancing the number of black and white students in the schools.

DEMOGRAPHIC ISSUES IN UNITARY STATUS HEARINGS

Much of the recent litigation in school desegregation cases is not about liability or remedy, but about whether the conditions for a return to unitary status have been met. Has the school district redressed the past de jure school segregation and complied with its remedial orders? Is the school district operating in a unitary fashion (as if there had never been a segregated school system)? Are any schools that were majority black before desegregation still majority black after desegregation (the so-called vestiges of a former dual system)? Are the changes in the schools that were desegregated the result of demographic changes or school board actions? Has the school system done all it can? Are additional changes to create greater desegregation, possible? The answers to these questions are embedded in the changing demography of large school districts. The following discussion of population change, both in the aggregate and in specific city neighborhoods, illustrates the constraints within which school districts are functioning, and uses case studies to examine specific school enrollment changes.

Vestiges, and Changing Neighborhood and School Composition

The central question in any unitary hearing is whether the school district desegregated the school system "to the extent practicable." In many hearings on unitary status, the arguments and court decisions therefore focus on the existence of predominantly one-race schools. The courts have noted, beginning with *Swann* in 1971, that although neither neighborhood schools nor the existence of a few one-race schools offends the constitution, the burden is on the school board to show that one-race schools are not the result of past or present discriminatory action. The proof may come from an analysis of local demographic change that includes the results of school board actions such as attendance-zone changes. This proof must demonstrate that the one-race school is the result of demographic change, independent of any school board actions.

Two questions are often raised with respect to existing one-race schools, especially to determine whether they are vestiges from prior de jure school systems. First, was there an attempt to remedy the formerly one-race schools by altering attendance zones or pairing and clustering the school with other schools, and was it effective? Second, was the occurrence of a majority-black school an outcome of demographic changes that occurred after the initial desegregation plan, or was it the role of subsequent board decisions?

Thus, a central issue in a hearing about unitary status and school district decision-making with respect to school enrollment composition is the nature of attendance-area changes and their effect on school racial and ethnic composition. To put it simply, are changes in the composition of the student population in the individual schools in the district a result of boundary adjustments by the school district or to other factors, including the changes brought about by changing demography?

Vestiges can be examined in a number of ways and for a number of different scenarios. Table 5.1 helps us to visualize the possible situations.

In the simplest situation, an originally one-race school is not changed. If it was impractical to change the school composition because there were insufficient white students to balance all the black one-race schools, or the

Table 5.1
Alternative Scenarios for the Vestige Status
of Predominantly One-Race Schools

	Vestige	Not Vestige
1. Originally one-race Still one-race, impractical to change		*
2. Originally one-race Still one-race, practical alternatives (e.g. zoning and pairing)	*	
3. Originally one-race, balanced by plan Becomes one-race - Due to demographic change - Due to board actions	*	*
4. Originally integrated Becomes one-race - Due to demographic change - Due to board actions	*	*

school was very far from the nearest residential area that could be used to integrate the school, then it is not a vestige. Alternatively if practical alternatives were available, the existence of a one-race school could be a vestige of the former dual school system. Two other general possibilities are one-race schools that were racially balanced by the plan, but which later returned to one-race status, and originally integrated schools which become one-race schools. Many of the instances of vestiges involve a situation in which a school's composition is largely black and is brought into compliance with a court-ordered guideline, but the school later falls out of compliance. It is in these instances that the general demographic changes discussed in the previous section influence the ability to keep adjusting the racial balance in the school. Examples of these situations occur in most school districts that are considering unitary status and are illustrated in the following discussion of neighborhood and attendance area population change.

Neighborhood Change

Metropolitan-wide demographic change creates changes in smaller communities and neighborhoods and these changes do not occur evenly throughout the neighborhoods and communities. Moreover, these changes are often at the heart of the changes in individual school enrollments.

In most American metropolitan areas, once an African American population has moved into a neighborhood, there is a tendency for the neighborhood to continue the process of transition from white to African American in population composition. There are exceptions to the pattern of white transition to black, especially where a large number of Hispanics are moving into central city neighborhoods (Lee and Wood 1991), but transition from white to ethnic neighborhoods is still the norm. Increasingly, the patterns of change in inner-city areas have now "spilled over" into surrounding suburban communities. Both St. Louis and Prince George's County show the classic pattern of the "spillover" of the black population expansion from the inner city to the suburbs.

In St. Louis, as in many American inner-city communities, a small and relatively local black population in 1950 increased and migrated throughout the city and then into the county suburbs closest to the city itself (figure 5.4). In 1950, the black population was largely concentrated in a few census tracts to the west and northwest of the downtown area. However, by 1970, there was a concentration of almost totally black tracts in a sector radiating out from the downtown area to the boundary of the city and into the northern suburbs of St. Louis County. During the 1980s, the black population also moved south and became a significant proportion of the population in the tracts in south St. Louis. The changing neighborhood resident population would in turn affect individual attendance areas, which changed their enrollment composition as a result of changes in the resident population.

In Prince George's County in 1970, there were only a dozen neighborhoods that were majority African American (figure 5.5). Almost all of them were adjacent to the Washington D.C. boundary. Some of the more distant suburbs also had small percentages of African American households that were also numerically small. Between 1970 and 1990, the neighborhood composition changes were large scale and widespread. Even by 1980, much of the county was at least one-quarter African American and very large areas inside the Beltway were majority African American.

By 1990, the only communities still majority white were in the College Park area and in the very far western portion of Prince George's County (figure 5.5). Many of the neighborhoods in the county were more than 75 percent African American and at least half of the County neighborhoods were majority African American. Thus, in the classic fashion of African American in-migration and white out-migration, the African American population has expanded throughout Prince George's County and changed the neighborhoods. The process of increasing African American proportions has not stopped with the 1990 census and the next census will undoubtedly show a continuing spread of the majority African American neighborhoods in Prince George's County.

Figure 5.4
**Changing Spatial Patterns of the 5–17 Black Population in St. Louis City
and Surrounding St. Louis County**

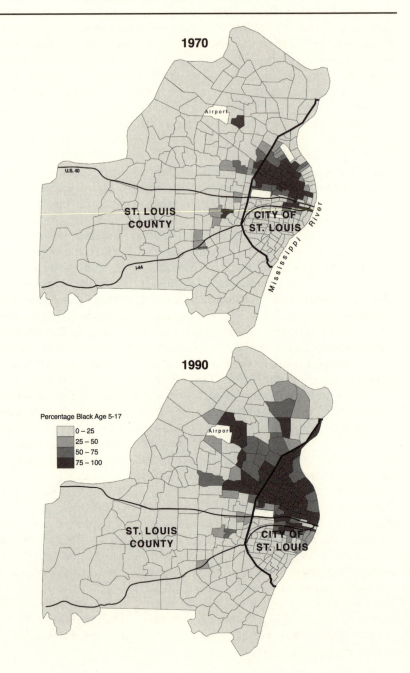

In Charlotte-Mecklenburg, where the aggregate changes have not been so dramatic, there are still substantial changes in the distribution of the black population and of the neighborhoods in the city and county (figure 5.6). In 1970, most of the black population was concentrated in the inner-city tracts near the downtown. By 1990, the black population had spread southwest and southeast and there were extensive areas of the county with majority black populations.

The figure also illustrates another facet of neighborhood change. In 1970, there were rural black populations in outlying sections of the county, especially to the north. In some cases, the percentages were over one-quarter. As whites suburbanized into these formerly rural areas, the black communities became whiter in composition, not because of black population losses but because of white population growth.

The process of spatial changes in inner-city neighborhoods leads to localized losses and gains. Both Prince George's County and Charlotte-Mecklenburg demonstrate different facets of how the changes are concentrated in particular neighborhoods. In Prince George's, the changes were concentrated within the Beltway, the area in Prince George's County which is inside Interstate 495 and closest to the predominantly black District of Columbia. The losses and gains were almost completely reversed between the white and African American populations (figure 5.7).

There were large white losses in all communities within the Beltway, especially in New Carrollton, Capitol Heights, Hyattsville and Lewisdale. In these same areas inside the Beltway, there were very large increases in the African American residential population, especially in Takoma Park in the north, and in Coral Hills and Hillcrest Heights in the southeastern parts of the county. Almost every community in Prince George's County had an increase in the African American population. Some of the increases were small, especially in the most distant suburbs from the Washington D.C. region. Prince George's County is thus a good illustration of what happens in suburban counties that are adjacent to large metropolitan inner-city areas with large minority populations. In these cases, the flow of minorities from the inner city to the suburbs fundamentally changes the suburban communities.

In Charlotte-Mecklenburg, the general changes are those of inner-city loss and suburban gain of the white population (figure 5.8). At the same time, there has been a transformation of several neighborhoods that have had black gains and white losses. For the most part however, Charlotte-Mecklenburg demonstrates the transformations that come from suburban gains that are several times greater than those of the black populations. These changes have transformed formerly rural areas into suburban residential development.

St. Louis is an example of the impact on the school-age population and on school desegregation that occurs when both the white and the black

Figure 5.5
Spatial Pattern of the Black Population Ages 0–17 in Prince George's County

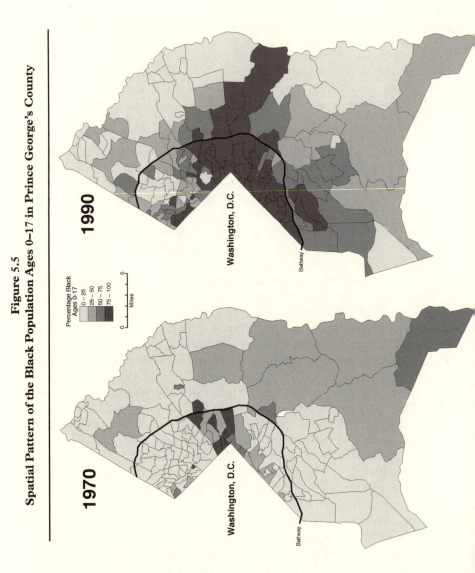

Figure 5.6
Spatial Patterns of the Black Population Ages 0–17 in Mecklenburg County

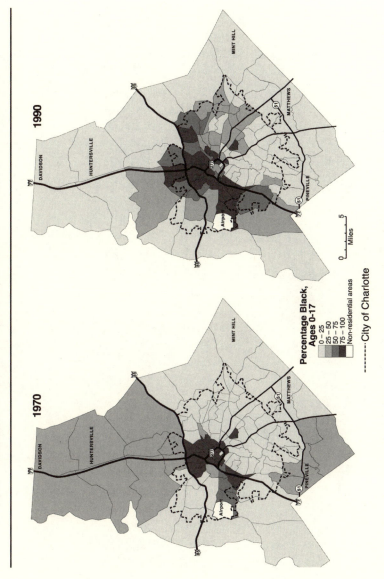

Figure 5.7
Population Gains and Loses in Prince George's County, 1970–1990

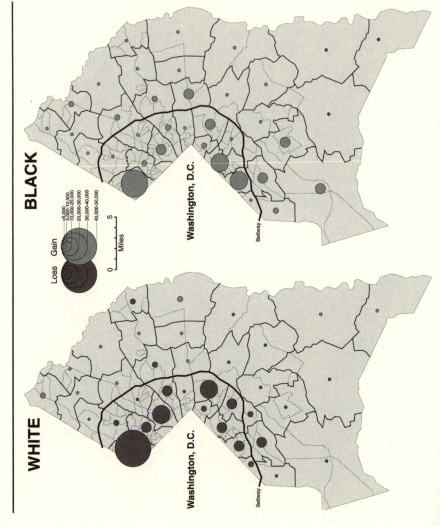

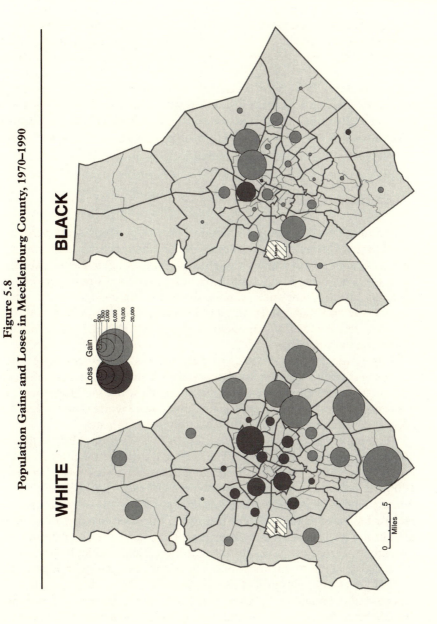

Figure 5.8
Population Gains and Loses in Mecklenburg County, 1970–1990

population are declining (figure 5.9). In these cases, the school district is faced with the need to maintain racial balance while also addressing declining enrollment and the need to close schools. The figure illustrates losses in black and white school-age population over a two-decade period, an important additional dimension to the changing composition portrayed in figure 5.4. During the 1970s, almost all the communities in the northern half of the city experienced very high total population losses of both blacks and whites. Between 1980 and 1990, the school district continued to have large neighborhood losses of blacks and whites also in the southern part of the school district. It is these losses and gains that transformed the composition of the attendance areas of the schools and which created practical difficulties for the St. Louis school district in maintaining integrated schools as ordered by the federal district court.

Analyzing Attendance-Area Changes

The demographic changes examined in the previous section are the forces that enable and limit the ability of the school district to racially balance its schools and to eliminate one-race schools. Attendance-area changes are at the heart of assessing the effectiveness of school district policies in integrating formerly one-race schools. By examining changes in the attendance areas and their effect on paired/clustered schools, it is possible to assess the relative roles of demographic change and school board actions in addressing the vestige issue.

Four examples from St. Louis directly address the vestiges issue raised in table 5.1. Two of the schools, Henry and Hogden, were formerly all-black schools that were integrated with predominantly white satellite zones. The other two schools, Froebel and Shenandoah, were white schools that had black satellite attendance areas attached to integrate them.

The Henry elementary school was near or at 100 percent black in the late 1960s and through the 1970s. The 1980–81 court order integrated the Henry elementary school. The enrollment changed immediately from nearly 100 percent black to a little under 60 percent black and because of additional changes in the noncontiguous zoning, it was possible to create a racially balanced school that approximately mirrored the city. But, beginning in the late 1980s, the increasing proportion of the black population throughout the city of St. Louis made it increasingly difficult to maintain the racial balance in such schools. The Henry and Hogden elementary schools are classic examples of the tension of racially balancing individual schools and maintaining that balance in the face of a changing urban demographic structure. Both elementary schools are representative of a class of formerly black schools which at various times have been integrated, but where it has not been possible to maintain racial balance because of the

Figure 5.9
St. Louis School-Age White and Black Population Gains and Losses,
1970–1990

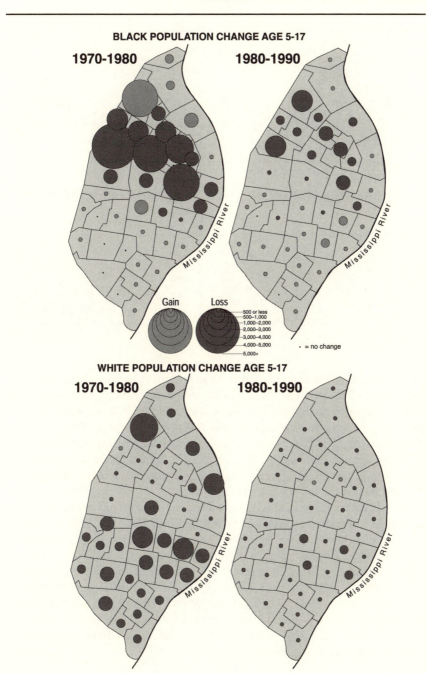

BLACK POPULATION CHANGE AGE 5-17

1970-1980   1980-1990

Gain   Loss
                  500 or less
                  500–1,000
                  1,000–2,000
                  2,000–3,000
                  3,000–4,000
                  4,000–5,000
                  5,000+

· = no change

WHITE POPULATION CHANGE AGE 5-17

1970-1980   1980-1990

Figure 5.10
Percent Black Enrollment in School-Age Resident Population
of Attendance Zones of Example Schools.

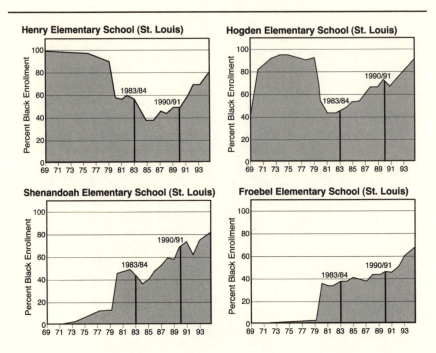

larger demographic changes. Even when the court-approved variations are as large as 15–65 percent black and exclude two-thirds of the schools from the mandatory reassignment desegregation plan, as in St. Louis, it is often impossible to racially balance all the schools when the district is rapidly changing from a 50/50 district to one approaching 80 percent minority.

When schools are largely white, or all white, they create a different scenario from the Henry and Hogden elementary schools. Froebel and Shenandoah (figure 5.10) are elementary schools that were integrated by attaching black satellite areas. The school district used paired attendance areas to racially balance the schools at near 40 percent black in 1980 as required by the court order. These schools illustrate the difficulty of maintaining racial balance. Demographic change in the formerly white schools, namely white loss, has increased the percent minority in both schools. An examination of the residential attendance zones reveals that the home attendance zone of both schools has changed substantially (figure 5.11). The percentage black has increased in a large part of the attendance area. Other ancillary zones that were used to balance the school initially have also increased their resident black population.

Figure 5.11
Residential Change in Two Attendance Areas

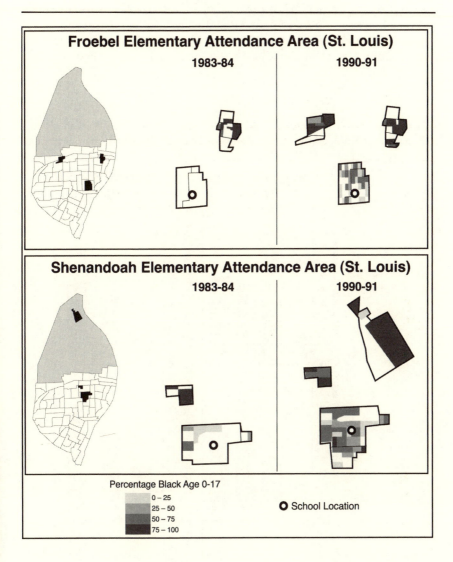

Three communities in Charlotte-Mecklenburg add further details to the discussion. Westerly Hills and Devonshire were both predominantly white suburban residential areas in 1970 in the western and eastern parts of Mecklenburg at some distance from the inner city. The more inner-city Highland attendance area, located between the two areas, was already experiencing residential change in 1970 and the attendance area was about one-quarter black. Both Devonshire and Westerly Hills were integrated with satellite pairing, and magnet programs in the case of Devonshire. Thus, by the mid-1970s, all three schools were integrated. Figure 5.12 shows that the school enrollment was between 30 and 40 percent black in 1974–75. The residential areas continued to change and by 1980, as the graph of the school-age resi-

Figure 5.12
Composition of the Change in School Enrollment and Neighborhoods in Elementary School Attendance Zones in Central Charlotte-Mecklenburg

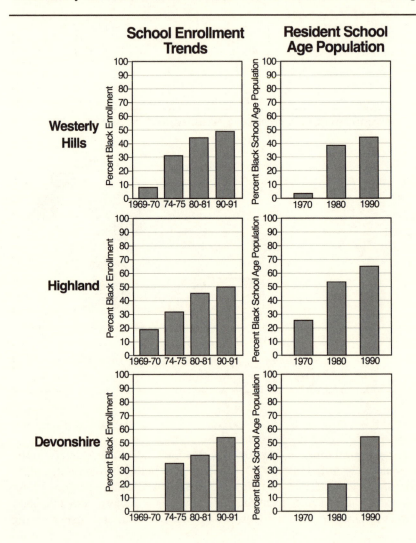

dent population shows, the resident population was similar to the school-age population, except in the case of Devonshire. The Devonshire attendance area continued to be more white than the school enrollment and in the Highland attendance area, the residential black population was higher than that of the black school enrollment. In both cases the school district used a variety of strategies to keep the school composition balanced.

The case studies of attendance areas show that in the first instance it is possible to maintain a large number of schools with black enrollments of less than 50 percent, the school composition that seems in general to be important to both black and white parental populations. However, as the black population increased and moved to neighborhoods outside of the inner city, and as the white population declined in the inner-city neighborhoods, it became increasingly difficult to maintain black enrollments below the 50-percent goal. In specific instances, as in St. Louis in 1980, it was possible to use the white student population in the southern section of the city to integrate some schools by attendance-linking between areas in the northern parts of the city and the southern parts of the city. However, the increasing proportion of blacks in the neighborhoods in the south after 1980 and the continuing overall white student losses from the city school system made it impracticable, or at the least very difficult, to make further attendance-zone adjustments to maintain a court-ordered racial balance.

CONCLUSIONS AND OBSERVATIONS

As we start the new century there are major changes sweeping through our metropolitan areas. They are no longer black and white; they are increasingly a multicultural hue of different races and ethnicities. The multicultural mix is reflected in the decision to allow multiple race/ethnicity answers to the race question on the 2000 U.S. census.

It is true that this demographic change has yet to overtake many smaller metropolitan areas, but the changes are on the way. These changes will increasingly redirect attention away from issues of racial balance in inner-city schools and to the broader and more complex issues of educational quality and funding for education. In this context it is possible that unitary status, making sure that there are no identifiable vestiges of former black schools, will be less relevant. The central issues are likely to increasingly turn on issues of educational adequacy and the delivery of high-quality education to all racial and ethnic groups. In school districts like Prince George's County, which is 85 percent black, there is little to be gained in continuing to debate the issue of racial balance. In school districts like Dallas where the school district is now, or will be soon, majority Hispanic, the issue of racial balance, narrowly conceived in black and white terms, is clearly irrelevant.

The demographic changes are still a contested territory, and while district court judges who are in the community recognize the strength and inevitability of the changes occurring, many appellate courts are only recently accepting the centrality of these changes and the difficulty of continuing court supervision in multiracial contexts. None of this obviates the need to vigilantly continue monitoring decisions by local school boards to provide an integrated education to all students. At the same time, to ignore the reality of the ethnic change sweeping U.S. cities is to ignore the demographic reality of the 21st century.

ENDNOTE

1. Unitary status is granted when a school district is deemed to have removed all evidence of a former dual school system.

REFERENCES

Armor, David. 1980. White flight and the future of school desegregation. In *School Desegregation*, edited by W.G. Stephen and J.R. Feagin. Plenum.

———. 1995. *Forced Justice: School Desegregation and the Law.* Oxford University Press.

Armor, David, and W.A.V. Clark. 1995. Housing segregation and school desegregation. In David Armor, *Forced Justice: School Desegregation and the Law,* 117–53. Oxford UP.

Clark, William A.V. 1980. Residential mobility and neighborhood change: Some implications for racial residential segregation. *Urban Geography* 1: 101–24.

———. 1986. Residential segregation in American cities: A review and interpretation. *Population Research and Policy Review* 5: 95–127.

——— 1991. Residential preferences and neighborhood racial segregation: A test of the Schelling model. *Demography* 28: 1–19.

——— 1995. The expert witness in unitary hearings: The six *Green* factors and spatial demographic change. *Urban Geography* 16: 664–79.

Frey, William H. 1995. The new geography of population shifts: Trends towards balkanization. In *State of the Union*, edited by R. Farley, vol. 2. Russell Sage Foundation.

Galster, G. 1988. Residential segregation in American cities: A contrary review. *Population Research and Policy Review* 7:113–21.

Galster, G., and W. Keeney. 1988. Race, residence, discrimination and economic opportunities. *Urban Affairs Quarterly* 24: 87–117.

Lee, B., and P. Wood. 1991. Is neighborhood social succession, place specific? *Demography* 28: 21–40.

Long, L. 1987. Trends in the residential segregation of blacks, Hispanics and Asians 1970–1980. *American Sociological Review* 52: 802–25.

———. 1988. *Migration and Residential Mobility in the United States.* Russell Sage Foundation.

Massey, Douglas S. and Nancy A. Denton. 1987. Trends in the residential segregation of blacks, Hispanics, and Asians. *American Sociological Review* 52:
802–25.

Rossell, Christine H. 1987. The Buffalo controlled choice plan. *Urban Education* 22:
328–54.

———. 1988. Is it the busing or the blacks? *Urban Affairs Quarterly* 24: 138–48.

Schelling, T. 1971. Dynamics models of segregation. *Journal of Mathematical Sociology* 1: 143–86.

Welch, Finis, and Audrey Light. 1986. *New Evidence on School Desegregation.* Los
Angeles: Unicon.

Yinger, J. 1995. *Closed Doors, Opportunities Lost: The Continuing Costs of Housing Discrimination.* Russell Sage Foundation.

Chapter 6

Desegregation and Academic Achievement

∞

David J. Armor

The debate over school desegregation and academic achievement started with the historic *Brown* decision and its famous "footnote 11" about segregation and psychological harm. While social scientists at that time were in general agreement that state-enforced school segregation inflicted psychological harm on African American children, constitutional scholars disagreed over the legal significance of the harm thesis. Most argued that state-enforced segregation was unconstitutional on its face; it was "inherently unequal," whether or not it could be traced to some adverse effect on the social or psychological well-being of black children (Goodman 1972; Yudof 1978). Others argued that it was necessary to find major adverse effects of segregation in order to overturn the earlier "separate but equal" doctrine of *Plessy* (Wilkenson 1978).

Whatever the Supreme Court intended by footnote 11, the issue of academic achievement took a back seat during the first twenty years or so of school desegregation. Instead, early remedial efforts focused on the desegregation of students, faculty, and programs, which were difficult enough challenges. Moreover, many educators and civil rights advocates believed that if schools, staff, and programs were thoroughly integrated, and resources allocated equitably, the problem of black achievement would be alleviated if not resolved. Full desegregation would eliminate the psychological and educational harms of segregation, and African American children would ultimately be able to compete with whites on an even footing. Elsewhere, this belief has been called the "harm and benefit thesis" of segregation and desegregation (Armor 1995).

Unfortunately, the harm and benefit thesis has not proven viable, at least in its original form. Today many urban school systems are still struggling with low academic achievement of black and other minority groups, and large achievement gaps persist today despite decades of school desegregation and other efforts to promote equity in schools. The reasons for this continuing problem of minority achievement are much debated. Was the original harm and benefit thesis of *Brown* simply wrong, or were there mitigating conditions that made the thesis inoperable?

Those who support desegregation policies often claim that despite desegregated student bodies and faculties, true integration has rarely been achieved in all aspects of school operations. That is, most desegregated school systems have within-school segregation in classrooms or programs (e.g., ability grouping, advanced placement) or else quality teachers and other resources are not distributed equitably.[1] This viewpoint generates a "revised" harm and benefit thesis that adds conditions to the relationship between desegregation and achievement not contemplated in the early remedial history of school desegregation. These new conditions can include assigning faculty according to experience or education, in addition to race; providing even greater resources to minority children than what they would receive under a simple "equity" rule (e.g., smaller classes); and a requirement for within-school desegregation which can mean elimination of ability grouping, race-norming criteria for gifted and talented programs, and elimination of prerequisites for honors or advanced placement courses.

Others have argued that the harm and benefit thesis was erroneous in the first place because it failed to identify the main causes of the achievement gap. These critics believe that the achievement gap cannot be remedied by school policies or programs alone, because it is caused mainly by the socioeconomic differences between minority and white families (Armor 1995; Walberg 1984). Low socioeconomic status (SES) causes achievement deficits at the very outset of schooling, and it is extremely difficult, if not impossible, to overcome these deficits as children move through school, at least without enormous resources beyond the reach of most school systems.

Still others agree that African American socioeconomic status (SES) does contribute to lower achievement, but they assert that low SES is itself a result or "vestige" of the former segregated school system.[2] This "intergenerational" version of the harm and benefit thesis contends that parents of contemporary black school children attended segregated schools during the 1950s or 1960s, and this school segregation caused black parents to have lower SES levels. Thus even if family SES differences explain most of the current achievement gap, school segregation is still the cause, but through the segregation of the parents rather than the children. The causal process simply takes place over two (or possibly more) generations.

This chapter discusses the relationship between desegregation and academic achievement, focusing on these different explanations for the continuing achievement gap. First, what is the state of empirical evidence on the relationship between school desegregation and achievement? Can one fairly conclude that desegregation has or has not improved minority achievement and closed the achievement gap to a significant degree? Second, where desegregation has failed to produce achievement gains for minority students, to what extent can it be explained by failure to attain true integration or parity in all areas, including within-school desegregation and resource equity? Finally, assuming that SES characteristics of minority families explain much of the achievement gap, what is the evidence on the intergenerational thesis, that SES effects are simply an effect of segregation two generations removed?

To answer these questions, the chapter begins with a review of several important historical studies which bear on the relationship between desegregation and achievement. While these early studies are important, many are of limited value for a rigorous evaluation of the several harm and benefit theses, because most of them occurred prior to the onset of comprehensive school desegregation as implemented during the 1970s. The chapter also relies on recent national studies using the National Assessment of Educational Progress, not so much for rigorous hypothesis testing, but rather for examining the overall status of the achievement gap and the simple relationship between school racial composition and achievement.

In this chapter, the most important evidence on the relationship between desegregation and achievement, particularly newer versions of the harm and benefit thesis, are provided by case study data. Unlike the historical studies and more recent national studies, case studies provide long-term data on achievement trends and much more detail on the nature and scope of desegregation plans that might affect the overall relationship between desegregation and achievement.

EARLY STUDIES

Without question, the most important early study of the relationship between desegregation and achievement was contained in the famous Coleman report, *Equality of Educational Opportunity* (Coleman 1966). Ironically, while the Coleman report was the basis of early expert testimony that desegregation could improve black achievement, including testimony by Dr. Coleman himself in the Denver case, neither the original report nor subsequent replication studies found that school segregation was a significant predictor of achievement (Armor 1972b; Smith 1972).

The original Coleman report did find a significant correlation between black achievement and a school's racial composition. When individual and school SES were controlled, however, racial composition did not contribute significantly to explaining variation in black verbal achievement scores. This led the Coleman report to conclude that it was the socioeconomic composition of the school rather than its racial composition that improved black achievement. Given the strong correlation between race and SES, however, Coleman inferred that if blacks were in higher SES schools, they would be schools with a majority of middle class white students, and therefore they would be desegregated.

Commenting on Coleman's inference in a 1972 study, Jencks and others correctly pointed out that most studies based on the Coleman data did not take into account the initial ability of black students in desegregated schools (Jencks et al. 1972). This was especially important in 1965, when most desegregated schools attained that status naturally by housing choices rather than being induced by court-ordered plans and student reassignment. As such, naturally desegregated schools might simply reflect self-selection by middle-class black families with high-achieving children who seek out more affluent, desegregated neighborhoods. If so, the association between racial composition and achievement would be spurious, driven by the housing choices of black families who already have high-achieving children.

Jencks and others acknowledged this potential self-selection effect and tried to control for it by looking at the effects of racial composition on first grade scores and comparing them to effects for sixth grade scores. Using these results, along with reviews of other studies, they concluded that "our best guess is that desegregation raises black scores by 2–3 points. Eliminating all predominately black schools might therefore reduce the overall black–white gap from 15 to 12 or 13 points (Jencks et al. 1972: 106)."

It might be useful to recap the Coleman data on this important point. Figure 6.1 shows the relationship between verbal achievement and school racial composition for sixth graders in the Coleman data.[3] In 1965, black verbal scores in majority-black schools (which enrolled most black students) averaged 24 points, while white verbal scores in majority-white schools (which enrolled most whites) averaged 36 points. This was a black–white gap of 12 points, which represented about one standard deviation or about one grade level on the verbal test. Blacks in majority-white schools averaged about three points higher than those in majority-black schools, or about 27 points. Even without any controls for student or school socioeconomic status, then, and assuming this difference represents the effect of desegregation rather than self-selection or SES effects, desegregation in 1965 would reduce the gap by only three points or about one-quarter of a school year. A sizeable black–white gap of nine points, or three-quarters of a school year, would remain.

As shown in figure 6.2, however, black students in majority-white schools had higher SES than blacks in predominately black schools, where SES was measured by an household items index. If the black test scores are regressed on school percent black, controlling for black SES in these schools, the black SES effect is strong and statistically significant but the effect of school

Figure 6.1
Verbal Achievement by School Percent Black, 1965 (Coleman Data)

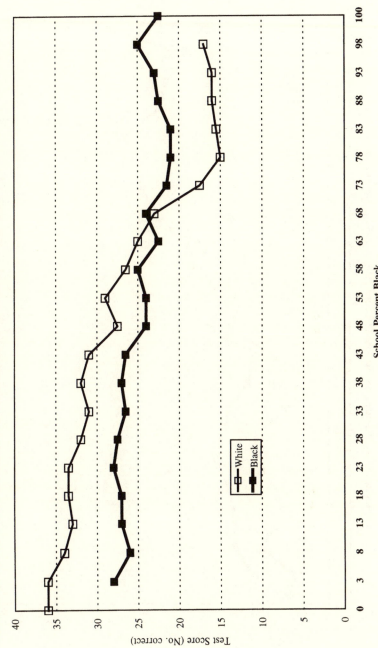

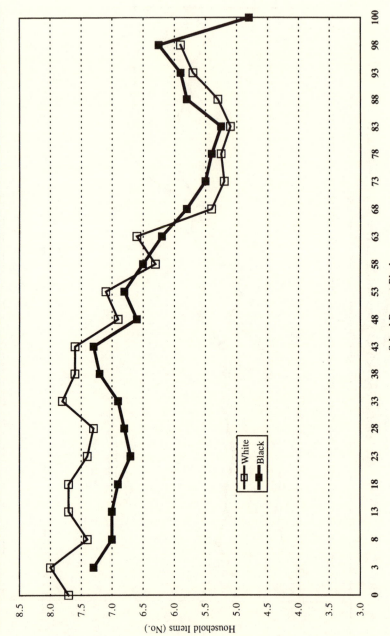

Figure 6.2
Household Items Index by School Percent Black, 1965 (Coleman Data)

percent black is weak and not statistically significant.[4] The effect of black SES is about two points higher on verbal achievement for each point higher on the household items index, while the effect of school racial composition is only .2 points higher achievement for every ten points higher in the percent of white enrollment. In other words, even if the race composition effect was significant, a group of black students moving from a ninety percent black school to a twenty percent black school, controlling for their average SES levels, would realize a gain of only 1.4 points on the verbal test.

The fundamental problem with the Coleman data, as acknowledged by nearly everyone who has analyzed it, is that the data comes from a one-time, non-experimental survey. Therefore, the Coleman data does not show achievement changes over time, nor can one control for self-selection effects. For this reason, post-Coleman research relied more on experimental or quasi-experimental studies, which were becoming increasingly feasible as increasing numbers of school systems began implementing desegregation plans. Not only did some of these studies have more rigorous research designs, capable of stronger causal inferences, but the policy relevance was also greater because black students were actually moving from segregated to desegregated schools.

Three of the earliest reviews of these studies were conducted by Armor (1972a), St. John (1975), and Crain and Mahard (1978). In 1972, Armor reviewed a Boston voluntary city-to-suburbs busing program (METCO) along with six other evaluations of induced desegregation plans from different parts of the country, all of which had control groups as well as pre- and post-desegregation measures of achievement. He concluded that none of these desegregation plans had produced significant gains in achievement. In 1975, St. John reviewed thirty-six studies with control groups and pre–post measures, and she concluded that "the achievement of black children is rarely harmed thereby, but they provide no strong or clear evidence that such desegregation boosts their achievement . . . a report of no significance is more common than a report of a significant gain" (St. John 1975: 31). In 1978, Crain and Mahard published the first meta-analysis of the effect of desegregation on black achievement based on ninety-three studies (including some studies without control groups or pre-desegregation measures). They did find significant effects of desegregation on achievement, although the most significant effects were confined to the early grades (usually kindergarten and first grade).

Finally, in 1984 a panel of seven experts was convened by the National Institute of Education (the research arm of the U.S. Department of Education) in an attempt to find consensus on the issue of desegregation and black achievement. The panel established minimal methodological criteria for selecting studies, including having a control group and having pre–post measures using the same achievement test.[5] Only nineteen such studies were identified, generating a total of thirty-five observations (counting each grade level tested as an observation). Each panelist then conducted his own analysis, but not all panelists used the same studies (for various method-ological reasons) and each used somewhat different techniques for measur-ing effect sizes. Not surprisingly, the panelists did not arrive at a consensus about the effects of desegregation on black achievement.

For this reason, the conclusions of Thomas Cook, who served as a re-viewer of the reviews, are especially important. Considering the analyses of the other panelists, he made the following observations: (1) desegregation did not lower black achievement; (2) desegregation had no significant effect on math achievement; (3) desegregation raised mean reading achievement from two to six weeks of a school year; (4) median reading gains were posi-tive but lower than mean gains and were not statistically significant. Because of the considerable differences in results across the nineteen studies, he then concluded "I have little confidence that we know much about how desegre-gation affects reading 'on the average' and, across the few studies examined, I find the variability in effect-sizes more striking and less well understood than any measure of central tendency" (Cook et al. 1984: 41).

Given the historic importance of the thesis that desegregation will im-prove minority achievement and reduce the achievement gap, it is remark-able that no comprehensive national studies were ever commissioned on this question, and that by 1984 the entirety of the most rigorous case studies could not generate a reliable conclusion.

NATIONAL STUDIES

The most extensive national data on academic achievement has been compiled by the National Assessment of Educational Progress (NAEP), a U.S. Department of Education project that has been administering achieve-ment tests to national representative samples since 1970 (Campbell et al. 1997). Test scores in reading, mathematics, and science are available for three age groups (9, 13, and 17) over a period spanning nearly three decades. Not only is this data the primary source of information about national achieve-ment trends, it is also the primary source of information about achievement gaps among white, black, and Hispanic students.

One of NAEP's most important findings is that the achievement gap be-tween black and white students narrowed significantly between 1970 and the late 1980s (Armor 1992). Since this phenomenon occurred during the same time period that saw the most extensive desegregation of the public schools, some have argued that the two trends are causally related, that school desegregation is one of the factors responsible for this narrowing of the gap.

One recent study that supports this argument is by Grissmer, Flanagan, and Williamson (1998). Using NAEP data and other information about changes in family characteristics and in school resources, they conclude that a combination of higher black SES, school desegregation (in the sense of student racial balance), smaller class sizes, and more demanding course work all contributed to the reduced achievement gap between black and white students. Most of their analysis was aggregate in nature, so they do not show the specific contributions of each of these factors (except family SES) to a reduction in the achievement gap. Also, their analysis did not consider all family characteristics, such as changes in parenting behaviors and parent IQ, so that the impact of family SES may be underestimated.

Trends in the black–white reading gap are shown in figure 6.3 for the NAEP data. The gap is expressed in standard deviation units to compare gaps across different years. Since students gain about one standard deviation per year on most achievement tests during the elementary school years, a difference of one standard deviation represents a difference of at least one grade level (or more at secondary grade levels). In 1971, black students were more than one grade behind white students at all three ages.

The black–white reading gap narrowed dramatically between 1971 and 1988, to about .7 standard deviation for age nine and about one-half standard deviation for age thirteen. White scores were virtually constant during this time, so that the reduction in the gap was due exclusively to gains by black students. Unfortunately, after 1988 the reading gap began increasing again for all three age groups and by 1996 it had returned to where it was in the early 1980s. Unlike the earlier period, the increasing gap between 1988 and 1996 was due to a combination of declining black scores and rising white scores. As of 1996, blacks in all three age groups remained between .7 and .8 standard deviation behind white students.

The trend in the mathematics achievement gap, shown in figure 6.4, is similar except the swings have not been quite so large. The black–white math gap for ages thirteen and seventeen narrowed until 1986 or 1990 and then began increasing again, but it has been relatively constant during the 1990s. The gap for age nine shows a somewhat different pattern; it narrowed, widened, and then began narrowing again so that it is about as narrow in 1996 as it was in 1986. By 1996, then, the math gap ranged from .75 to .9 standard deviation depending on age. For ages thirteen and seventeen, it is important to note that the widening of the gap is due almost exclusively to higher performance by white students, while the scores of black students remained fairly constant.

These trends and changes in the black–white achievement gap are obviously complex and cannot be easily explained. In fact, the Grissmer study does not offer an explanation for the recent increase in the black–white gap. For our purposes, the important question is to what extent school desegregation might be a factor in explaining these changes in the achievement gap. If school desegregation was partly responsible for the reduction in the gap, could it also be partly responsible for the increase in the gap?

Figure 6.3
National Trends in Black–White Reading Gap (NAEP)

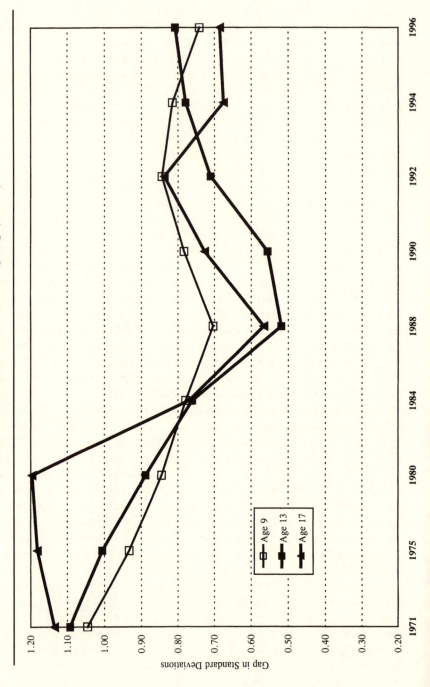

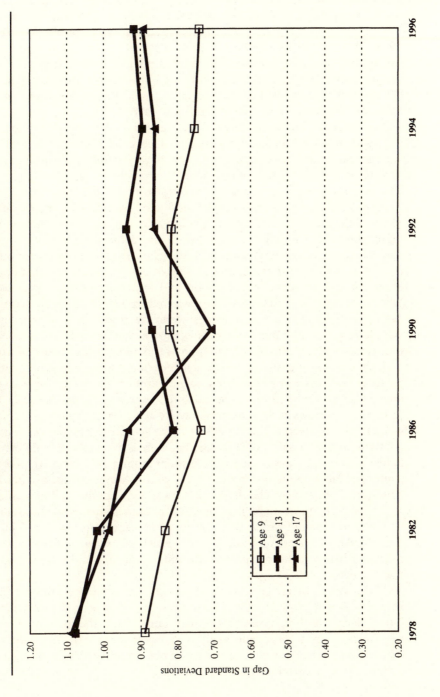

Figure 6.4
National Trends in the Black–White Math Gap (NAEP)

As shown in figure 4.3 in chapter 4, schools were highly segregated in 1968, particularly in very large school districts (enrollment over about 27,000), but desegregation was rapid until 1972 and then tapered off by 1982. There has been very little change in overall desegregation levels between 1982 and 1995, despite the fact that many school districts attained unitary status during this period and are no longer under court supervision. Whatever the legal status of desegregation plans, and by whatever means, most school districts maintain some level of racial balance.

At the national aggregate level, then, there is no relationship between the increasing black–white achievement gaps during the 1990s and school desegregation levels. Since school resources have generally improved during this decade, perhaps the cause should be sought in family changes or changes in school program content and academic standards.

Aggregate analyses such as those conducted by Grissmer and those already mentioned are not a very satisfying way to test the effect of school desegregation, because they do not relate the achievement of individual students to the racial composition of their school while controlling for other factors. It is likely, for example, that school desegregation brought about other changes in school organization and structure which impacted all schools whether or not they had desegregated student bodies, and these organizational and structural changes were the true causes of improved achievement. For example, desegregation also brought racially balanced faculties and a more equitable distribution of school programs and resources; perhaps this was the reason for black achievement gains, not school racial balance. The only way to confirm a role for student desegregation is to examine achievement within segregated and desegregated school settings.

Figure 6.5 shows average black and white achievement by school percent white for age thirteen in the 1992 NAEP; the achievement scores have been adjusted for individual SES.[6] For reading, there is no appreciable difference in black scores in schools that range from predominantly minority (0–20% white) to high white majorities (61–80% white), although black scores are considerably higher in schools over 80% white. Given the lack of relationship elsewhere, this is more likely an effect of unmeasured SES characteristics or other factors rather than an effect of racial composition. This is confirmed by a regression analysis in which school percent white is not significant when controls are present for individual SES and school district poverty level.[7]

The adjusted black math scores do show a six- or seven-point increase between 21–40% and 41–60% white, but so do white scores. Thus the adjusted black–white gap remains fairly constant across differing school compositions. Again, a regression analysis shows that the percent white in a school does not have a significant effect on black math achievement once individual SES characteristics and school district poverty levels are taken into account.

Figure 6.5
School Percent White and Achievement, 1992 NAEP Age 13 (Adjusted for Individual SES)

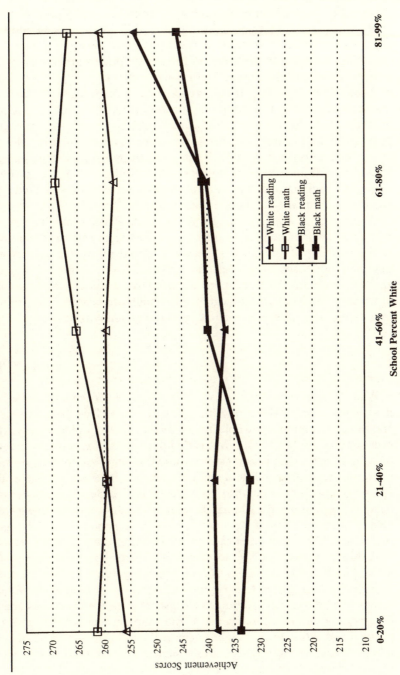

We find, therefore, that NAEP does not lend much support to the thesis that a school's racial composition has a significant relationship with black achievement or with the achievement gap. This analysis of individual achievement, however, is still unsatisfactory from several standpoints. First, the NAEP survey samples consist of relatively small numbers of students from many schools and school districts across the country, and the data says nothing about whether a district actually has a desegregation plan, much less its type, extent, and duration. Second, while NAEP collects achievement data over time, the sample of school districts can and does change over time, so that we cannot be sure that we are always comparing the same group of schools when we look at achievement trends over time. Third, the individual SES measures are collected from students themselves, they are limited in number, and they may not be as reliable as data collected from parents or from official school district records.

Finally, and perhaps most important, the NAEP data suffer from the same problem that emerged in the Coleman report. There is no way to control for the initial ability of students in segregated versus desegregated schools, which might be influenced by self-selection effects. Thus in figure 6.5 we do not know whether the small variations occurred as a result of school programs, or whether the families in desegregated schools are systematically different from families in segregated schools in ways we cannot measure.

CASE STUDIES

A case study, as the term is used here, is a study of school desegregation in a particular school district. Although case studies lack the ability to generalize for the nation as a whole, they often have methodological advantages over national studies when investigating the effects of school desegregation on achievement. One is that case studies yield achievement data on an entire population of schools and students, not just small samples of students and schools within school districts as in the NAEP. Second, usually a great deal is known about the nature, scope, and duration of the desegregation plan in question; there is virtually nothing known about school desegregation in the NAEP data other than the racial composition of a school.

A third advantage of case studies is that achievement trends can be examined over extended periods of time, following student achievement from near the beginning of a desegregation plan (when most students were segregated) to periods when students have spent their entire school careers in desegregated schools. Finally, the relationship between school racial composition and achievement can be examined for all students within the same school district who are exposed to the same desegregation and other school policies, thereby eliminating idiosyncratic school district policy or program effects that might be confounded with school racial balance.

The five school districts chosen for case studies have certain features in common. They are all very large school districts, representing large metro-politan areas with enrollments exceeding 40,000 students. They have all im-plemented comprehensive desegregation plans that arose under some type of litigation, and they have attained substantial desegregation (racial bal-ance) in all or in a significant portion of their schools. In all cases, the achievement gap between black (or minority) and white students was an issue at some period during the litigation, either during the initial liability phase of the lawsuit or during some later stage in the case when low achieve-ment of minority students became an issue (e.g., petitions for unitary sta-tus or for further relief). As a result, extensive achievement data by race is available and has been subjected to detailed analyses.

In certain other respects the school districts are diverse. Three are from southern states that had dual school system laws: Dallas, Kansas City, and Charlotte-Mecklenburg; and two are northern districts with different kinds of liability problems: Minneapolis and Wilmington. Charlotte and Wilm-ington are large county-wide districts that included most of the suburban population when their plans began, while the other three are central-city districts surrounded by numerous suburban (and mostly white) school dis-tricts. Finally, Dallas and Kansas City had become majority–black by the time their major plan was implemented and have always had some schools that were not racially balanced, while Charlotte and Wilmington remained predominately white despite long-term racial balance in nearly all of their schools. Minneapolis started out as a predominately white school district with high racial balance but later became predominately minority with much less racial balance. This diversity presents an opportunity to examine the relationship between desegregation and achievement under a variety of conditions.

Dallas, Texas

Like many urban school systems in the South, the Dallas case has a long history of litigation and a corresponding multiplicity of desegregation plans. After adopting geographic zoning in the late 1960s, the first busing plan was implemented in 1971 for secondary schools only, while an elementary plan was stayed by an appellate court. A second and more comprehensive plan was adopted in 1976 that created a number of desegregated primary schools (grades 4–6) and junior highs (grades7–8), although some areas remained with K–6 neighborhood schools. All K–3 schools remained as neighborhood schools, and most of these were racially imbalanced. Like many other urban school districts that implemented mandatory busing, Dallas experienced se-vere white flight. Dallas was 57 percent white in 1970 prior to the first de-segregation plan, but by the time the elementary plan was implemented in

1976 the white enrollment had dropped to only 38 percent, and it continued to fall reaching 20 percent by the mid-1980s.

The 1976 plan did not attempt to desegregate all of the elementary schools in Dallas. Many K–6 schools were not desegregated by rezoning and mandatory busing and therefore remained predominately black; there was also a small number of predominately white schools. The predominately black schools received various compensatory programs. This circumstance gives an opportunity to examine whether achievement trends differed for those schools that were desegregated versus those that remained predominately black.

Figure 6.6 shows the trends in Dallas sixth grade reading achievement tests (ITBS) reading scores for sixth grade students, from 1977 to 1991. Prior to 1980, the scores for all students were very low, and even white students were below the national norms, which is uncommon in urban school systems. Starting in 1980 and continuing to about 1983, scores of both white and minority students improved substantially and then leveled off; few important changes occurred between 1983 and 1991.[8] The gains for both black and Hispanic students were greater than those for white students, and as a result the black–white gap was reduced from about 23 points (one standard deviation) to 13 points (about two-thirds of a standard deviation).[9]

Was this gap reduction a result of school desegregation or other causes? Because some elementary schools were desegregated and others were not, we can compare the overall black reading gains in schools that were either desegregated or that remained predominantly minority between 1977 and 1985. These trends, shown in figure 6.7, make it clear that black achievement gains occurred in both desegregated and predominantly minority schools. Thus it was not racial balance itself that caused minority achievement to improve and the gap to close, but rather some other factors. Although it is not clear exactly what those factors were, the low scores of white students in the late 1970s suggest a possibility that the curriculum was not well-aligned with the ITBS content. In addition, it is known that Dallas did work to improve basic skills teaching in all of its schools during the early 1980s. Whatever the causes, the gains were not caused by the racial balancing of its elementary schools.

Wilmington–New Castle County, Delaware

Desegregation in Wilmington–New Castle County, Delaware has a singular history that provides a compelling case study of the relationship between desegregation and academic achievement. In 1978, a federal district court ordered the predominately black Wilmington school district, serving the city of Wilmington, to be consolidated with several predominately white suburban school districts in New Castle County to create a single, new county-

Figure 6.6
Trends in Dallas 6th Grade Reading Achievement (ITBS)

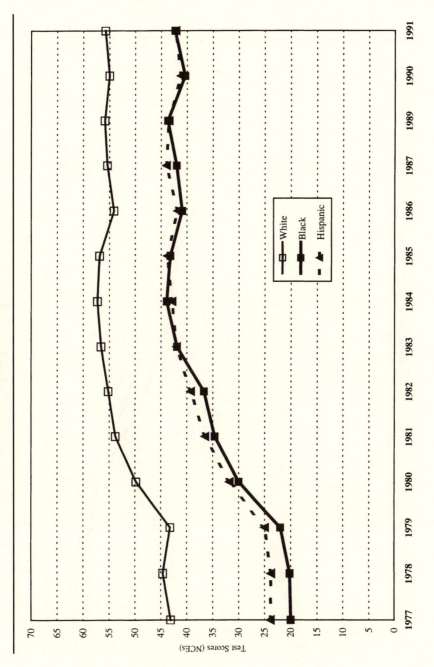

Figure 6.7
Dallas 6th Grade Black Reading Achievement by Type of School

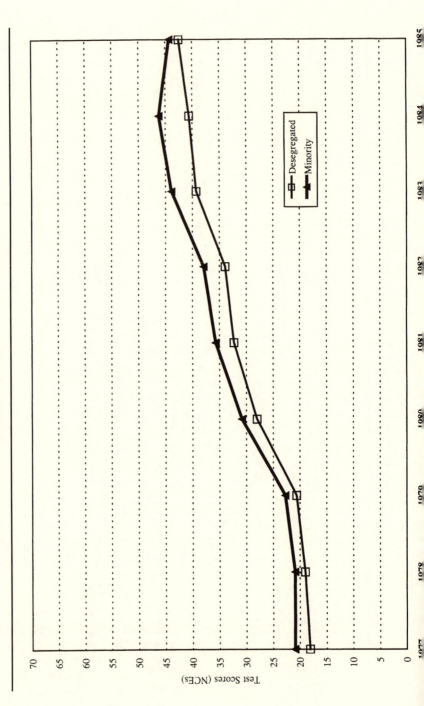

wide school district. Although the legal history of this case is quite interesting, for present purposes it suffices to say that a countywide desegregation
plan was ordered, which required two-way mandatory busing of black students into formerly white suburban schools and white students into formerly
black inner-city schools. It is the only large metropolitan consolidation and
busing plan ordered by a federal court that was actually implemented.[10]

The case is of special interest to achievement studies because, in contrast
to city-only desegregation plans, the inclusion of suburban districts meant
that large numbers of black students attended most of their school years (9
out of 12) in majority-white and generally affluent suburban schools. Suburban white students were bused into former Wilmington city schools for
only three years, usually during the late elementary or the middle school
years, which tended to limit the magnitude of white flight. While there was
significant white flight in the years immediately following the start of busing, the consolidated system began with such a high white–black ratio
(80–20) that the white loss was sustained without converting New Castle
County into a majority–black school system. Moreover, in 1981 the single
consolidated district was split into four independent subdistricts, with former Wilmington city schools being divided up and apportioned to four new
districts whose population bases were predominantly suburban and white.
The result of all these factors is that New Castle County became one of the
most racially balanced districts in the nation, with the white–black ratio stabilizing at about 65:35.

Indeed, in 1991, 96 percent of its schools were racially balanced at a very
narrow allowable variance (plus or minus ten percentage points from their
respective districtwide ratios). More than 90 percent of all schools in the
county met this rigorous criterion between 1981 and 1993, except for the
years 1986 to 1989, when 85 percent met the criteria. Nearly all schools
ranged from 60 to 75 percent white during this period, and only two out of
50 elementary schools had a majority black enrollment for more than one
year. In other words, this school system had a level of school desegregation
that many would consider ideal, a level and duration rarely attained in large
desegregated school districts.

If school desegregation can have a significant impact on the achievement
gap, we would expect it to occur here, given the high degree of stable racial
balance and the fact that most elementary-age black students attended
majority-white schools in the suburbs. But figure 6.8 shows that the achievement gap in sixth grade reading remained large and constant between 1985
and 1993. A break in the trend lines denotes a change from the California
Achievement Test (CAT) to the Stanford Achievement Test (SAT). In 1985,
the first year that sixth graders would have attended racially balanced
schools since kindergarten, we see a black–white gap of fifteen points, or
about three-fourths of a standard deviation on the CAT. Although black students were scoring only five points below national norms on the CAT, when

Figure 6.8
Trends in New Castle County 6th Grade Reading Achievement*

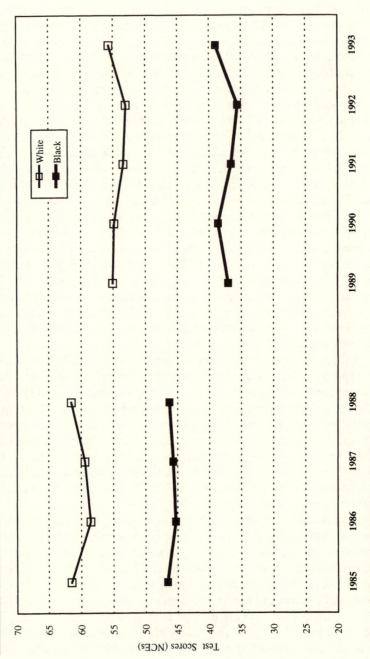

* 1985-1988 CAT; 1989-1993 Stanford Achievement.

the SAT was introduced, black scores fell to the upper thirties in NCE units. The black–white gap for the SAT, which averages seventeen points, is also about three-fourths of a standard deviation, which is comparable to the national achievement gap for 9-year olds (see figure 6.1). Despite the substantial school desegregation in New Castle County and its extended duration, there is no indication of improvement in black test scores nor a reduction in the black–white achievement gap during this time.

Kansas City, Missouri

In 1986, a federal court ordered Kansas City, Missouri to implement what may well be the most expensive remedial plan in history. Kansas City had been operating a major desegregation plan since 1977, but in 1986 the Court ordered an expanded plan involving extensive new construction, renovation, and addition of magnet programs to all of its secondary schools and to more than half of its elementary schools. With a unique court-ordered tax levy and court-ordered funding from the state, total school expenditures reached $10,000 per pupil by 1990, with total funding exceeding $1.5 billion over an eight-year period or so.

As revealed by the achievement trends in figure 6.9, this extraordinary degree of expenditures and program enhancements did little to raise the achievement levels of black students or to close the black–white achievement gap. In 1988, before most of the improvements were completed, black fifth grade students averaged about 40 on the ITBS composite test (NCE units), or about twelve points below white students. By 1994, black scores had risen slightly to 43 but white scores rose also, so the gap remained at twelve points. When a new version of the ITBS test was introduced in 1995, black scores fell to 38 and white scores fell to the same extent, so the black–white gap again remained at twelve points. The pattern for Hispanic students is similar to that for black students, although the Hispanic–white gap has actually increased from eight to thirteen points.

Although the black–white achievement gap is narrower in Kansas City than in New Castle County or in national data, this arises from low white scores rather than high black scores. For example, in 1995, Kansas City whites score just at the national norm of 50, while New Castle County whites score considerably above the national norm at 56. Unlike New Castle County, Kansas City has lost much of its middle-class white population, and elementary school enrollment is down to 25 percent white students. The white families remaining in Kansas City public schools have relatively high poverty rates: 50 percent of fifth grade students are on free lunch compared to less than 15 percent for New Castle County. Based on this poverty difference alone, the achievement gap should be narrower in Kansas City than New Castle County.

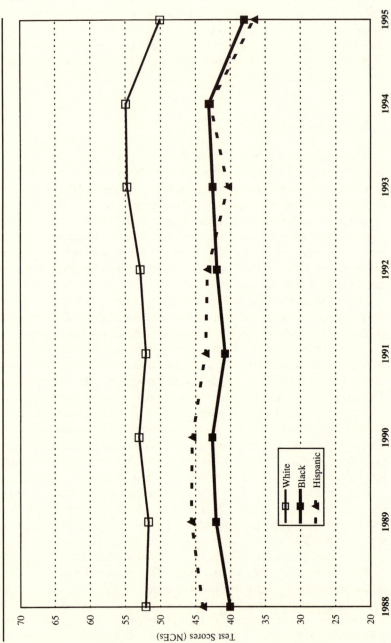

Figure 6.9

Trends in Kansas City 5th Grade Achievement (ITBS Composite Score)

Unlike New Castle County, Kansas City has a wide variation in the racial composition of its elementary schools, most of which are magnet schools with a considerable degree of racial balance, and others of which are "traditional" neighborhood schools that are predominately minority. This variation in racial composition allows examination of another aspect desegregation and achievement, namely the relationship between degree of racial balance and achievement within the same district. Examining this relationship within a single district has a distinct advantage over the NAEP analysis in figure 6.5 because it eliminates the problem of differing school district policies and practices which might affect achievement. That is, in the NAEP data, schools with differing racial composition generally come from different school districts, while in this analysis the schools are all from Kansas City.

Figure 6.10 shows Kansas City black fifth grade achievement by school racial composition in 1995. Although there is variation in test scores for schools with differing racial compositions, there is no particular pattern to this variation, and in particular there is no indication that higher concentrations of minority students is associated with lower black achievement. Black students in schools ranging from 55 to 65 percent minority (the whitest elementary schools in the system) score at about the same level as black students in racially isolated schools that are 95 to 100 percent minority. One school at 90 percent minority has very high black scores, but it is either an anomaly or it may be caused by a large concentration of gifted students at this school. Interestingly, the category that represents the most racially balanced schools—75 percent minority, equaling the district-wide ratio—has the lowest achievement level of all schools.

One limitation of the Kansas City data, of course, is that in 1995 none of its elementary schools would be considered desegregated by a traditional absolute standard, since they all have more than 50 percent minority enrollments. A better test of the relationship between school composition and achievement would be in a school district that has some racially balanced schools that are majority–white and some imbalanced schools that are predominantly black or minority. Such a district will be reviewed next.

Charlotte-Mecklenburg, North Carolina

Charlotte-Mecklenburg is one of the more celebrated desegregation cases in the country. It was the source of the Supreme Court's famous *Swann* decision in 1971, which set the stage for massive mandatory busing and racial-balance plans that were implemented throughout the country over the next ten years. After strong opposition initially, the Charlotte school board finally embraced the plan and set out to become an exemplary example of school desegregation. They maintained one of the most racially balanced school systems for more years than most school systems in the nation;

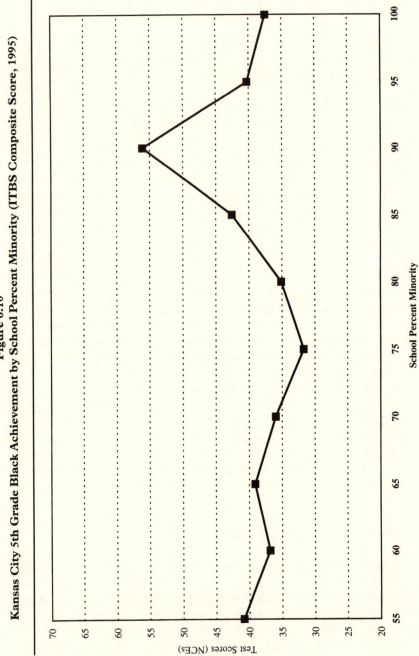

Figure 6.10
Kansas City 5th Grade Black Achievement by School Percent Minority (ITBS Composite Score, 1995)

its degree of racial balance during the 1970s and 1980s is equaled or exceeded only by Wilmington–New Castle County and perhaps a few other county-wide school districts in the South.

Although Charlotte also experienced significant white flight during the early years of their busing plan, they started out with a white–black ratio of 70:30, eventually stabilizing at about a 60:40 ratio. In 1992, Charlotte changed its desegregation strategy to some degree, replacing some of the mandatory busing with magnet schools and stopped trying to racially balance all of its schools in response to demographic change. As a result, by the late 1990s there was more variation in the racial composition of schools. While the majority of students still attended well-balanced schools, there were a number of schools with high and low percentages of black students.

Figure 6.11 shows the trends in composite (reading and math) achievement between 1978 and 1997. Although the gap looks larger in Charlotte than other districts reviewed here, it must be noted that the scores between 1978 and 1992 are median percentiles, rather than NCEs, and an achievement gap of thirty percentile points is equal to an NCE gap of about twenty points, or one standard deviation. Thus in 1978, the Charlotte black–white gap was over one standard deviation, higher than the national gap, even though Charlotte students had spent their entire elementary school career in desegregated schools. Like Dallas, both black and white students improved dramatically until 1982, but the gap shrank somewhat to about one standard deviation.

When a new version of the CAT test was introduced in 1986, scores of both black and white students dropped, and the black–white gap returned to just over one standard deviation. Thus, whatever caused the rapid rise in test scores between 1978 and 1983, it was not school desegregation. When the scores dropped in 1986, black students in Charlotte had attended schools and a school system that had been fully desegregated for fifteen years. In 1994, Charlotte dropped the CAT test because the state introduced a mandatory statewide mastery test program. The scores on the state tests, given to grades three to eight, are expressed as the percentage of students "proficient," according to state standards. There are no national norms for this test, but the Charlotte scores for black students are several points below the state averages for black students. Clearly, none of these Charlotte achievement test results, whether early or recent, provide evidence that school desegregation has improved black achievement or closed the achievement gap.

The variation in school racial composition in Charlotte, which has increased during the 1990s, allows a better test of the relationship between racial balance and recent achievement than was provided by the Kansas City data. Although most elementary schools meet a court-imposed standard of 25 to 55 percent black, by 1998 there were a number of schools with black enrollments as low as 10 percent and as high as 90 percent. If there is

Figure 6.11

Trends in Charlotte-Mecklenburg Achievement (Composite Score*)

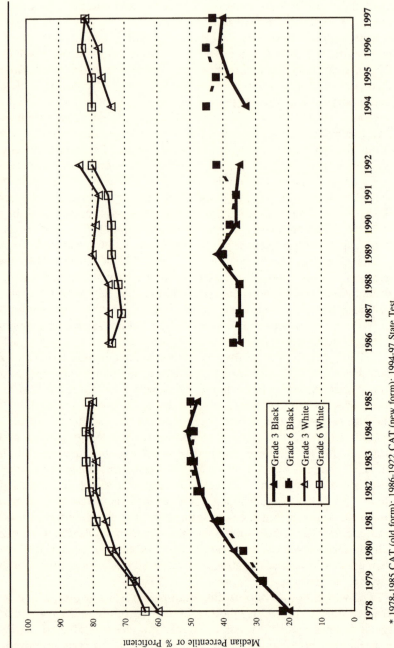

* 1978-1985 CAT (old form); 1986-1922 CAT (new form); 1994-97 State Test.

a causal relationship between racial balance and achievement, we should see it in Charlotte.

Figure 6.12 shows the relationship between school percent black and achievement on the state mastery tests, which are shown as scale scores. There is no significant trend or pattern in the achievement results. Although a small number of black students (160) in schools less than 16 percent black score two or three points higher than other schools, many more blacks in other schools with a majority of white students (1200 black students in schools 16 to 35 percent black) score just about the same as blacks in schools with a large majority of black students (900 black students in schools 66 percent or more black). Thus there is virtually no relationship between current school composition and achievement in elementary schools.

Minneapolis, Minnesota

Minneapolis is the second case study for a northern school district. It adopted its first desegregation plan under court order in 1974 when it was more than 80 percent white, and it made several major plan modifications and extensions in 1977 and 1982, after which it achieved very substantial racial balance. In addition to the federal litigation, the state of Minnesota enforced one of the more rigorous state laws requiring school racial balance regardless of whether there was intentional (de jure) segregation. Thus even though the federal court case was dismissed in 1983, Minnesota continued its desegregation plan under a state mandate.

Partly because of the changing and expanding desegregation plans, including mandatory busing, Minneapolis lost more than half of its white enrollment between 1972 and 1982. While it was still majority white in 1982, it continued to lose white enrollment until about 1991, when it became over 50 percent minority for the first time. The state stopped enforcing its racial balance law in 1995, and Minneapolis started relying less on busing and more on community (neighborhood) schools. But by 1995, Minneapolis had become a predominantly minority schools district, and its white enrollment had dropped to 36 percent with blacks outnumbering whites for the first time. Given these substantial changes, Minneapolis offers an excellent example of a desegregated district which changed from predominantly white to predominantly minority over the period of our study.

Figure 6.13 shows the Minneapolis trends in sixth grade reading between 1982 and 1996, after the district had attained a high degree of racial balance. Again, there is no evidence that school desegregation has improved black achievement or reduced the achievement gap. In fact, it appears that during the 1990s, black achievement declined and the black–white gap widened. This decline may have been caused in part by

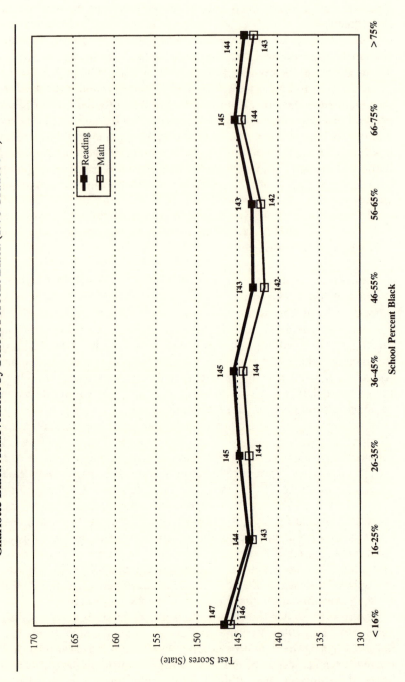

Figure 6.12
Charlotte Black Achievement by School Percent Black (1998 Grades 3–5)

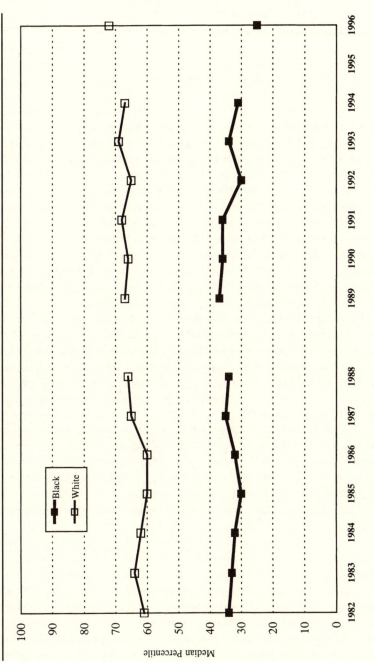

Figure 6.13

Trends in Minneapolis 6th Grade Reading Achievement*

* 1982-1988 Stanford Achievement; 1989-1994 CAT; 1995-1996 CAT-5.

175

rising black enrollment and an increasing percentage of black students in poverty. The percentage of black students on free lunch increased from 62 percent in 1991 to 72 in 1996.

The Revised Harm and Benefit Thesis

It seems clear from the case studies that school desegregation, both in terms of substantial school racial balance and enhancements such as integrated magnet programs, has done little to close the achievement gap between black and white students. Black achievement did rise significantly in two of the districts, Dallas and Charlotte, but so did white achievement, albeit somewhat less than black achievement, and thus the gap did close somewhat. In Charlotte, the gains were mostly temporary, and when a new test was introduced in 1986 the gap returned to where it was before the gains, even though racial balance had been maintained. In Dallas, the gains appear to be permanent, but the gains were just as large in predominately minority (that is, non-desegregated) schools as in desegregated schools. Thus, to whatever we might attribute the black and white gains in Dallas and Charlotte, it would not be to racial balance per se.

One possibility is that desegregation led to substantial programmatic changes, such as greater emphasis on basic skills instruction or possibly adoption of higher academic standards, and this change benefited black students more than white students. However, these types of programmatic changes would not require school racial balance, as demonstrated clearly in the Dallas case. Another possibility is greater alignment between instruction and standardized test content—and greater emphasis on teaching test content—which may pertain especially to Charlotte, given the steep rise in test scores and then the sharp drop. Whatever the reasons for these gains in Dallas and Charlotte, given the lack of black gains or gap reductions in Kansas City, Minneapolis, or New Castle County, they cannot be attributed to desegregation in the sense of school racial balance.

This leaves one other explanation of the lack of black gains or gap closure, which is the revised harm and benefit thesis. To what extent can one attribute the lack of progress in closing the black–white gap to various intervening conditions, such as within-school segregation or inequitable allocation of resources?

Regarding within-school segregation, none of these school districts practiced routine ability grouping in their elementary schools, and generally speaking, desegregated elementary schools had desegregated classrooms. Most of the districts offered gifted and talented programs, in which black students were often underrepresented (due to test score differences), which was an issue in some of the litigation hearings. But since gifted and talented programs generally serve only a small fraction of the population, it cannot be reasonably argued that the racial imbalance that might exist in these programs is responsible for the gap that exists between the vast majority of students who are not in gifted programs.

With regard to the equitable allocation of resources, formal studies have been conducted as part of unitary hearings (or preparation for hearings) in Dallas, Kansas City, and Charlotte. In New Castle County, resource allocation was never raised as an issue, simply because black students from the former Wilmington district spent nine out of their twelve years in majority white suburban schools. In Dallas, pupil–teacher ratios were slightly smaller (by one pupil) and per capita expenditures were substantially higher (by $500) in predominately minority elementary schools as compared to desegregated schools.[11] Teacher experience was one year lower in minority schools, and the percent with master's degrees was about five percent higher, as compared to desegregated schools. With the exception of expenditures, these differences are quite small, and in any event, there was little difference in black achievement in these two types of schools (see figure 6.7).

In Charlotte, pupil–teacher ratios were substantially smaller, by two to three pupils, in majority-black elementary schools compared to racially balanced schools. Given the high correlation between expenditures and pupil–teacher ratios, per-pupil expenditures very likely favored majority black schools as well (Trent 1999; and Armor 1999). Like Dallas, there was only a one-year difference in teacher experience favoring balanced schools, and also a difference of 4 to 7 percent of teachers with advanced degrees (depending on the year of the evaluation). Not only are these differences small in absolute terms, they were not at all related to student achievement once student SES was controlled.

In Kansas City, there were no significant differences in teacher experience or teacher education between predominately minority schools and racially balanced elementary schools. Since all racially balanced elementary schools in Kansas City were magnet schools, it is not surprising that balanced schools had somewhat smaller pupil–teacher ratios (by one pupil) and substantially higher expenditures (by $600) as compared to predominately minority schools. Again, these resource differences had no impact on student achievement, as demonstrated by the relationship between test scores and school racial composition in figure 6.10.

There is no solid evidence in any of these five cities that within-school segregation or inequitable allocation of resources can explain a significant portion of the long-lasting achievement gap, or the failure of black scores to rise after desegregation in three of the cities. There is ample evidence in all five districts that family SES characteristics are strongly related to student achievement, and this is the most likely explanation for the perpetuation of the black–white gap. There is one additional theory, however, that attempts to attribute SES effects to prior segregation, to which we now turn.

THE INTERGENERATION THEORY

The intergeneration theory of school segregation is a special case of a much broader theory of segregation and its effects, which has its origins in the famous vicious-circle thesis of Gunnar Myrdal (1944) in his classic study of race in America. The Myrdal thesis, simply put, was that racial prejudice, segregation, and black disadvantage were sustained by a vicious circle of beliefs and behaviors that found their origins in slavery. Slavery caused objective economic and social disadvantages for blacks, which in turn reinforced beliefs that blacks were inherently inferior, which led to segregation laws after slavery was abolished. These segregation laws perpetuated black disadvantages, which then reinforced racial prejudice. Like slavery, the segregation forced upon one generation perpetuated further economic and social disadvantages for the next generation, which then sustained existing prejudicial beliefs, and so on in a never-ending cycle of mutually reinforcing beliefs and behaviors passed on from one generation to the next.

The intergeneration theory asserts that school segregation, as practiced until at least the late 1960s in the South, caused or contributed to the lower educational, occupational, and economic attainment of black parents. It is well established that lower socioeconomic status is strongly associated with lower academic achievement. Therefore, if lower SES is caused by the segregation of black parents, the intergeneration theory would be a valid explanation of low black test scores. This theory was advanced by Dr. Robert Crain in testimony during the Kansas City, Missouri, unitary status hearing.[12] The basic causal sequence for the intergeneration theory can be represented schematically as follows:

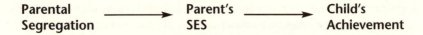

Parental ⟶ **Parent's** ⟶ **Child's**
Segregation   **SES**   **Achievement**

Dr. Crain carried out the only known attempt to test the intergenerational theory of segregation effects. He commissioned a telephone survey of about 900 Kansas City parents of children in three grade levels (5, 8, and 10), which included about 600 black parents. Information was collected about the parents' socioeconomic status (education, income, assets), their experience with segregation in their elementary school, other forms of discrimination, and attitudes about the Kansas City school system. Parent survey data was combined with school district information including 1995 achievement test scores.

Not surprisingly, a high proportion of black Kansas City parents attended segregated elementary schools when they were children; about 64 percent had attended schools in Kansas City. On average, these black parents had completed sixth grade by 1968, and over 90 percent had completed elementary school by 1977, which is the first year of Kansas City's major desegregation plan. About 70 percent of the black parents interviewed reported that they had attended elementary schools that were all or nearly all black. Another 6 percent attended a majority–black school, 14 percent had attended desegregated schools with about a 50–50 enrollment, and only 10 percent had attended majority-white schools.

If the causal process hypothesized above is true, one would expect a simple correlation between the racial composition of a parent's school and a child's achievement test scores. Figure 6.14 shows, however, that there is virtually no relationship between black parents' school segregation and a child's reading or math scores in 1995. In fact, black children whose parents attended predominately black schools average 38 on the reading test compared to 35 for those whose parents attended desegregated schools, although this is not a statistically significant difference. There is virtually no difference for math scores. The Pearson correlations between the full parent segregation measure and black achievement are .03 for reading and –.02 for math.

In contrast, and as expected, there are strong relationships between black parent SES measures and their children's academic achievement, as shown in figure 6.15. Black children whose parents did not finish high school score only 35 points on the reading test, while those who completed college score 53 points, which is above the national average. A similar relationship is documented for math scores. The relationship between parent segregation and income (not shown) is somewhat weaker. Children from black families earning less than $15,000 per year score 39 on the reading test compared to 47 for families earning over $54,000 per annum. The differences for math are 42 and 48 points, respectively. The correlations between black reading scores and the full SES measures are .18 for parent education and the somewhat higher value of .20 for parent income. The correlations with math scores are slightly lower (.12 and .15, respectively).

Other family SES variables were measured in the survey, including number of savings instruments (savings bonds, mutual funds and stocks, and savings for college) and an index of household reading/technology items, which includes number of books, subscriptions to magazines and newspapers, having a library card, and owning a personal computer. The correlation between black reading scores and these two measures is .20 for number of savings instruments and .15 for the household items index. These two variables also have somewhat lower correlations with math scores (.15 and .07, respectively).

The intergeneration theory does not require a direct relationship from parent segregation to child's achievement; it is possible that the causal process works entirely through the family SES factors. Since we have shown that family SES has a strong impact on achievement for black students, it remains to determine whether parent segregation has significant effects on parent SES characteristics. Generally, black parent segregation is only

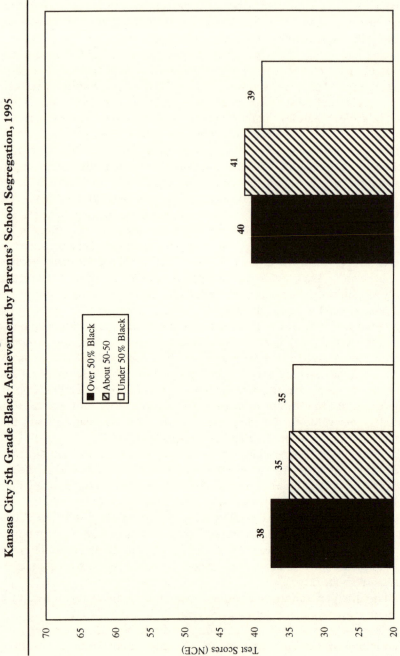

Figure 6.14
Kansas City 5th Grade Black Achievement by Parents' School Segregation, 1995

Figure 6.15

Kansas City 5th Grade Black Achievement by Parent's Education, 1995

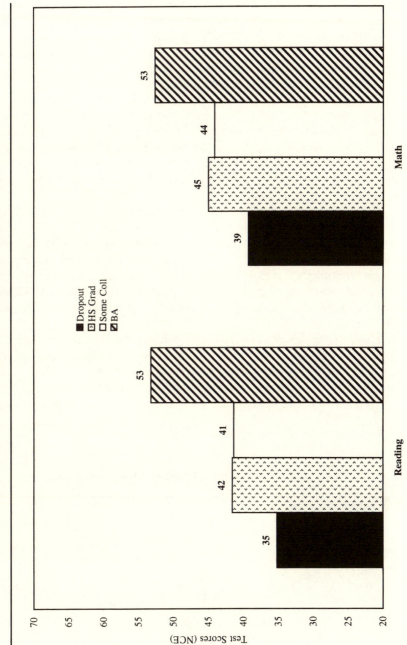

weakly related to SES, and the relationships are much weaker than those between SES and achievement. The correlation between black parent segregation and education is only −.03, and the correlation between black parent
segregation and income is only −.07. Neither of these correlations is statistically significant. In other words, a parent's school segregation experience is
not significantly related to their education or income status, which are two
of the strongest predictors of student achievement.

The correlations between parent segregation and two other SES measures are somewhat higher. The correlation with number of savings instruments is −.09, and the correlation with household items is −.10. Both of
these correlations are statistically significant. Is it possible that parent segregation affects children's achievement indirectly through effects on the number of savings instruments and the number of household reading/technology
materials?

The proper way to test for the indirect effects of a potential causal factor
is by means of path analysis. In the path diagram below (figure 6.16), the arrows show the hypothesized causal effects of parent segregation on savings
and household items, which then have causal effects on child's achievement.
The assumption is also made that having more savings instruments is an in-
dicator of wealth, thereby causing higher accumulations of household items.
Finally, an arrow also indicates a possible direct effect of parent segregation
on reading achievement.

The numbers shown next to the arrows are the path coefficients as derived from a path analysis.[13] Note that, controlling for SES characteristics,
the direct effect of parent segregation on achievement is positive, which is
contrary to the hypothesis. However, this path coefficient is not statistically significant, and neither of the other two path coefficients for parent

Figure 6.16
Intergeneration Model of Black Reading Achievement

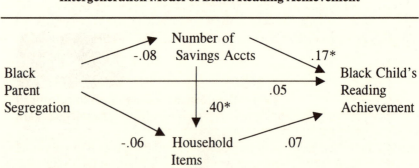

* Statistically significant at < .05.

segregation are significant. Finally, the path coefficient from household items to achievement is not significant. The two path coefficients for number of savings are both statistically significant. Even if the coefficients for parent segregation were statistically significant, the combined indirect negative effects of parent segregation operating through both savings and household items (e.g., $-.08 \times .17$, $-.06 \times .07$) would be smaller than the positive direct effect.

Other more complex models can be tested. For example, parent education can be added to the model, but this does not add anything because the path coefficients for parent education (both from segregation and to achievement) are smaller than those for savings. Another possible model uses only education and income (neither savings nor household items is significant when education and income are both included in the model). In this model, the effect of parent segregation is larger for income $(-.09)$, but smaller for education $(-.03)$, and while income has a slightly larger effect on achievement $(.19)$, the direct effect of parent segregation on achievement is also larger and in the wrong direction $(.07$, not significant).

Similar path models were tested for math achievement, but even weaker relationships emerged. No matter how the models are constructed, there is no evidence that the prior school segregation of parents has a negative influence on black achievement, either directly or indirectly operating through negative effects on parental socioeconomic characteristics. At least for Kansas City students, the intergeneration theory finds little support from the Crain data.

CONCLUSIONS

The answer to the first question addressed in this chapter, whether school desegregation has or has not had a significant affect on black achievement and the black–white gap, is a qualified "no." The answer is qualified not because the data is equivocal, but because the question may be interpreted in different ways. The ambiguity arises from the possibly differing meaning of the term, "desegregation." If it refers primarily to the racial balancing of student bodies and faculty—the main thrust of desegregation plans during the 1970s—then the answer is an unequivocal "no." Whether one examines data from historical studies, more recent national studies, or district-level case studies, it is quite clear that the racial composition of student bodies, by itself, has no significant effect on black achievement, nor has it reduced the black–white gap to a significant degree.

If by desegregation one includes all of the policy, instructional, and programmatic changes that may take place as a result of the desegregation process itself, such as raising academic standards, greater basic skills instruction, more remedial programs, improved alignment of curriculum to test content, better preparation for standardized tests, and so forth, then desegregation may have improved black achievement and closed the black–white gap to a limited but significant degree. Judging by the NAEP results and by the two case studies with achievement trends starting in the 1970s, minority achievement appears to have risen and the gap closed by about two-tenths of a standard deviation, or about four points on an NCE scale. If this improvement is due to changes in schools, it must be a programmatic change because it is not dependent on racial composition. Of course, the change could be due to changes outside the school system, such as improved black family SES.

Remarkably, this result is very close to Jencks' prediction nearly three decades ago that nationwide desegregation might raise black achievement by three out of fifteen points on the Coleman tests. It is important to emphasize that these gains could have occurred (and in fact did occur) regardless of school racial balance, which has been the major focus of desegregation plans as well as the greatest source of controversy. It appears from the data and analyses here that the modest gains could have occurred by various types of school reform (although this study does not say precisely which ones) without the years of mandatory busing that have contributed greatly to the loss of the middle class from many urban school districts.

To what extent might the absence of large reductions in the achievement gap be due to various intervening conditions that were not anticipated in *Brown*, which is the second question addressed in this chapter? To believe this proposition would be to ignore two of the most desegregated and equitable school systems in the nation, New Castle County and Charlotte-Mecklenburg, which have long been viewed as having among the most successful and exemplary desegregation plans in the nation. While Charlotte has been criticized for its reduction of mandatory busing after 1991, during the 1980s Charlotte was one of the most desegregated systems in the country, and yet its test scores still reveal very large achievement gaps (Morantz 1996). The same can be said of New Castle County. Not only were nearly all black students enrolled in majority–white schools during these years, there was very little within-school segregation and no one questioned the equity of school resources and programs. Moreover, in New Castle County, black students spent most of their school career in formerly white suburban schools.

Finally, we explored the possibility that the intergeneration theory explains the absence of larger black gains, whereby parental segregation causes lower family parental SES. Based on the Crain Kansas City study, this thesis was not confirmed. Family SES remains the primary explanatory factor for achievement differences, both between and within races, and there is little evidence in the Kansas City study that family SES differences are caused by the segregation of the parent generation.

A more likely explanation for the persistence of the black–white achievement gap is that family socioeconomic status is passed on from one generation to the next, thereby sustaining both low SES and low achievement among black families. In this respect, there may well be a vicious circle operating to maintain the black–white achievement gap, but it is unlike the one posited by Gunnar Myrdal. In particular, the circle has not been broken by eliminating school segregation, which was one possible linkage in his theory, and it is also safe to say the vicious circle has not been broken by the substantial reduction in racial prejudice, which was another link. What we may have is a much simpler vicious circle, whereby socioeconomic status tends to be passed from one generation to the next, and given the strong association between SES and achievement, the achievement gap is likewise perpetuated from one generation to another.

ENDNOTES

1. This was the position taken by Gary Orfield and other signatories in a social science statement submitted as part of an amicus brief for the Supreme Court hearing in *Freeman v. Pitts*, the DeKalb County, Georgia, case. See Social Scientists (1991).

2. This was the position taken by Dr. Robert Crain in a 1997 expert testimony in *Jenkins v. Missouri*.

3. The data in figures 6.1 and 6.2 and in the discussion are taken from Armor (1972b, tables 7 and 12, and figure 3).

4. This regression uses average black achievement and the average black household items index for the 21 groups of schools in figures 6.1 and 6.2. The coefficient for SES is 1.95 (t=3.02) and the coefficient for school percent black is –.024 (t=1.55).

5. Not all panelists agreed that studies should have a pretest measure, but since control groups were not always assigned randomly, the majority of the panel believed that pretests were essential to eliminate the possibility of self-selection effects, since most of the desegregation studies involved voluntary plans.

6. The individual SES variables are parents' education, family structure, and an index of household reading items. The reader may contact the author for the regression results.

7. The reader may contact the author for the regression results.

8. Scores for 1977 and 1978 used ITBS 1971 norms; for 1979 to 1985 ITBS 1978 norms; and for 1986 to 1991 ITBS 1985 norms.

9. The standard deviation for the 1977 and 1978 reading test was 23, and for the 1983 test it was 20.

10. The first metropolitan consolidation order by a federal district court was for Detroit, Michigan and its surrounding suburbs, but this order was overturned by the Supreme Court in its famous *Milliken I* decision in 1974. Another well-known consolidation involving Jefferson County and Lexington, Kentucky was actually brought about by a consolidation action of the state legislature.

11. See Dallas Independent School District: Motion for unitary status.

12. *Jenkins v. Missouri*.

13. The reader may contact the author for details of the path analysis.

REFERENCES

Armor, David J. 1972a. The evidence on busing. *The Public Interest* 28: 90–126.

———. 1972b. School and family effects on black and white achievement. In *On the Equality of Educational Opportunity*, edited by F. Mosteller and D.P. Moynihan. New York: Random House.

———. 1992. Why is black educational achievement rising? *The Public Interest* 108: 65–80.

———. 1995. *Forced Justice: School Desegregation and the Law*. New York: Oxford UP.

———. 1999. Rebuttal Report, *Capacchione v. Charlotte-Mecklenburg Schs.*, 57 F.Supp. 2d 228 (1999) (1999 U.S. Dist. LEXIS 13990).

Campbell, Jay et al. 1997. *NAEP 1998 Trends in Academic Progress*. Washington, D.C.: National Center for Education Statistics.

Coleman, James, E.Q. Campbell, C.J. Hobson, J. McPartland, A.M. Mood, F.D. Weinfield, and R.L. York. 1966. *Equality of Educational Opportunity*. Washington, D.C.: U.S. Government Printing Office.

Cook, Thomas et al. 1984. *School Desegregation and Black Achievement*. Washington, D.C.: National Institute of Education, U.S. Department of Education.

Crain, Robert L., and Rita Mahard. 1978. Desegregation and black achievement, A review of the research. *Law and Contemporary Problems* 42: 17–58.

Dallas Independent School District. 1993. Motion for unitary status. *Tasby v. Woolery, General Superintendent, Dallas Independent School District*, Civil Action no. 3-4211-H, 869 F. Supp. 454 (1994) (1994 U.S. Dist. LEXIS 16583).

Goodman, Frank I. 1972. De facto school desegregation: A constitutional and empirical analysis. *California Law Review* 60: 275–437.

Grissmer, David, Ann Flanagan, and Stephanie Williamson. 1998. Why did the black–white gap narrow in the 1970s and 1980s? In *The Black–white Test Score Gap*, edited by C. Jencks and M. Phillips. Washington, D.C.: The Brookings Institution.

Jencks, Christoper et al. 1972. *Inequality*. New York: Basic Books.

Jenkins v. Missouri, U.S. 8th Cir. 1997.

Morantz, Allison. 1996. Desegregation at risk. In *Dismantling Desegregation: The Quiet Reversal of Brown v. Board of Education*, edited by Gary Orfield and Susan E. Eaton. New York: New Press.

Myrdal, Gunnar. 1944. *An American Dilemma: The Negro Problem and Modern Democracy*. New York: Harper and Row.

Smith, Marshall. 1972. The basic findings reconsidered. In *On the Equality of Educational Opportunity*, edited by F. Mosteller and D.P. Moynihan. New York: Random House.

Social Scientists. 1991. School desegregation: A social scientist statement. In NAACP et al. brief as amicus curiae in support of respondents. *Freeman v. Pitts*, U.S. Supreme Court on writ of cerciorari (U.S. 11th Cir. 21 June 1991) signed by 52 social scientists.

St. John, Nancy. 1975. *School Desegregation*. New York: Wiley and Sons.

Trent, William T. 1999. Expert Report, *Capacchione v. Charlotte-Mecklenburg Schs.*, 57 F. Supp. 2d 228 (1999) (1999 U.S. Dist. LEXIS 13990).

Walberg, Herbert J. 1984. Improving the productivity of America's schools. *Educational Leadership* 41(8): 19–27.

Wilkenson, J.H. III. 1978. *From Brown to Bakke.* New York: Oxford UP.

Yudof, Mark G. 1978. School desegregation: Legal realism, reasoned elaboration, and social science research in the Supreme Court. *Law and Contemporary Problems* 42: 57–109.

Chapter 7

Ability Grouping and Classroom Desegregation

⬡

Christine H. Rossell

LEGAL STATUS OF TRACKING AND ABILITY GROUPING AND CLASSROOM SEGREGATION

Compared to school racial-balance plans, court-ordered classroom racial balance is relatively uncontroversial. The big disruption in school districts is desegregating the schools; it is only *after* the schools have been desegregated that anyone notices the classrooms. For this reason, the issue of tracking and ability grouping is sometimes called a "second generation" desegregation problem along with race relations, achievement, discipline, and attitudes (Levin and Moise 1975). Although most classrooms appear to have been reasonably desegregated at the time of their school desegregation plan, there have been a number of districts where there was a noticeable problem that prompted complaints. But, in the few instances when the courts responded by ordering a remedy, there have not been any demonstrations or boycotts, although it is possible there was some additional white flight.

Classroom segregation, like school segregation, is a simple concept to understand. If all the whites learn in one set of classrooms and all the blacks learn in another, the classrooms are segregated. But if the segregation is not complete and there is an educational justification for the resulting racial imbalance—for example, that it is more efficient to teach children in classrooms that are homogeneous in ability and therefore they will learn more in such an environment—the issue becomes an educational one. This educational issue is called tracking, or ability grouping.

The term "tracking," defined as ability-grouping *between* classrooms, is typically used rather broadly to refer to all school ability-grouping practices involving curricular differentiation which produce classrooms that vary in the average ability of the students, even if the process is student choice. The more restricted definition of tracking—the practice of school administrators assigning students to classrooms based on their ability—fell out of favor with policymakers and intellectuals by the mid-1970s, largely because differences in the average achievement of the races and ethnic groups resulted in racial and ethnic segregation within schools (Goldberg, Passow, and Justman 1966; Findley and Bryan 1971; Esposito 1971, 1973; U.S. Commission on Civil Rights 1974; Rist 1970).

Nevertheless, some form of ability grouping, whether it is by student choice or administrative design, is apparently practiced everywhere in the United States. According to a 1994 U.S. Department of Education survey of U.S. high schools, only 1 percent of large high schools (those with grade 10–12 enrollment at or above 800), had undifferentiated courses with open access to enrollment. Argys, Rees, and Brewer's (1996) analysis of NELS public school data found only 11 percent of tenth grade math students and 15 percent of tenth grade English students were in heterogeneous classes.

Tracking and ability grouping may be controversial educational policy, but it is only a constitutional issue when it results in racial isolation within schools. In the first important case on this issue, *Hobsen v. Hansen* (269 F. Supp. 401 [1967]), the district court judge, Skelly Wright, found ability grouping in the District of Columbia public schools to be unconstitutional because black students were disproportionately in the lower tracks. The fact that the ability grouping was not intentionally racially motivated did not exonerate the school district.

On appeal, the circuit court refused to "plunge into a sea of . . . difficult issues of educational policy" such as the appropriate balance between the practical need to group students by ability, and the need to ensure equal educational opportunity to every student. The court made it clear that it was not the process itself that was unconstitutional, but the way in which it was practiced in the Washington D.C. public schools (*Smuck v. Hobson*, 408 F.2d [1969]).

In school districts under a court order to remedy de jure segregation, a significant segregative effect resulting from achievement grouping can only be justified by demonstrating that it is not a vestige of the dual school system. Many federal courts have held that it is.[1] One of the earliest of these decisions was *Singleton v. Anson County Board of Education* (1968). Here, the court stated:

Ability groupings or the so-called "track method" may have academic justification and may be an educational rather than a constitutional issue, but the track system or "ability grouping" is suspect when it first begins to flourish on the eve of or during a desegregation suit.[2]

On the other hand, six years later, a district court came to an apparently opposite conclusion in *Morales v. Shannon* (366 F.Supp. 813 [1973]; 516 F.2d 411 [1975]) when it concluded that an inference of discrimination could not be made from the overrepresentation of minorities in lower grouping levels. Two later court decisions in the 1970s, however, upheld and expanded the principle that tracking is to be avoided until the effects of discrimination have worn off. In *Reed et al. v. Rhodes* (455 F.Supp. 569 [1978]), the Cleveland school desegregation case, the district court was persuaded by testimony that the assignment of a previously segregated student to a low-achieving group resulted in a self-fulfilling prophecy of continuing low achievement. Although the court forbade ability grouping, it was only for a period sufficient to ensure that the underachievement of certain groups was not due to the educational inequities caused by prior segregation.

In the same year, a district court went even further in *United States v. Gadsden County School District* (359 F.2d 1369 [1976]; 572 F.2d 1049 [1978]) in reversing the burden of proof. In a district that was not unitary, the plaintiffs did not have to prove that ability grouping was a vestige of the dual school system. The burden was on the school district to prove it was not a vestige. The court ruled it had not done so and the school district was ordered to create a new system that did not result in racial imbalance.

In 1987, in *Montgomery v. Starkville* (665 F.Supp. 487 [1987]), a U.S. district court went around the burden-of-proof obstacle by declaring that, for all intents and purposes, the Starkville School District was unitary as of 1971, although it had never been declared so. Because it was "unitary," any classroom racial imbalance caused by ability grouping did not reflect the effects of past segregation or a contemporary segregative intent.

The courts have also considered tracking and ability grouping in the context of a formal unitary hearing and in most cases ruled in favor of the districts. In *Quarles v. Oxford* (868 F.2d 750 [1989]), the district court judge found the Oxford, Mississippi school district to be unitary despite allegations by the plaintiffs that their achievement-grouping practice was racially discriminatory. The appeals court upheld the district court and ruled that, since all classes were open to all students, student choice, not racial discrimination, explained why there were more white than black students enrolled in accelerated classes.

Evidence has also been presented in unitary hearings that classroom imbalance is not a result of racial discrimination, but of differences in achievement between the races. This occurred in 1993 in *Tasby v. Woolery, Dallas Independent School District* (Dallas Independent School District et al. 1993), in 1993 in *Diaz v. San Jose Unified School District* (Rossell 1993a, 1993b), in 1995 and 1996 in *Coalition to Save Our Children v. State Board of Education of the State of Delaware, the Board of Education of the Brandywine School District, the Christina School District, the Colonial School District, and the Red Clay School District and Delaware House of Representatives* (Rossell 1994), in 1998 in *Reed v. Rhodes* [Cleveland] (Rossell 1997), in 1998 in *Vaughns et al. v. Prince George's County et al.* (Peterkin, Rossell, Shoenberg, and Trent 1997), in 1999 and 2000 in *People Who Care v. Rockford* (Rossell 1999; 2000c), and in 2000 in *Hoots et al. v. Commonwealth of Pennsylvania et al.* (Rossell 2000a, 2000d). Dallas was declared unitary on this issue in a three-year phaseout (*Tasby v. Woolery*, 869 F.Supp. 454 [1994]) and *Diaz* was settled by a consent decree.[3] The New Castle County, Cleveland, and Prince George's County cases were decided in favor of the defendant school districts.[4] The *Hoots* decision was a partial unitary decision. The court declared the district unitary in all respects except the curriculum, because the math curriculum had not been fully detracked (*Hoots et al. v. Commonwealth of Pennsylvania et al.*, Civil Action No. 71-538, U.S. District Court for the Western District of Pennsylvania, January 16, 1991). The Rockford district court declared the district not unitary on any factor but was overturned by the seventh Circuit Appeals Court in a stinging rebuke (*People Who Care v. Rockford Board of Education*, April 2001).

The *Capacchione v. Charlotte-Mecklenburg* unitary decision[5] also rejected the plaintiffs claim that tracking and ability grouping were racially discriminatory. The court cited Judge Posner's 1997 seventh Circuit decision, probably the strongest defense of tracking in a legal decision:

Tracking is a controversial educational policy, although just grouping students by age, something no one questions, is a form of "tracking." Lawyers and judges are not competent to resolve the controversy. The conceit that they are belongs to a myth of the legal profession's omnicompetence that was exploded long ago. To abolish tracking is to say to bright kids, whether white or black, that they have to go at a slower pace than they're capable of; it is to say to the parents of the brighter kids that their children don't really belong in the public school system; and it is to say to the slower kids, of whatever race, that they may have difficulty keeping up, because the brighter kids may force [**26] the pace of the class. "The vast majority of public school students in the United States are tested, ranked, and segregated into separate ability groups and classes based on standardized test performance." Note, "Teaching Inequality: The Problem of Public School Tracking," 102 Harv. L. Rev. 1318 (1989) (footnote omitted). This may be deplorable, as the author of the student note (who at the time of writing the note was neither a public school student nor, it is a safe guess, a parent) believes, id. at 1340-41; but as the consensus of the nation's educational authorities, it deserves some consideration by a federal court.[6]

THE EDUCATIONAL EFFECTS OF
TRACKING AND ABILITY GROUPING

As with the demand for racial balance in the schools, the demand for racial balance in the classrooms is motivated by a harm and benefit thesis. Racially imbalanced classrooms, it is alleged, are bad because they harm black children educationally. Black children are disproportionately low achieving, so a predominantly black classroom is a predominantly low-achieving class. Teachers teach at a slower pace in low-achieving classes and thus further lower the achievement of their low-achieving (black) students. Finally, the thesis argues that remedying this harm by assigning children to academically heterogeneous classes will benefit the low achievers without harming the high achievers.

Despite the low esteem with which tracking and ability grouping is held by intellectuals and policymakers, the research does not show that it harms low-achieving children. In 1975, Levin and Moise summarized the research as being "so contradictory that it cannot be said with any sense of conviction whether ability grouping does or does not lead to increased achievement and improved self-esteem of children" (Levin and Moise 1975: 121).[7] A meta-analysis by Robert Slavin (1990b) found ability grouping at the secondary level to have no effect on academic achievement, regardless of the academic ability of the student. He explains:

[It] is surprising to find that assignment to the low-ability group is not detrimental to students' learning. A substantial literature has indicated the low quality of instruction in low groups (e.g., Evertson, 1982; Gamoran, 1989; Oakes, 1985) and a related body of research has documented the negative impact of ability grouping on the motivations and self-esteem of students assigned to low groups . . . Studies contrasting teaching behaviors in high- and low-track classes usually find that the low tracks have a slower pace of instruction and lower time-on-task (e.g., Evertson, 1982; Oakes, 1982). Yet the meaning and impact of these differences are not self-evident. It may be that a slower pace of instruction is appropriate with lower-achieving students, or that pace is relatively unimportant because a higher pace with lower mastery is essentially equivalent to a lower pace with higher mastery . . . In this regard, it is important to note that Evertson, Sanford, and Emmer (1981) found time-on-task to be lower in extremely heterogeneous junior high school classes than in less heterogeneous ones because teachers had difficulty managing the more heterogeneous classes. (Slavin 1990a: 490–91)

In a subsequent response to a critic, Slavin (1990a) points out that the two lines of research cited to support the idea that ability grouping has detrimental effects for low-achievers are descriptive and cannot demonstrate cause and effect. He notes that:

[M]any studies find that there is less content covered in low-track classes. But is this by its nature an indication of low quality? Might it be that low-track classes need a slower pace of instruction? The whole idea of ability grouping is to provide students with a level and pace of instruction appropriate to their different needs. Similarly, time-on-task is found to be lower in low-track classes. Might it be that low-achieving students are more likely to be off-task no matter where they are? (Slavin 1990a: 505)

But there is one group, the gifted, that consistently benefits from ability grouping. Slavin excluded grouping for gifted students from his synthesis on the basis that it was too unique. Kulik and Kulik, however, have included this in their meta-analyses of ability grouping (1982; 1991; 1992). They found that, overall, grouping for instruction has only a small positive effect on the achievement of average and above-average students, and no negative effect on low achievers.

Grouping did, however, have a consistently positive effect on the achievement of high ability or "gifted" students when they were put into special classes with enriched or accelerated instruction in their secondary school subjects. Ekstrom (1961) and others have also noted the effectiveness of honors classes in their reviews of grouping research. High-ability students apparently benefited from the stimulation provided by other high-aptitude students and from the special curricula that grouping made possible.

In addition, students in grouped classes

clearly developed more positive attitudes toward the subjects they were studying. Grouping practices, however, did not appear to influence students' attitudes toward themselves and their schools. (Kulik and Kulik 1982: 425)

In 1991, Kulik and Kulik summarized the research on ability grouping as showing that "academic benefits are striking and large in programs of acceleration for gifted students" (Kulik and Kulik 1991: 191).

Several other studies have found that high-ability classes benefit high-achieving students (Argys, Rees, and Brewer 1996; Hoffer 1992; Gamoran 1987; Gamoran and Mare 1989; Kerkhoff 1986; Vanfossen, Jones, and Spade 1987). One of these studies, however, found ability grouping to also have a small negative effect on low achievers. Argys, Rees, and Brewer concluded from their analysis of NELS data:

These estimates suggest that detracking schools would create winners and losers. Students currently in below-average classes would benefit, while students in the average and above average classes would be harmed. On net, these estimates suggest that detracking all students currently enrolled in homogeneous classes would produce approximately a 2 percent drop in the average mathematics test score. (Argys, Rees, and Brewer 1996: 637)

In short, in their national data set, the high-achieving students were harmed more than the low-achieving students benefited from heterogeneous grouping. But the overwhelming body of research on classroom desegregation, like the research on school desegregation, finds grouping practices have no effect on the achievement of the lowest-achieving students. Unlike *school* desegregation, however, there is a considerable and consistent body of evidence showing harm to the highest-achieving students from eliminating high-ability classes. In short, detracking does have losers— the highest-ability students.

HOW MUCH CLASSROOM SEGREGATION EXISTS?

Very little analysis has been conducted of the extent of classroom segregation in the United States. Unlike schools, classroom racial-composition data is not collected every year by the federal government. Moreover, the data is quite bulky in size—there being many more classrooms than there are schools—so the issue is rarely analyzed or even summarized in desegregation reports to the court. Indeed, this may be why there is not a lot of litigation on this issue, in comparison to the amount of litigation on schools.

Morgan and McPartland (1981) conducted one of the few studies of classroom racial balance using Office for Civil Rights (OCR) data collected in 1976. In that year, 3,617 school districts across the nation were directed to submit classroom enrollment by race from a sample of eighteen classrooms in each school in their district. Morgan and McPartland used the relative exposure index to measure racial balance because they believed its properties were better than the index of dissimilarity.[8] The formula is

$$Rbw = (pw - Sbw)/pw$$

where pw is the proportion white in the school and Sbw is the interracial exposure index for the classrooms in that school.[9]

Appendix 7.1 displays their analysis by region and for the United States as a whole. The level of racial imbalance for classrooms across the United States (far right column) was quite low in 1976: .06 for elementary schools, .07 for middle schools, and .11 for high schools. This was also the case for *schools* in the United States which at that time had a relative exposure index of .08. In other words, both schools and classrooms were quite racially balanced in 1976. The greatest classroom imbalance was found at the secondary level, and among regions, the greatest imbalance was in the South.

One reason the relative exposure index is so low for both schools and classrooms is that the average school was 66 percent white in 1976. The relative exposure index gives credit for having a higher percentage white in the average black child's school, all other things being equal.

Appendix 7.2 shows the average relative interracial exposure index for classrooms in the United States (first line), a sample of fifty-seven school districts from a national sample of 119 school districts that I was studying in the 1980s (second and third lines) and school districts studied in connection with unitary hearings (lines 4–12). The districts selected from the Rossell sample are those that were under a court order to desegregate their schools. The classroom enrollment data for the court-ordered districts come from the OCR survey in 1980 for elementary, middle, and high schools, and in 1988 for elementary schools only. The court-ordered sample has much more classroom imbalance than the United States did in 1976 for two reasons. First, the data in the court-ordered sample is four to twelve years later than the U.S. sample (Morgan and McPartland data) and classroom imbalance has been increasing over time as the percentage white has been declining. Second, the Rossell court-ordered sample is only 37 percent white compared to 66 percent white for the national sample. It is more difficult to racially balance classrooms and schools when a school district is predominantly minority than when it is predominantly white.

There are eight additional districts in appendix 7.2 that either attained or sought unitary status and had classroom racial balance as a requirement of their court order (Brandywine, Christina, Colonial, and Red Clay, Delaware; Rockford, Illinois; and Woodland Hills, Pennsylvania), or an issue raised by the plaintiffs at the time of their unitary motion (Dallas, Texas,[10] San Jose, California in 1992–93, and Prince George's County, Maryland). This is probably not the universe of districts seeking unitary status on classroom racial imbalance or curriculum, but they are the most important cases of the 1990s. In 1992–93, San Jose began the process of attaining unitary status, but ultimately settled with the plaintiffs.[11] In 1998–99, Brandywine, Christina, Colonial, and Red Clay, Delaware sought unitary status together and received it in all areas including classroom racial balance.[12] Prince George's County, Maryland sought unitary status in 1996–97, but, at their request, were given a phase-out plan for unitary status in 2002 if there were no outstanding lawsuits against them. As of June 25, 2002, they are unitary. Rockford, Illinois sought unitary status in 1999–2000, requesting a three-year phase-out, which was granted by the seventh Circuit overturning the district court. Woodland Hills, Pennsylvania sought unitary status in 1999–2000, also requesting a three-year phase-out, and was pronounced unitary in all areas except the curriculum.

Appendices 7.1 and 7.2 show that in general, there is not much classroom imbalance[13] in the United States or in the school districts seeking unitary status. The Rossell court-ordered districts were the most imbalanced, but even they were only between .26 and .30 on a scale that could go to 1.00. Thus, the civil rights movement seems to have been successful not only in achieving school racial balance, but in achieving classroom racial balance as well.

Appendix 7.2 shows differences between school levels in racial imbalance. In 1976, there were five points more imbalance in the United States at the high school level than the elementary school level and one point more imbalance at the middle school level than the elementary school level. Across all the districts shown, there was an average seven points more high school imbalance and two points more middle school imbalance than at the elementary level.

Appendix 7.3 shows the percentage of students in classrooms within ± 20 percentage points of the school's racial composition. This measure was not calculated for the national sample, so only the school districts that sought unitary status are displayed. Between 89 and 100 percent of the elementary students in these districts are in classrooms within ± 20 percentage points of the school's racial composition. Between 71 and 95 percent of the middle school students are in racially balanced classrooms. Brandywine, Delaware had the least middle school balance with 71 percent of its classrooms balanced at ± 20 percentage points. Nevertheless, this was deemed sufficient for unitary status. Finally, between 64 and 87 percent of the high school students are in racially balanced classrooms. Red Clay, Delaware and Rockford, Illinois have the least high school balance with 64 and 65 percent in racially balanced classrooms—a level deemed sufficient for unitary status.

As with the other racial balance measures, there are fewer balanced classrooms at the high school or middle school level than at the elementary school level. The average is 18 percentage points fewer racially balanced classrooms at the high school level than the elementary level. The greatest high school difference is in Rockford, which was under a 1996 classroom racial balance order.

DETRACKING IN SAN JOSE, WOODLAND HILLS, AND ROCKFORD

San Jose, Woodland Hills, and Rockford are the three most recent school districts that have agreed to, or been ordered to, eliminate ability grouping in order to racially balance classrooms. San Jose detracked in 1994 as part of a settlement agreement, the Rockford school district was ordered in 1996 to produce racial balance in its classrooms, and the Woodland Hills school district was ordered in 1991 to detrack its secondary curriculum. Both Rockford and Woodland Hills sought unitary status after implementing their detracking orders and so their record on classroom racial balance and detracking became evidence in the trial.

San Jose Unified School District[14]

San Jose, like virtually all school districts in the United States, had secondary courses differentiated by levels of difficulty, even after a court-ordered school desegregation plan was implemented in the Fall of 1986 that racially balanced all the schools (*Diaz v. San Jose Unified School District*, 633 F.Supp. 808 [1985]). When they applied for unitary status in 1993, racial imbalance at the secondary level was raised by the plaintiffs as a reason they were not unitary. After lengthy deliberations, the district entered into a consent decree[15] in 1994 that required eliminating ability levels in core subjects in middle school and the ninth grade of high school, and eliminating ability criteria as prerequisites for enrollment in any secondary level advanced courses. The consent decree also required that all class-rooms be ethnically balanced.[16] The gifted program was exempt from these requirements.

Middle Schools. Before the consent decree, the middle schools had a district-wide course catalog that resembled the high school course catalog. Each grade was divided into subjects and each subject area into grade level and accelerated courses. Not surprisingly, given their differences in socioeconomic status and academic achievement, Hispanic and black students were overrepresented in the grade-level courses and underrepresented in the accelerated courses.

There have been no accelerated courses since 1994 and the middle school course catalog has disappeared. Where once there were two ability levels in every subject, there is now only one heterogeneous course.

It is possible, however, to take off-grade courses in math. That is, a sixth grader could take seventh grade math and vice versa. In addition to sixth, seventh, and eighth grade math, two high school courses, algebra and geometry (replaced in 1997–98 with Integrated Math I and II), are offered in middle school. Thus, although accelerated math courses have been eliminated, accelerated math students still exist.

The middle schools were also required to achieve the following racial balance within three years:

- no less than 80 percent of its regular educational classrooms within ± 15 percentage points of that school's Hispanic *and* white percentage for regular education classes at the grade level of the class;
- 100 percent of its regular education classrooms within 25 percentage points of the school's percent Hispanic for the grade level of the class;
- Mixed-ability composition in all of its core curriculum classes.[17]

San Jose was able to accomplish these goals in the first year of the consent decree. Across all seven middle schools, in every year since the 1994–95 consent decree, at least 80 percent—and in most schools at least 90 percent—of the regular classrooms were desegregated by the ±15 percentage-point standard. Moreover, without exception, the classes that did not meet the ± 15 standard were desegregated to within ± 25 percentage points as the consent decree required. Thus, 100 percent of the middle schools were in compliance with the desegregation standards of the consent decree from 1994–95 to the present.

This represents considerable improvement over the period before the consent decree. In 1992–93, an average of 55 percent of the classrooms were within ± 15 percentage points. Some schools had as few as 41 percent of their schools within that range and no school was above 70 percent. Nor were the remaining schools within 25 percentage points. The average adherence to that standard was 82 percent and the highest percentage was 94 percent.

High Schools

The consent decree's high school detracking requirements are as complex as the middle school's, but they focus primarily on the ninth grade core curriculum. As with middle schools, all course differentiation by ability levels was eliminated in the ninth grade, although students can still take off-grade math courses.

In 1992–93, two years before the consent decree, every core subject had an accelerated or honors level course at each grade for a total of sixteen accelerated or honors courses in the high school core curriculum. In 1994-95, all accelerated courses were eliminated from ninth grade English, science, and social studies.

The consent decree also affected grades 10–12, albeit to a lesser degree. It required that:

By the 1994–95 school year, the District will eliminate all high school prerequisites, except for bona fide course-sequencing prerequisites. No student will be denied enrollment in a high school course or activity, except for bona fide course-sequencing prerequisites.

The year before the consent decree, 69 percent of the English courses, 63 percent of the social science courses, 79 percent of the science courses, and 18 percent of the math courses required some measure of a student's ability— either a teacher's recommendation, a specific letter grade in the prior course, or a placement test—as a condition for enrollment. After the consent decree, none of the high school core courses required these criteria. Indeed, the high school English and social science courses do not even require a lower sequence of the same course. The consent decree thus resulted in a change in the entire high school curriculum, not just the ninth grade.

The racial balance requirements, however, only affected the ninth grade. They required that by the 1995–96 school year, the district's ninth grade core instructional courses will be taught in desegregated and mixed-ability classes defined as:

- for classrooms with more than 20 students:
  within plus or minus 15 percentage points of that school's Hispanic and white enrollment for regular education classes at the grade level of the class;
- for classrooms with 20 or fewer students:
  within plus or minus 25 percentage points of that school's Hispanic and white enrollment for regular education classes at the grade level of the class.

As with the middle schools, 100 percent of the ninth grade core courses in the six high schools met the consent decree racial balance criteria in the first year, two years before they were required to do so, and they have maintained that. This represents considerable improvement from before the consent decree, when only 50 percent of the ninth grade core classes were within ±15 percentage points ranging from 35 percent at two schools to almost 70 percent at one.

San Jose was obligated to design a plan to recruit Hispanic and other minority students to participate in advanced and elective courses. Beginning with the 1995–96 school year, if the percentage of Hispanic students in any core instructional or advanced course in any grade in a high school differed by more than 20 percentage points from the percentage of Hispanic students in the pool of students at that school who had met any "bona fide course sequencing prerequisites" for that specific course, the school would have to develop a plan to bring Hispanic enrollment in the course to within the 20-point band during the following school year. For example:

[I]f Hispanics at a school comprise one-half (50%) of the students at that school who have completed the prerequisites for Algebra 3, then the school's plan will provide measures so that the enrollment in the course will be at least thirty percent (30%) Hispanic by the following school year.[18]

Unfortunately, there is no pre-consent decree data on students who completed such prerequisites in order to calculate the extent of improvement. According to the Compliance Monitor's annual reports, however, the district has fully complied with this requirement, despite the fact that no one really knows the research basis for any of these numbers. District staff invest an enormous amount of time producing these outcomes and reporting them in annual desegregation compliance reports, but they are never asked to prove that meeting these goals has any effect on anything else, such as race relations, achievement, or self-esteem. Nor did the plaintiffs produce such evidence when they first demanded them. As with desegregation plans, the numbers seem to acquire an importance of their own that transcends any rationale for imposing them in the first place.

The effect of these requirements on racial imbalance in grades 10–12 can be seen in appendix 7.4. There is an average ten-point decline in racial imbalance in grades 10–12 after the consent decree. In some schools, the decline is almost twenty points. But racial imbalance did not go to zero.

The analysis shown in figure 7.1 assesses whether detracking in grade nine, and eliminating course prerequisites in all grades, has achieved its goal of improving Hispanic representation in advanced courses. Hispanic representation in the advanced courses is calculated as the ratio of the advanced-course percentage Hispanic to the high school percentage Hispanic.[19] If

Figure 7.1

Ratio of High School Advanced Course percent Hispanic to High School percent Hispanic Pre- and Post-Consent Decree, San Jose

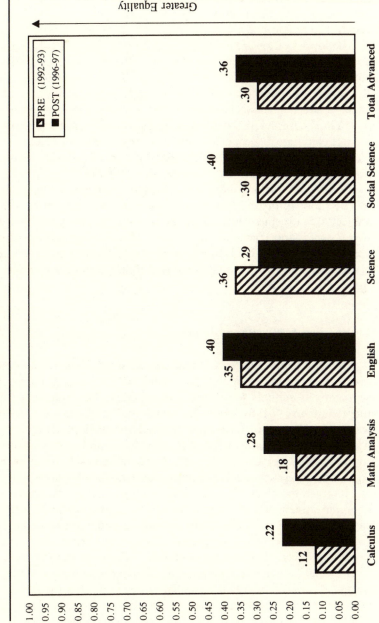

Hispanics were enrolled in advanced courses at the same rate as their percentage in the high school student body, the ratio would be 1.0. Instead, Hispanics are underrepresented in advanced classes because the Hispanic percentage in advanced courses is about 22 to 40 percent of their percentage in the student body.

The lowest ratios are in the advanced math classes—calculus and math analysis—where the opportunity to take off-grade courses produces some ethnic imbalance in the last math courses offered in a sequence at a school. But, there is still considerable Hispanic underrepresentation in English, science, or social science classes where no such opportunity exists in grades 6–9. Thus, completely detracking the middle schools and the ninth grade did not eliminate disproportionality in advanced courses in any subject area. This is not surprising, given the large differences in socioeconomic status between Hispanics and whites in the school district.

Although detracking did not eliminate disproportionality, it has reduced it. The ratios improved about ten points after the consent decree in every subject area except science, although socioeconomic status differences between whites and Hispanics increased.[20] Thus, the most likely cause of this small improvement in advanced course enrollment in eleventh and twelfth grade is the ninth grade detracking and elimination of course prerequisites that occurred in 1994.

Woodland Hills, Pennsylvania

The Woodland Hills School District is a small, 52-percent white, school district just outside of Pittsburgh, which has been under a court order to desegregate its schools for almost twenty years. The first plan was implemented in the 1981–82 school year when the Woodland Hills school district was created by a court order that merged one predominantly black district with four predominantly white districts. The secondary schools were desegregated in the first year in 1981–82; the elementary schools in the next year. At that time, the schools were almost perfectly racially balanced.

However, the plaintiffs continued to complain about vestiges of discrimination in student activities, guidance and discipline, curriculum, and staff assignments. A 1988 consent decree was signed by the district and the plaintiffs (but not the state, who was also a defendant) to remedy these vestiges. The parties, however, could not agree on how it was to be implemented.

A special master was appointed to hold hearings on these plans, and a report was issued. The 1991 Remedial Order[21] adopted the special master's recommendations with only a few modifications. The special master's report (Fatla 1990) determined that the district had eliminated tracking at the elementary level entirely, and in the basic courses at the secondary level, but not in the advanced courses. According to the master, despite improvements in standard courses, significant racial disparities remain in advanced-level courses. In part these disparities are a product of the recently dismantled tracking system. Many minority students lack the skills and knowledge required to succeed in advanced level courses, not because of an innate lack of ability, but because they have been tracked in low or average courses for many years, receiving limited instruction in limited skills, and therefore have been effectively denied the opportunity to compete for higher placement. This is particularly evident in science and mathematics. (Fatla 1990: 33)

Thus, the master blamed the prior tracking system for the underrepresentation of minorities in advanced classes. He singled out the math sequence because students could decide to take pre-algebra at any point between the seventh and tenth grade. A student who took it in seventh or eighth grade could progress through algebra, geometry, and calculus by twelfth grade. A student who waited until tenth grade would not be able to complete this sequence.

The special master's position, which was accepted by the court in its 1991 remedial order, was that racial disparities in course enrollment were a vestige of the dual school system:

This stratification of students is found throughout the curriculum in varying degrees. Minority students tend to be concentrated in standard courses while being virtually absent from advanced level courses. This stratification is the most critical disparity in the system because it is a direct measure of the educational deprivation suffered by minority students as a direct result of the formerly segregated system. It is the most pernicious of evils and likely the most difficult to eradicate. (Fatla 1990: 36)

Nevertheless, the special master's report and the court's 1991 remedial order did not specify any particular racial balance or specific curriculum changes, as was the case in San Jose. The court did adopt the plaintiffs' proposal to hire additional staff to redesign the curriculum and testing, presumably to eliminate the elements of the curriculum that were thought to have produced unequal achievement. After 1991, the only differentiation within courses that remained was the AP–non-AP course distinction in the eleventh and twelfth grade.

The level of racial imbalance produced by the requirement to detrack in Woodland Hills is shown in appendices 7.2 and 7.3. The relative exposure index for Woodland Hills is the lowest of all the districts at the elementary and high school level, and one of the lowest at the middle school level. On the plus or minus 20 percentage-point standard, Woodland Hills has 100 percent of its elementary classrooms, 85 percent of its middle schools, and 87 percent of its high schools racially balanced.

The problem identified by the master in his 1980 report, that minority students tend to be concentrated in standard courses and absent from advanced level courses (Fatla 1990: 36), still existed ten years later at the time of the unitary hearing. Students were allowed to choose which math courses they took in middle school and when they took them. In high school, they were allowed choice in many more courses. At every secondary grade, whites were more likely than blacks to choose the advanced courses.

Junior High Schools

Junior High Schools in Woodland Hills include grades 7–9. Although all junior high school students take Science 7 and Science 8, there is a choice in ninth grade of taking Physical Science or Biology. At one of the junior high schools this resulted in unequal racial percentages in these two courses.

As in most school districts, the poverty rate for black students is two to three times the rate for white students.[22] As David Armor demonstrated in the same court case (Armor 2000) and as other research has found (e.g., Coleman et al. 1966; Jaynes and Williams 1989; and Armor 1995), differences in socioeconomic status are likely to produce differences in achievement.

Figure 7.2 shows the average math achievement of black and white students in each math course offered at the junior high schools. Although the achievement of black students is lower than white students and there is considerable heterogeneity in these courses, the average math test score of all students increases with each sequential step in the math curriculum.

I assess the degree to which there is racial discrimination in the advanced math and science courses by controlling for these achievement differences. Although the existence of achievement differences between the races is a compliance issue in and of itself in these unitary hearings, and the plaintiffs allege that achievement differences are a vestige of the dual school system, its use as a control variable in the classroom-segregation portions of the unitary cases is not challenged by the plaintiffs and is accepted by the courts. Indeed, the plaintiffs' experts typically also use ability as a control variable in their assessment of the cause of racial disproportionality in course enrollment. But even in the districts where the plaintiffs' experts did not do this—for example, Dallas in 1994 and Prince George's County, Maryland in 1998—controlling for achievement was apparently accepted by the courts.[23]

One way to control for achievement is to compare the current percentage black of the advanced courses to the percentage black of the advanced courses if only the highest scoring students enrolled. This kind of analysis was conducted in Dallas, San Jose, Brandywine, Christina, Colonial, Red Clay, Prince George's County, Rockford, and Woodland Hills. A number of different definitions of high scoring are used, including at or above the fiftieth percentile.

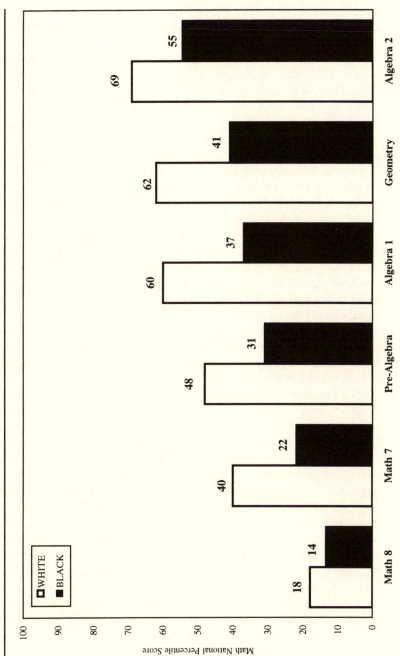

Figure 7.2

Average Achievement Scores of White and Black Students in Junior High Math Courses, Woodland Hills School District, 1999–2000

Despite enormous racial differences in achievement in Woodland Hills, there were no imbalanced courses in the seventh grade and only one imbalanced course in eighth grade (Algebra I) at East Junior High School. If that course had admitted only average and above-average students (50–100th percentile), it would have been 7 percent black. Without ability criteria, the most advanced math course in the eighth grade was 24 percent black. Thus, there were more eighth grade black students enrolled in Algebra I than would be predicted from the pool of average and above-average black students.

The analysis shown in figure 7.3 for West Junior High School shows a similar outcome. There is a higher percentage black in advanced courses— biology (27%), geometry (29%), and algebra (16%)—than would occur if only the highest scoring students enrolled in, or if the highest scoring students were simply assigned, to these courses, whether the high-scoring population includes the top 10 percent or the top 50 percent.

Figure 7.4 shows the same comparison for Biology, Geometry and Algebra 2 at East Junior High School. This shows a higher percentage black than would occur if only the highest scoring ninth graders enrolled, regardless of how high scoring is defined. Indeed, no black students would be enrolled if high scoring is defined as 70–100; even if it is defined as 50–100, only 29 percent would be enrolled.

Another way to analyze this data is to look at the percentage of black students and percentage of white students who are in each math class for their grade, controlling for their achievement. Dr. Jan de Leeuw compared the percentage of black students and white students in each achievement category in Woodland Hills who were enrolled in each of the math courses offered for that grade.

Appendix 7.5 is a reanalysis of data presented by de Leeuw in his report on Woodland Hills of three seventh grade math courses: Math 7 (the least advanced), Pre-Algebra, and Algebra 1 (the most advanced). The highest achievement category is 10, which encompasses 90–100 NCEs. In that category, 66.7 percent of the black students are enrolled in Pre-Algebra and 33.3 percent are enrolled in Algebra 1, the more difficult course. By contrast, 31.8 percent of the white students in that category are enrolled in Pre-Algebra and 68.2 percent are enrolled in Algebra 1. Thus, a much higher percentage of white students in that achievement category are enrolled in the highest level math course for that grade. However, there are only three black students in this achievement category.

The point of the analysis in appendix 7.5 is to reveal how few students would have to be moved to produce parity in the percentages. In the highest achievement category, moving just one seventh grade black student from Pre-Algebra to Algebra would produce percentages in each course that are the same as the white percentages in that achievement category. In the next highest achievement group, 80–90, there is a higher percentage of

Figure 7.3

Percent Black of 9th Graders in Biology, Geometry, and Algebra 2 and if Restricted to the Highest Scoring Students, West Junior High, Woodland Hills, 1999–2000

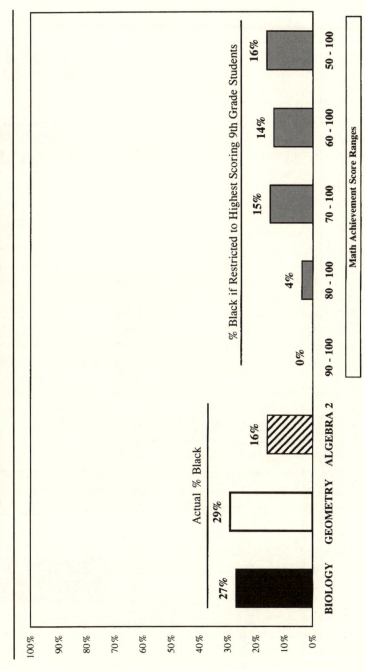

% Black if Restricted to the Highest Scoring 9th Grade Students

Math Achievement Score Ranges

Figure 7.4
Percent Black of 9th Graders in Biology, Geometry, and Algebra 2 and if Restricted to the Highest Scoring Students, East Junior High School, Woodland Hills, 1999–2000

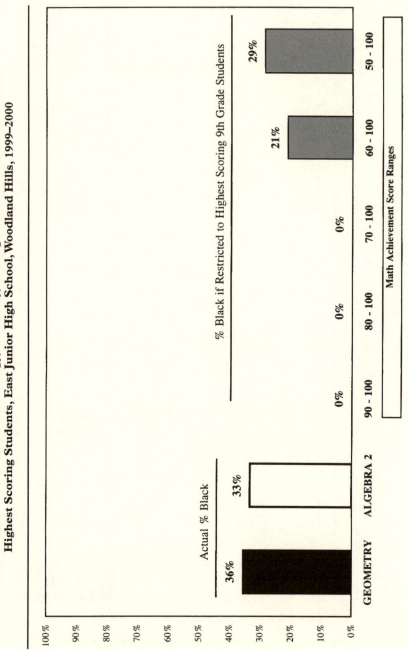

black students than white students enrolled in Algebra 1, so black students would need to be taken out of the highest level math course in order to produce equal percentages. Across all categories of achievement (shown on the far right of appendix 7.5), equal percentages can be achieved by simply moving four black students out of Math 7 and into Algebra 1.

Among the eighth grade math courses shown in appendix 7.6, de Leeuw's own data, converted to numbers, shows that across all achievement categories, black students are underrepresented in Math 8, the lower level course, and overrepresented in Pre-Algebra and Algebra 1, the higher level courses. To achieve percentages equal to whites, thirty black students would have to be taken out of the higher level math courses—Pre-Algebra and Algebra 1—and put into the lower level math class. Only one more black student would have to be enrolled in Geometry to produce parity with whites. Thus, de Leeuw's data shows that when achievement is controlled for, eighth grade black students are favored in Math 8, pre-Algebra and Algebra I and equally represented in Geometry.

Woodland Hills High School

The percentage of black high school students who are poor is four times that of whites[24] and they have lower achievement. Although the high school courses vary between them in level of difficulty, the only differentiation within courses is the advanced placement (AP)–non-AP distinction in the following core subject areas: English, History, Biology, Chemistry, Calculus, Environmental Science, Physics, and Computer Science. Students who take AP courses get college credit if they attain the necessary score on the AP exam. In addition, their grade is weighted to reflect the greater difficulty of the course. The high school also gives weighted grades for about a dozen other courses.

As shown in figure 7.5, although whites have higher achievement than blacks, students of each race who enroll in weighted courses have substantially higher achievement than the students of the same race who do not. Figure 7.6 controls for this by comparing the current percentage black of the total weighted courses, and the AP courses alone, to the percentage black if only the highest scoring eleventh and twelfth grade students enrolled or were assigned. As shown, there is currently a higher percentage black in all weighted courses and in the AP courses alone than there would be if only the highest scoring students were enrolled, even if high scoring is simply anyone above the fiftieth percentile.

The Woodland Hills Unitary Decision

The district was found unitary in all respects except the curriculum, based on the judgment that the math curriculum had not been fully detracked. The

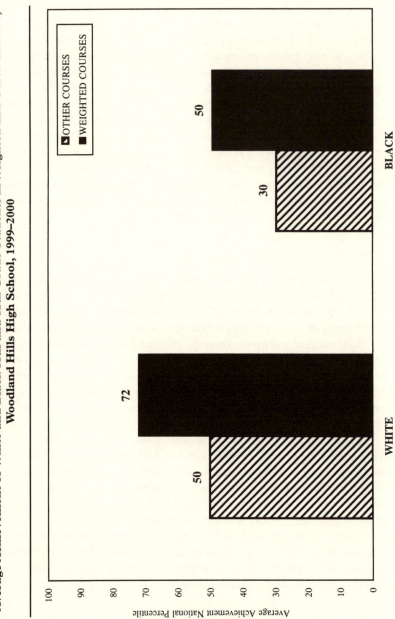

Figure 7.5

Average Achievement of White and Black 11th and 12th Grade Students in Weighted and Other Courses, Woodland Hills High School, 1999–2000

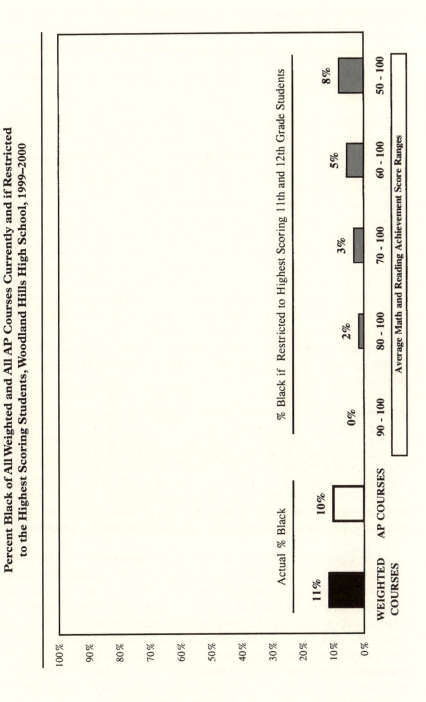

Figure 7.6
Percent Black of All Weighted and All AP Courses Currently and if Restricted
to the Highest Scoring Students, Woodland Hills High School, 1999–2000

judge who ruled on unitary status is the judge who ordered detracking in 1991, and he has apparently not changed his position since then:

"Tracking" is the process of assigning students to classes based on their perceived ability. Most academicians now agree that it is better to mix rather than assign students in this manner.[25]

Judge Cohill did not conclude, however, that the higher percentage white in the AP and weighted courses was problematic, although there is less student choice in AP course enrollment than in math courses. Nor had the plaintiffs ignored the AP courses—they alleged that the AP courses, like the math courses, were a vestige of the old discriminatory tracking system.

Perhaps a major problem with the math curriculum was that the superintendent had admitted on cross-examination that it would not be fully detracked until PUMP Algebra and a cognitive tutors program were in place the following year. PUMP Algebra is a computer-assisted instructional program that allows students of different math abilities and interests to be instructed in the same classroom because the computer delivers individualized instruction. Students cannot progress until they have mastered the material in each section. Thus, this program allows for heterogeneous classrooms because there is little or no whole-class instruction.

Citing the superintendent's testimony,[26] the judge concluded that the district would be unitary when the superintendent's program had been implemented:

The District shall complete detracking in the mathematics curriculum by eliminating lower-level courses and providing a single, detracked math curriculum for all the secondary level. Implementation of the District's present plans, which were the subject of much testimony at the hearing and which have been detailed elsewhere in this Opinion, would satisfy our order to provide a single, detracked curriculum . . . We do not intend to micromanage the District's curriculum, which is properly the function of the schools and the school board. However, these changes were proposed by the District, and would meet our requirements to detrack the curriculum. The other curricula have been successfully revised and no longer require the Court's attention.[27]

Judge Cohill also stated that in reaching his conclusion he was nevertheless "persuaded more by the defendants' evidence than by the plaintiffs' witnesses," and he did "not adopt the plaintiffs' opinions on this subject."[28] It is inevitable, however, that at the end of PUMP Algebra, there will be some students ahead of others. If the history of San Jose's experiment is any indication, forcing students into the same course, even if taught individually by a computer, will only improve minority representation in the later advanced courses; it will not equalize it. Although the Court seems willing to find the district unitary on classrooms simply because they will have implemented the superintendent's program, the plaintiffs may object when the program doesn't produce equality.

Rockford, Illinois

Unlike San Jose and Woodland Hills, Rockford was only under a court order to racially balance its classes. The district did not have to eliminate course ability levels if it could balance its classrooms without doing so.

The Comprehensive Remedial Order of 1996, as modified by the Seventh Circuit and subsequent federal district orders, established the following criteria:

SCHOOL LEVEL	CLASSROOM STANDARD	COMPLIANCE POOL
Elementary School	All classes within ± 12 % points of compliance pool racial composition[29]	% of minority students at each K-5 (K-8 for magnets) grade level in each building
Middle School	Core courses within ± 12% points of compliance pool racial composition	% of minority students enrolled in each "core course" at each building
High School	Core courses within ± 12% points of compliance pool racial composition	% of minority students enrolled in each "core course" at each building

Electives were excluded from the court order, although high school honors courses were not, despite the fact that enrollment in them is by student choice. At the middle-school level, the core courses are the required seventh and eighth grade English, social studies, math, and science courses, which are about half of the courses offered. At the high school level, the core courses are English, government, U.S. history, economics, biology and chemistry, Algebra 1, Algebra 2, and geometry, which are about a quarter of the courses offered. They are, of course, the most important courses, and presumably attaining racial balance in these courses will have a reciprocal effect on the other courses.

The district also has a gifted program, with separate courses and classrooms at every school level, that is exempted from the racial-balance criteria. The middle-school curriculum had no course differentiation except for the gifted program.

The extent of classroom imbalance in Rockford is shown in appendix 7.2. The relative exposure index includes all courses, not just the core courses. At all three school levels, Rockford had a level of racial imbalance similar to the other districts that applied for unitary status.

Appendix 7.3 shows the percentage of classrooms imbalanced at ± 20 percentage points. Using this standard, Rockford did better than the other districts at the elementary and middle-school level, but worse at the high-school level. Indeed, Rockford had the same level of imbalance as Red Clay—less than two-thirds of its classrooms were balanced. Nevertheless, that level was apparently sufficient for unitary status for Red Clay at the district court level as well as the appellate court level.

Figure 7.7 shows an analysis of the gifted program in Rockford across all school levels. As is typical of gifted and talented programs in districts under court order, there was no absolute cutoff used to classify a student as gifted nor was one used to assign students to the program. Figure 7.7 compares the actual percentage minority in fall 1999 in the elementary, middle, and high schools, on the left, to the percentage minority at each school level if the program were restricted to the highest scoring students. Several different definitions of high scoring are used in this and other figures, including one that encompasses the sixtieth percentile. The actual percentage minority is about twenty-five to forty points higher for the elementary gifted, 20 to 30 points higher for the middle school gifted, and 10 to 15 points higher for the high school gifted than it would be if only the highest scoring students were enrolled.

There are eight middle schools in Rockford with a 6–8 grade span. Figure 7.8 is an analysis of eighth grade algebra (gifted and regular), the only advanced course at the middle school level. There is a higher percentage minority in eighth grade algebra than in any high-scoring group until the high-scoring group includes those who score at the fiftieth percentile.

There are six high schools in Rockford with a 9–12 grade span. Figure 7.9 is an analysis of high school honors and gifted English and social studies. Figure 7.10 shows the same analysis for the honors and gifted science and math courses. All of these analyses suggest that there is a higher or similar percentage of minorities in the honors or gifted level of these subjects than you would expect from their percentage in the high scoring population.

Another way to analyze this data is to look at the percentage of each race enrolled in honors or gifted courses across the entire achievement spectrum. In this calculation, the number of black students in the advanced courses is divided by the number of black students in an achievement category. This is an attempt to replicate an analysis presented by Dr. Jeannie Oakes in this case. As shown in appendix 7.7, there is a higher percentage of whites than blacks enrolled in two of the higher achievement categories, but a lower percentage in three of the higher achievement categories.

However, there are very few black students in the higher achievement categories. Appendix 7.8 shows how few students would have to be moved to equalize the percentage of each race in an achievement category enrolled in an honors or gifted course. In the 90–100-percentile category, only three more black students would have to enroll in an honors/gifted class in order to produce parity with white students. On the other hand, black students in the achievement categories between 60 and 89 percentiles are overrepresented in advanced courses. Across all achievement categories, there are eight black students too many enrolled in honors and gifted to achieve parity with whites. In short, this analysis shows there is a

Figure 7.7

Percent Minority of the Gifted Program and Percent Minority if Restricted to the Highest Scoring Students, Rockford Elementary, Middle, and High Schools, Fall 1999

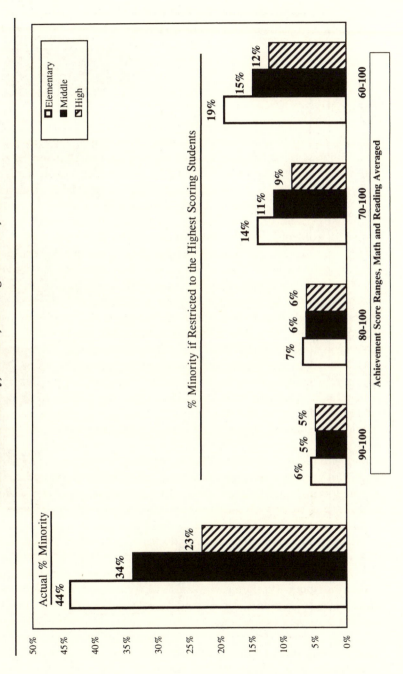

Figure 7.8
Percent Minority of 8th Grade Algebra/Gifted Classes and Percent Minority if Restricted to the Highest Scoring Students, Rockford, 1999

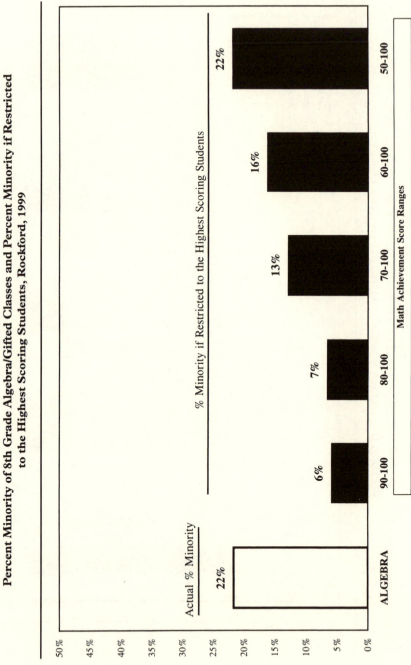

Figure 7.9

Percent Minority of High School English and Social Studies Honors/Gifted Classes and Percent Minority if Restricted to the Highest Scoring Students, Rockford, 1999

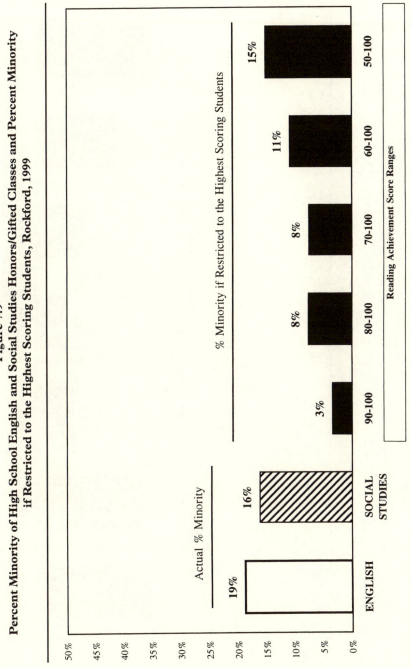

Figure 7.10
Percent Minority of High School Science and Math Honors/Gifted Classes and Percent Minority
if Restricted to the Highest Scoring Students, Rockford, 1999

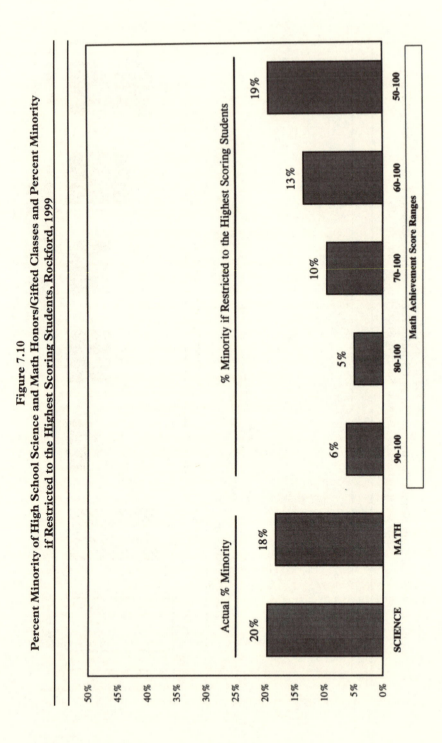

slightly higher percentage of black students enrolled in honors and gifted classes than you would predict from their achievement.

CONCLUSION

Tracking and ability grouping are one of the many areas of public policy in which policymakers pay lip service to one set of ideals, but practice another. Judge Cohill's conclusion that most academicians now agree it is better to mix rather than assign students to classes based on their perceived ability is probably correct. Nevertheless, there are differences in average achievement and racial composition in high school classes, and in math courses at the middle school level, all over the United States, including those that have supposedly detracked and/or racially balanced their classrooms.

Appendix 7.9 summarizes the requirements of the court orders on classroom and curriculum desegregation in the districts analyzed in this chapter. The first column is the year of the court order on classroom desegregation. As shown, the issue of classroom desegregation was raised by the plaintiffs in Dallas and Prince George's County at the time of their unitary motion although they had no specific court order requiring it. In the other districts, the issue was raised earlier and a court had ordered detracking and/or classroom racial balance, or, in the case of San Jose, the district had voluntarily agreed to do it. The four Delaware districts had no specific court order, but a standard nevertheless.[30] Compliance with these within-school integration court orders was thus evidence that had to be assessed at the unitary hearing.

The second column summarizes the racial balance requirements of these districts. Dallas, Prince George's County, and Woodland Hills did not have classroom racial-balance requirements. Brandywine, Christina, Colonial, Red Clay, San Jose, and Rockford did. Indeed, San Jose and Rockford's racial balance requirements were extremely detailed and complex and the attempt to achieve compliance each year was a major undertaking involving enormous resources, personnel, and analysis.

The curriculum was basically left unchanged in Dallas, the four Delaware districts, Prince George's County, and Rockford, although five of these districts had racial-balance requirements. Since most court opinions have held that it is not tracking and ability grouping that offends the Constitution, but the racial isolation that it produces, these court decisions were efficient in a policy analysis sense because they let the school districts decide how best to eliminate racial imbalance in their classrooms. Presumably, eliminating ability grouping would be only one of several options available to the school district.

Woodland Hills was under an order to eliminate ability grouping in its secondary courses even when it resulted from student choice, but not required to achieve any specific racial balance. The Rockford standard applies to all secondary grades, but it only applies to core courses. In some ways, the most radical plan is that of San Jose, since it had to achieve racial balance and eliminate ability levels in courses. On the other hand, the most radical aspect of the plan—the elimination of course ability levels and student choice—went no further than ninth grade, and did not really include math because math ability differientiation is between-course rather than within courses.

In almost every school district with explicit racial-balance or curriculum requirements, there were some programs that were exempted. The gifted program was exempted from racial-balance requirements in every district that had a self-contained gifted program. In addition, self-contained special education and bilingual education classes were also exempt. In Woodland Hills, the judge decided at the unitary hearing that AP courses were exempt from the requirement to detrack.

The next column in Appendix 7.9 shows the basic structure of the student-assignment process. Perhaps one of the great successes of the detracking movement is that very few school districts in the United States now assign students to different levels of courses solely on the basis of an ability criterion (e.g., achievement scores, grades, teacher recommendations). Virtually all school districts allow student choice, either as the primary process by which students are assigned to classes, as in San Jose, Woodland Hills, and Rockford, or as a secondary process, as in Brandywine, Christina, Colonial, and Red Clay. For example, the four Delaware districts had eligibility requirements for advanced courses, but if a student who was not eligible wanted to enroll, they were allowed to do so. San Jose, Woodland Hills, and Rockford, have a total student-choice system. Rockford, for example, continued to offer honors courses after their detracking order, but students decided for themselves whether they wanted to enroll. Even the Woodland Hills AP courses, which had a seventeen-point eligibility criterion for enrollment, allowed students who did not meet that criterion to enroll provisionally. If they performed satisfactorily, they could remain in the class.

Thus, the major civil rights success story in this area of school desegregation may be the almost universal acceptance by school administrators of the notion that students should be allowed to choose advanced courses and not be restricted by ability criteria. The most ardent advocates of detracking, however, are not satisfied with what results from student choice because it looks too much like what results when administrators assign students on the basis of academic ability. As has become evident from the detracking experiments in San Jose and Woodland Hills, as long as high schools feel obligated to offer a variety of courses that vary in difficulty, and students are free to choose their courses and at what time in their school career they enroll in them, these courses will differ in the achievement levels of the students in them. Students seem to be almost as efficient at sorting themselves on the basis of academic ability as counselors and administrators. Indeed, the San Jose experiment shows that it is possible to eliminate course prerequisites without substantially affecting the kind of students who take these courses. Students understand that if they take Algebra II without taking Algebra I first, they will have a very difficult time getting a passing grade, even if Algebra 1 is not formally required. It is a rare student who would want to do that.

As a result of the tendency for students to sort themselves when given choice, the plaintiffs' experts in Brandywine, Colonial, Christina, Red Clay, San Jose, Rockford, and Woodland Hills advocated that students be forced to take the same courses at the same point in their academic careers. It is, they argue, the only way to eliminate ability differences between courses and racial disproportionality in course enrollment.

And they are right. But so far, no school district has been willing to completely eliminate all student choice in all secondary level courses. Nor could they be ordered to do so by a court if the classrooms were nevertheless racially balanced. It is only the racial imbalance that makes the educational practice of tracking or ability grouping a constitutional issue.

As with school desegregation, the court decisions on classroom desegregation that have required racial balance or detracking have gone beyond the original violation of racial discrimination. The question is, why? The answer is that the plaintiffs have convinced the court that there is an educational benefit to a black child from having them sit next to a white child that would not accrue to them by simply eliminating racial discrimination. As with school desegregation research, however, the best that can be said is that there is no research evidence to support this notion. Indeed, if the black child in question happens to be very high achieving or gifted, the most likely outcome is that they will be harmed by being forced into academically heterogeneous classes.

But as more and more school districts attain unitary status, the issue of tracking and ability grouping should wane as a legal issue. There are few instances of a court intervening in the curriculum and classroom assignment process of a school district that had not already been found guilty of intentional segregation of their schools. The enthusiasm for school racial balance has clearly waned as the original sin of the dual school system has become more and more distant. Accordingly, there should be fewer and fewer courts willing to require classroom racial balance and curriculum modifications. On the other hand, there were never that many to begin with in comparison to the school cases.

The final scorecard on the success of the tracking and ability-grouping decisions is mixed. If the goal of these court orders is to eliminate all differences in student achievement between secondary courses, they have failed. Even when ability levels within courses and ability criteria for enrollment

are eliminated, differences in the average achievement of the students enrolled in different courses remain. On the other hand, if the goal of the court
orders is to eliminate racial discrimination, they have succeeded. The elementary classrooms are highly racially balanced. At the secondary level,
there is the same, or a higher percentage, minority in the advanced courses
or gifted programs than would be predicted from their achievement. Minority children are actively encouraged to enroll in advanced courses or
gifted programs and there is simply no school administrator today who
would do otherwise.

It cannot be said enough that this is the great triumph of the civil rights
movement—there is an almost universal acceptance among whites of the
principle that racial discrimination is a sin. On the other hand, there is still
an achievement gap between the races that will result in racially imbalanced
classrooms. There cannot be any decent person who does not feel regret
when they look into an advanced course classroom in an ostensibly desegregated school and see mostly white students. But as with other complex
policy areas, we have important competing values, such as freedom, choice,
academic efficiency and competitiveness, that we are unwilling to abandon.
Indeed, I suspect that black parents are no more willing to abandon these
principles than Americans in general.

ENDNOTES

1. *Singleton v. Jackson Municipal Separate School District*, 419 F.2d 1211 (1969);
U.S. v. Sunflower County School District, 430 F.2d 839 (1970); *Carter v. West Feliciana
Parish School Board*, 396 U.S. 290 (1970); *Lemon v. Bossier Parish School Board*, 444
F.2d 1400 (1971); *Moses v. Washington Parish School Board*, 330 F.Supp. 1340
(1971); *McNeal v. Tate County School District*, 508 F.2d 1017 (1975).

2. *Singleton v. Anson County Board of Education*, 283 F. Supp. 895 (1968), cited
in Levin and Moise (1975: 121).

3. Stipulated Modified Remedial Order, *Vasquez et al. v. San Jose Unified School
District et al.*, Case No. C 71-2130 RMW (SJ), U.S. District Court, 18 February
1994.

4. The New Castle County decisions are *Coalition to Save Our Children v. State
Board of Education*, 901 F.Supp. 784 (1995); *Coalition to Save Our Children v. State
Board of Education*, 90 F.3d 752 (1996); the Cleveland decision is *Reed et al. v. Rhodes
et al.*, 1 F.Supp. 2d 705 (1998); the Prince George's County decisions are *Vaughns
et al. v. Prince George's County et al. and National Association for the Advancement of
Colored People (NAACP) et al. v. Prince George's County et al.*, 18 F.Supp. 2d 569
(1998) and *Vaughns et al. v. Prince George's County et al. and NAACP et al. v. Prince
George's County et al.*, Civil No. PJM 72-325 and PJM 81-2597, June 25, 2002. What
is interesting about the Prince George's County case is that the motion for unitary
status was initiated not by the defendants, but by the court in response to a school
board decision to eliminate racial quotas in the magnet program, something they
could do only if they were unitary. The judge appointed a four-person expert panel—

Robert Shoenberg, Robert Peterkin, William Trent, and me—to assess whether the district had complied with its court orders, and subsequently held hearings on the report and the school district's compliance. After the hearings, an agreement was worked out between the district, the county, and the state to continue funding for the next four years during a transition period to unitary status.

5. *Capacchione v. Charlotte-Mecklenburg Schools.*, 57 F. Supp. 2d 228 (1999). This was overturned by the 4th circuit, but then affirmed by an en banc panel of the 4th circuit in 2001.

6. *People Who Care v. Rockford School District et al.*, 111 F. 3d 528 (1997) as cited in *Capacchione v. Charlotte-Mecklenburg Schools*, 57 F. Supp. 2d 228 (1999): 167.

7. The studies they cited are Esposito 1973, Goodlad 1960, and Passow 1962.

8. They do not elaborate, but I have noticed that when one of the racial groups is quite small, the relative exposure index is likely to give more reasonable results than the index of dissimilarity. For example, in a hypothetical 99 percent white school district with six schools and nine minorities and 600 whites distributed so that there are three minorities in each of three schools and 100 whites in each of the six schools, the relative exposure index is .01, but the index of dissimilarity is .50, which is a fairly high level of imbalance. Yet, it strikes me that every minority is going to school with substantial numbers of whites and is in a highly integrated environment. When the races are equal in size and evenly distributed, the two indices are the same.

9. The formula is given in chapter 4 for schools. Classrooms should be substituted for schools in that formula. Each classroom's exposure (proportion white times the number of blacks) is calculated, then summed across classrooms in a school, and divided by the number of blacks in all the classrooms.

10. Racial balance indices were not computed for Dallas, Texas.

11. Stipulated Modified Remedial Order, *Vasquez et al. v. San Jose Unified School District et al.*, Case No. C 71-2130 RMW (SJ), United States District Court, Northern District of California, 18 February 1994.

12. In the original 1978 desegregation suit (*Evans v. Buchanan*, 447 F. Supp. 982, [1978]), eleven predominantly white suburban school districts were ordered to merge with the predominantly black Wilmington district to divide into the desegregated New Castle County school district. In 1981, the court permitted them to form four districts—Brandywine, Christina, Colonial, and Red Clay—each with a part of Wilmington.

13. The relative exposure indices in appendix 7.2 are for blacks and whites for all districts except the four Delaware districts and Rockford. In the latter districts it is blacks and Hispanics combined, and in San Jose, it is all minorities. The indices are broken down by elementary, middle and high school.

14. This analysis appears in more detail in Rossell 2000b.

15. Stipulated Modified Remedial Order, *Vasquez et al. v. San Jose Unified School District et al.*, Case No. C 71-2130 RMW (SJ), United States District Court, Northern District of California 18 February 1994.

16. The computation was to be based on the enrollment count within ten days of the opening of school.

17. The gifted program, and self-contained classrooms for LEP and special education students, are excluded from this calculation. In addition, highly specialized electives (such as jazz band and string quartet) are excluded, not to exceed five percent of the total regular education classes offered.

18. Stipulated Modified Remedial Order (1994: 30).

19. For example, the ratio of .12 for Hispanic enrollment in calculus in 1992–93 was derived as follows. First, the Hispanic percentage in calculus courses was computed by dividing the Hispanic enrollment (10) in calculus by the total number of students enrolled (224) in calculus. Hispanics were 4.5 percent of the enrollment in calculus. Second, the Hispanic percentage of the high school enrollment is calculated by dividing the number of Hispanics (3,251) by the high school enrollment of 8,212. Hispanics were 37.2 percent of the high school enrollment. Third, the ratio is computed as 4.5 divided by 37.2 percent, which is .12.

20. In 1992–93, 54.2 percent of Hispanics were on free or reduced lunch compared to only 9.6 percent of whites for a disparity of almost 45 percentage points. By 1996–97, the disparity had increased to 53 percentage points with 66.5 percent of Hispanic students eligible for free or reduced lunch compared to only 13.1 percent of white students.

21. *Hoots et al. v. Commonwealth of Pennsylvania et al.*, Civil Action No. 71-538, U.S. District Court for the Western District of Pennsylvania 16 January 1991.

22. At East Junior High, the percentage of black students who were poor, that is, eligible for free or reduced lunch, was 83 percent compared to 49 percent for whites. At West Junior High, the percentage of black students who were poor was 69 percent compared to 25 percent for white students.

23. Nor do I remember it being challenged in cross examination.

24. The free lunch eligibility is 54 percent for blacks and 15 percent for whites.

25. *Hoots et al. v. Commonwealth of Pennsylvania et al.*, Civil Action No. 71-538, U.S. District Court for the Western District of Pennsylvania 25 July 2000: 6.

26. *Ibid.*, 36.

27. *Ibid.*, 73.

28. *Ibid.*, 37.

29. When the percentage minority in the relevant pool at any school level is less than twice the compliance standard, then the bottom of the compliance range is adjusted to half of the percentage of minority students in the compliance pool. In other words, if the minority percentage in the relevant pool is 22 percent (less than two times 12), the standard for classrooms is 11 to 34 percent minority.

30. The requirement to have classrooms 10–49 percent minority was suggested by the plaintiffs in the four Delaware school districts. At some point, the court asked the district to include the number of classrooms that met this standard in their annual desegregation reports, but it is not clear that meeting that standard was actually required. Nevertheless, evidence on the extent to which the district had met this standard was presented at the unitary hearing.

Appendix 7.1
Classroom Racial Imbalance* in U.S. by Region and School Level, 1976

	Northeast	Midwest	South	West	U.S.
Elementary	0.05	0.05	0.07	0.03	0.06
Middle or Jr. High	0.05	0.06	0.09	0.05	0.07
High	0.09	0.09	0.13	0.07	0.11

Source: Morgan and McPartland (1981: 25).

* 1.0 is complete segregation; 0 is perfect racial balance.

Appendix 7.2
Classroom Racial Imbalance* in U.S., 1976, Rossell Court-Ordered Sample, 1982 and 1998, and Districts Declared or seeking Unitary Status, 1992–1993 to 1999–2000

	Elementary	Middle	High
1976 U.S. Sample	0.06	0.07	0.11
1980 & 1982 Rossell Sample	0.28	0.26	0.30
1988 Elementary Only - Rossell Sample	0.32		
1993-94 Brandywine DE	0.11	0.12	0.16
1993-94 Red Clay, DE	0.04	0.08	0.18
1993-94 Christina, DE	0.08	0.11	0.18
1993-94 Colonial, DE	0.04	0.05	0.10
1996-97 Prince George's Co., MD	0.06	0.11	0.12
1992-93 San Jose, CA	0.16	0.11	0.17
1997-98 San Jose, CA	0.04	0.11	0.10
1999-00 Woodland Hills, PA	0.02	0.08	0.08
1999-00 Rockford, IL	0.06	0.05	0.11

* 1.0 is complete segregation; 0 is perfect racial balance.

Appendix 7.3
Percent of Students in Classroom ± 20 Points of School's Percent Black in Districts Declared or Seeking Unitary Status, 1992–1993 to 1999–2000

	Elementary	Middle	High
1992-93 San Jose, CA	96%	78%	71%
1993-94 Brandywine, DE	89%	71%	78%
1993-94 Red Clay, DE	92%	86%	64%
1993-94 Christina, DE	96%	88%	81%
1993-94 Colonial, DE	97%	95%	82%
1996-97 Prince George's Co., MD	92%	84%	84%
1997-98 San Jose, CA	98%	89%	83%
1999-00 Woodland Hills, PA	100%	85%	87%
1999-00 Rockford, IL	99%	94%	65%
AVERAGE	95%	86%	77%

Appendix 7.4
The Effect of 9th Grade Detracking and Eliminating Course Prerequisites on the Racial Imbalance of 10th–12th Grade Classrooms, San Jose, 1992–1993 through 1997–1998

	1992-93	First Year of Detracking 1994-95	1995-96	1996-97	1997-98
Lincoln High	.25	.25	.21	.14	.13
San Jose High	.30	.22	.24	.20	.19
Willow Glen High	.21	.21	.14	.13	.10
Pioneer High	.39	.22	.19	.14	.21
Leland High	.03	.03	.03	.06	.06
Glunderson High	.03	.07	.04	.06	.05
High School Average	**.20**	**.17**	**.14**	**.12**	**.12**

Appendix 7.5

A Re-analysis of Dr. de Leeuw's Table 3, 7th Grade Math Class Enrollment, Woodland Hills Junior High Schools

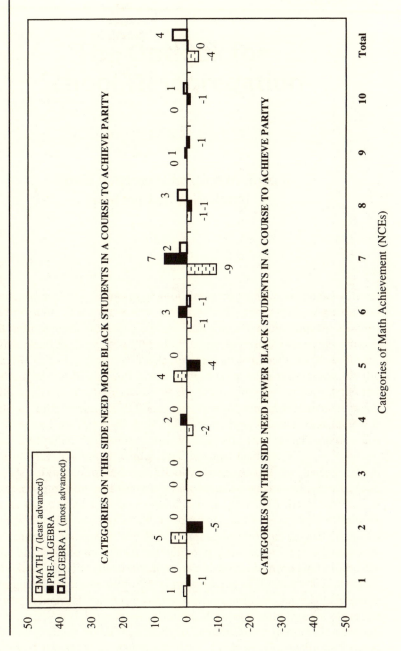

Appendix 7.6

A Re-analysis of Dr. de Leeuw's Table 4, 8th Grade Math Class Enrollment, Woodland Hills Junior High Schools

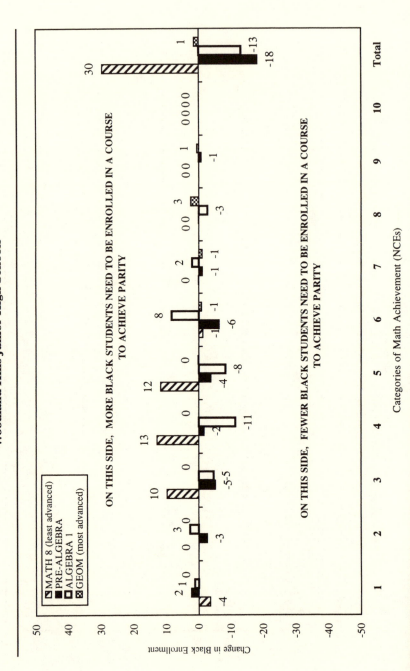

Appendix 7.7

Percentage of Minority and Majority Students Enrolled in Honors and Gifted Core Courses among Students Enrolled in Core Courses by 10-Point Slices of Achievement, Rockford, 1999

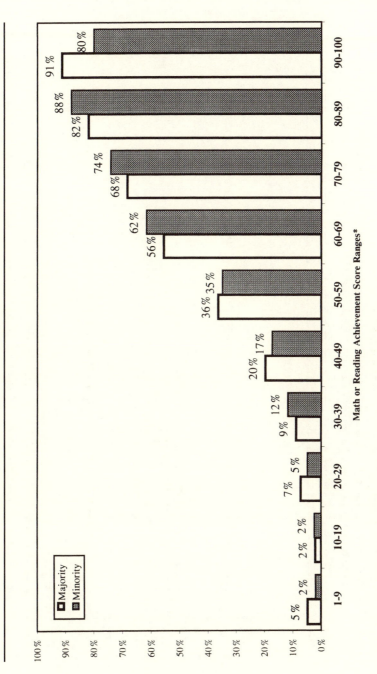

* Reading score for English and social studies classes; math score for math and science classes.

Appendix 7.8

Change in Number of Minority Students in Honors/Gifted Classes Needed to Produce Parity in the Percent of Each Race in Each Achievement Category in Honors/Gifted Classes, Rockford, 1999

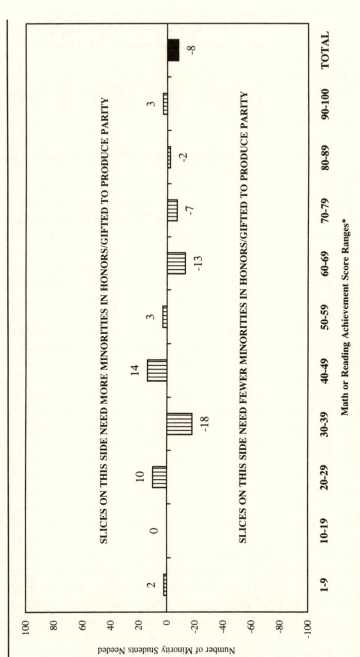

* Reading score for English and social studies classes; math score for math and science classes.

Appendix 7.9

Requirements of Court Orders on Classroom Desegregation in Districts Seeking Unitary Status

School District	Year of Order on Classrooms	Racial Balance	Curriculum	Exceptions[a]	Secondary Assignment Process	Found Unitary on Classrooms
Dallas, TX*	N/A	NONE	NONE	N/A	Elig. Req.	Prelim. 1994, final 1997
Brandywine, De		10-49% Min.	NONE	NONE	Elig. & Choice	1995
Christina, De		10-49% Min.	NONE	NONE	Elig. & Choice	1995
Colonial, De		10-49% Min.	NONE	NONE	Elig. & Choice	1995
Red Clay, DE		10-49% Min.	NONE	NONE	Elig. & Choice	1995
Prince George's Co., MD**	N/A	NONE	NONE	N/A	Elig. & Choice	Prelim. 1998, final 2002
San Jose, CA	1994	ELEM: +/- 15 % pts. of grade % Hisp. MIDDLE: 80% of classes at +/- 15 % pts. of grade % Hisp.; 100% at +/- 25 % pts. of grade % Hisp. HIGH: classes >20 at +/- 15 % points of grade % Hisp.; classes 20 or less at +/- 25% points of grade % Hisp.	Elim. Ability Levels; Elim. Ability Levels; Elim. Ability Levels	GIFTED; GIFTED; GIFTED, GRADES 10-12	Student Choice; Student Choice	HAS NOT APPLED
Woodland Hills, CA*	1991	NONE	Elim. Ability Levels	N/A	Student Choice	Partial 2000, final 2003
Rockford, Il*	1996	ELEM: +/- 12 % pts. Of grade MIDDLE & HIGH: +/- 12 % pts. Of core course % Min.	NONE	NON-CORE, GIFTED; NON-CORE, GIFTED	Student Choice	Preliminary 2001 (Overturning District Court 2000); Final Unitary 2003

* Three year phase out to unitary status.

** Four year phase out to unitary status.

[a] All districts with racial balance requirements were allowed to exclude self-contained special education and bilingual education classes.

REFERENCES

Argys, Laura M., Daniel E. Rees, and Dominic J. Brewer. 1996. Detracking America's schools: Equity at zero cost? *Journal of Policy Analysis and Management* 15(4): 623–45.

Armor, David J. 2000. Expert Report, *Hoots et al. v. Commonwealth of Pennsylvania et al.*, Civil Action no. 71-538 (U.S. Dist. WD Pa. Feb.).

———. 1995. *Forced Justice: School Desegregation and the Law.* New York: Oxford UP.

Coleman, James S., E.Q. Campbell, C.J. Hobson, J. McPartland, A.M. Mood, F.D. Weinfield, and R.L. York. 1966. *Equality of Educational Opportunity.* Washington, D.C.: U.S. Government Printing Office.

Dallas Independent School District with Christine H. Rossell, and David J. Armor. 1993. Unitary Status Motion to the Court. (U.S. Dist. ND Texas 1994).

Ekstrom, R.B. 1961. Experimental studies of homogeneous grouping: A critical review. *The School Review* 69: 216–26.

Esposito, Dominick. 1971. *Homogeneous and Heterogeneous Ability Grouping: Principal Findings and Implications for Evaluating and Designing More Effective Educational Environments.* New York: Teachers College, Columbia University.

———. 1973. Homogeneous and heterogeneous ability grouping: Principal findings and implications for evaluating and designing more effective educational environments. *Review of Educational Research* 43: 163–79.

Evertson, Carolyn M. 1982. Differences in instructional activities in higher- and lower-achieving junior high english and math classes. *Elementary School Journal* 82: 329–50.

Evertson, Carolyn M., Julie P. Sanford, and Edmund Emmer. 1981. Effects of class heterogeneity in junior high school. *American Educational Research Journal* 18: 219–32.

Fatla, Mark. 1990. Report and recommendation regarding desegregation remedies. *Dorothy Hoots et al. v. Commonwealth of Pennsylvania et al.*, Civil Action no. 71–538 (U.S. Dist. WD Pa. 20 Aug.).

Findley, Warren G., and Miriam M. Bryan. 1971. *Ability Grouping, 1970: Status, Impact and Alternatives.* Athens: University of Georgia, Center for Educational Improvement.

Gamoran, Adam. 1987. The stratification of high school learning opportunities. *Sociology of Education* 60 (July): 415–35.

———. Measuring curriculum differentiation. *American Journal of Education* 60: 135–55.

Gamoran, Adam, and Robert D. Mare. 1989. Secondary school tracking and educational inequality: Compensation, reinforcement, or neutrality? *American Journal of Sociology* 94(5): 1146–83.

Goldberg, Miriam L., A. Harry Passow, and Joseph Justman. 1966. *The Effects of Ability Grouping.* New York: Teachers College, Columbia University.

Goodlad, John L. 1960. Classroom organization. In *Encyclopedia of Educational Research: A Project of the American Educational Research Association*, edited by Chester W. Harris. New York: Macmillan.

Hoffer, Thomas B. 1992. Middle school ability grouping and student achievement in science and mathematics. *Educational Evaluation and Policy Analysis* 14(3): 205–27.

Jaynes, Gerald D. and Robin M. Williams, eds. 1989. *A Common Destiny.* Washington, D.C.: National Academy Press.

Kerckhoff, Alan C. 1986. Effects of ability grouping in British secondary schools. *American Sociological Review* 51: 842–58.

Kulik, Chen-Lin C., and James A. Kulik. 1982. Research synthesis on ability grouping. *Educational Leadership* (May): 619–21.

Kulik, James A., and Chen-Lin C. Kulik. 1982. "Effects of ability grouping on secondary school students: A meta-analysis of evaluation findings." *American Educational Research Journal* 19(3): 415–28.

———. 1991. "Ability grouping and gifted students." In *Handbook of Gifted Education,* edited by Nicholas Colangelo and Gary A. Davis, 178–95. Boston: Allyn and Bacon.

Levin, Betsy, and Philip Moise. 1975. School desegregation litigation in the seventies and the use of social science evidence: An annotated guide. *Law and Contemporary Problems* 34(1): 50–133.

Morgan, Phillip R., and James M. McPartland. 1981. *The Extent of Classroom Segregation within Desegregated Schools.* Baltimore: Johns Hopkins University, Center for Social Organization of Schools.

———. 1982. The reproduction of inequity: The content of secondary school tracking. *Urban Review* 14: 107–20.

———. 1985. *Keeping Track: How Schools Structure Inequality.* New Haven: Yale UP.

Passow, A. Harry. 1962. The maze of research on ability grouping. *Educational Forum* 26: 281.

Peterkin, Robert, Christine H. Rossell, Robert Shoenberg, and William Trent. 1997. Report of the court-appointed panel in *Vaughns et al. v. Prince George's County Board of Education et al.* Submitted to Judge Peter J. Messitte 30 June.

Rees, Daniel I., Laura M. Argys, and Dominic J. Brewer. 1996. Tracking in the United States: Descriptive statistics from NELS. *Economics of Education Review* 15(1): 83–9.

Rist, Ray C. 1970. Student social class and teacher expectations: The self-fulfilling prophecy in ghetto education. *Harvard Educational Review* 40: 411–51.

Rossell, Christine. H. 1993a. An analysis of the San Jose unified school district's compliance with the court order in the areas of student assignment (school and classroom segregation), transportation and bilingual education. Report, *Vasquez et al. v. San Jose Unified School District et al.* Case no. C 71-2130 RMW (SJ), (US Dist. ND Cal. 29 June).

———. 1993b. Supplemental report analyzing the San Jose unified school district's compliance with the court order in the area of student assignment (school and classroom segregation). Report, *Vasquez et al. v. San Jose Unified School District et al.* Case no. C 71-2130 RMW (SJ), (US Dist. ND Cal. 1. Nov.).

———. 1994. School and classroom desegregation in the New Castle County, Delaware desegregation area (Brandywine, Red Clay, Christina, and Colonial school districts). Report, *Coalition to Save Our Children v. State Board of Education,* 901 F. Supp. 784, (U.S Dist. Dela. 30 Nov).

———. 1997. Rebuttal report analyzing the Cleveland city school districts Compliance with remedial components. Report, *Reed v. Rhodes,* 1 F.Supp. 2d 705 (US Dist Ohio 6 Oct.).

———. 1999. Within-school integration in the Rockford school district, fall 1999. Report, *People Who Care et al. v. Rockford Board of Education, School District No. 205* 111 F. 3d at 536 (10 December).

———. 2000a. Compliance with the *Green* factors in Woodland Hills, Pennsylvania. Report, *Hoots et al. v. Commonwealth of Pennsylvania et al.*, Civil Action no. 71-538 (U.S. Dist. WD Pa. 1 March).

———. 2000b. Is it possible to detrack? Report to San Jose Unified School System. 10 January.

———. 2000c. Rebuttal report on within-school integration in the Rockford school district. Report, *People Who Care et al. v. Rockford Board of Education, School District No. 205* 111 F. 3d at 536 (20 February).

———. 2000d. Supplemental report on tracking and ability grouping in the Woodland Hills school district. Report, *Hoots et al. v. Commonwealth of Pennsylvania et al.*, Civil Action no. 71-538 (U.S. Dist. WD Pa. 9 May).

Slavin, Robert E. 1990a. Ability grouping in secondary schools: A response to Hallinan. *Review of Educational Research* 60(3): 505–07.

——— 1990b. Achievement effects of ability grouping in secondary schools: A best-evidence synthesis. *Review of Educational Research* 60(3): 471–99.

U.S. Commission on Civil Rights. 1974. Towards quality education for Mexican Americans. *Mexican American Education Study, Report No. 6.* Washington, D.C.: U.S. Government Printing Office.

U.S. Department of Education, National Center for Education Statistics. 1994. Curricular differentiation in public high schools. Office of Educational Research and Improvement, NCES 95-360.

Vanfossen, Beth E., James D. Jones, and Joan Z. Spade. 1987. Curriculum tracking and status maintenance. *Sociology of Education* 60: 104–22.

Chapter 8

Racial Disparities
in School Discipline

∞

Charles M. Achilles

INTRODUCTION

School desegregation has provided many benefits. Much progress in education from 1954 until now would have been impossible without the national emphasis upon dismantling the unlawful segregation of America's schools as required by *Brown v. Board of Education* (347 U.S. 483 [1954]).

School safety and quality and the fair (equal, equitable) treatment of pupils and students in American public schools deserve serious attention. The values of equality and equity and of quality schools that are safe and conducive to learning should not conflict, nor should school administrators sacrifice one for the other. These philosophic and ethical positions are more than semantics. Pupils are usually required by law to attend school until some state-determined age, and they are not empowered to change that condition.

The importance of the goals of safety, equality, equity, and quality extends beyond pupils (those who are required to attend) to students (those who voluntarily attend). Historically, high-visibility court cases, especially civil rights (desegregation) cases, have emphasized equality and equity. In recent years, school safety and school quality concerns are growing on the public consciousness.[1]

Landmark school desegregation decisions have emphasized the fair, equal, and equitable treatment of African American students in school systems found to be segregated and not providing equal treatment to one or more groups. Early school desegregation court cases challenged de jure segregation to have laws changed so that all students, not just one group or another, could enjoy equal access to and opportunities from public education. Later, court cases began also to address de facto segregation brought about by actions that had the effect of creating segregation, or resegregation, even though the laws themselves were not biased. Plaintiffs often presented data on the proportion of minority youth in the student body compared to their proportion in a treatment variable such as disciplinary action, or assignment to special education, as evidence of continuing segregation. That is, plaintiffs argued that the disproportionate overrepresentation of minorities in schooling actions perceived as negative and their underrepresentation in positive schooling events such as advanced placement (AP) courses were prima facie evidence of unequal treatment and of discrimination. Using this approach, the continuance of disproportionate representation, for example, in student disciplinary actions such as assignment to out-of-school suspensions (OSS), is considered a vestige of the prior segregated system.

That the distribution of consequences of student misbehavior in schools often is not proportionate is easily demonstrated by analyzing discipline-action outcomes compared to various groups of students defined by variables such as race, gender, age, poverty, and so on. In this chapter, the discussion of the concept of "disproportionate representation" specifically focuses on student behavior using detailed data related to student behaviors that are required for desegregation monitoring. In desegregating school systems, administrators have developed uniform codes of student conduct in order to achieve equity in responding to student misbehavior. These codes typically include categories of the severity of student misbehavior (and corresponding corrective actions) ranging from school-related indiscipline such as truancy, class cutting, and disruption to crimes that would require arrest, adjudication, and punishment if committed by anyone in or out of school (e.g., aggravated assault, weapons, arson, rape).

Disciplinary data collected at schools can be disaggregated by many variables such as race, gender, free and reduced lunch, et cetera, and analyses can be made for each year to check for consistency, severity, improvement, and other variables. Results for a single system can be compared to outside sources or benchmarks, such as to similar systems in the state, to school systems that have been declared unitary by court decisions, or to national statistics, and so on. These analyses show consistency and comparative relationships.

The questions this chapter will address using school-district data on student misbehavior and administrative response will provide answers to some questions that a court would be interested in. For example, do reported student misbehaviors seem to be connected to discrimination in the school setting? How is administrative discretion in disciplinary actions toward a specific group connected to disproportionate representation? What about disproportionate representation that occurs when the student misbehaviors are severe and require legal action over which the administrator has little discretion? Is the misbehavior in some way connected to past school segregation?

This chapter answers these questions by explaining (a) the concept of proportionality connected to student behavior, (b) the development, assessment, and use of a Uniform Code of Student Conduct (Code), (c) the results of applying the Code, and (d) the procedures used in some court cases to determine if the evident disproportion in student discipline actions is discriminatory and related to a prior condition of segregation (a vestige of prior segregation). The chapter includes examples of steps taken to determine if the disproportionality evident in student behavior outcomes is discrimination.

THE CONCEPT OF
DISPROPORTIONALITY IN STUDENT DISCIPLINE

Disproportionality in outcomes of student misbehavior, such as suspension, derives from an assumption that the connection between behavior outcomes and a status variable (e.g., gender or race) will approximate a ratio of one to one. In some desegregation cases, plaintiffs have argued that the observed disproportionality in student discipline outcomes is a vestige of prior segregation or that it is the result of discrimination. An alternative approach is to start with the data as presented and consider other factors. In this approach, one (a) accepts the data as offered, (b) attempts to determine why a discrepancy or difference exists, (c) compares local outcomes to outcomes elsewhere, and then (d) attempts to explain why the outcomes are what they are.

Groups establish rules of behavior, presumably to advance the purposes of the organization or group. Pushing, shoving, tackling and other aggressive physical behaviors are not valued behaviors in a school; they are respected on a football field (regardless of the race of the perpetrator). This extreme example demonstrates the need for standards of behavior (rules or Code) that govern the behavior valued in the group or organization to help achieve the group's goals. If a person on a football team pushes, shoves, or tackles better than another, the more successful person "makes" the first team. People are on the team because they excel in a valued behavior. A person who misses practice without a good excuse or violates team rules is likely to be suspended or even kicked off the team. Typically, the better the player—that is, the more the player excels at what is valued and conforms to the team rules, the more likely the person is to play regularly and not to be disciplined. "Proportions" derive from the valued behavior. If conditions to get on the team are fair, would disproportion of team members by race be discrimination? Would the issue of disproportion carry over to each position within the team?

The assumption that there is a one-to-one proportionality in individual behavior within or between status variables such as race, gender and age is tenuous. It is productive to start with the observed (empirical) data and then to explain why outcomes are as they are. In an analysis, there is a need for some standard of comparison of groups and of the outcomes being studied. Achilles (1994, 1997, 2000) has used an index of proportionality to guide such comparisons. The example provided here uses data from the *Hoots et al. v. Commonwealth of Pennsylvania* analysis of discipline in the Woodland Hills School District (WHSD) (Achilles, 2000: 4–5).

Two proportionality indices are useful in discussing out-of-school suspension (OSS) as the result of student misbehavior. One index can be computed for total school suspensions (that is, for a duplicated count that includes multiple suspensions of a student), and another can be computed for students suspended (unduplicated count) where each student is counted only once, regardless of the number of OSS.

The total suspension index (TSI) is calculated as a group's percentage of suspensions (duplicated count) divided by a group's percentage of enrollment. The formula, and its solution for Woodland Hills, is

$$\text{TSI} = \frac{\text{Group's \% of Suspensions}}{\text{Group's \% of Enrollment}} \qquad \begin{array}{c} \text{Black} \\ \dfrac{71}{44} = 1.61 \end{array} \qquad \begin{array}{c} \text{White} \\ \dfrac{29}{55} = .53 \end{array}$$

Thus, in the Woodland Hills School District, 71 percent of all OSS went to black youth, 29 percent of all OSS went to white youth. Black students were 44 percent of the WHSD student population and white students were 55 percent (1 percent of the students were "other"). The 71 percent of OSS received by black students divided by the black percentage of the school population (44 percent) provides an index of proportionality of 1.61 for suspensions to blacks. This means there is a higher percentage of suspensions that are black than black students exist in the enrollment because an index of 1.0 represents equal proportions. The index of proportionality for OSS for whites is 29 percent divided by 55 percent, which equals .53. This means there is a lower percentage of suspensions that are white than the percentage of enrollment that is white.

The students suspended index (SSI) is an unduplicated count of students suspended. The formula, and its solution for Woodland Hills, is

$$\text{SSI} = \frac{\text{Group's \% of Students Suspended}}{\text{Group's \% of Enrollment}} \qquad \begin{array}{c} \text{Black} \\ \dfrac{67}{44} = 1.52 \end{array} \qquad \begin{array}{c} \text{White} \\ \dfrac{33}{55} = .60 \end{array}$$

For Woodland Hills, the SSI is calculated by dividing the black percentage of students suspended, which is 67 percent, by the black percentage of enrollment, which is 44 percent. The result is 1.52 for black students. The same calculation for white students who compromise 33 percent of students suspended divided by their 55 percent of enrollment yields an index of .60. The difference between the TSI of 1.61 and the SSI of 1.52 for black students shows that black students received more multiple OSS than did white students in 1998–1999. A "likelihood ratio" results from dividing the index for one group by the index for another group. For students (SSI—unduplicated count) receiving OSS, the ratio is 1.52 divided by .60, or 2.53. Similar indices and ratios can be calculated for other school districts, and for other indicators of misbehavior.

The indices represent a useful and uncomplicated way to develop descriptive data and comparisons. In row (a) and column 1 below, minorities are 60 percent of the population, but 40 percent of the students suspended. The SSI for the minority population is 60 divided by 40, equaling 1.5. Whites are the remaining 40 percent of suspended pupils and the remaining 60 percent of the population producing an SSI of .67, shown in column 1 of row (b). The likelihood ratio in row (c) is the ratio of the minority index (1.5) to the white index (.67). Note the change in indices in row (c) as the suspension minority percentage is held at 60 percent (row a) and the suspension white percentage at 40 percent (numerator in row b) but the population percentages change until they are the same as the suspension percentages. At that point, each index is 1.0 and the likelihood ratio is 0. If we keep increasing the percentage minority and decreasing the percentage white in the enrollment, but continue to keep the racial percentages for students suspended constant, we end up with the final column where blacks are suspended at lower rates than their percentage in the population, and whites are suspended at higher rates than their percentage in the population, producing a minority suspension likelihood ratio of .38.

(a)	$\frac{60}{40} = .1.5$	$\frac{60}{45} = .1.33$	$\frac{60}{50} = .1.2$	$\frac{60}{55} = .1.09$	$\frac{60}{60} = .1.0$	Etc.	$\frac{60}{80} = .75$
(b)	$\frac{40}{60} = .67$	$\frac{40}{55} = .73$	$\frac{40}{50} = .8$	$\frac{40}{45} = .89$	$\frac{40}{40} = 1.0$	Etc.	$\frac{40}{20} = 2.0$
(c)	2.23	1.82	1.5	1.22	.00	Etc.	.38

The index of proportionality is useful in analyzing data on student behavior for several reasons. If appropriate data, such as data on student misbehaviors and outcomes, can be reported in percentages, then the index allows comparisons of one group or one study to another. For example, data on student behavior and outcomes was available for analysis by defendants in desegregation suits in New Castle County, Delaware (*Coalition v. State Board of Education* 1995), in Cleveland (*Reed v. Rhodes* 1997), and in Woodland Hills School District (*Hoots et al. v. Commonwealth of Pennsylvania*

2000). The TSI and SSI could be compared between and among these districts, and also to national data as compiled by the Office for Civil Rights (OCR) in annual surveys.

Appendix 8.1 demonstrates the parsimony and validity of the index by comparing the WHSD data to relevant data from Office for Civil Rights (OCR) reports for the nation as a whole. When OCR data are analyzed by computing and using the appropriate percentages to create an index, results similar to Woodland Hills are obtained. The nation had a proportionality index in 1993 of 2.53 and in 1999 of 2.38 compared to a WHSD index of 2.58.

THE UNIFORM CODE OF STUDENT CONDUCT

A formal statement of student behavior, usually called a Uniform Code of Student Conduct (Code), is the foundation for deciding what is acceptable or unacceptable pupil or student behavior. The Code must meet two tests in a discussion of desegregated schools.

- On its face, a Code must be unbiased, fair, and equitable.
- A Code must be applied in a fair, equitable, and unbiased manner.

The Code must guide student behavior toward equal opportunity and treatment; it cannot contain any element that discriminates against any group (race, gender, age, disability) that must abide by the code. But it is not enough just to have a code that is unbiased, fair and equitable: those who administer the Code must apply it fairly.

Step One: The Code Itself

All school disciplinary actions should be governed by, and emanate from, an unbiased application of the Code. But first, is the Code itself free of bias and do its provisions allow for all persons to be treated equitably and fairly? The language in a code can be legalistic and difficult and educators must take steps to help students and parents to understand the code and discipline rules. The Code is distributed to students and parents each year and the code and discipline system are explained to parents, students, educators, and others each year. Four school systems in New Castle County, Delaware were joined into a single district as part of the desegregation remedy in 1978. The combined New Castle County School Board adopted a student code of conduct derived from *Milliken v. Bradley* (418 U.S. 717, 740–41 [1974]), *Milliken II* (433 U.S. 267 [1977]), and from research and literature on student codes of conduct (e.g., Moody, Vargon, and Williams, 1974). The general criteria that were developed by this process in *Coalition v. State Board of Education* (1995) were refined by additional research (e.g., Avery 1998; Burke 1981; Harris and Dowe 1980), and used to guide analyses of codes in *Reed v. Rhodes* (1997) in Cleveland; and *Hoots et al. v. Commonwealth of Pennsylvania* (2000). The resulting criteria for assessing a code of conduct can be summarized as follows. The code should

- Be planned cooperatively
- Be reviewed annually
- Comply with laws
- Emphasize due process
- Have some room for interpretation

- Have clear behavior expectations
- Be presented annually to students
- Be instructive and goal oriented
- Be written clearly and be understandable
- Express student rights

Appendix 8.2 shows some state governments (Delaware, Illinois, Michigan, New Jersey, North Carolina, Pennsylvania, Texas), courts (*Milliken v. Bradley; Coalition v. State Board of Education*; *Reed v. Rhodes*), school districts (Rockford, Cincinnati, Portland, Woodland Hills School District) and national organizations (National School Safety Center) where these criteria have been used in more detailed form. Fourteen criteria are listed and most entities met at least ten of them.

An Example of Assessing a Code of Conduct

In *Coalition v. Delaware State Board of Education*, *Reed v. Rhodes* (Cleveland Public Schools), and *Hoots et al. v. Commonwealth*, shown in columns 2, 8, and 15 of Appendix 8.2, each school district's Code was compared to the criteria summarized above. Using *Reed v. Rhodes* as the example here, the Code in the Cleveland Public Schools (CPS) fully met all criteria but one: it was not particularly readable or user-friendly because it was written in highly legalistic terms and in language some parents and many elementary-age pupils might not easily understand.[2] To meet this criterion, the CPS Code was (a) explained each year in homeroom or small groups, (b) explained to each new student entering school, (c) sent home, (d) provided in different languages, etc. In elementary schools, portions of the Code were posted as behavior rules. Some teachers role-played parts of the Code to help pupils understand the rules and consequences.

Once the code has met the test of being equitable as a document, the question becomes more complex. Is a bias-free Code applied in a fair and equitable manner to students? Removal of a student from school, especially for any extended period of time, may influence that student's academic progress and potentially post-secondary school admissions and even future earning power. Given the potential harmful effect of removal from school and subsequent loss of academic time, an OSS action must meet all conditions of due process. Moreover, regarding disproportionate representation, no disciplinary action can violate the equal protection clause.

The typical code of conduct sets out positive statements about behavior expectation; the rights and responsibilities of students, educators, parents, and other involved people, and the due-process protections afforded to students through the appeals process at various levels of the discipline process.

Misbehaviors are typically presented in several levels of severity, with consequences that reflect both the severity of the misbehavior and steps taken when students repeatedly commit an offense. Being tardy to a class is less serious than fighting, which is less serious than possession of a weapon. Consequences for these misbehaviors might include verbal reprimand or a call home, in-school or out-of-school suspension, or expulsion and a report to another agency such as the police. Because a code also guides a student toward self-discipline, the code will allow some room for administrative interpretation and discretion except when the laws require "zero tolerance" such as possession of a weapon. Thus, if a code calls for an after-school detention after a third tardy, an administrator might waive the detention if the student presents a strong case of extenuating circumstances.

The ten summary criteria discussed previously are expressed in appendix 8.3 as a checklist that the author used to evaluate the codes in several court cases. The checklist has space for comments about important features of the code that influence a judgment about it's fairness and utility.

ANALYZING STUDENT BEHAVIOR

In *Coalition* (1995), *Reed v. Rhodes* (1997), and *Hoots et al.,* (2000), plaintiffs argued that unitary status should be denied to the defendants—the local school district or state—because, among other things, there was disproportionate representation of minority students in disciplinary actions in the schools, and in *Hoots et al.,* that minorities received harsher consequences and that discipline was excessive.

The question of whether or not discipline is excessive is open to interpretation, and may be less contentious than the issue of proportionality. That there has been an increase in consequences of student behavior, and behavior in the general population, is evident in the following discussion.

Rossell (1980) reported that "According to the Office of Civil Rights 1972–73 survey . . . one out of every twenty-four students . . . was suspended at least once during the school year" (p. 262). According to the Office of Civil Rights (OCR) 1990 survey, adjusted national estimated data (OCR 1993), one out of every twenty-one students was suspended at least once, and according to OCR (1999) one of every seventeen students was suspended at least once in 1997. This increase in the numbers of students receiving OSS at least once in a school year may reflect both an increase in student misbehavior and a decreasing dropout rate in schools. A similar change in misbehavior is also seen outside of schools where between 1990 and 1999, "The rate of incarceration increased from 1 in every 218 U.S. residents to 1 in every 147" (U.S. Department of Justice: 1).

The "Plaintiff's Brief in Opposition" (1997: 10) in *Reed v. Rhodes* defined the proportionality issue explicitly: "In 1994–96, African American students accounted for approximately 70 percent of the students in the district and for 80 percent of the suspensions. . . ." This statement was presented as evidence of vestiges of segregation in the area of student rights. Added data or analyses may not have been included because past decisions generally held that the simple numerical finding of disproportionate representation in such measurable school-discipline outcomes as OSS and expulsions constituted prima facie evidence of discrimination. Defendants have seldom accepted the task of analyzing the data, specifying and studying the problems, and presenting alternatives to plaintiff claims. Unequal representation of one group or another in actions taken by empowered representatives[3] of a school might stem from prior de jure or de facto segregation, but disproportionate representation might also be from other causes.

In other areas of desegregation, such as assignment of staff or students to schools, the courts have established a band of ±10 percentage points, or ±15 percent points, variation from the district proportion of a particular segment of the population as the target to be achieved. With a district population of 60 percent African American and 40 percent other students, and a ± 10 percent band, school leaders would seek a racial mix in the schools between about 50 percent and 70 percent African American and 50 percent and 30 percent other. It is but a short step from this desired assignment proportion based on a status characteristic (e.g., race) to arguing that the same proportions should apply to behavioral action outcomes such as suspensions. Is this logical?

Would a suspension rate by race that fell within a ± 10 percentage-point or ± 15 percentage-point band be considered no discrimination by plaintiffs in a desegregation case? Would that proportion be required for all other comparisons of behaviors with status variables for there to be no discrimination?

Deciding What Categories to Use in Specifying "Representation"

In the case of disciplinary action for violating a student code of conduct (or for arrests, or for speeding tickets, for example), proportionate representation suggests that the proportion of people involved in the disciplinary action will approximate that group's proportion in the population. With a population of 50 percent males and 50 percent females, proportionate representation means that about 50 percent of school misbehavior and 50 percent of OSS are to males and 50 percent to females. Would this same result be true for other variables, too, such as students in various age groups or grades, students on free and reduced lunch versus no free lunch; students in the top quartile of their academic class as opposed to students in the bottom quartile (or even for non-top-quartile students)? Based on experience, the distinctions just provided show that proportionality is complex when applied to behavior. In schools, males are suspended more frequently than are females; students in the bottom academic quartile or students on free lunch are suspended more frequently than are students not on free lunch or students who have top academic standing. Middle-school-age students are suspended more frequently than younger students. These conditions were true in *Coalition v. State Board of Education*, *Reed v. Rhodes* and *Hoots et al.*, as well as in other cases.

The example in appendix 8.4 of suspensions by age categories uses the school levels in WHSD (K–3, 4–6, 7–9, 10–12) as a surrogate for age. Using 1998–1999 data, each group's proportion of the total student body is shown (31 percent, 23 percent, 24 percent, and 22 percent). Each group's percentage of total suspensions is also reported (6 percent, 17 percent, 64 percent, and 12 percent respectively). Those percentages are compared to "bands" that might be considered to govern assignments ($\pm$ 10 percent and $\pm$ 15 percent). Only school level D, grades 10–12 with 22 percent of the population and 18 percent of the suspensions falls within both bands. The other groups are outside. If a group's suspension percentage were the same as that group's percentage of the population, the student suspension index would be 1.0. The index column shows that in this example, two age groups (K–3 and 4–6) are far below the 1.0 desideratum, one group (7–9) is far above, and one group (10–12), at .82, is fairly close to 1.0. Dividing the smaller of pairs of indices into the larger shows that a student in grades 7–9 is about twenty-one times more likely to be suspended than is a student in K–3. A student in grades 10–12 is about six times more likely to be suspended than is a student in grades K–3. Using these indicators, most age groups are disproportionately suspended when compared to some other group.

Are the data in appendix 8.4 necessarily evidence of discrimination? Most parents and educators would agree that older students engage in behaviors that lead to disciplinary action more frequently than do younger students. For these data, does relying on disproportionate representation demonstrate age discrimination against older students?

Similar computations are possible using any groups in the population: race, gender, academic standing, or SES, for example. Given the many combinations of variables, is an index of 1.0 between or among all comparisons of groups reasonable? Between what group comparisons is it reasonable to expect this? What are some alternative explanations for disproportionate representation besides discrimination? Is it possible that in 2000, forty-six

years after *Brown*, public-school administrators consistently apply disciplinary actions to specific groups in a consciously discriminatory manner?

Exploring the Arguments

Data on representation of one group or other in some action or activity—
in the present discussion, representation of a group in OSS—is usually read-
ily available. In fact, in desegregation orders, courts often have required data
collection and monitoring processes that provide indicators of equal treatment of students.

Court Opinions that Provide Guidance for Analysis

Hoots et al. (unreported no. 71-538 W.D.P.A. [1997]) makes it clear that
although defendants must prove that disparities are not the result of the
prior de jure segregation, they do not have to achieve equality of results
nor any specific number or ratio. Most instructive is the following from
Freeman:

Racial balance is not to be achieved for its own sake, but is to be pursued only when
there is a causal link between an imbalance and the constitutional violation. Once
racial imbalance traceable to the constitutional violation has been remedied, *a school
district is under no duty to remedy an imbalance that is caused by demographic factors.*
(*Freeman v. Pitts*, 503 U.S. 467 at 494 [1992]; emphasis added)

Judicial opinions have provided indications that statistical information
alone, or disproportionality issues alone, are not of themselves indications
of intentional discrimination. Consider the following excerpts from the
opinion by Posner, chief judge of the U.S. Court of Appeals for the Seventh
Circuit.

... *he based his finding of intentional discrimination on statistical disparities, which need
not reflect discrimination, intentional or otherwise* ... (at 534) (Emphasis added.) ... *a
statistical study that fails to correct for salient explanatory variables, or even to make the
most elementary comparisons, has no value as causal explanations and ... is therefore in-
admissible in a federal court.* (*People Who Care et al. v. Rockford Board of Education,
School District No. 205*, 111 F.3d 528 at 537–38 [1997]; emphasis added)

In desegregation cases where disproportionality was an issue in the original findings, it is clear that defendants have the obligation to demonstrate
that any remaining disproportionality is not because of vestiges of prior segregation in the school or system. Consider the impact that variables outside
of the school could have on in-school behavior.

Parental Involvement and Peer Influence: Always Good?

The Coleman et al. (1966) study pointed out that home life influenced student performance in school. Indicators that a student may be at-risk include such things as a sibling who is in a gang or in trouble with the law, a parent in jail, poverty, single-parent households. Family, peers, and others all influence a student's school behavior. Problems in schools need careful and targeted help from beyond the classroom, including help from parents and other adults (Steinberg, Brown and Dornbusch, 1997). Peer culture also shapes student behavior. Youngsters who participate in school and school-related activities succeed at school (Finn, 1993). Controlling peer influences, television viewing habits, participation in school, and so forth takes adult care (Singer et al. 1999).

An Alternative Approach to the Analysis of Disproportionality

Rather than accepting uncritically that disproportionality by itself indicates discrimination, school and community leaders should determine if observed disproportionality is discriminatory. The following steps provide a framework for analyzing the disproportionality issue:

1. Obtain and verify the data. Assume that the data are neutral.
2. Categorize data to explore the magnitude of the difference between actual (empirical) and ideal, or desired, conditions.
3. Analyze each observed discrepancy to determine why it exists. Analyses should lead to plausible alternative explanations of the discrepancy.
4. Search for information to explain the discrepancy. Because the data are neutral, the discrepancy (disproportion) is not the problem or cause. Hypothesize one or more probable causes of the discrepancy.
5. Establish questions or hypotheses to guide an exploration of possible and plausible alternatives to disproportion by race (or gender, age, etc.).
6. Make analyses and comparisons that allow considered judgments about possible causes of disproportions.

Examples of Analyses for Disproportionate Representation[4]

Examples of disproportionate representation are derived from *Coalition to Save Our Children v. State Board of Education* (1995), *Reed v. Rhodes* (1997), and *Hoots et al.* (2000). The approach and analyses used in *Reed v. Rhodes* and in *Hoots et al.* were essentially those used earlier in *Coalition*. In each case, defendants (the school system or state) sought unitary status. They had to demonstrate that disproportions in student disciplinary actions were not vestiges of prior segregation. Although the conditions in the cases were very similar, most examples used here are taken from *Reed v. Rhodes* and *Hoots et al.* because later cases incorporate the ideas from earlier cases.

In *Reed v. Rhodes*, data on student behavior and on OSS by race were clear. Approximately 70 percent of the student body was African American and 80 percent of disciplinary actions were received by this group. The 70 percent figure had been constant ($\pm$ 2 percent) for approximately ten years. Data were available on student disciplinary actions and suspensions for that same time, and for additional years of the court-ordered desegregation process. I accepted as correct the plaintiff's assertion, as expressed in the "Plaintiffs' Brief in Opposition" (1997), that minorities were 70 percent of enrollment but 80 percent of disciplinary actions.

Fair and equitable application of the Code can be determined and judged in several ways. If the court allows it, the Code can be assessed by evaluating outcomes of the Code's use against a standard of $\pm$ 10–15 percentage points of the distribution of students by such things as race, gender, age, or free lunch. Although easy to compute, this approach has shortcomings. For example, applying a $\pm$ 15 percent-point standard in a district that has 85 percent of one race means that if 100 percent of disciplinary actions are imposed on that racial group, it is equitable. A more serious problem, however, is that the standard relies on a stated desired outcome rather than on a more realistic assessment guided by the Code.

Student misbehaviors in *Reed v. Rhodes* had been categorized into four classifications of severity as stipulated in the Code. Class I was essentially school-related misbehaviors such as disturbance in class or talking back to the teacher. Class II misbehaviors included such things as fighting, failure to report for a legitimate discipline or corrective action for a Class I behavior, smoking, or other such infraction. Class III misbehaviors included such things as assault, violence, a weapon look-alike, or repeated violations of Class I or Class II misbehaviors. Finally, Class IV included misbehaviors for which the student would most probably receive an expulsion. Class III or Class IV misbehavior would result in an adult being called to the attention of the legal system. The Code in *Hoots et al.* also provided four levels of misbehaviors ranging from mild to serious.

Given the court requirement that school-district defendants must maintain extensive databases including student misbehavior by race, gender, et cetera, it was a fairly simple task to categorize all suspensions and OSS (a) by classes (I–IV) of misbehavior, (b) by the race (gender, age, etc.) of the person who received the corrective action for a misbehavior, and (c) by other factors. The next step was to analyze the individual and aggregate data.

Employing Criteria to Evaluate the Disproportionality Issue

Besides looking historically at a district's record of handling student behavior, it is possible to compare that district's discipline index to indices of
similar school systems, to districts that achieved unitary status, to national
data, to other reports that use comparable percentages, and so on. Another
approach is to compare OSS by race (or gender, etc.) to arrest records, juvenile court records or to incarceration rates in the immediate vicinity of the
school system, in the state, and in the nation. Each comparison can serve as
a means to evaluate the extent of disproportionality in disciplinary actions
internal to the system and to external benchmarks. Other comparisons include disaggregating the discipline data by individual schools, by the race of
the administrator who handles OSS, by student academic standing, by SES
(free lunch), by age, and by combinations of the variables.

Analyses by severity of offense are instructive because in serious offenses,
an administrator has little or no discretion to act. The administrator's discretion decreases as the seriousness of the misbehavior increases. Consistency can be analyzed between and among groups and school districts and
over time by the race of the suspending school official, or others to discover
if discrimination exists or not.

Some comparisons are useful to help in decisions about discrimination
and in considering OSS in general. For example, in *Reed v. Rhodes*, it was
possible to compare the three-year average OSS in Cleveland Public Schools
(CPS) with the same rates in six comparable but smaller urban school systems in Ohio. The OSS rates per one hundred students ranged from 58.9 to
11.9, with an average of 40.2. The rate for CPS, at 27.5, was higher than only
one other urban system and considerably below the average.

Figures 8.1 through 8.3 show selected comparisons used in *Reed v.
Rhodes* to determine if any evident disproportion indicated discrimination.
Figure 8.1 shows the consistency of OSS over time in the CPS. From
1981–1997, the range of the TSI for black students (percentage black of
suspensions divided by the percentage black of enrollment) was between
1.04 and 1.14. This consistency was maintained for sixteen years in spite of
social and demographic changes, through many changes of teachers and administrators, and as the student population and racial percentages in the
school district changed. Such consistency would hardly be possible unless
disciplinary actions closely followed a Code that provided guidance to educators in administering discipline consistently.

Figure 8.2 shows that in CPS the disproportionality of OSS increased
as the administrator's discretion to act decreased because of the severity of
the misbehaviors. This phenomenon was also true in *Coalition* and in *Hoots
et al.* When the misbehavior was a Class I or minor offense, the percentage of OSS received by black students (69.5%) was essentially the same as
the percentage of black students in the CPS (70%), creating a black TSI of

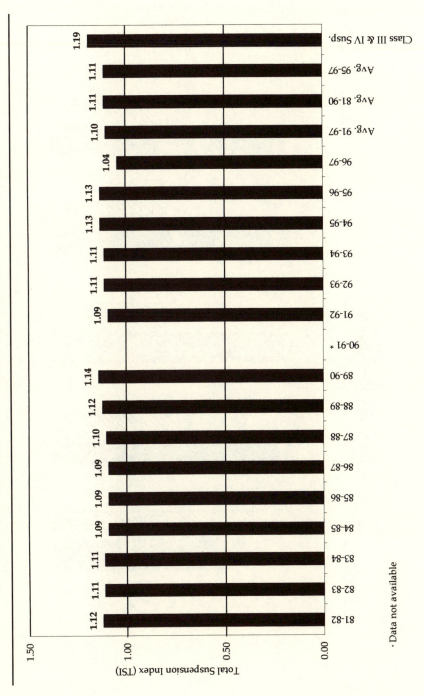

Figure 8.1
Out-of-School Suspensions (OSS) in the Cleveland Public Schools Over Time, 1981–1997

Total Suspension Index (TSI)

Category	TSI
81-82	1.12
82-83	1.11
83-84	1.11
84-85	1.09
85-86	1.09
86-87	1.09
87-88	1.10
88-89	1.12
89-90	1.14
90-91 *	
91-92	1.09
92-93	1.11
93-94	1.11
94-95	1.13
95-96	1.13
96-97	1.04
Avg. 91-97	1.10
Avg. 81-90	1.11
Avg. 95-97	1.11
Class III & IV Susp.	1.19

* Data not available

Figure 8.2
Disproportionality of OSS by Administrator Discretion

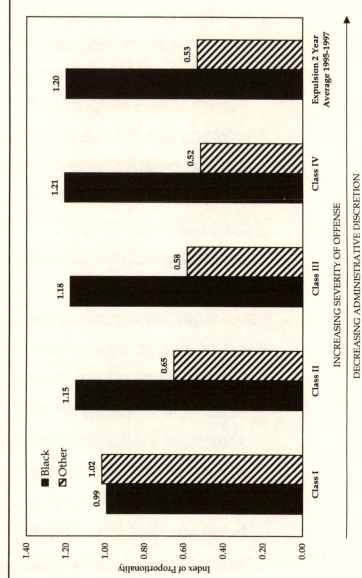

.99. There is increasing disproportion with each class of offense as (a) administrative discretion decreases, (b) the student is afforded more due process options, including informal and formal hearings, and (c) more people, such as the police, are involved in decisions. When the misbehavior is a Class IV offense—a violent or dangerous event—the percentage of OSS received by black students (84.5%) is disproportionate (1.21) when compared to the percentage of black students (70%) in the CPS. Thus, outcomes of disciplinary action are related to the behavior and the disproportion is caused mainly by student behaviors that do not allow school personnel any option but to take the actions prescribed in the Code.

Figure 8.3 compares the student suspension index (SSI) for black students among the four Delaware districts that achieved unitary status in 1994, the Woodland Hills Schools District (WHSD) (1997–98, 1998–99), the Cleveland Public Schools (CPS) (1993–94, 1996–98), and the United States, using OCR data. The index is the percentage of students ever suspended who are black divided by the percentage black of the enrollment. In this analysis, a student who is suspended many times is represented only once. The four Delaware districts all had higher suspension indices than did WHSD or CPS, but the national indices were even higher than the Delaware indices.

Appendix 8.5 shows these comparisons in several districts and also includes the TSI, or total suspensions index, which includes multiple suspensions of the same students. The indices for total suspensions and for students suspended are very similar.

Appendices 8.6 through 8.8 show racial disproportionality for consequences of misbehaviors outside of the school systems, and therefore not subject to school or school administrator bias. Appendix 8.6 shows disproportionality in U.S. jail populations. The proportionality indices from 1992 through 1994 for black prisoners are 3.38, 3.38 and 3.23 and .64, .64, .67 for other prisoners, and the ratios (the black index divided by the other index) range from 4.8 to 5.3. The indices and ratios for males and females are much more disproportionate than those for race. The male–female ratio ranges from 9.2 to 10.3, whereas the black–white ratio only ranges from 4.8 to 5.3.

Appendix 8.7 offers comparative data on the proportionality of black and white juveniles confined in training schools based on a rate per 100,000 juveniles. This analysis compares one CPS and two WHSD suspension indices with the rates of juveniles placed in training schools in Pennsylvania (*Hoots et al.*), in Ohio (*Reed v. Rhodes*), and in the United States. The racial disproportionality for juvenile detainees in training schools, which ranges from 15.63 in Pennsylvania to 6.04 in the United States to 7.58 in Ohio, greatly exceeds the disparities by race in WHSD (between 2.53 and 3.68) or in CPS (between 1.53 and 1.16) for student discipline actions.

Figure 8.3
Students Suspended Index for Black Students

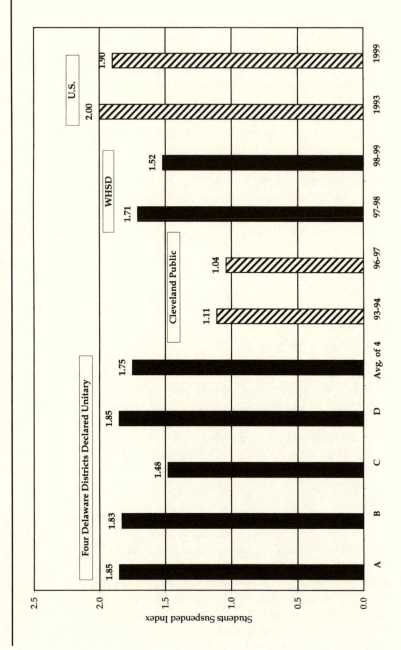

Data in appendix 8.8 shows arrest rates (per 1000) of persons eighteen years old and older as designated by race and by gender in the municipalities that comprise WHSD (*Hoots et al.*), in Pennsylvania, and in the United States in the top half of the table. Indices of proportionality are shown for the Cleveland metropolitan area which includes CPS and areas outside of CPS (Cuyahoga County). The arrest rates reflect the relative levels of crime in the communities where students reside, including various socioeconomic factors in the communities, such as poverty and low educational attainment, that lead to misconduct in schools (Singh 1999). Given the racial disparity in arrest rates, it is not surprising to see a disparity in the discipline rates in WHSD and in the CPS, shown in the bottom half of the table. In fact, the racial disparity in school suspensions is much smaller than the racial disparities in arrest rates.

SUMMARY

This chapter has reviewed key issues in school desegregation that relate to student behavior in schools, the consequences of student misbehavior, and emerging issues in analyzing racial and other disparities in student discipline. Rather than accept that disproportionate representation of one or another group in school disciplinary actions is prima facie evidence of discrimination, defendant school districts are beginning to seek explanations for the evident disparity and to present data to the courts about other probable causes.

The idea that a behavior outcome is connected to a single, or to any, status variable is suspect. There are several reasons to question the assumption that school discipline and outcomes of disciplinary action are solely the result of discrimination:

- The prevalence of more pronounced disparities in outcomes related to behavior in agencies outside of the school (courts, arrests, incarcerations) than in schools suggests that school behavior reflects behavior in the larger society.
- The interrelationships of many of the variables used in analyses of disciplinary outcomes (e.g., poverty, race, single-parent households, age, etc.) suggest that the univariate explanation of racial discrimination is simplistic.
- The finding that—although the incidences of misbehavior are fewer in elementary schools than in later grades—there is still racial disproportionality suggests that (a) students come to school exhibiting varying behavior readiness for school, and (b) that school activities help ameliorate the disproportions.
- Internal consistency in suspension indices over time, across groups or categories, and within groups undermines the argument that discipline is applied inequitably and not in accordance with a fair and unbiased code of conduct.

- The findings that (a) disproportionality increases as the severity of the infraction increases and administrator discretion to act decreases, and (b) that indices of proportionality do not vary by the race of the disciplinarian undermine the notion that disproportionality is caused primarily by discrimination.

The court-ordered compilation of discipline data has provided a rich resource for the analysis of student behavior. Recent court decisions in desegregation cases have opened the way for analyses of new questions about probable causes of the evident disparities in school discipline outcomes when they are analyzed by important groupings of students.

In his opinion in *Hoots et al. v. Commonwealth of Pennsylvania*, Judge Cohill noted that, "We are not the first court to struggle with whether a racial disparity in student discipline is a vestige of the constitutional violation, or remains despite the school district's having done all that is practicable to eliminate this imbalance" (*Hoots* at 68). In support of this position, Judge Cohill recognized the findings in *Coalition* (90 F.3d at 774), and *People Who Care v. Rockford Board of Education*, (111 F.3d 528, 538 [7th Cir. 1997]) that reversed a remedial relief requiring students to be disciplined in proportion to their percentage in the school population. In that opinion, chief Judge Posner noted that

Racial disciplinary quotas violate equity in its root sense. They entail either systematically overpunishing the innocent or systematically under punishing the guilty. They place race at war with justice. They teach school children an unedifying lesson of racial entitlements. (*People Who Care v. Rockford Board of Education*, 1997 at 538)

Concluding Thoughts

Although the concern about disproportionality in school disciplinary actions gets much attention, a second fact should be noted. How well are students behaving relative to Uniform Codes of Conduct? Most students are behaving quite well indeed. For example, in the Cleveland Public Schools in 1967–98, approximately 7 percent of CPS students accounted for 73 percent of CPS suspensions (Achilles, 1997: 19). In the Woodland Hills School District (*Hoots et al.*) 4 percent of WHSD students in 1997–98 accounted for 58 percent of the total suspensions (Achilles, 2000: 27) and in 1998–99 fewer than 4 percent of the students accounted for 66 percent of misbehaviors leading to suspensions.

In *Coalition, Reed v. Rhodes*, and *Hoots et al.* the defendants presented evidence that discipline actions in the schools generally should be and are based upon (a) a fair and unbiased Code of Student Conduct, (b) applied in a fair and unbiased manner, (c) that yields consequences for students that are directly and most plausibly related to the observed student behavior. In student parlance, "You do the crime, you serve the time."

Defendant school districts have provided considerable testimony and evidence that student misbehavior in schools has strong connections to social conditions beyond the direct control of the school: poverty syndrome, single-parent homes, peers, violence in neighborhoods and homes, television violence. Defendant school districts also have shown that relying on a single status variable, usually race in desegregation cases, may not be a productive way to explain racial disparity in discipline outcomes.

The line of evidence and testimony in recent cases suggests that the prior assumption that racial disparity in student discipline is a prima facie vestige of prior segregation and can be remedied by court orders might better be replaced with attention focused on new questions. Why is there a racial disparity in school misbehavior? How might forces in family, community and society cooperate to reduce this disparity? This redirection of energy has potential for positive outcomes and better school environments because it focuses on the cause, not the outcome, of the racial disparities in school behavior.

ENDNOTES

This material is a revision of the Achilles, C.M., and Achilles, S.H. (1998, August) "Disproportionate representation or not? A disciplinarian's dilemma," paper presented at the National Council of Professors of Educational Administration (NCPEA) 53rd Annual Conference, Juneau, Alaska, and draws heavily upon data reviewed or expert reports prepared for defendants in court cases in New Castle County, Delaware (1994); Cleveland, Ohio (1997); Rockford, Illinois (2000), and Woodland Hills, Pennsylvania (2000).

1. Even in some recent highly visible years, the schools were by far more safe than other places that youths aged 5–17 frequent. In 1997–1998 there were eleven high-visibility deaths in schools from the violence of guns, but more than 3,000 violent deaths in public places such as malls, and in homes or neighborhoods. Education quality is also quite consistently a "hot topic" for politicians and others, as demonstrated by the 1950s Sputnik issue, the 1983 report, "A Nation at Risk," and the late 1990s push for charter schools, vouchers, privatization, and choice.

2. The Codes in *Coalition v. Board of Education* and in *Hoots et al. v. Commonwealth* also fell short on this criterion and all districts used similar processes to help students and others understand the Code.

3. In the present discussion, empowered representatives are the educators in the system, such as teachers and administrators. Persons affected by the decisions are pupils who may be in the school setting because of mandatory attendance laws, or older students who are attending schools but who are older than mandatory attendance ages.

4. The examples are drawn from recent cases (1994–2000) in which the author testified as an expert for defendants (Achilles 1994, 1997, 2000).

Appendix 8.1
A Comparison of OCR and WHSD Data
Using the Students Suspended Index

A.   **OCR Data (1993)**

    1.   **Suspension Rates**

Black Students Suspended Black Student Enrollment	$\dfrac{632,833}{6,616,308}$	= 9.6%
White Students Suspended White Student Enrollment	$\dfrac{1,063,158}{27,727,008}$	= 3.8%
Black & White Students Susp. Black & White Student Enroll.	$\dfrac{1,695,991}{34,343,316}$	= 4.9%
Total Students Suspended Total Student Enrollment	$\dfrac{1,979,862}{40,847,916}$	= 4.8%

Dividing 9.6% by 3.8% = 2.53; that is, black students are suspended 2.53 times more than white students. 1993 OCR data.

    2.   **Proportionality Indices**

	1993	1999
Black: % Students Suspended % Black of Enrollment	$\dfrac{32\%^{a}}{16\%} = 2.0$	$\dfrac{32\%}{17\%} = 1.9$
White: % Students Suspended % Black of Enrollment	$\dfrac{54\%^{b}}{68\%} = .79$	$\dfrac{51\%}{64\%} = .80$

The likelihood ratio is 2.0/.79 = 2.53; that is, black students are suspended 2.53 times more than white students in 1993; in 1999 the ratio is 1.9/.8 = 2.38.

B.   **WHSD Data (1998-99)**

Black Student Index	$\dfrac{67\%}{41\%} = 1.52$
White Student Index	$\dfrac{33\%}{55\%} = .60$

The likelihood ratio is 1.52/.60 = 2.53; that is, black students are suspended 2.53 times more than white students in the Woodland Hills School District in 1998-99.

---

[a] This is 632,833 black students suspended divided by 1,979,862 total suspended.
[b] This is 1,063,157 white students suspended divided by 1,979,862 total suspended.

Appendix 8.2
Validation of Criteria for Assessing a Uniform Code of Student Conduct[a]

Code Provisions, Issues (Avery 1998: 63-77)	Summary (X = Yes)															
	Milliken v. Bradley	Coalition (DE)	DE State Committee	State of Illinois	State of Michigan (1971)	State of New Jersey	State of N. Carolina	Reed V. Rhodes (Ohio)	State of	State of Texas	Nat. Sch. Safety CTR	Rockford (IL)	Cincinnati, OH (a)	Portland, OR (b)	WHSD	Total (of 15)
Distributed to all students and parents.	X	X	X	X	X	X	X	X	X	X	X	X	X	X	X	15
Formally written; adopted by Bd. of Ed.		X	X	X	X	X	X	X	X	X	X	X	X	X	X	14
Broad input from students, teachers, parents, and administrators.		X	X	X	X	X	X	X	X	X	X	X	X	X	X	14
Due process rights are explained.	X	X	X	X	X	X	X	X	X	X	X	X	X	X	X	15
Expected behaviors are clearly stated.			X	X		X	X	X	X	X	X	X	X	X	X	12
Anticipated consequences are clearly stated.			X	X		X	X	X	X	X	X	X	X	X	X	12
Code applies equally to all without discrimination. (Code is not biased)	X	X	X	X		X	X	X	X			X	X	X	X	12
Complies with local, state, federal laws.		X	X	X	X	X	X	X	X	X	X	X	X	X	X	14
Explained clearly to all students/others.		X	X	X	X	X	X	X			X	X	X	?	?	11
Administrative flexibility in assigning consequences			X			X	X	X		X	X	X	X	X	X	10
Training for all staff in applying the code.	X		X					X	X		X	X	?	?	X	7
Rights and responsibilities are clearly stated.	X		X		X	X	X	X	X			X	X	X	X	11
Reviewed and updated annually (Periodically)	X	X	X			X	X	X	X	X	X	X	?	?	X	11
Used consistently. (Determined by court ruling).	X	X	X					X	X			?	?	?	X	6
TOTAL	7	9	14	9	7	12	12	14	12	10	11	13	10	10	14	164

? Not determined from document itself. More analyses are required.

(a) Cincinnati Public School Districtwide Code of Behavior (K-6 and 7-12), 1994-95. Two documents. Also, Board Resolution, 8/9/93 and two discipline summary sheets.

(b) Portland. Guide to Policies, Rules, and Procedures on Student Responsibilities, Rights, and Discipline (1989 and 1999).

Appendix 8.3
Checklist for Evaluating a Uniform Code of Student Conduct

CRITERIA FOR CODE	YES/ NO/? *	COMMENTS/ DATA **
Are the elements of The Code planned cooperatively involving: parents, students, school personnel, others?		
Behavior expectations are clearly stated.		
Rules are instructional, goal-oriented (realistic, age-sensitive), and constructive. Allows for some interpretation by persons administering The Code.		Consequences within levels of infractions have several options. No options in "zero tolerance," such as weapons.
Is The Code revised periodically or annually by stakeholders?		
Is The Code in compliance with laws and policies? (Local, State, Federal).		
Rules and Consequences are: Readable Explicit Precise Clear "Reader-Friendly."		
Rules are presented to students and parents annually: People receive instruction about the Code. ***		
Stakeholder rights and responsibilities and Code purpose are stated.		
Is there an explanation of student due process rights? (In general and for both suspension and expulsion).		
Code is fair and equitable (Summary).		No evidence of discrimination or bias in The Code itself.

* A designation such as (?) in the "Yes/No" column could indicate a need for further exploration before a clear yes or no would be warranted. "Yes" does not indicate no room for improvement. "Fair" might suggest that cosmetic improvements seem warranted.
** Two comments from the actual review of the Code in *Reed v. Rhodes* are provided as examples.
*** A Code Implementation Plan might contain dissemination activities and a plan to get information to students, parents, professional and teaching staff, and administrators.

Example of Proportionality Based on School-Level Suspensions (OSS) for Violations of a School Uniform Code of Student Conduct[1]

| | School Level | Percentages of WHSD | | Compliance With Absolute Indicators | | Index [2] | Proportion Indicators |
		Population	Suspension	± 15%	± 10%		Ratios [3]
(A)	K-3	31	4	NO	NO	.13	$\frac{B}{A}=3.69$; $\frac{C}{A}=21.46$; $\frac{D}{A}=6.31$
(B)	4-6	23	11	YES	NO	.48	$\frac{C}{B}=5.48$; $\frac{C}{D}=3.40$
(C)	7-9	24	67	NO	NO	2.79	
(D)	10-12	22	18	YES	YES	.82	$\frac{D}{B}=1.71$
TOTAL		100	100				

[1] School level is a proxy for age (Achilles, 2000: 25).

[2] Computed as % group's suspensions ÷ % group's population.

[3] Ratio of two indices, larger divided by smaller. A person in group C (Grades 7-9) is 21.46 times more likely to be suspended, on average, than is a person in group A (Grades K-3). In other words, $\frac{IndexC}{IndexA} = \frac{2.79}{.13} = 21.46$

Appendix 8.5
A Comparison of Selected Unitary Systems and the United States

| | OSS SUSPENSION INDEXES | | | |
| | SUSPENSIONS (TSI) | | STUDENTS SUSPENDED (SSI) | |
ENTITIES	MIN. (BL)	MAJ.(WH)	MIN. (BL)	MAJ.(WH)
Brandywine, DE (1993-94)	1.90	.61	1.85	.63
Christina, DE (1993-94)	1.94	.58	1.83	.63
Colonial, DE (1993-94)	1.54	.72	1.48	.75
Red Clay, DE (1993-94)	1.86	.56	1.85	.57
Avg. of 4 DE Districts	1.81	.62	1.75	.64
Cleveland (1993-94)	1.11	.73	(R)	(R)
Cleveland (1996-97)	1.04	.90	1.04	.90
WHSD (*Hoots*) (98-99)	1.61	.53	1.52	.60
WHSD (*Hoots*) (97-98)	1.73	.47	1.71	.51
OCR: U.S. (1993)			2.00	.79
OCR: U.S. (1999)			1.89	.80

(R) = Data not available.

* The comparisons are not always on identical categories, but they serve as indicators. For example, some data are for different years, or the reporting categories may be Black or minority, or White/Other. Nevertheless, the similarity of the indices, in general, is noteworthy. OCR reports Black, White. Delaware used Black, White, Hispanic.

Appendix 8.6

Jail Population in the United States, 1992–1994, by Gender and by Race: Black and Other

Year	POPULATION	POPULATION BY CATEGORIES			
	TOTAL	OTHER	BLACK	MALE	FEMALE
1992					
Number	444,584	249,428	195,156	403,768	40,816
%		56%	44%	91%	9%
Index		.64	3.38	1.86	.18
Ratio			5.28	10.31	
1993					
Number	459,804	256,341	203,463	415,576	44,228
%		56%	44%	90%	10%
Index		.64	3.38	1.84	.20
Ratio			5.28	9.18	
1994					
Number	490,442	284,164	206,278	441,219	49,223
%		58%	42%	90%	10%
Index		.67	3.23	1.84	.20
Ratio			4.82	9.18	

* Percentages in population: Male 49%; Female 51%; Black 13%; Other 87%. *Other* includes all persons in the analysis not classified as Black. Source: Statistical Abstract of the United States. 1996, U.S. Department of Commerce, October 1996: 21-23, the National Data Book.

Appendix 8.7

**U.S. Public Juvenile Training Schools: One-Day Counts by Race and Rates
per 100,000 Juveniles for the United States, Ohio, and Pennsylvania
(1991)[1]—Compared to OSS in School Systems in Litigation**

	JUVENILE DETAINEES					
	White		Nonwhite		Total	
Location	N	Rate	N	Rate	N	Rate
PA	169	16	442	250	611	51
USA	9620	50	18915	302	28535	112
OHIO	984	95	1375	720	2359	192

Dividing the non-white training-school detainee rate by the white detainee rate produces the following ratios:

OHIO: $720 \div 95 = 7.58$ PA: $250 \div 16 = 15.63$ USA: $302 \div 50 = 6.04$

	OUT OF SCHOOL SUSPENSIONS			DETAINEES	
	Black Index	White Index	Ratio [2]	PA Ratio	US Ratio
1998-99 WHSD (Students)	1.52	.60	2.53		
" (Suspensions)	1.61	.53	3.04	15.63	6.04
1997-98 WHSD (Students)	1.70	.51	3.33		
" (Suspensions)	1.73	.47	3.68		
				Ohio Ratio	
1993-94 CPS (Students)	1.12	.73	1.53	7.58	6.04
1996-97 CPS (Students)	1.04	.90	1.16		

[1] Schwartz & Hsieh (1994: 46-47).

[2] The likelihood ratio is calculated by dividing the Black index by the White index for students suspended, (or total suspensions) for example, $1.52 \div .60 = 2.53$.

Appendix 8.8
**1997 Rates (per 1,000) of Persons 18 Years and Older Arrested by
Race/Gender in Woodland Hills (WHSD), Pennsylvania (PA),
Cleveland Public Schools (CPS), and U.S. Compared to Out-of-School
Suspensions in Litigating Districts**

	ARRESTS[1]					
	Race			Gender		
	Black	White	Ratio [2]	Male	Female	Ratio
WHSD	112	19	5.89	54	11	4.91
PA	111	30	3.70	61	15	4.07
U.S.	107	35	3.06	68	18	3.78
CPS INDEX[3]	1.67	.45	3.71	1.87	.29	6.45

	STUDENTS SUSPENDED					
	Race			Gender		
	Black	White	Ratio[2]	Male	Female	Ratio
1997-98 (WHSD)	1.70	.51	3.33	1.35	.63	2.14
1998-99 (WHSD)	1.52	.60	2.53	1.35	.64	2.14
1996-97 (CPS)	1.04	.90	1.16	1.33	.69	1.93

[1]Arrest data for WHSD and Pennsylvania are from Singh (1999).

[2] The ratio, using rates per 1000, is equivalent to the Likelihood Ratio where the black index is divided by the white index.

[3] Achilles (1997: 28, C-4); Bania (1997).

REFERENCES

Achilles, C.M. 1994. Delaware desegregation case: Student discipline analysis. Report for *Coalition v. Board of Education*.

———. 1997. The Cleveland public schools: An analysis of student rights with an emphasis on student discipline practices and concerns regarding "disproportionate representation" by race in student suspensions and expulsions. Report for *Reed v. Rhodes*.

———. 2000. Evaluation of discipline in the Woodland Hills School District. Report for *Hoots et al. v. Commonwealth of Pennsylvania*.

Achilles, C.M., and S.H. Achilles. 1998. Disproportionate representation or not? A disciplinarian's dilemma. Paper at the National Conference of Professors of Educational Administration (NCPEA). Juneau.

Avery, J.W. 1998. *A Comparative Review of Student Codes of Conduct For Schools in Wayne County, MI.* Ypsilanti: Eastern Michigan University. Unpublished Dissertation.

Bania, N. 1997. Economic and social indicators for blacks and whites living in the Cleveland public school district. Report for *Reed v. Rhodes*.

Burke, F.G. 1981. *Handbook for Developing a Code of Conduct for Students*. 2–8. Trenton: N.J. State Dept. of Education.

Coalition to Save our Children v. Delaware State Board of Education, 901 F.Supp. 784 1995.

Coleman, J.S., E.Q. Campbell, C.J. Hobson, J. McPartland, A.M. Mood, F.D. Weinfield, and R.L. York. 1966. *Equality of Educational Opportunity.* Washington, D.C.: U.S. Government Printing Office.

Finn, J.D. 1993. *School Engagement and Students at Risk.* Washington, D.C.: OERI. NCES: 93–470.

Harris, K.A. and R.R. Dowe. 1980. *Detroit High School Profiles: Criteria-Based Monitoring of Desegregation.*

Hoots et al. v. Commonwealth of Pennsylvania et al. 2000. Opinion by Judge D. J. Cohill. Civil Action no. 71–538, (U.S. Dist. W.D. Pa. 25 July).

Moody, C.D., C.B. Vargon, and J. Williams. 1974. *Student Behavior, Rights and Responsibilities and the Fair Administration of Discipline: Conference Proceedings.* 239–73. Ann Arbor.

Office of Civil Rights. 1993. *Fall 1990 Elementary and Secondary School Civil Rights Survey: Revised National Statistical Estimates* (DBS under subcontract).

———. 1999. *1997 Elementary and Secondary School Civil Rights Compliance Report.* U.S. Department of Education.

People Who Care et al. v. Rockford Board of Education. 1997. Opinion by chief Judge Posner. 111 F.3d 528 (7th Cir 1997); 1997 U. S. App. LEXIS 7143.

Rossell, C.H. 1980. Social science research in educational equity cases: A critical review. In D. C. Berliner, ed. *Review of Research in Education.* 237–95. Washington, D.C.: American Educational Research Association.

Schwartz, I.M. and C. Hsieh. 1994. *Juveniles Confined in the United States, 1979–1991*. Philadelphia: University of Pennsylvania School of Social Work, Center for the Study of Youth Policy.

Singer, M.I., D.B. Miller, S. Guo, D.J. Flannery, T. Frierson, and K. Slovak. 1999. Contributors to violent behavior among elementary and middle school children. *Pediatrics* 104: 878–84.

Singh, V.P. 1999. Hoots et al. v. Commonwealth of Pennsylvania et al. *Twelve Socioeconomic Characteristics.* Pittsburgh: University of Pittsburgh.

Steinberg, L., B. Brown, and S.M. Dornbusch. 1997. *Beyond the classroom: Why school reform has failed and what parents need to do.* New York: Simon and Schuster.

U.S. Department of Commerce. 1996. *Statistical Abstract of the United States, 1996 and The National Data Book.* 22, 23, 210. Washington, D.C.: Author. Bureau of the Census.

U.S. Department of Justice. 2000. *Prison and Jail Inmates at Midyear, 1999 OJP.* Bureau of Justice Statistics Bulletin. Author (A. J. Beck, BJS Statistician).

Chapter 9

Improving Intergroup Relations in the Schools

Walter G. Stephan

Few social policies in the post-World War II period have created such sustained controversy as school desegregation. Powerful forces exist on both sides of the issue. Desegregation was one of the mainstays of the civil rights movement and the 1954 *Brown* decision was one of its first great victories. African Americans saw desegregation as a way to obtain a better future for their children. It called for Americans to change one of their basic social institutions and many whites were reluctant to do so; they did not want to see their segregated way of life eroded by the tides of history. Some of the opposition to desegregation was couched in terms of principles, such as states' rights, and some of it was phrased in terms of practicalities, such as the difficulties and costs of implementing busing, but another reason for white opposition to desegregation was based on a desire to maintain the racial status quo. Large numbers of whites were reluctant to send their children to school with African Americans. Thus, the hopes of African Americans and the fears of whites clashed on the battleground of school desegregation.

We are now in a position to look back nearly a half-century and ask what the effects of desegregation on race relations have been. Did desegregation in the schools change relations between the races? That is the first question I will address in this chapter. The answer, as I will show shortly, is decidedly mixed. The second question I will address stems from the answer to the first. If desegregation did not lead to improvements in intergroup relations, is there anything that can be done in the schools to improve relations between the races? The answer to this question is a clear yes.

THE EFFECTS OF SCHOOL DESEGREGATION

In the court cases leading up to the *Brown* decision, many of the social scientists who testified expressed the belief that segregation fostered negative relations between African Americans and whites. For instance, Kenneth Clark testified that "discrimination, prejudice and segregation have definitely detrimental effects on the personality development of the Negro child. The essence of this detrimental effect is a confusion in the child's self-concept of his own self-esteem—basic feelings of inferiority, conflict, confusion in his self-image, resentment, hostility toward himself, and *hostility toward Whites*" (Clark cited in Kluger 1975: 356, emphasis added). Thus, Clark was suggesting that segregation led African Americans to be prejudiced toward whites. Another social scientist, David Krech, testified that segregation leads to stereotyping and prejudice among whites. He said, "Legal segregation, because it is obvious to everyone, gives . . . environmental support for the belief that Negroes are in some way inferior to white people, and that in turn supports and strengthens beliefs of racial differences, or racial inferiority" (cited in Kluger 1975: 361). Krech also believed that eliminating segregation in the schools and in other arenas of American society would reduce prejudice. As he wrote in a textbook on social psychology "any step which can be taken to break down segregation . . . can make a significant contribution to the removal of racial prejudice in this country" (Krech and Crutchfield 1948: 516).

In the post-World War II period, there was also a widespread belief among social scientists that contact between the races could improve intergroup relations (Allport 1954; Williams 1947). The social scientists who filed an amicus curiae brief in the *Brown* case offered a version of this contact hypothesis.

Under certain circumstances desegregation . . . has been observed to lead to the emergence of more favorable attitudes and friendlier relations between the races . . . There is less likelihood of unfriendly relations when change is simultaneously introduced into all units of a social institution . . . The available evidence also suggests the importance of consistent and firm enforcement of the new policy by those in authority. It indicates also the importance of such factors as the absence of competition . . . the possibility of contacts which permit individuals to learn about one another as individuals: and the possibility of equivalence of positions and functions among the participants. (Allport and 35 co-signers 1953: 437–38)

At the time, it was believed that such conditions could be created in the schools. As we shall see, the actual conditions under which school desegregation was implemented rarely fulfilled these conditions, but we shall also see that the social scientists' faith in the favorable effects of this type of intergroup contact were not misplaced.

Short-Term Effects of School Desegregation on Intergroup Relations

Little desegregation occurred in the decade after *Brown* as the South fought to evade the Supreme Court decision in every way it could. With the passage of the Civil Rights Act of 1964, the federal government acquired the capacity to withhold funds from school districts that did not comply with the mandate contained in *Brown* (Stephan 1980). This led to an increase in school desegregation and to the first studies of its effects. School desegregation proceeded in fits and starts for the next two decades, but the pace of new mandatory court-ordered desegregation slackened in the 1980s and came to a near standstill in the 1990s, as did the studies of its short-term effects on intergroup relations (Orfield and Eaton 1996).

Studies of desegregation provide a mixed picture of its effects on intergroup relations (Stephan 1978; 1986; 1991; 1999). Taken together, these studies show that in 16 percent of the desegregated schools examined, the attitudes of whites toward African Americans became more favorable over time or were more favorable than those in comparison schools that were segregated. In the remaining schools, there were either no changes over time or no differences between desegregated and segregated schools (36%), or attitudes became, or were, more negative (48%). For the attitudes of African Americans, the picture is slightly more positive. In 38 percent of the schools studied, the attitudes of African Americans toward whites became or were more positive, while there were no differences in 38 percent of the schools, and attitudes became more, or were, negative in 24 percent of the cases. These studies were nearly all done during the first year after the implementation of desegregation and many involved mandatory desegregation plans with all of the controversy, turmoil, and tension that is usually attendant on the implementation of such plans. There are other reasons to be cautious about drawing conclusions from these studies about the effects of desegregation on race relations. The students examined in these studies varied a great deal in age and socioeconomic status (SES); the studies were done in different parts of the country; the types of desegregation plans examined varied considerably; the samples were very small in some studies; and the designs often left a lot to be desired (including cross-sectional as well as longitudinal designs).

Desegregation clearly did not have the beneficial effects on intergroup relations that were anticipated by the social scientists who participated in the *Brown* case. In retrospect, it is not difficult to understand why. Mandatory desegregation, as it was implemented in most communities, did not fulfill any of the contact conditions thought to be associated with the creation of favorable intergroup relations (Cook 1984; Schofield 1991). It was rarely instituted in all segments of a school system at the same time; it rarely had firm or consistent support from authority figures such as school boards, administrators, teachers, or parents; it was not voluntary; relations between students in the classroom were competitive not cooperative; the students from the different groups often came from different social class backgrounds; and the students frequently remained segregated within the desegregated schools and therefore had few opportunities to learn about one another as individuals.

Long-Term Effects of Desegregation on Intergroup Relations

The long-term effects of desegregation have been more consistent and more positive than the short-term effects. These studies, many of them national in scope, have generally examined the effects of attending desegregated schools on a variety of indices of willingness to interact with members of racial outgroups. For instance, a number of studies indicate that African Americans who attended desegregated schools are more likely to be working in integrated settings as adults than African Americans who attended segregated schools (Braddock, Crain, and McPartland 1984; Braddock and McPartland 1983; Braddock and McPartland 1989; Braddock, McPartland and Trent 1984). The effects found in these studies are not large, but they are consistent in suggesting that interacting with whites in the school setting makes African Americans more likely to apply for, or more likely to be hired into, jobs that involve working with whites. Other studies indicate that a parallel effect occurs for whites (Braddock, McPartland and Trent 1984). African Americans who attended desegregated schools are also more likely to attend traditionally all-white universities than African Americans who attended segregated schools (Braddock 1987; Braddock and McPartland 1982). In addition, African Americans who attended desegregated schools are more likely to have white friends as adults than African Americans who attended segregated schools (Crain 1971; Ellison and Powers 1994; Green 1981). Both African Americans and whites are also more likely to live in integrated neighborhoods and send their own children to desegregated schools than are people who attended segregated schools (Crain 1971; U.S. Commission on Civil Rights 1967).

Thus, it appears that experience with interacting with members of other racial groups in the schools carries over to adulthood and increases the chances of interracial interaction. Unfortunately, none of these studies distinguished between the types of desegregation plans these students had experienced so they do not shed any light on whether mandatory or voluntary desegregation has a greater impact on these social-outcome variables. In addition, in some of these studies, the students attending desegregated schools were a select group and the results for these students may not generalize to other students.

Why would the picture for the long-term effects of desegregation be more positive than the picture for the short-term effects? One reason is that after the turmoil of the initial years of mandatory desegregation, desegregation became accepted as the status quo. Accommodations are now made both within and outside of school that allow for more normal interactions between members of different racial and ethnic groups. Students of one racial or ethnic group learn how to interact effectively with members of other racial and ethnic groups, make friendships, work together in school and play together on the same teams. Negative incidents occur, of course, but by and large, students acquire knowledge about how to relate to people who are different from them that students in segregated schools have no opportunity to learn.

There have also been some negative effects of desegregation on intergroup relations. In their initial phases, certain types of desegregation plans, especially mandatory plans involving large urban school districts with adjacent suburban districts, prompted some whites to flee these school districts (Armor 1980; 1988; Rossell and Armor 1996; Wilson 1985). There was also a great deal of controversy over mandatory desegregation plans in many communities and this undoubtedly exacerbated relations between the races for a period of time in those communities. And, within the desegregated schools themselves, there were opportunities for intergroup conflict that could not arise in segregated schools, just as there were opportunities for positive intergroup contact in such schools, and these conflicts undoubtedly had negative effects on some students' relations to members of other racial and ethnic groups.

The research on the short- and long-term effects of desegregation makes it quite clear that desegregation is not a panacea for problems in intergroup relations. As the research on the mixed effects of desegregation began to emerge, researchers began to develop and assess techniques of improving intergroup relations in the schools. The question they asked was, "If desegregation itself does not promote favorable relations, what will?" The answers to this question will occupy the remainder of this chapter.

TECHNIQUES OF IMPROVING INTERGROUP RELATIONS IN THE SCHOOLS

For decades there has been a gulf between knowledge about the causes of prejudice, stereotyping, and discrimination and knowledge about their cures. The gulf has been slowly disappearing as social scientists acquire more and more knowledge about techniques of improving intergroup relations. I will review six of these techniques that are the most relevant to improving intergroup relations in the schools.

Cooperative Learning Groups

The most extensively researched technique of improving intergroup relations in the schools consists of the use of small cooperative groups compris-
ing members of different racial or ethnic groups. The initial impetus for
these techniques was research on cooperation and research on the contact
hypothesis. Research on cooperation had established that cooperation in
small groups could have beneficial effects on interpersonal relations, while
research on the contact hypothesis had begun to establish the conditions
under which contact was most likely to lead to improvements in intergroup
relations. The research on the contact hypothesis had used the initial for-
mulations of the contact hypothesis by Allport (1954) and others (Williams
1947) and built on this foundation. The basic findings of this research are
that cooperative contact involving participants who hold positions of equal
status, who interact under conditions that allow for individualized contact,
are supported by relevant authority figures, and that results in achieving valued goals, leads to improvements in relations between groups (Aronson,
Blaney, Stephan, Sikes, and Snapp 1978; Hertz-Lazarowitz and Miller
1992; Johnson and Johnson 1992a; Slavin 1978; Weigel, Wiser, and Cook
1975). Specifically, it has been found that cooperative learning groups increase cross-ethnic helping and friendships (DeVries and Edwards 1974;
Johnson and Johnson 1992b; Slavin 1992; Weigel et al. 1975, Ziegler 1981)
as well as empathy and liking for other students (Blaney, Stephan, Rosenfield, Aronson, and Sikes 1977; Bridgeman 1981).

In actual practice, this approach usually involves bringing students of two
or more racial or ethnic groups together in groups of four to six students to
learn standard academic materials (Aronson et al. 1978; Aronson and Patnoe 1997; Aronson and Thibodeau 1992; Bruffee 1993; Cohen 1992; Johnson, Johnson and Holubec 1994; Slavin 1991). However, the academic
materials are tailored for group use. For instance, in one of these techniques, known as the jigsaw classroom, the materials are divided into as
many segments as there are students in each group (Blaney et al. 1977;
Aronson and Patnoe 1997; Aronson and Thibodeau 1992). Each student in
the group is required to learn his or her materials and teach them to the
other students in the groups, usually during sessions lasting a hour or so a
day. The range of materials taught using cooperative techniques is very
broad including social studies, history, math, geography, and language. Depending on the type of cooperative technique being used, the students are
either tested and graded individually as they would be ordinarily, or they are
graded as a group. In some techniques, the cooperative groups compete
against one another, while in others there is no competition between the
groups. Tests of the achievement of students in these groups indicate that
they learn as much as they would learn in teacher-taught classrooms (Johnson and Johnson 1992a, 1992b), and there is some evidence that minority

groups actually perform better in cooperative groups than in teacher-taught classrooms (Blaney et al. 1977; Devries, Edwards, and Slavin 1978; Johnson and Johnson 1992a, 1992b; Lucker, Rosenfield, Aronson, and Sikes 1977; Sharan and Shachar 1988).

The early studies of these techniques indicated that they changed attitudes toward other members of the cooperative groups, but these changes in attitudes often did not generalize to the racial and ethnic groups to which the other students belonged. Later research indicated that more generalizable attitudes could be fostered in cooperative groups by assigning students to groups on a nonracial basis (Miller, Brewer, and Edwards 1985; Miller and Harrington 1990), insuring that the interactions are positive in nature (Desforges, Lord, Ramsey, Mason, Van Leeuwen, West, and Lepper 1991), and encouraging an interpersonal focus during the cooperative interactions (Rogers 1982, cited in Brewer and Miller 1988; see also Miller and Harrington 1990). Another way to increase the chances of creating attitude changes that generalize to the groups as a whole is to change the composition of the groups periodically so that the students are exposed to multiple members of other racial and ethnic groups. Another potential problem that can arise in cooperative groups concerns how to handle differences in ability. To overcome this problem, Cohen (1986; 1990) has students work in small mixed groups on tasks that require a variety of skills (intellectual, spatial, artistic, dramatic, etc.). The students are rotated through roles requiring a variety of skills so that they all have opportunities to display their particular talents. Her studies indicate that in these cooperative groups there is an increased acceptance of lower status (usually minority) students and increased achievement (Cohen 1986, 1990, 1992).

Multicultural Education

A substantial number of schools now incorporate aspects of multicultural education into their curriculum. They typically do so in recognition of the need to prepare students to work in our racially and ethnically diverse society. Although some of the schools that include multicultural educational materials in their curriculum are desegregated, many of them are segregated. Multicultural education curricula usually consist of materials on the history and cultural practices of a wide array of American racial and ethnic groups (Banks 1987, 1988, 1997; Grant and Sleeter 1989; NCSS Task Force 1992). The material is often presented in a didactic manner accompanied by interactive exercises. An attempt is often made to present history from the perspective of minority groups, rather than the more traditional perspective of the dominant majority. The goal of these programs is to "participate in public discourse and civic action with people who are different from them in significant ways" (NCSS Task Force 1992: 274). In addition, an explicit goal of most multicultural programs is to reduce prejudice and improve relations between groups.

Despite its widespread adoption, there do not appear to be any systematic, longitudinal studies of the effectiveness of multicultural education (Banks and McGee-Banks 1995; Sleeter and Grant 1987). There, are however, a considerable number of studies of more limited curricula that cover relatively short time spans. These short-term programs usually present information about different racial and ethnic groups in classroom settings for periods ranging from a few hours to as long as six to ten weeks. Reviews of these programs indicate that the majority of them are effective, but it is also clear that many of them have little or no effect. In my own review of these studies, I found that 62 percent of them led to decreases in prejudice, 35 percent found no effects and one study found an increase in prejudice (Stephan and Stephan 1984). Similarly, a more recent review of this literature found that the majority of these programs were successful in reducing prejudice (McGregor 1993). A recent study of one such program was done in Canada by Aboud and Fenwick (1999). This study examined the effects of an eleven-week curriculum designed to teach students about peers from different racial and ethnic groups using a variety of didactic presentations and interactive exercises. The students received instruction for one or two classes per week. The program reduced the prejudice of high-prejudiced white children, but had little effect on the attitudes of African American students.

Stephan and Stephan (1984), reported that the most successful programs appeared to be those that were longer in duration and those that involved more active participation on the part of the students, including the use of role-playing techniques and discussions of values and behaviors related to intergroup relations. McGregor (1993) found that programs using younger students (elementary and secondary school students) were generally more successful than those with older students and that classes with lower teacher-to-student ratios showed the largest positive effects. Specific techniques shown to be effective in these studies included: stressing the positive similarities between groups (Kehoe and Hood 1978 cited in Ijaz 1984), learning about the norms, roles, and values of the other group (Triandis 1975), dividing students into arbitrary groups and having them experience discrimination on the basis of this arbitrary distinction (Byrnes and Kiger 1990; Weiner and Wright 1973), writing essays supporting increased opportunities for minority groups (Gray and Ashmore 1975; Lieppe and Eisenstadt 1994), acting out cases of discrimination that can occur in school settings such as making racially insensitive remarks or "jokes" or the use of racial epithets (Breckheimer and Nelson 1976), role-playing being a member of another group (Hohn 1973; Kehoe and Rogers 1978; Smith 1990), negotiating agreements with a member of an outgroup (Thompson 1993), having low-prejudice children discuss their racial attitudes with high-prejudice children (Aboud and Doyle 1996), and keeping journals related to intergroup relations (Katz and Ivey 1977). Nearly all of these studies examined white students' attitudes toward African Americans so the results cannot necessarily be generalized to other ethnic groups. Another problem with these programs is that they are narrowly focused, rather than comprehensive. They teach children about a particular ethnic group or impart a particular skill, but they fail to take into consideration the full complexity of actual intergroup relations in our society.

In addition to these studies, there is also a small number of studies that have examined the effects of training prospective teachers to teach multi-cultural education courses. Several of these studies indicate that this type of training changes actual behavior in the classroom, as well as racial attitudes (Grant and Grant 1985; Mahan 1982, Noordhoff and Kleinfeld 1993). However, there is also a group of studies that show that this type of training has little or no effects on racial attitudes (Grant and Tate 1995; Sleeter 1992). Again, it appears that the longer programs have more positive effects than the shorter programs.

Intergroup Dialogues

Intergroup dialogue programs are currently being used most extensively in university settings (Gurin, Lopez and Nagda 1998; Schoem, Frankel, Zuniga and Lewis 1993), however there seems to be no reason they would not work well with high school students. They involve bringing students of different racial and ethnic groups together under highly favorable contact conditions (i.e., equal status, individualized, cooperative, supported by authority figures). The group size varies from fifteen to twenty-five, but the technique could also be used with smaller groups. The typical dialogue group includes members of only two groups—groups that have historically had difficulties relating to one another (e.g., African Americans and whites). On some campuses, these dialogue opportunities are offered as full credit classes, while on other campuses they are optional non-credit classes. The non-credit classes meet several times a week, but usually for time periods less than a semester long, and sometimes only for a weekend.

The groups engage in semi-structured interactions under the supervision of trained facilitators. They discuss topics related to intergroup relations such as stereotyping, prejudice, and discrimination and they read and discuss assigned materials about current events and issues. Experiential exercises are employed to stimulate discussion. The stress is on dialogue between groups, so many opportunities are provided for people to voice their own individual experiences. Students are also often asked to keep journals of their thoughts and experiences related to the dialogues. The groups are analytically oriented and are intended to cause introspection as well as teach students to take the perspective of members of other groups. It is expected that students will learn how the power and privilege of groups that dominate the social structural hierarchy affect education, job opportunities, job advancement, and political power, as well as the day-to-day behavior of members of all groups. Although students are encouraged to focus on group differences during the dialogues, toward the end of the dialogue program students are usually encouraged to explore areas of commonalities that they can use as a basis for forming coalitions to work on specific problems together in the future.

Several studies of the effectiveness of dialogue programs have been done. In one it was found that students who had participated in a semester-long dialogue course had a better understanding of the social structural factors associated with racial inequalities and poverty (Lopez, Gurin and Nagda 1998). In a second study, it was found that the greatest changes in attitudes concerning the causes of inequality occurred among the students who most actively participated in the dialogue groups (Lopez, Gurin and Nagda 1998). A related study found that discussions of racial identity-related personal experiences were particularly influential in changing racial attitudes among participants in dialogue groups (Yeakley 1998). A four-year follow-up of students participating in dialogue groups found that white students perceived greater commonalities with peoples of color, and students of color perceived that there was less racial divisiveness in our society as a result of participation in the dialogues—compared to students who had not participated in this program (Gurin, Peng, Lopez and Nagda [forthcoming]). This research suggests that discussing racial issues under controlled conditions can change attitudes and it offers some suggestions about how these changes occur.

Moral-Development Training Programs

Most moral-development programs are based on Kohlberg's theory of moral development (Kohlberg 1969; 1981). All of these programs are intended to raise the level of children's moral reasoning and improve intergroup relations. Empirical studies have shown that dramatizing moral dilemmas and role-playing exercises do increase children's levels of moral reasoning (Blatt and Kohlberg 1975). Some moral-development programs include discussions of group differences in perceptions, backgrounds, and cultures in an attempt to improve intergroup relations. The specific techniques that have been used in such programs include describing social practices in different groups and noting the similarity in moral values underlying them; creating booklets of family history or maps of family origins; arranging visits to the class by representatives of various groups; playing tape recordings of older relatives; and role playing or brief dramas using racial or ethnic themes (Davidson and Davidson 1994). Clearly, some of these techniques are closely related to those employed in multicultural education, the primary difference being that they are used in a context emphasizing moral education. To date, no empirical studies have been done on the effectiveness of these techniques.

Another type of moral-development program has been used in high schools in an attempt to encourage students to confront prejudice by examining moral aspects of the Holocaust. The "Facing History and Ourselves" program uses an examination of the Holocaust to sensitize students to anti-Semitism and a host of related issues (Stoskopf and Strom 1990). The "Facing History" curriculum is designed to be a one-semester history-related course (Fine 1993, 1995). It focuses on a particular historical period, Nazi Germany before and during World War II, but guides the students to use these historical incidents to reflect on the present-day problems of prejudice and racism. The curriculum materials also encourage students to analyze their own values and identities as they analyze the Holocaust. The concluding segments of the curriculum address students' responsibility for protecting civil liberties. The goals of this program are to foster perspective-taking, critical thinking, and moral decision-making. An effort is made to present the materials in a way that is relevant to the students' own experiences of prejudice and stereotyping. This program may well change intergroup relations, but no studies of its effects are available.

Conflict-Resolution Techniques

Another technique that was not originally designed to improve intergroup relations, but which could be adapted for such purposes, concerns the teaching of conflict-resolution skills to students. Over the last decade, programs that teach mediation skills to students have been introduced into a number of schools (Araki 1990; Johnson and Johnson 1995a, 1995b; Johnson, Johnson, Dudley and Acikgoz 1994; Tolson, McDonald and Moriarity 1992). For example, one program was created for inner-city high schools in New York City. It was found that the conflict-resolution training improved the students' abilities to manage conflict, increased their social support from other students, and decreased victimization by others (Deutsch 1993). The students also experienced increases in self-esteem, decreases in anxiety, and greater feelings of self-control. In another study, it was found that providing elementary students with nine hours of mediation training improved their mediation skills as indicated by their reactions to hypothetical conflict situations (Johnson, Johnson, Dudley and Magnusson 1995).

Coleman and Deutsch (1995) argue that introducing conflict-mediation curricula in schools creates a climate in which students are more willing to voluntarily submit their conflicts to resolution. When conflicts are submitted for resolution, they suggest that there should be mediators from each of the parties to the dispute. They also suggest that the mediators should try to help the disputants to recognize the role that ethnic and cultural background plays in shaping their views of the dispute and the other parties to the dispute. Although these programs were not specifically designed to improve intergroup relations, the skills that are acquired are clearly relevant to resolving intergroup conflicts. There is no reason these programs could not be specifically designed to help students resolve intergroup conflicts.

Intercultural Training Programs

Programs designed to help people learn about and adapt to foreign countries may also be relevant to improving relations between racial and ethnic groups in this country. These programs are intended to improve interpersonal relations skills, lead to greater understanding of the other group, and increase the accuracy of perceptions of the other group (Brislin and Yoshida 1994). Reviews of their effectiveness indicate that these programs are generally successful in improving relationship skills and the accuracy of intergroup perceptions (Black and Mendenhall 1990). Among the effective techniques are simulation games, role-playing interactions, exercises that present information about the other culture, case studies, and interactions with individuals from the other culture (Bhawuk 1990; Brislin, Landis, and Brandt 1983; Gudykunst and Hammer 1983; Cushner and Landis 1996).

One technique, known as the cultural sensitizer, teaches individuals from one culture about cultural differences using a programmed learning approach that involves the analysis of specific instances of intercultural misunderstanding or conflict (Cushner and Landis 1996; Triandis 1972). A number of studies indicate that this technique leads to a better understanding of the other culture using pre-test, post-test comparisons (e.g., Cushner 1989; Landis, Brislin and Hulgus 1985; Landis, Day, McGrew, Thomas, and Miller 1976; Weldon, Carlston, Rissman, Slobodin, and Triandis 1975). The goal of this technique is to teach the subjective culture of the other group—those aspects of culture such as norms, values, and beliefs that are often unquestioningly accepted by members of that group, but typically remain hidden from outsiders. Subjective culture consists of the implicit worldview of the group and the goal of cultural sensitizers is to make this implicit worldview explicit.

The premise of all intercultural training techniques is that it is primarily the differences between cultures that lead to misunderstandings and conflicts, not the similarities. The emphasis on differences runs directly counter to the assumptions of more colorblind approaches that tend to stress that members of all groups are fundamentally similar. The intercultural techniques might be especially useful in school systems that draw students from different cultural backgrounds. When information about group differences is presented, it is important that it be presented in a nonevaluative manner; otherwise it may simply reinforce preexisting stereotypes and prejudices.

SUMMARY

Perhaps the best way to conceptualize the elements of these programs that may be responsible for their success is to use the contact hypothesis. The original contact hypothesis and its successors contained five elements whose effectiveness has now been well-established in the research literature (Allport 1954; Amir 1976; Pettigrew 1998; Stephan 1987; Stephan and Stephan 1996; Williams 1947). Intergroup contact is most likely to improve intergroup relations when it is cooperative, equal-status, involves common goals, the interactions are individualized, and the contact is supported by authority figures. In addition, reviews of the contact literature suggest that a number of other situational elements also facilitate positive changes in intergroup relations. The research suggests that the contact should be voluntary, non-superficial, interpersonally oriented, have a high potential for friendship development and provide opportunities for informal interaction. In addition, there should be an attempt to create multiple opportunities for contact with different outgroup members in a variety of settings, opportunities for stereotype disconfirmation, an emphasis on superordinate or cross-cutting categories (i.e., emphasizing overarching groups that encompass all those present or emphasizing groups that cut across racial and ethnic lines), low threat, and the contact should result in achieving valued outcomes.

The success of cooperative groups is easily understood within this framework. The intergroup contact that occurs in cooperative groups fulfills all of the basic conditions set forth in the contact hypothesis. Not only is the contact cooperative, it involves equal status within the groups, the students have common goals, they get to know one another as individuals, and it is supported by the relevant authority figures (teachers, administrators). In addition, contact in cooperative groups creates a superordinate identity with the learning groups (which tend to be racially balanced), it has the potential to lead to intergroup friendships, and it involves multiple opportunities for contact with different outgroup members in a setting that often leads to stereotype disconfirmation. It also tends to be non-threatening and the students report liking cooperative groups.

If cooperative groups have such beneficial effects, why haven't they been more widely adopted? One answer is that cooperative learning techniques require training as well as organizational support. Some teachers seem to resist using them because they fear that they may not adequately prepare their students to function in a competitive society. Teachers also worry that using cooperative groups may undercut the motivation of their high-achieving students and provide their low-achieving student with a free ride, and many are uncomfortable giving group grades. The developers of these techniques argue that none of these criticisms is valid, but the fact that many teachers subscribe to them does deter them from using cooperative techniques (Cohen 1990; Deutsch 1993; Johnson and Johnson 1995b).

To a greater or lesser extent, each of the other intergroup-relations programs also draw heavily on the elements of the contact hypothesis for their success. Intergroup dialogue programs have nearly all of the advantages of cooperative groups, plus some unique advantages of their own. They are usually voluntary, the contact is non-superficial, they are interpersonally oriented, and the interactions between group members tend to be informal. They also have a high potential for friendship development.

Multicultural education is often used in both single-race and multiracial schools. These programs provide information that disconfirms prevailing societal stereotypes and present information about multiple outgroup members in many settings. Typically, they are not threatening and the programs themselves are supported by authority figures. Intercultural-relations programs contain all of the favorable elements of multicultural education. In addition, participation is usually voluntary, and sometimes they involve intergroup contact under conditions approximating those stipulated in the contact hypothesis. Moral-development programs, such as "Facing History and Ourselves," place less emphasis on disconfirming stereotypes than multicultural and intercultural programs and more emphasis on issues concerning moral values, but in many respects they are similar to multicultural and intercultural programs in providing historical and cultural information about outgroups, creating a superordinate identity, and in being supported by authority figures. The teaching of conflict-resolution techniques fits the conditions of the contact hypotheses less well than the other techniques, unless they are specifically oriented toward resolving intergroup conflicts. If they are oriented toward intergroup conflicts, they are likely to involve stereotype disconfirming information, cooperation among multiple participants of different groups, non-superficial interaction with outgroup members, pursuit of a common goal, and support by relevant authority figures.

It is quite clear from this review of intergroup-relations programs that it is possible to improve intergroup relations in the schools. Some of the techniques that can be used to improve intergroup relations, such as the use of cooperative groups, intergroup dialogues, or intergroup conflict-resolution training, require the participation of members of different groups. Obviously, these techniques can only be used in multiracial schools. But many of the other techniques, including multicultural education, moral education, and intercultural training, can be used in single-race, as well as multiracial schools. Some of the techniques, such as cooperative groups, seem especially suited to primary school students, while others, such as intergroup dialogues, seem best suited to secondary school students, but all of these techniques can probably be adapted for use with students of different ages. The effectiveness of some of these techniques, including cooperative groups and intercultural training, has been well-established, while other techniques such as intergroup dialogues and conflict-resolution training, have yielded some promising results. The effectiveness of the remaining techniques (multicultural education and moral education applied to racial and ethnic groups) has not yet been established. It is possible that all of these techniques are more likely to be successful when they take place in settings in which intergroup contact is voluntary, but that is no reason not to use these techniques in school districts that still have mandatory desegregation plans. There are curriculum materials available for all of these techniques (a list of them is provided at the end of the chapter).

To some extent, the future of race relations in our society depends on the schools. The tools now exist that would enable schools to promote more positive relations among different racial and ethnic groups. We will all benefit if administrators, teachers, and parents decide that the schools should take advantage of these tools and start taking a more active role in improving intergroup relations.

REFERENCES

Aboud, F.E., and A.B. Doyle. 1996. Does talk of race foster prejudice or tolerance in children? *Canadian Journal of Behavioral Science* 28: 161–70.

Aboud, F.E., and V. Fenwick. 1999. Exploring and evaluating school-based interventions to reduce prejudice. *Journal of Social Issues* 55(4): 767–86.

Allport, F.H., and others. 1953. The effects of segregation and the consequences of desegregation: A social science statement. *Minnesota Law Review* 37: 429–40.

Allport, G.W. 1954. *The Nature of Prejudice*. Reading: Addison–Wesley.

Amir, Y. 1976. The role of intergroup contact in change of prejudice and race relations. In *Towards the Elimination of Racism*, edited by P. Katz and D.A. Taylor, 245–308. New York: Pergamon.

Araki, C. 1990. Dispute management in the schools. *Mediation Quarterly* 8: 51–62.

Armor, D.J. 1980. White flight and the future of desegregation. In *School Desegregation: Past, Present, and Future*, edited by W. Stephan and J. Feagin. New York: Plenum.

———. 1988. School busing: A time for change. In *Eliminating Racism: Profiles in Controversy*, edited by P.A. Katz and D.A. Taylor, 259–80. New York: Plenum.

Aronson, E., N. Blaney, C. Stephan, J. Sikes, and M. Snapp. 1978. *The Jigsaw Classroom*. Beverly Hills: Sage.

Aronson, E., and S. Patnoe. 1997. *The Jigsaw Classroom*. New York: Longman.

Aronson, E., and R. Thibodeau. 1992. The jigsaw classroom: A cooperative strategy for reducing prejudice. In *Cultural Diversity in the Schools*, edited by J. Lynch, C. Modgil, and S. Modgil. Vol. 2, 231–56. London: Falmer Press.

Banks, J.A. 1987. *Teaching Strategies for Ethnic Studies*. 4th ed. Boston: Allyn and Bacon.

———. 1988. *Multicultural Education*. 2nd ed. Boston: Allyn and Bacon.

———. 1997. *Educating Citizens in a Multicultural Society*. New York: Teachers College Press.

Banks, J.A., and C.A. McGee-Banks. 1995. *Multicultural Education: Issues and Perspectives*. 2nd ed. Boston: Allyn and Bacon.

Bhawuk, D.P.S. 1990. Cross-cultural orientation programs. In *Applied Cross-Cultural Psychology*, edited by R.W. Brislin. Thousand Oaks: Sage.

Black, J.S. and M. Mendenhall. 1990. Cross-cultural training effectiveness: A review and theoretical framework for future research. *Academy of Management Review* 15: 113–36.

Blaney, N., C. Stephan, D. Rosenfield, E. Aronson, and J. Sikes. 1977. Interdependence in the classroom: A field study. *Journal of Educational Psychology* 69: 121–28.

Blatt, M.M., and L. Kohlberg. 1975. The effects of classroom moral discussion on children's level of moral reasoning. *Journal of Moral Education* 4: 129–61.

Braddock, J.H. II. 1987. The impact of segregated school experiences on college and major field choices of black high school graduates: Evidence from the high school and beyond survey. Paper presented at the National Conference on School Desegregation. University of Chicago.

Braddock, J.H. II, R. Crain., and J. McPartland. 1984. A long-term view of desegregation: Some recent studies of graduates as adults. *Phi Delta Kappan* 66: 259–64.

Braddock, J.H. II, and J. McPartland. 1982. Assessing school desegregation effects: New directions in research. *Research in Sociology of Education and Socialization*, vol. 3: 59–182.

———. 1983. More evidence on the social psychological processes that perpetuate minority segregation: The relationship of school desegregation and employment desegregation. Baltimore: Center for Social Organization of Schools, Johns Hopkins University.

———. 1989. Social psychological processes that perpetuate racial segregation: The relationship between school and employment desegregation. *Journal of Black Studies* 19: 267–98.

Braddock, J.H., II, J. McPartland, and W. Trent. 1984. Desegregated schools and desegregated work environments. Paper presented at the American Educational Research Association, New Orleans, LA.

Breckheimer, S.E., and R.O. Nelson. 1976. Group methods for reducing racial prejudice and discrimination. *Psychological Reports* 39: 1259–68.

Brewer, M.B., and N. Miller. 1988. Contact and cooperation: When do they work. In *Eliminating Racism: Profiles in Controversy*, edited by P.A. Katz and D.A. Taylor, 315–26. New York: Plenum.

Bridgeman, D. 1981. Enhanced role-taking through cooperative interdependence: A field study. *Child Development* 52: 1231–38.

Brislin, R.W., D. Landis, and M.E. Brandt. 1983. Conceptualizations of intercultural behavior and training. In *Handbook of Intercultural Training*, edited by D. Landis and R.W. Brislin. Vol. 1. New York: Pergamon.

Brislin, R.W., and T. Yoshida, eds. 1994. *Improving Intercultural Relations.* Thousand Oaks: Sage.

Bruffee, K.A. 1993. *Collaborative Learning.* Baltimore: Johns Hopkins University.

Byrnes, D.A., and G. Kiger. 1990. The effect of a prejudice-reduction simulation on attitude change. *Journal of Applied Social Psychology* 20: 341–56.

Cohen, E. 1986. *Designing Groupwork: Strategies for Heterogeneous Classrooms.* New York: Teachers College Press.

———. 1990. Teaching in multiculturally heterogeneous classrooms. *McGill Journal of Education* 26: 7–22.

———. 1992. *Restructuring the Classroom: Conditions for Productive Small Groups.* Madison: Wisconsin Center for Education Research.

Coleman, P.T., and M. Deutsch. 1995. The mediation of interethnic conflict in schools. In *Toward a Common Destiny*, edited by W.D. Hawley and A.W. Jackson, 371–96. San Francisco: Jossey-Bass.

Cook, S.W. 1984. The 1954 social science statement and school desegregation: A reply to Gerard. *American Psychologist* 39: 819–32.

Crain, R. 1971. School integration and academic achievement of Negroes. *American Journal of Sociology* 44: 1–26.

Cushner, K. 1989. Assessing the impact of a culture-general assimilator in intercultural training. *International Journal of Intercultural Relations* 13: 125–46.

Cushner, K., and D. Landis. 1996. The intercultural sensitizer. In *Handbook of Intercultural Training*, edited by D. Landis and R.S. Bhagat, 2nd ed., 185–202. Thousand Oaks: Sage.

Davidson, F.H., and M.M. Davidson. 1994. *Changing Childhood Prejudice: The Caring Work of the Schools.* Westport: Greenwood Publishing.

Desforges, D.M., C.G. Lord, S.L. Ramsey, J.A. Mason, M.D. VanLeeuven, S.C. West, and M.R. Lepper. 1991. Effects of structured cooperative contact on changing negative attitudes toward stigmatized social groups. *Journal of Personality and Social Psychology*, 60: 531–44.

Deutsch, M. 1993. Cooperative learning and conflict resolution in an alternative high school. *Cooperative Learning* 13: 2–5.

DeVries, D.L., and K.J. Edwards. 1974. Student teams and learning games: Their effects on cross-race and cross-sex interaction. *Journal of Educational Psychology* 66: 741–49.

DeVries, D.L., K.J. Edwards, K.J., and R.E. Slavin. 1978. Biracial learning teams and race relations in the classroom: Four field experiments on Teams-Games-Tournaments. *Journal of Educational Psychology* 70: 356–62.

Ellison, C.G., and D.A. Powers. 1994. The contact hypothesis and racial attitudes among black Americans. *Social Science Quarterly* 75: 385–400.

Fine, M. 1993. Collaborative innovations: Documentation of the Facing History and Ourselves program at an essential school. *Teachers College Record* 94: 771–89.

———. 1995. *Habits of the Mind: Struggling over Values in America's Classrooms.* San Francisco: Jossey-Bass.

Grant, C.A., and G.W. Grant. 1985. Staff development and education that is multicultural. *British Journal of In-Service Education* 12: 6–18.

Grant, C.A., and C.E. Sleeter. 1989. *Turning on Learning.* New York: Macmillan.

Grant, C.A., and W.F. Tate. 1995. Multicultural education through the lens of the multicultural education research literature. In *Handbook of Research on Multicultural Education,* edited by J.A. Banks and C.A. McGee-Banks. 145–65. New York: Macmillan.

Gray, D.B., and R.D. Ashmore. 1975. Comparing the effects of informational, role-playing, and value-discrepant treatments of racial attitudes. *Journal of Applied Social Psychology* 5: 262–81.

Green, K. 1981. Integration and achievement: Preliminary results from a longitudinal study of educational attainment among black students. Paper presented at the American Educational Research Association, Boston, MA.

Gudykunst, W.B. and M.R. Hammer. 1983. Basic training design: Approaches to intercultural training. In *Handbook of Intercultural Training,* edited by D. Landis and R.W. Brislin. Vol. 1. New York: Pergamon.

Gurin, P., G. Lopez, and B.R. Nagda. 1998. *Context, identity, and intergroup relations.* Ann Arbor: University of Michigan.

Gurin, P., T. Peng, G. Lopez, and B.R. Nagda. Forthcoming. Context, identity, and intergroup relations. In *Cultural Divides: The Social Psychology of Intergroup Contact,* edited by D. Prentice and D. Miller.

Hertz-Lazarowitz, R., and N. Miller. 1992. *Interaction in Cooperative Groups.* New York: Cambridge UP.

Hohn, R.L. 1973. Perceptual training and its effects on racial preferences in kindergarten children. *Psychological Reports* 32: 435–41.

Ijaz, M.A. 1984. Ethnic attitude change. In *Multiculturalism in Canada,* edited by R.J. Samuda, J.W. Berry, and M. Laferriere. 128–38. Toronto: Allyn and Bacon.

Johnson, D.W., and R.T. Johnson. 1992a. Positive interdependence: Key to effective cooperation. In *Interaction in Cooperative Groups,* edited by R. Hertz-Lazarowitz and N. Miller. 174–99. New York: Cambridge UP.

———. 1992b. Social interdependence and crossethnic relationships. In *Cultural Diversity in the Schools,* edited by J. Lynch, C. Modgil, and S. Modgil. Vol. 2, 179–90. London: Falmer Press.

———. 1995a. *My Mediation Notebook.* 3rd. ed. Edina: Interaction Book Co.

———. 1995b. *Teaching Students to be Peacemakers.* 3rd. ed. Edina: Interaction Book Co.

Johnson, D.W., R.T. Johnson, B. Dudley, and K. Acikgoz. 1994. Effects of conflict resolution training on elementary school students. *Journal of Social Psychology* 134: 803–17.

Johnson, D.W., R.T. Johnson, B. Dudley, and D. Magnusson. 1995. Training elementary school students to manage conflict. *Journal of Social Psychology* 135: 673–86.

Johnson, D.W., R.W. Johnson, and E.J. Holubec. 1994. *Cooperative Learning in the Classroom.* Alexandria: The Association for Supervision and Curriculum Development.

Katz, J.H., and A. Ivey. 1977. White awareness: The frontier of race awareness training. *Personnel Guidance* 55: 485–89.

Kehoe, J.W., and T.W. Rogers. 1978. The effects of principle testing discussions on student attitudes toward selected groups subject to discrimination. *Canadian Journal of Education* 3: 73–80.

Kluger, R. 1975. *Simple Justice: The History of* Brown v. Board of Education *and Black America's Struggle for Equality*. New York: Knopf.

Kohlberg, L. 1969. Stage and sequence: The cognitive developmental approach to socialization. In *Handbook of Socialization Theory and Research*, edited by D.A. Goslin. Chicago: Rand McNally.

———. 1981. *Essays on Moral Development*. New York: Harper and Row.

Krech, D., and R.S. Crutchfield. 1948. *Theory and Problems of Social Psychology*. New York: McGraw-Hill.

Landis, D., R.W. Brislin, and J.F. Hulgus. 1985. Attributional training versus contact in acculturative learning: A laboratory study. *Journal of Applied Social Psychology* 15: 466–82.

Landis, D., H.R. Day, P.L. McGrew, J.A. Thomas, and A.B. Miller. 1976. Can a "Black" cultural assimilator increase racial understanding? *Journal of Social Issues* 32: 169–83.

Lieppe, M.R., and D. Eisenstadt. 1994. Generalization of dissonance reduction: Decreasing prejudice through induced compliance. *Journal of Personality and Social Psychology* 67: 395–413.

Lopez, G.E., P. Gurin, and B.A. Nagda. 1998. Education and understanding structural causes for group inequalities. *Political Psychology* 19: 305–29.

Lucker, G.W., D. Rosenfield, E. Aronson, and J. Sikes. 1977. Performance in the interdependent classroom. *American Educational Research Journal* 13: 115–23.

Mahan, J.M. 1982. Community involvement components in culturally-oriented teacher preparation. *Education* 103: 163–72.

McGregor, J. 1993. Effectiveness of role-playing and antiracist teaching in reducing student prejudice. *Journal of Educational Research* 86: 215–26.

Miller, N., M.B. Brewer, and K. Edwards. 1985. Cooperative interaction in desegregated settings: A laboratory analogue. *Journal of Social Issues* 41: 63–81.

Miller, N., and H.J. Harrington. 1990. A model of category salience for intergroup relations: Empirical tests of the relevant variables. In *European Perspectives in Psychology*, edited by P.J.D. Drenth, J.A. Sergeant, and R.J. Takens. Vol 3, 205–20. New York: John Wiley and Sons.

NCSS Task Force. 1992. Curriculum guidelines for multicultural education. *Social Education* (September): 274–94.

Noordhoff, K., and J. Kleinfeld. 1993. Preparing teachers for multicultural classrooms. *Teaching and Teacher Education* 9: 27–39.

Orfield, G., and S.F. Eaton. 1996. *Dismantling Desegregation*. New York: New Press.

Pettigrew, T.F. 1998. Intergroup contact theory. *Annual Review of Psychology* 49: 65–85.

Rossell, C.H., and D.J. Armor. 1996. The effectiveness of school desegregation plans, 1968–1991. *American Politics Quarterly* 24(3): 267–302.

Sharan, S., and H. Shachar. 1988. *Language and Learning in the Cooperative Classroom*. New York: Springer.

Schofield, J.W. 1991. School desegregation and intergroup relations: A review of the literature. *Review of Education* 17: 335–409.

Schoem, D., L. Frankel, X. Zuniga, and E. Lewis. 1993. *Multicultural Teaching in the University*. Westport: Praeger.

Slavin, R.E. 1978. Student teams and achievement divisions. *Journal of Research and Development in Education* 12: 381–87.

————. 1991. *Student Team Learning: A Practical Guide to Cooperative Learning.* Washington, D.C.: National Education Association.

————. 1992. Cooperative learning: Applying contact theory in the schools. In *Cultural Diversity in the Schools,* edited by J. Lynch, C. Modgil, and S. Modgil. Vol. 2, 333–48. London: Falmer Press.

Sleeter, C.E., and C.A. Grant. 1987. Race, class, gender and disability in current textbooks. In *The Politics of the Textbook,* edited by M.W. Apple and L.K. Christian-Smith. New York: Routledge.

Sleeter, C.E. 1992. *Keepers of the American Dream.* London: Falmer Press.

Smith, A. 1990. Social influence and antiprejudice training programs. In *Social Influence Processes and Intervention,* edited by J. Edwards, R.S. Tisdale, L. Heath, and E.J. Posavic, 183–96. New York: Plenum.

Stephan, W.G. 1978. School desegregation: An evaluation of predictions made in *Brown vs. The Board of Education. Psychological Bulletin* 85: 217–38.

————. 1980. A brief historical overview of school desegregation. In *Desegregation: Past, Present and Future,* edited by W. Stephan and J. Feagin, 3–24. New York, Plenum.

————. 1986. Effects of school desegregation: An evaluation 30 years after *Brown.* In *Advances in Applied Social Psychology,* edited by L. Saxe and M. Saks. Vol. 4. New York: Academic Press.

————. 1987. The contact hypothesis in intergroup relations. In *Group Processes and Intergroup Relations,* edited by C. Hendrick. Beverly Hills: Sage.

————. 1991. School desegregation: Short-term and long-term effects. In *Opening Doors: Perspective on Race Relations in Contemporary America,* edited by H.J. Knopke, R.J. Norrell, and R.W. Rogers, 100–18. Tuscaloosa: University of Alabama.

————. 1999. *Reducing Stereotyping and Prejudice in the Schools.* New York: Teachers College Press.

Stephan, W.G., and C.W. Stephan. 1984. The role of ignorance in intergroup relations. In *Groups in Contact: The Psychology of Desegregation,* edited by N. Miller and M. B. Brewer, 229–57. New York: Academic Press.

————. 1996. *Intergroup Relations.* Boulder: Westview.

Stoskopf, A.L., and M. Strom. 1990. *Choosing to Participate: A Critical Examination of Citizenship in American History.* Brookline: Facing History and Ourselves National Foundation.

Thompson, L. 1993. The impact of negotiation on intergroup relations. *Journal of Experimental Social Psychology* 29: 304–25.

Tolson, E., S. McDonald, and A. Moriarity. 1992. Peer mediation among high school students: A test of effectiveness. *Social Work in Education* 14: 86–93.

Triandis, H.C. 1972. *The Analysis of Subjective Culture.* New York: John Wiley and Sons.

————. 1975. Culture training, cognitive complexity, and interpersonal attitudes. In *Cross-cultural Perspectives on Learning,* edited by R.W. Brislin, S. Bochner, and W.J. Lonner. New York: Wiley.

U.S. Commission on Civil Rights. 1967. *Racial Isolation in the Schools.* Washington, D.C.: U.S. Government Printing Office.

Weigel, R.H., P.L. Wiser, and S.W. Cook. 1975. The impact of cooperative learning experiences on cross-ethnic relations and helping. *Journal of Social Issues* 31: 219–44.

Weiner, M.J., and F.E. Wright. 1973. Effects of undergoing arbitrary discrimination upon subsequent attitudes toward a minority group. *Journal of Applied Social Psychology* 3: 94–102.

Weldon, D.E., D.E. Carlston, A.K. Rissman, L.F. Slobodin, and H.C. Triandis. 1975. A laboratory test of effects of culture assimilator training. *Journal of Personality and Social Psychology* 32: 300–10.

Williams, R.M. Jr. 1947. *The Reduction of Intergroup Tensions*. New York: Social Science Research Council.

Wilson, F.D. 1985. The impact of school desegregation on white public school enrollment. *Sociology of Education* 58: 137–53.

Yeakley, A.M. 1998. The nature of prejudice change: Positive and negative processes arising from intergroup contact experiences. Ph.D. Dissertation. Ann Arbor: University of Michigan.

Ziegler, S. 1981. The effectiveness of cooperative learning teams for increasing cross-ethnic friendship: Additional evidence. *Human Organization* 40: 264–68.

Resource Literature

Adams, M., L.A. Bell, and P. Griffin. 1997. *Teaching for Diversity and Social Justice*. New York: Routledge.

Akin, T. 1995. *Character Education in America's Schools*. Spring Valley: Innerchoice Publishing.

Aronson, E., and S. Patnoe. 1997. *The Jigsaw Classroom*. New York: Longman.

Banks, J.A. 1994. *An Introduction to Multicultural Education*. 3rd ed. Boston: Allyn and Bacon.

———. 1997. *Educating Citizens in a Multicultural Society*. New York: Teachers College Press.

Banks, J.A. and A.A. Clegg. 1990. *Teaching Strategies for Social Studies*. 4th ed. New York: Longman.

Bowers, V., and D. Swanson. 1988. *More than Meets the Eye*. Vancouver: Pacific Educational Press.

Bowser, B.P., G.S. Auletta, and T. Jones. 1993. *Confronting Diversity Issues on Campus*. Thousand Oaks: Sage.

Brislin, R.W., and T. Yoshida. 1994. *Improving Intercultural Interaction: Modules for Cross-Cultural Training Programs*. Thousand Oaks: Sage.

Bruffee, K.A. 1993. *Collaborative Learning*. Baltimore: Johns Hopkins UP.

Burke, B. 1995. *Celebrate Our Similarities*. Huntington Beach: Teacher Created Materials Inc.

Cech, M. 1991. *Globalchild: Multicultural Resources for Young Children*. Menlo Park: Addison-Wesley.

Cohen, E.G. 1992. *Restructuring the Classroom: Conditions for Productive Small Groups*. Madison: Wisconsin Center for Education Research.

Cohen, J.J., and M.C. Fish. 1993. *Handbook of School Based Interventions*. San Francisco: Jossey-Bass.

Cushner, K., and R. Brislin. 1996. *Intercultural Interaction: A Practical Guide*. 2nd ed. Thousand Oaks: Sage.

Davidson, F.H., and M.M. Davidson. 1994. *Changing Childhood Prejudice: The Caring Work of the Schools.* Westport: Greenwood Publishing.

Derman-Sparks, L. 1995. *Anti-bias Curriculum: Tools for Empowering Children.* Washington, D.C.: National Association for the Education of Young Children.

Diaz, C.E., ed. 1992. *Multicultural Education for the 21st Century.* Washington, D.C.: National Education Association.

Fine, M. 1995. *Habits of Mind: Struggling over Values in America's Classrooms.* San Francisco: Jossey-Bass.

Fowler, S.M., and M.G. Mumford. 1995. *Intercultural Sourcebook: Cross-Cultural Training Methods.* Vol. 1. Yarmouth: Intercultural Press.

Halstead, J.M., and M.J. Taylor. 1996. *Values in Education and Education in Values.* Bristol: Falmer Press.

Hawley, W.D., and A.W. Jackson, eds. 1995. *Toward a Common Destiny: Improving Race and Ethnic Relations in America.* San Francisco: Jossey-Bass.

Johnson, D.W., and R.T. Johnson. 1995a. *My Mediation Notebook.* 3rd ed. Edina: Interaction Book Co.

———. 1995b. *Teaching Students to be Peacemakers.* 3rd ed. Edina: Interaction Book Co.

Johnson, D.W., R.T. Johnson, and E.J. Holubec. 1994. *Circles of Learning: Cooperation in the Classroom.* 4th ed. Edina: Interaction Book Co.

Jones, J. M. 1998. *The Cultural Psychology of African-Americans.* Boulder: Westview.

Kohls, L.R., and J.M. Knight. 1994. *Developing Intercultural Awareness.* Yarmouth: Intercultural Press.

Landis, D., and R.S. Bhagat. 1996. *Handbook of Intercultural Training.* Thousand Oaks: Sage.

Looking for America: Promising School Based Practices in Intergroup Relations. Vol. 1. 1997. Boston: National Coalition of Advocates for Students.

Niedergang, M., and M.L. McCoy. 1994. *Can't We All Just Get Along: A Manual for Discussion Programs on Racism and Race Relations.* 2nd ed. Pomfret: Study Circles Resource Center.

Parker, W.M., J. Archer, and J. Scott. 1992. *Multicultural Relations on Campus.* Muncie: Accelerated Development Inc.

Power, F.C., A. Higgins, and L. Kohlberg, eds. 1989. *Lawrence Kohlberg's Approach to Moral Education.* New York: Columbia UP.

Rothenberg, P.S., ed. 1997. *Race, Class, and Gender.* 4th ed. New York: St. Martin's Press.

Seelye, H.N., ed. 1996. *Experiential Activities for Intercultural Learning.* Yarmouth: Intercultural Press.

Seelye, H.N., and H. Wasilewski. 1996. *Between Cultures: Developing Self-Identity in a World of Diversity.* Yarmouth: Intercultural Press.

Simon, Kenneth T. et al. 1996. *Lessons on Equal Worth and Dignity.* New York: United Nations Association of the United States of America (485 Fifth Ave. 10017–6104).

Slavin, R.E. 1991. *Student Team Learning: A Practical Guide to Cooperative Learning.* Washington, D.C.: National Education Association.

Stahl, R.J., ed. 1994. *Cooperative Learning in Social Studies: A Handbook for Teachers.* Menlo Park: Addison-Wesley.

Thomson, B.J. 1992. *Words Can Hurt You: Beginning a Program of Anti-Bias Education.* Reading: Addison-Wesley.

Resource Centers

Center for Teaching Peace, 4501 Van Ness St. NW, Washington, DC 20016.

Educators for Social Responsibility, 23 Garden St., Cambridge, MA 02138.

Facing History and Ourselves, 25 Kennard Rd., Brookline, MA 02146.

The Grace Cotrino Abrams Peace Education Foundation, 3550 Biscayne Blvd. Suite 400, Miami, FL 33137.

Human Rights Resource Center, 615 B St., San Rafael, CA 94901.

National Association for Mediation in Education, 425 Amity St., Amherst, MA 01002.

The Southern Poverty Law Center, 400 Washington Ave., Montgomery, AL 36104.

Chapter 10

Attitudes on Race and Desegregation

∞

Christine H. Rossell and David J. Armor

INTRODUCTION

School desegregation plans had a profound impact on the citizens and communities where they were implemented. Some of the effects were anticipated and positive, but others were unexpected and negative. Perhaps the greatest achievement of the civil rights movement both anticipated and positive was the ultimate endorsement by whites of the principle of integration, attained early in the North and eventually in the South.

Despite this overwhelming support for the principal of integration, whites continued to show strong opposition to certain methods of desegregation, and especially to the forced busing of the 1970s. Demonstrations, boycotts, bus burnings, and other expressions of white hostility met the mandatory busing orders of the federal courts, in the North as well as the South. Although not as spectacular, the steady white flight that accompanied many of these desegregation plans further contributed to an unprecedented transformation of these communities and their school systems.

There has been much debate among social scientists about these seemingly contradictory attitudes and behaviors, on the one hand the increasing tolerance of the principal of integration and certain types of interracial experiences, and on the other hand persistent opposition and resistance to particular desegregation methods. Some experts have chosen to devalue the reduction of classic racial prejudice, instead elevating the willingness to accept mandatory busing to a litmus test of racial tolerance. These experts have invented a new type of racial prejudice called "symbolic racism," which would apply to parents who oppose mandatory busing regardless of how many nonracial reasons they might have for their position. Others point out that the ends do not necessarily justify the means, and that the values of racial tolerance do not require abandonment of nonracial means of assigning children to school.

This chapter attempts to sort out the different strains in this debate, showing some of the broad changes in attitudes about race in general and school desegregation in particular. Some attitudes have changed dramatically, others have not. We believe the differences in these trends is meaningful, and we offer an interpretation that does not require a choice between racism on the one hand and white beneficence on the other.

METHODOLOGY

Much of the discussion in this chapter relies on national survey data collected by professional polling organizations, namely the Gallup Polls, the National Opinion Research Center (NORC) at the University of Chicago, and the Institute for Social Research at the University of Michigan. For some topics and some years, however, we analyze surveys of parents undertaken by the authors of this chapter in sixteen medium-to-large school districts throughout the nation.[1]

Although not a national sample, the parents surveyed in these districts were randomly selected from among those with children in the public schools in districts that were considering a new or evaluating an existing desegregation plan. These surveys show levels of support or opposition to various desegregation techniques similar to levels in national surveys, and therefore we believe they offer a fair representation of the attitudes of white and minority parents throughout the nation. We have also reviewed other research that touches on the issue of how school desegregation affects the attitudes and behavior of the citizens who live in desegregating school districts.

ATTITUDES ON INTEGRATION PRINCIPLES

The white response to integration in the South in the 1950s, when desegregation meant a few black children attending a white school, was obviously an example of classic racial prejudice. Indeed, the 1954 *Brown* decision was made at a time when less than a majority of whites supported the principle of school integration[2] and at least 80 percent of southern whites objected to having a few black children in their child's school.

Appendix 10.1 shows that by 1963, one year before the U.S. Civil Rights Act of 1964, 64 percent believed in the principle of integration. By the beginning of busing in 1970, 75 percent of whites believed in the principle of integration. By 1985, the support of whites had reached its peak of 93 percent, which caused the National Opinion Research Center (NORC) to stop asking the question because there was so little variation in responses.

One could reasonably conclude that today only the lunatic fringe—perhaps about 6 percent of the white population—does not believe in the principle of school integration. The same thing could be said of blacks. Indeed, the only difference between blacks and whites on this issue is that blacks have always shown high support for the principle of school integration, at least since they were first asked this question in a 1972 national poll.[3] By 1991, there was only a two percentage-point difference between whites and blacks in their attitudes toward school integration. Furthermore, contrary to predictions of a resurgence of segregationist attitudes among blacks and whites, these data show no retreat on the principle of integration—about 90 percent of blacks and whites support the principle of integration.

Appendix 10.1 also illustrates responses to another set of questions that tap support for the principle of integration, but in a concrete fashion. This question is "Would you yourself have any objection to sending your children to a school where a few of the children are (Negroes/blacks)?" In 1959, 72 percent of southern[4] whites objected to sending their child to a school with a few blacks, in contrast to less than 10 percent of nonsouthern whites at any time during this time period. These results show that the hostile behavior of southern whites in response to the integration of a few black children into their schools was quite consistent with their attitudes at that time. By 1969, however, as the influence of the civil rights movement increased and the reality of desegregation settled in, only 20 percent of southern whites objected to a school with a few blacks in it. By 1980, there was no regional difference and by 1993 only four percent of whites objected to sending their child to a school with a few blacks in it.

The next variation on this question shows a more impressive increase in white acceptance of blacks from 1959 through 1993. In 1959, almost 85 percent of southerners and 35 percent of northerners objected to sending their child to a school that was half black. In 1969, only 46 percent of southern whites and 28 percent of nonsouthern whites objected to half-black schools. Although there was still a regional difference in 1980, southerners were only 5 percentage points more likely than northerners to object to sending their child to a school that was half black. By 1993, only 17 percent of whites objected to sending their child to a school that was half black.

The final variation on this question in appendix 10.1 shows responses that are even more extraordinary. Although in 1959 almost 90 percent of southerners and 60 percent of northerners objected to sending their child to a school that was majority black, by 1980 there was only a 15 percentage-point difference between southerners and northerners. By 1993, only 42 percent of whites objected to sending their child to a school that was majority black, although this is still a relatively high rate of opposition when compared to opposition to a half-black school.

The national surveys might be criticized on the grounds that they are based on a random sample of adults, many of whom either do not have school-age children or do not live in a school district with a sizeable black population. Thus, for these respondents, questions regarding the racial composition of a school they would be willing to send their child to may be too abstract. For this reason, we turn to surveys of parents in communities with large minority populations where desegregation plans were either being debated or were already implemented.

Figure 10.1 and appendix 10.2 show the percentage of white parents objecting to sending their child to their current neighborhood school if it became one-half black/Hispanic or two-thirds black/Hispanic in Los Angeles; Chicago; Worcester, Massachusetts; DeKalb County, Georgia; Topeka, Kansas; Stockton, California; Knox County, Tennessee; and Baton Rouge, Louisiana. DeKalb, Stockton, and Baton Rouge had comprehensive desegregation plans, the latter two being mandatory. The bar on the right is the average percentage of white parents from 1989 to 1993 who would object to these racial compositions in their neighborhood school.

There is a clear time difference in the results, with the Los Angeles (1977) and Chicago (1981) surveys showing much higher opposition to half-black schools than the later surveys. Starting in 1989, the percentage of white parents objecting to a half-black school ranges from only 4 to 13 percent, with an average of 8 percent, even though these communities are in both southern and northern regions. There is greater white opposition to attending two-thirds minority schools, even in the later years, ranging from 25 percent in Stockton to 38 percent in DeKalb, with an average of 32 percent. Even so, this opposition is less than that shown in the national surveys—just over 40 percent—during this time period. This data suggests that the civil rights movement has been extraordinarily successful in achieving its symbolic goals. Almost no whites are upset if there are a few black children attending their children's school. The Little Rock crisis, and others like it, where angry white mobs protested a handful of black children entering their school are gone forever. By the late 1980s, only a small minority of white parents objected to their children attending a school that was half minority and half white. Blacks are no longer official pariahs, and racial prejudice in the old-fashioned sense is simply socially unacceptable for all but a small minority of whites. This is a remarkable revolution in white attitudes that must be credited to the moral leadership of the civil rights movement.

There is more white opposition to attending predominately minority schools, but even here it might be surprising that many whites do not object. For those that do, it is hard to call this racial prejudice in the traditional sense, because whites are a majority in most communities and a predominately minority school is not a desegregated school in those communities.

Figure 10.1

Percentage of White Parents Objecting to Neighborhood School 1/2 or 2/3 Black/Hispanic

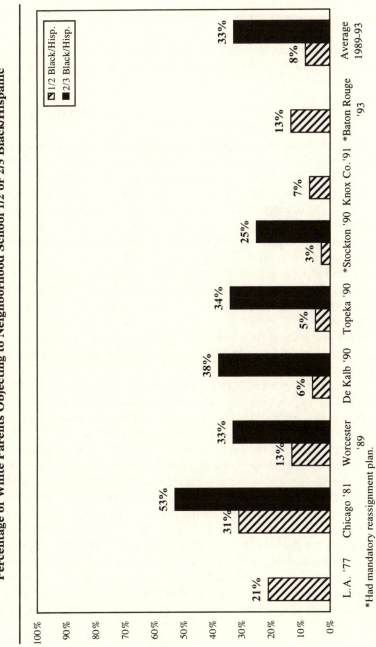

*Had mandatory reassignment plan.

There may also be other concerns about a predominately minority school that are not based on racial prejudice, such as a perception (not necessarily accurate) of academic problems, given the lower academic achievement levels of many black and Hispanic students. It is this opposition to predominately minority schools, coupled with mandatory reassignment methods, that gives rise to the white flight problem documented in chapter 4.

POLITICAL PROTEST

Although these pro-integration attitudes were well established by the onset of busing, the ugly scenes of the 1950s and 1960s in the South were replayed in the North when mandatory busing began in Pontiac and Boston in the early 1970s. Comprehensive mandatory busing plans in larger districts typically reassign nearly one-half the white children to schools across town in black neighborhoods (the same applies to black children assigned to schools in white neighborhoods). The assumption among many intellectuals and academics was that objecting to a few black children entering one's school and objecting to one's children being reassigned across town were both caused by racism. It is our opinion, however, that objecting to mandatory busing can be viewed as a "rational" act based on personal cost-benefit assessments.

Those who engage in protest demonstrations and boycotts are not just parents whose children are being forcibly desegregated. The available research on the characteristics of such protesters indicates that they tend to be working class (Hayes 1977; Taylor and Stinchcombe 1977; and McConahay and Hawley 1978), and more alienated, authoritarian, and racially prejudiced than those who do not protest (Hayes 1977; Taylor and Stinchcombe 1977; McConahay and Hawley 1978; and Begley and Alker 1978). More importantly, because protest is a deviant form of behavior, it requires a supportive social environment, particularly at the neighborhood level, before it will occur (Kirby, Harris, Crain, and Rossel 1973; Hayes 1977; and Taylor and Stinchcombe 1977). Only Giles, Gatlin, and Cataldo's (1976) study of Florida school districts found greater protest among higher social class people. Rossell (1978) found that the greater the white student reassignments, the greater the protest. Because the Boston plan was the most extensive in the United States in terms of white reassignments—indeed, entire white neighborhoods were reassigned—it experienced an enormous amount of protest. The proximity of the affected individuals apparently reduced informational costs and the psychological costs of participating in an otherwise deviant act.

Furthermore, the occurrence of protest is not a function of a "lack of leadership" as is often alleged. Rossell (1978) found that during the year preceding the implementation of court-ordered desegregation, public pronouncements for or against school desegregation by the political, business, and civic elite had little effect on protest demonstrations. This is probably because such techniques rarely influence what is important to protesters: the social support of the neighborhood and the tangible costs and benefits of the plan.

Protest voting, like protest demonstrations, is positively related to the extent of desegregation. But Rossell (1975) also found that the defeat of school tax referenda had no influence whatsoever on court or even school board orders in her sample of sixty-nine northern cities. Even more surprisingly, neither did the defeat of school board members in regular or recall elections.[5] Once a mandatory reassignment plan has been implemented, however, one of its negative consequences has been the inability of the school district to pass bonds for school construction and renovation. This is one way communities can express their opposition to court-ordered school policies that they cannot otherwise control through the normal political process. Indeed, protest voting and white flight have been the two unanticipated consequences of mandatory desegregation with the strongest and most long-term adverse effects.

OPINIONS ON DESEGREGATION TECHNIQUES

Although whites support the principle of integration, they overwhelmingly oppose the most widely used method of desegregating schools—mandatory reassignment or "busing." The first national data we have on this issue comes from the Institute for Social Research (ISR), University of Michigan, surveys in 1972, 1974, 1976, and 1980,[6] in which they asked the following question:

There is much discussion about the best way to deal with racial problems. Some people think achieving racial integration of schools is so important that it justifies busing children to schools out of their own neighborhoods. Others think letting children go to their neighborhood schools is so important that they oppose busing. Where would you place yourself on this scale, or haven't you thought much about this?

1. Bus to achieve integration (1–4)

2. Keep children in neighborhood schools (5–7)

3. Haven't thought much about this.

As shown in figure 10.2, white respondents show a consistent lack of support for busing to achieve integration—rarely greater than 10 percent—when the alternative is keeping children in their neighborhood schools. Black respondents are, however, not overwhelmingly supportive either—only a minority, or in a few years a slight majority, support mandatory reassignment.

Figure 10.2

Percentage Supporting Busing to Achieve Integration Rather than Neighborhood Schools 1972 through 1998

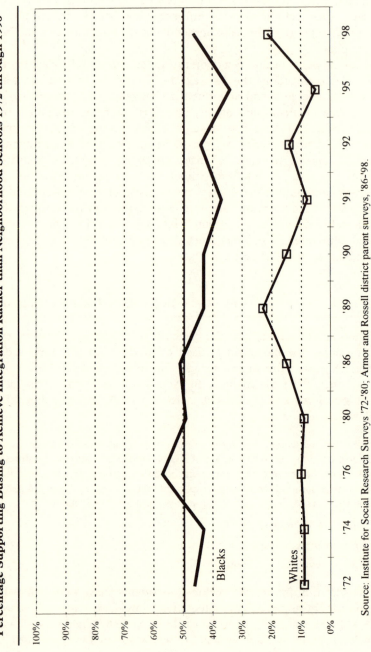

Source: Institute for Social Research Surveys '72-'80; Armor and Rossell district parent surveys, '86-'98.

The data in figure 10.2 from 1986 to 1998 is based on parent surveys in school districts considering desegregation-plan alternatives.[7] When parents are asked how they feel about mandatory reassignment in their own district, there is the same lack of support as in the ISR national surveys of adults. In addition, although only a minority of black parents support busing, black parents are still about 25–30 points more supportive than white parents.

Appendix 10.3 disaggregates the averages shown in figure 10.2 that are from the parent surveys and also presents earlier findings separately by district and ordered by year of the survey. The question used in figure 10.2 is the question at the bottom of the table. These surveys suggest declining support for mandatory reassignment among black parents, from a high of almost 70 percent in Los Angeles in 1977 to a low of 34 percent in the St. Paul–Minneapolis metropolitan area in 1998. The level of white support for mandatory reassignment is much lower and varies only from 6 to 28 percent; there seems to be no pattern over time. Across all years and districts, an average of only 13 percent of white parents support mandatory desegregation techniques compared to 47 percent of black parents.

The parent surveys also asked about a number of specific desegregation techniques that varied as to the degree of choice and the maintenance of neighborhood schools. The techniques surveyed distinguish among six types of plans that can be arrayed on a continuum from greater to less choice:

Voluntary plan with magnet schools

Voluntary transfer plan (M to M)

Redrawing contiguous attendance zones

Controlled Choice

Mandatory reassignment with magnets

Mandatory reassignments, no magnets

As shown in figure 10.3 and appendix 10.3, black and white parents show substantial agreement that the most desirable desegregation policy alternative for their district is neighborhood schools with choice (the four bars on the far left of the graph)[8] followed by redrawing attendance zones of adjacent schools ("Rezoning ").[9] What both groups want least for their child is a mandatory reassignment plan, whether it is controlled choice or the other two mandatory options. Interestingly, among the mandatory options, controlled choice is supported most by white parents and least by black parents. The reason may be that controlled choice represents more opportunity for whites to avoid predominately minority schools than the other two options, while for blacks it represents less certainty about getting into a majority white school.[10] Thus, having neighborhood schools and choice not only explains white (and probably middle-class black) behavioral response[11] to

Figure 10.3

Average Percentage of Parents Supporting Alternative Desegregation Plans

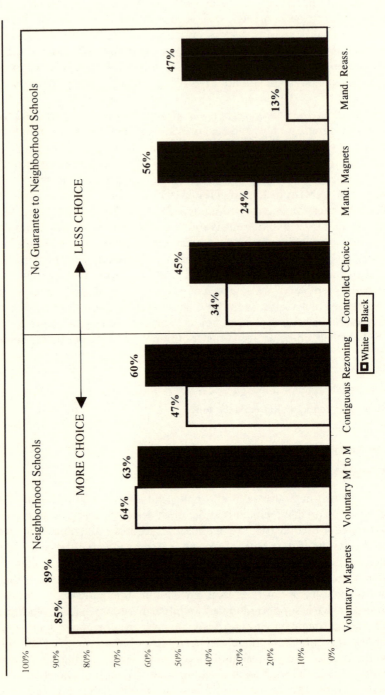

Source: Armor and Rossell surveys, '86, '88, '90, '91; Armor surveys, '89, '92, '93, '98; Rossell surveys, '95, '98.

school desegregation plans, it also seems to explain both black and white parental support for desegregation alternatives.

Appendix 10.2 shows the behavioral intentions of public school parents if a mandatory reassignment plan were adopted in their school district and their own child were reassigned to an opposite-race school. The percentage of white parents who would object ("not go along") declines slightly over time, but it increases for black parents until its peak in 1991 in Knox County, Tennessee, which at the time of the survey was about 85 percent white. In this district, which had not previously had a formal desegregation plan, 71 percent of white parents and 70 percent of black parents would not go along with a mandatory reassignment plan that assigned their child to an opposite-race school. Unwillingness to go along among black parents declined dramatically in the next three surveys to almost half that of Knox County, although white unwillingness stayed fairly high. Across all years and districts, 73 percent of white parents and 39 percent of black parents claimed they would not go along with the mandatory reassignment of their own child.

Finally, appendix 10.2 shows the percentage of parents in eleven school districts from 1977 to 1993 who said they would definitely transfer their child to a magnet school in an opposite-race neighborhood. Given all the publicity about the poor quality of black schools and the high level of support for magnet schools, it is surprising that only 30 percent of black parents, on average, would definitely choose to transfer their child to a magnet school in an opposite-race neighborhood. This is consistent, however, with black parents' estimation of discrimination in the quality of education for black students in their district. As shown in appendix 10.2, on average, only about a third of black parents believe that black students get a worse education than do white students.

Thus, contrary to the assumption of most of the court decisions of the 1970s and the academic writing on this subject, only a minority of African Americans support mandatory reassignment and a majority would not go along with a mandatory reassignment of their own child to an opposite-race school. Most black parents, like most white parents, prefer their neighborhood school to being bused to a school they did not choose. Even more surprisingly, a large majority of black parents prefer their current neighborhood school to a special magnet school they could choose themselves, perhaps because most of them believe that black children are currently receiving an education that is at least as good as white children receive.

Given these survey results, it is not unreasonable to ask why the civil rights community has ignored black parents and their preferences. In "Serving Two Masters," Derrick Bell (1976), a black law professor at New York University, concludes that the NAACP Legal Defense and Educational Fund (LDF), the major plaintiff attorney in school desegregation cases, ignores their clients' preferences because they have a conflict of interest—their most important clients are the intellectuals and elites who provide financial support for the organization and who not only believe fervently in school integration, but in a kind of "domestic domino theory" in which failure on the busing issue would trigger a string of defeats in other civil rights arenas. Their local clientele, ordinary black parents, have little or no contact with the LDF once they are solicited as a plaintiff for litigation. Ron Edmonds (1974), another black educational expert and scholar, agrees with Bell on this point.

Nathaniel Jones, NAACP General Counsel, defends the organization's behavior with the argument that "it would be absurd to expect that each and every black person should be polled before a lawsuit is filed, or a plan of desegregation is proposed."[12] He said that he did not need to ask black parents about their preferences because he himself was black and could draw on his own life experiences.[13] But this cannot possibly be true and it is precisely the problem with class-action suits—lawyers are a highly educated, highly paid elite who, regardless of their origins, are not capable of knowing what their clients want without asking them.[14]

One watchdog group charges that the reason class-action suits often do not represent the preferences of their clients is not just because of a conflict of interest, but because of egotism. Class-action suits "have the capacity to provide large sources of narcissistic gratification . . . and the psychological motivations which influence the lawyer in taking on 'a fiercer dragon' through the class action may also underlie the tendency to direct the suit toward the goals of the lawyer rather than the client."[15]

Indeed, it is interesting to note that in the Chicago, Yonkers, Worcester, and Stockton cases, the legal counsel for the plaintiffs offered a mandatory reassignment plan supported by only a minority of black parents, and in none of the court cases in the school districts shown in appendix 10.2 and 10.3 did the plaintiffs' attorney offer the plan supported by the most black parents—a neighborhood school plan with magnets—despite being given the results of parent surveys in their districts showing that they were not considering the preferences of their "clients."[16]

THE EFFECT OF DESEGREGATION ON ATTITUDES

National surveys, and the parent surveys in districts considering a plan, cannot tell us the effect of a desegregation plan on the attitudes of individuals who live in that community. Four of the districts in which parent surveys were conducted—Savannah, Stockton, Baton Rouge, and Hattiesburg—had formal desegregation plans, all of them mandatory reassignment, at the time of their survey. The other eleven districts did not have a formal plan at the time of the survey and had never had one. One way to look at the effect of desegregation is to compare attitudes in districts with formal plans to those without plans.

Table 10.1 shows the percentage of parents who think black and white students should go to the same school broken down by race and whether a district had a plan. Interestingly, for both racial groups, parents in the districts without a plan had a higher percentage believing black and white students should attend the same school. This may underestimate the actual positive effect of not having had a plan because the public school parents in districts with plans are mainly those willing to stay who are presumably more positive toward integration to begin with. The parents in districts without a plan also include those who are not willing to stay, who are presumably less positive toward integration to begin with. It is quite possible that experiencing desegregation can make one fully aware of how difficult it is to truly integrate a school system.

What is especially interesting is how little difference having children in desegregated schools makes on a parent's assessment of whether black children get a worse education than white children. Only a third of black parents believe this is true, and the belief in inequity is only five percentage points lower if they have their children in racially balanced schools. Only 10 percent of white parents think black children get a worse education, and it is only five points lower if they have their children in racially balanced schools. In short, neither group of parents sees a great deal of educational inequity, and the perception of inequity is not significantly affected by desegregation. Yet this has been one of the major claims for desegregation made by intellectuals and civil rights attorneys.

Table 10.1
**Attitudes of Parents by Whether District Had Desegregation Plan
at Time of Survey**

		WHITE		BLACK	
		Plan*	No Plan	Plan	No Plan
Average Survey Year		1990	1990	1990	1990
Average % Minority in Survey Year		65%	50%	65%	50%
Number of Districts		(N=3)	(N=11)	(N=3)	(N=11)
Believe Black and White Students Should Go To Same School		89%	95%	93%	96%
Believe Black Students Get a Worse Education in Public Schools Than White Students		5%	10%	31%	36%
Object to School	50-50	9%	14%	4%	5%
	2/3 Minority	25%	40%	2%	6%

Table 10.1 also shows the percentage of white parents who would object if their current school became one-half or two-thirds minority. Unfortunately, the analysis may be confounded by differences in racial composition between the two groups of districts. The three districts with plans that were asked this question[17] were 65 percent minority, on average, whereas those without plans were only 50 percent minority. The average year of the survey is the same for the two groups.

Overall, the percentage of white parents objecting to a school that is one-half minority is generally low, but it is five points less in the districts with plans, and the percentage objecting to a school that is two-thirds minority is fifteen points less in districts with plans. There is some suggestion here that desegregation has reduced white opposition to attending high-minority schools, but it is also possible, given the racial compositions of these districts, that the districts with plans have lost many of the whites who object to attending a majority black school. In this case, what we are seeing is the more tolerant attitudes of the white parents who did not flee a mandatory busing plan.

Finally, figures 10.4 and 10.5 show support for various types of desegregation techniques according to whether the district had a formal plan. Figure 10.4 shows attitudes among white parents and figure 10.5 shows attitudes among black parents.[18] There is remarkably little difference in parental support for various types of plans between districts with and without plans. The largest difference regards support for changing contiguous attendance zones to improve integration. Whites in plan districts are thirty points more supportive of contiguous rezoning than whites in districts without plans, and blacks are thirteen points more supportive in plan districts. It appears that parents in districts with plans have become educated about contiguous rezoning as a way to maintain integration while reducing busing.

There is also a modest difference regarding mandatory reassignment. Both whites and blacks show greater support for mandatory reassignment in districts with a plan, but since the plan districts all have mandatory plans, this may reflect no more than the fact that parents who object most strongly to these types of plans have already left the district. In any event, the proportion of white parents who support mandatory assignment is very low even in districts that have mandatory plans. For the most preferred plan, voluntary magnet plans, there is very little difference according to plan status.

There are a few studies that have examined pre- and post-desegregation attitudes or compared a desegregated district to an undesegregated district (Estabrook 1980; Ross 1977; Abney 1976; and Serow and Solomon 1979). The Ross (1977) study of Boston (as well as the Estabrook Study, 1980) and the McConahay and Hawley (1978) study of Louisville indicate that at the end of the first year of desegregation, white parents with children in the public schools supported desegregation more than did parents of preschool children. In addition, the percentage of parents intending not to enroll their

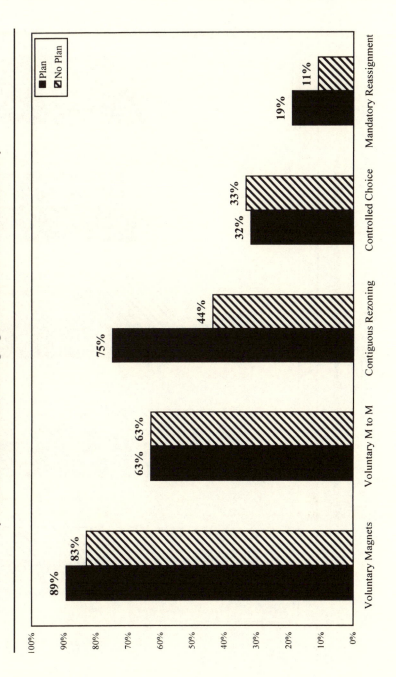

Figure 10.4
Percentage of White Parents Who Support Plan Alternative
by Whether District Had Desegregation Plan at the Time of Survey

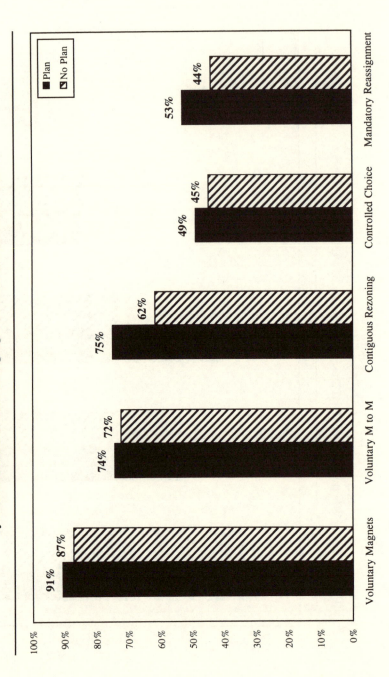

Figure 10.5

Percentage of Black Parents Who Support Plan Alternative by Whether District Had Desegregation Plan at the Time of Survey

preschool children in the public schools when they reached school age was four times greater for those with no school-age children than for those who already had some children in the public schools. Ross (1977) similarly found that whites whose children were bused in 1974–75 during Phase I of the Boston desegregation plan were generally more certain that black children benefited from integration and less certain about the negative effect of school desegregation on white children than those with preschool children.

Serow and Solomon (1979) conducted a survey of post-implementation attitudes in a countywide suburban school district in the South where desegregation was initially implemented in a subsample of twelve elementary schools in the school system. Both white and black parents who had children in the desegregated schools gave significantly greater support to the principle of school desegregation, various methods of desegregation, and the success of the new desegregation plan. They also rated their child's school experience as more successful than parents whose children were in schools that had not yet been desegregated.

These studies, like the parent survey results shown in table 10.1 and figures 10.4 and 10.5, are confounded by a self-selection bias. The parents of preschool children, or children in schools not yet desegregated, include not only those who will stay, but those who will withdraw their child from the school system, whereas those who have kept their children in the desegregated public schools consist almost entirely of those who will stay. Thus, they are more likely to be supportive of desegregation before the plan was implemented.

Abney's (1976) quasi-experimental study in Jackson, Mississippi, comes closest to eliminating the self-selection bias because it examines the same people over time in two surveys, and has a control group. The first survey was conducted in the summer after the court order, but before school opened. The second survey was conducted at the end of the first year of desegregation. Abney compared the attitude change of parents who had kept their children in the public schools to parents who had transferred them to private schools. Support for integration was measured by the maximum number of black students a parent felt he or she could tolerate in his or her child's class of thirty students. The highest number cited was fifteen. Among the parents who kept their children in the public schools, 20 percent would accept fewer black students than they had the year before, 43 percent would accept the same number, while 38 percent increased the number of black students they would accept in their child's classroom. Among those parents who transferred their children to private schools, 23 percent would tolerate fewer black students than the previous year, 62 percent would accept the same number, and only 15 percent were willing to have a larger number of black students in their child's classrooms. In short, there was a greater increase in racial tolerance among those who kept their children in the public schools and we can assume that at least part of this effect was due to their contact with black children because there were virtually no black children in the private schools.[19]

McConahay and Hawley (1978), however, found that experiencing school desegregation can increase one's fears about the quality of education in a de-segregated school. They found the percentage of whites who believed that the quality of education would decline with busing increased from 78 percent in 1976 (the first year) to 81 percent in 1977. In addition, the percentage who believed that "the differences in learning ability between most blacks and whites is so great that neither group benefits from going to school together" increased from 38 percent in the first year to 51 percent in the second year.

By contrast, they found black parents to be more favorable toward, and more positively affected by, their desegregation experience. School desegre-gation is, after all, a black demand. McConahay and Hawley (1978) found that among those supporting busing to achieve racial desegregation, almost all of whom were black, the percentage who believed that the quality of educa-tion would be adversely affected by busing declined from 32 to 22 percent and the percentage believing that "the difference in learning ability between most blacks and most whites is so great that neither group benefits from going to school together" decreased from 12 to 5 percent after a year of busing.

EXPLANATIONS FOR THE REJECTION OF
BUSING AND ACCEPTANCE OF INTEGRATION

What accounts for the high level of opposition to mandatory of busing and the strong support for neighborhood schools? Unfortunately, almost all of the research and writing has focused on white attitudes and opinions. But the attitudes and opinions of black parents are equally important, perhaps more important, because they are the victims of segregation, and should help determine the direction of remedies.

Black Attitudes

Schuman, Steeh, and Bobo (1985: 88–89) offer two hypotheses for the declining black support for mandatory reassignment and other government strategies for achieving racial equality in American society. Their first hy-pothesis is that after the incredible energy blacks put into the civil rights movement of the 1960s, there had to be some "natural falling away during the 1970s as the salience of these issues decreased" (Schuman, Steeh, and Bobo 1985: 88-89). Their second hypothesis is that some blacks may have retreated from the use of federal force for desegregation because of their perception that it was so intensely opposed by whites as to be impractical. In short, white opposition to busing and its resulting protest and flight, rather than their own preferences, may have caused the decline in black support (Schuman, Steeh, and Bobo 1985: 88–89).

Indeed, affluent black parents have filed lawsuits in several school districts around the country to prevent the adoption of a mandatory reassignment plan, as well as to dismantle one already in place. Watts (1993), a reporter for the *Atlanta Journal-Constitution*, characterizes the opinions of DeKalb County black parents, 52 percent of whom opposed busing, some intensely enough to intervene in the school desegregation suit, as believing that "mixed-race schools may sound good in theory, but in reality black children meet with harsh discrimination, suffer disproportionate punishment, are banned from leadership roles in clubs and activities, and in general have to live in an atmosphere that fails to respect their culture and history" (Watts 1993: 893). The black parents he talked to wanted neighborhood schools with facilities and resources that were equal to those in white neighborhood schools. Going to school with whites was not important to them.

Derrick Bell similarly assesses school desegregation and racial balance:

Yet, the remedies set forth in the major school cases following *Brown*—balancing the student and teacher populations by race in each school, eliminating one-race schools, redrawing school attendance lines, and transporting students to achieve racial balance—have not in themselves guaranteed black children better schooling than they received in the pre-*Brown* era . . . If benefits did exist, they have begun to dissipate as whites flee in alarming numbers from school districts ordered to implement mandatory reassignment plans. (Bell 1980: 531)

But Schuman, Steeh, and Bobo (1985) admit they find neither explanation satisfactory and there is little evidence to support either hypothesis. Another possible explanation, one that we favor, is that forced integration to achieve racial balance might not be in the self-interest of blacks even if whites supported it. After forty years of experience with desegregation and twenty-five years of racial balance plans, many blacks perceive no educational or social benefit, and serious costs, from forced integration. Before the desegregation movement, many black families believed that the cost of losing their neighborhood school was outweighed by the expected educational and social benefits of desegregation. As more black parents became aware that these benefits are minimal (see chapter 6), they have shifted back to greater support for neighborhood schools and choice. In short, a personal cost–benefit calculation by black parents could explain their favoring neighborhood schools even if these schools are predominately minority.

White Attitudes

Two major theories of the determinants of political attitudes and behavior have been used to explain white opposition to busing. The first theory is that whites are motivated by diffuse prejudicial attitudes formed in early childhood. In other words, racism explains white opposition to busing. This theory has been advanced most notably by Sears et al. (1979, 1980), McConahay (1982), and McConahay et al. (1981), in which they propose that busing is a manifestation of symbolic racism (Schuman, Steeh, and Bobo 1985; Jackman 1978, 1981; Jackman and Muha 1984; Kinder and Sears 1981; Sears, Lau, Tyler, and Allen 1980; Sears, Hensler, and Speer 1979; McConahay 1982; McConahay, Hardee, and Batts 1981).

One important problem with this theory is that the level of opposition to mandatory busing is so high that virtually the entire white population must be labeled racist, even though they also have a high level of tolerance (both attitudinal and behavioral) for schools that enroll substantial numbers of black and minority students. Another problem with the racism theory is that blacks are also increasingly likely to oppose mandatory busing, apparently because of its tangible costs and unrealized benefits.

The second theory of white opposition to busing is based on an application of rational choice theory, which posits that attitudes and behaviors are based on an individual analysis of the costs and benefits of alternative actions; we have put forward this explanation elsewhere (Armor 1995; Rossell 1995). On the benefit side, there is much less to offer whites than blacks, since blacks are the aggrieved and disadvantaged party that is supposed to receive social and, especially, educational benefits from desegregation, according to the classic harm and benefit thesis implied in *Brown v. Board of Education* (Armor 1995). While some might argue that whites will benefit by reduced racial prejudice, this is clearly not a benefit for nonprejudiced whites and it's not likely that prejudiced whites will see it that way. Most important, unlike blacks, whites have never been promised improved education as a result of desegregation, which is the main purpose of schools, so the educational benefits of desegregation are nonexistent for white parents.

On the cost side, a majority of both black and white parents prefer to attend schools that are closest to them, so mandatory reassignment to a distant school is perceived as a definite cost in time and convenience. Moreover, since predominantly black schools generally have lower achievement than white schools, and since many parents (perhaps mistakenly) attribute this condition to the school rather than to the students, being assigned to a black school can be perceived as an additional cost regardless of distance. Likewise, the opposite is true for black parents assigned to a majority white school.

Thus, from a cost–benefit perspective, it is clearly in the self-interest of whites to oppose mandatory busing plans that remove them from their current neighborhood schools and assign them to existing majority black schools some distance away. The cost–benefit theory also explains the increasing black opposition to mandatory desegregation as the perceived educational benefits seem to be diminishing.

CONCLUSIONS

Old-fashioned racism was pretty much gone by 1970. Surveys indicate that about 80 percent of whites did not object to white and black students attending the same school and only 20 percent of southern whites objected to a school with a few blacks. By 1985, there was no difference between blacks and whites in their support for the principle of integration and less than 20 percent of whites objected to half-black schools. Thus, the greatest achievement of the civil rights movement was an almost universal support for the principle of integration that was achieved early and nationwide, not just in districts that had implemented desegregation plans. This can be attributed to the moral leadership of the civil rights movement that literally changed the hearts and minds of white Americans.

Against the backdrop of enormous support for the principle of integration, the reaction of whites to forced busing came as a huge shock to the nation. The media and academics generally attributed opposition to busing to racism. The evidence presented here, however, indicates that racism probably explains opposition to the principle of integration, but it does not explain opposition to busing. Whites are willing to tolerate a large number of black children in their neighborhood school, but they are opposed to having their child bused across town to a black school. White tolerance of black children in their school and the similarity of white opinions to black opinions suggest strongly that opposition to busing is explained by self-interest, not racism. Most black parents are opposed to busing, but it is unlikely that this is because they are prejudiced against blacks. Black parents, like white parents, perceive forced integration as not in their self-interest.

Unfortunately, the civil rights attorneys who filed desegregation lawsuits all over the United States in the 1970s never consulted their clients. Experts for the NAACP, the Legal Defense Fund, the U.S. Justice Department, and the ACLU drew up and defended mandatory reassignment plans that were supported by only a minority of black parents in the districts in which they were implemented.

Indeed, an argument can be made that perhaps the greatest tragedy of school desegregation is that the plans that were supposed to protect the civil rights of African Americans ended up violating them. The survey research indicates that African Americans wanted the same right to choose to attend schools in white neighborhoods that whites had. They lost that right to choose with mandatory reassignment and were instead forced to attend a school chosen by some white planner or a computer. Just as under de jure segregation, black children were now being assigned to a school solely because of their race, albeit for noble purposes.

But we have little evidence that mandatory reassignment achieved these noble purposes. Nor did it change the attitudes and opinions of parents who resided in the school districts where it was implemented. Although whites who kept their children in the public schools after a desegregation plan was implemented are a self-selected group who would be expected to be more racially tolerant, the evidence shows very little difference in terms of attitudes toward desegregation, tolerance of black children, or the principle of integration between whites in districts with a plan and those without. This is also true of black parents.

Thus, the lackluster empirical evidence on outcomes and the current agreement between black and white parents on desegregation techniques provide strong evidence that opposition to busing—that is, to forced integration—is motivated by self-interest, not racism. Parents of both races prefer student assignment plans that offer more choice to those that offer less choice, because human beings always prefer more choice to less unless the expected benefits make giving up choice worthwhile. There is no evidence that school desegregation has achieved benefits that make that loss worthwhile and parents of all races seem to understand this.

ENDNOTES

1. The parent survey was designed by David Armor and first used in Los Angeles in 1977. The questions asked vary somewhat from district to district. The parent surveys analyzed in this chapter were conducted in sixteen school districts: Los Angeles, California (1977); Chicago, Illinois (1981); Yonkers, New York (1986); Savannah-Chatham County, Georgia (1986); Natchez-Adams, Mississippi (1988); Worcester, Massachusetts (1989); DeKalb, Georgia (1990); Topeka, Kansas (1990); Stockton, California, (1990); Knox County, Tennessee (1991); the Hartford Metropolitan Area, Connecticut (1992); East Baton Rouge Parish, Louisiana (1993), Rockford, Illinois, (1995), Hattiesburg, Mississippi (1998); and the St. Paul/ Minneapolis Metropolitan Area, Minnesota (1998). When parents in more than one district are interviewed in a single year, a weighted average of the district responses is computed by multiplying the percentage supporting by the number of responses of that race in that survey. All averages presented from these surveys are weighted in this way. The responses, shown in appendices 10.2 and 10.3, were obtained by telephone surveys administered by a professional polling firm with a CATI system. In each school district, parents were randomly selected from school district records— stratified by race—containing the student's name, race, grade, school assignment, address and telephone number. The response rate for each survey was at least 80 percent.

2. The question is "Do you think white students and black students should go to the same schools or to separate schools?" 1. Same 2. Separate. This question has been asked by the National Opinion Research Center at the University of Chicago since 1942 in their General Social Survey (NORC 1942–1985; Schuman, Steeh, and Bobo 1985). Dates for 1984 and 1985 were provided by Tom Smith at the NORC. Districts in which parents were asked this question are DeKalb, Georgia (1990), Topeka, Kansas (1990), Stockton, California (1990), Knox County, Tennessee (1991), and East Baton Rouge Parish, Louisiana (1993).

3. It is telling that the first national survey of the attitudes of black Americans on the principle of school integration and their opinions on school desegregation implementation techniques was in 1972, eighteen years after *Brown*, four years after *Green*, and one year after *Swann*, all court decisions which produced major changes in school integration and its strategies—changes which apparently did not need to be informed by information regarding what black parents wanted. Indeed, we are not aware of *any* plaintiff group that has polled black parents on the issue of mandatory reassignment.

4. Gallup and NORC use the following definition of the South: Alabama, Arkansas, Delaware, Florida, Georgia, Kentucky, Louisiana, Maryland, Mississippi, North Carolina, Oklahoma, South Carolina, Tennessee, Texas, Virginia, West Virginia, and the District of Columbia.

5. Moreover, in 1973 in *Keyes v. School District # 1*, the Supreme Court established the principle that deciding to desegregate and then rescinding the decision is evidence of intentional discrimination.

6. Cited in Schuman, Steeh, and Bobo (1985, 88–9).

7. Stockton parents were not asked the simple mandatory reassignment question. The question asked varies slightly from district to district, but generally informs public school parents that the school district is considering options or ideas for school desegregation and wants their opinion of them. For each desegregation alternative, parents are asked whether they strongly support, somewhat support, strongly oppose, or somewhat oppose the described alternative. In the case of mandatory reassignment plans, the question usually asked is how they feel about mandatory busing of students in order to attain racial integration. This is not exactly the same as asking people to choose one alternative over the other, as is the case with the ISR surveys.

8. In figure 10.3 "Vol. Magnet." = voluntary plan with magnet options; "Vol. M to M" = voluntary transfers to improve integration with transportation . The question generally begins with wording similar to the following: "As you may know, the _____ public schools are considering ways to improve school integration. I am going to read you a few ideas that could improve school integration in the _____ public schools, and I would like you to tell me if you strongly support, support somewhat, oppose somewhat, or strongly oppose each idea." The voluntary techniques are described as: "What about voluntary transfers to other schools to improve racial integration, with free transportation?" "What about a voluntary program in which children can attend integrated schools with special programs like intense computer or science studies, which are called magnet schools?"

9. The question is "What about improving integration by changing attendance boundaries of adjacent schools?"

10. The question is generally worded: "Another method for racial and ethnic integration is called a controlled choice plan. In this type of plan, all neighborhood attendance zones are eliminated and no one is guaranteed a neighborhood school. Instead, all parents choose what schools they would like their children to attend, which could include your current neighborhood school. The administration would make school assignments, and they would try to give everyone their first choices. But they would also have to make sure each school was integrated, so some students would be assigned to schools their parents did not choose. Free transportation would be provided if you chose or were assigned to a school other than your neighborhood school."

11. Unfortunately, because enrollment statistics are not kept by class, it is difficult to determine the extent of middle-class minority flight on anything but a case
study basis. Crain and Rossell (1989), documented black and Hispanic flight to
Catholic schools in Boston, Philadelphia, and Chicago. Indeed, as a result of middle-
class black and Hispanic flight, the parochial schools of Boston had more interracial
exposure (percentage white in the average black child's school) than the public
schools.

12. Jones letter to Bell, 31 July 1975, cited in Bell (1976).

13. Personal communication with Christine Rossell, 17 May 1994, Williams-
burg, Virginia.

14. Nor is listening to parent activists a good substitute. As any political scientist knows, activists have different attitudes and opinions from ordinary citizens.

15. Council on Legal Education for Professional Responsibility (1974), cited in
Bell, 1976.

16. In Stockton, an 80 percent minority school district, the plaintiffs finally
agreed after months of negotiations to enter into a settlement agreement offering educational enhancements, but only because the changing demographics of the school
district eventually caused them to conclude that desegregation was no longer achievable, not because it was not supported by their "clients." In Knox County, the plaintiff organization was not a black civil rights legal defense group, but the Office for
Civil Rights, and their position on mandatory reassignment was not very clear. The
only thing that was clear was that the district's prior M to M transfer plan and other
voluntary efforts were considered inadequate.

17. Hattiesburg parents were not asked this question. In fact, they were only
asked about desegregation techniques.

18. Mandatory with magnets is dropped from this analysis because only one of
the districts with a mandatory reassignment plan was asked this question.

19. There may be a selection–maturation interaction bias that limits the general-
izability of the results. That is, the same results might not be obtained if private
school parents were forced (truly forced) to keep their children in the public schools.

Appendix 10.1
Gallup and NORC National Survey Results

% of Adults Supporting White and Black Students Attending the Same School				% of Whites Objecting to a School of the Following Racial Composition:						
					Few Black		Half Black		Majority Black	
Years	White	Black		Years	Southern Whites	Non-Southern Whites	Southern Whites	Non-Southern Whites	Southern Whites	Non-Southern Whites
1942	32%			1959	72%	7%	83%	34%	86%	58%
1956	50%									
1963	65%									
1964	64%									
1965	70%			1965	37%	7%	68%	28%	78%	52%
1968	73%			1969	21%	7%	46%	28%	64%	54%
1970	75%									
1972	84%	96%								
1976	84%	97%		1975	15%	3%	38%	24%	61%	47%
1977	86%	93%								
1980	88%	98%		1980	5%	5%	27%	22%	66%	51%
1982	90%	96%		1983[b]	5%	5%	18%	18%	42%	42%
1984	92%	90%								
1985	96%	95%		1985[b]	4%	4%	16%	16%	39%	39%
1989[a]	90%	97%								
1990[a]	95%	96%		1990[b]	3%	3%	18%	18%	48%	48%
1991[a]	93%	96%		1991[b]	3%	3%	17%	17%	41%	41%
1993[a]	86%	92%		1993[b]	4%	4%	17%	17%	42%	42%

Source: NORC General Social Survey
1942-1985

Source: Gallup Polls, '59-'80 by region; NORC General Social Survey, '83-'93

[a] Armor and Rossell District Parent Surveys, 1989-1993
[b] 1983-1993 national sample not by region.

Appendix 10.2
Armor and Rossell Parent Survey Results

	L.A. CA WH	L.A. CA BL	Chicago IL WH	Chicago IL BL	Yonkers NY WH	Yonkers NY BL	Mand. Plan[b] Savannah-Chatham Co. GA WH	Mand. Plan[b] Savannah-Chatham Co. GA BL	Natchez-Adams Co MS WH	Natchez-Adams Co MS BL	Worcester MA WH	Worcester MA BL	DeKalb Co. GA WH	DeKalb Co. GA BL	Topeka KS WH	Topeka KS BL
Survey Year >	1977		1981		1986		1986		1988		1989		1990		1990	
% Min. in Survey Year >	66%		82%		50%		59%		65%		31%		62%		29%	
Respondent Race >	WH	BL	WH	BL	WH	BL	WH	BL	WH	BL	WH	BL	WH	BL	WH	BL
Sample Size >	572	473	599	315	551	231	419	347	400	400	525	102	439	501	503	396
QUESTIONS:																
Think Black and White Students Should Go to Same School	a	a	a	a	a	a	a	a	a	a	90%	97%	94%	95%	98%	98%
Believe Black Students Get a Worse Education in Public Schools than White Students	a	a	a	a	a	a	a	a	a	a	a	a	6%	25%	4%	28%
Object to a School																
50-50	21%	2%	31%	7%	a	a	a	a	a	a	13%	8%	6%	1%	5%	7%
2/3 Minority	a	a	53%	15%	a	a	a	a	a	a	33%	14%	38%	4%	34%	a
If Dist. Adopted Busing Would Not Go Along	88%	34%	85%	32%	69%	18%	60%	11%	65%	16%	80%	54%	91%	54%	56%	26%
Vol. Transfer to Magnet in Opposite Race Neighb. % Definitely	6%	16%	5%	14%	20%	47%	24%	39%	13%	46%	6%	12%	8%	27%	12%	34%

[a] Question not asked.
[b] Mandatory plan at time of survey.

	Mand. Plan[b] Stockton CA 1990 78%		Knox. Co. TN 1991 16%		Hartford Metro, CT 1992 37%		Mand. Plan[b] Baton Rouge LA 1993 58%		Rockford IL 1995 38%		Mand. Plan[b] Hattiesburg MS 1998 79%		Mpls./St.Paul Metro, MN 1998 22%		Weighted Average	
Survey Year > % Min. in Survey Year > Respondent Race >	WH	BL	WH	BL	WH	BL	WH	BL	WH	BL	WH	BL	WH	BL	WH	BL
Sample Size >	400	150	600	600	600	250	633	604	100	100	202	187	369	97		
QUESTIONS:																
Think Black and White Students Should Go to Same School	94%	98%	92%	96%			86%	92%							92%	95%
Believe Black Students Get a Worse Education in Public Schools than White Students	3%	27%	19%	51%			6%	32%							8%	34%
Object to a School																
50-50	3%	3%	7%	7%			13%	4%							13%	5%
2/3 Minority	25%	2%	a	a											38%	8%
If Dist. Adopted Busing Would Not Go Along	77%	46%	71%	70%	51%	23%	79%	49%	37%	8% Cont. Choice			70%	44%	73%	39%
Vol. Transfer to Magnet in Opposite Race Neighb. % Definitely	14%	32%	12%	36%			8%	26%							11%	30%

a Question not asked.
b Mandatory plan at time of survey.

317

Appendix 10.3
Armor and Rossell Parent Survey Results

	L.A. CA		Chicago IL		Yonkers NY		Mand. Plan[b] Savannah-Chatham Co. GA		Natchez-Adams Co MS		Worcester MA		DeKalb Co. GA		Topeka KS	
Survey Year >	1977		1981		1986		1986		1988		1989		1990		1990	
% Min. in Survey Year >	66%		82%		50%		59%		65%		31%		62%		29%	
Respondent Race >	WH	BL	WH	BL	WH	BL	WH	BL	WH	BL	WH	BL	WH	BL	WH	BL
Sample Size >	572	473	599	315	551	231	419	347	400	400	525	102	439	501	503	396
QUESTIONS																
Voluntary-Magnets	a	a	a	a	85%	95%	86%	87%	78%	82%	70%	73%	88%	91%	87%	88%
Voluntary-M to M	a	a	a	a	42%	65%	45%	60%	28%	54%	90%	94%	69%	73%	71%	76%
Contiguous Rezoning	a	a	a	a	54%	78%	84%	78%	20%	75%	63%	51%	43%	63%	55%	70%
Controlled Choice	a	a	a	a	a	a	a	a	a	a	37%	43%	31%	49%	31%	46%
Mandatory Reassignment with Magnets	a	a	a	a	a	a	a	a	a	a	a	a	15%	55%	35%	62%
Mandatory Reassignment for Integration	12%	68%	11%	46%	15%	51%	27%	59%	11%	65%	23%	43%	6%	38%	22%	50%

a Question not asked.
b Mandatory plan in place at time of survey.

	Mand. Plan[b] Stockton CA		Knox. Co. TN		Hartford Metro, CT		Mand. Plan[b] Baton Rouge LA		Rockford IL		Mand. Plan[b] Hattiesburg MS		Mpls./St.Paul Metro, MN		Weighted Average	
Survey Year >	1990		1991		1992		1993		1995		1998		1998			
% Min. in Survey Year >	78%		16%		37%		58%		38%		79%		22%			
Respondent Race >	WH	BL	WH	BL	WH	BL	WH	BL	WH	BL	WH	BL	WH	BL	WH	BL
Sample Size >	400	150	600	600	600	250	633	604	100	100	202	187	369	97		
QUESTIONS																
Voluntary-Magnets	91%	93%	88%	91%			90%	92%	87%	59%					85%	89%
Voluntary-M to M	73%	74%	71%	83%	67%	69%	63%	83%			82%	71%	58%	71%	64%	63%
Contiguous Rezoning	65%	67%	24%	42%											47%	60%
Controlled Choice	30%	39%	37%	42%			33%	52%	14%	40%					34%	45%
Mandatory Reassignment with Magnets	19%	41%	a	a											24%	56%
Mandatory Reassignment for Integration	a	a	8%	37%	14%	44%	11%	51%	5%	34%	28%	52%	17%	34%	13%	47%

[a] Question not asked.
[b] Mandatory plan in place at time of survey.

REFERENCES

Abney, G. 1976. Legislating morality: Attitude change and desegregation in Mississippi. *Urban Education* 11 (October): 333–38.

Armor, David J. 1995. *Forced Justice: School Desegregation And The Law*. Oxford UP.

Begley, T.M. and H.A. Alker. 1978. Attitudes and participation in anti-busing protest. Paper presented at the Annual Meeting of the American Sociological Association, San Francisco. August.

Bell, Derrick. 1976. Serving two masters: Integration ideals and client interests in school desegregation litigation. *Yale Law Journal* 85 (March): 470–516.

———. 1980. *Brown v. Board of Education* and the interest-convergence dilemma. *Harvard Law Review* 93 (January): 518–33.

Council on Legal Education for Professional Responsibility, Inc. 1974. *Lawyers, Clients & Ethics*, edited by M. Bloom. Cited in Bell (1976), note 44, p. 493.

Crain, Robert, and Christine Rossell. 1989. Catholic schools and racial segregation. In *Public Values, Private Schools*, edited by Neal Devins, 184–214. Falmer Press.

Edmonds, Ron. 1974. Advocating inequity: A Critique of the civil rights attorney in class action desegregation suits. 3 *Black Law Journal* 178 cited in Bell (1976), note 60, p. 490.

Estabrook, Leigh S. 1980. The effect of desegregation on parents' evaluation of schools. Ph.D. Dissertation, Boston University.

Giles, Michael, Douglas Gatlin, and Everett Cataldo. 1976. Determinants of resegregation: Compliance/rejection behavior and policy alternatives. Report to the National Science Foundation. Boca Raton: Florida Atlantic University.

Hayes, J.G. 1977. Anti-busing protest. Paper presented at the Annual Meeting of the North Carolina Educational Research Association. Charlotte. November.

Jackman, Mary R. 1978. General and applied tolerance: Does education increase commitment to racial integration? *American Journal of Political Science* 22(3): 302–24.

———. 1981. Education and policy commitment to racial integration. *American Journal of Political Science* 25: 256–69.

Jackman, Mary R. and Michael J. Muha. 1984. Education and intergroup attitudes: Moral enlightenment, superficial democratic commitment, or ideological refinement? *American Sociological Review* 49: 751–69.

Kinder, Donald R. and David O. Sears. 1981. Prejudice and politics: Symbolic racism vs. racial threats to the "good life." *Journal of Personality and Social Psychology* 40: 414–31.

Kirby, David J., Robert T. Harris, Robert L. Crain, and Christine H. Rossell. 1973. *Political Strategies In Northern School Desegregation*. D.C. Heath.

McConahay, John B. 1982. Self-interest versus racial attitudes as correlates of anti-busing attitudes in Louisville. *Journal of Politics* 44: 692–720.

McConahay, John B., and Willis D. Hawley. 1978. Reactions to busing in Louisville: Summary of adult opinions in 1976 and 1977. Durham: Institute of Policy Sciences and Public Affairs.

McConahay, John B., Betty B. Hardee, and Valerie Batts. 1981. Has racism declined in America? It Depends on Who Is Asking and What Is Asked. *Journal of Conflict Resolution* 25: 563–79.

Ross, J. Michael. 1977. Does school desegregation work? A quasi-experimental analysis of parental attitudes toward the effect of desegregation on student achievement. Paper presented at the Annual Meeting of the Society for the Study of Social Problems. Chicago. September.

Rossell, Christine. 1975. School desegregation and electoral conflict. In *The Polity of the School*, edited by Frederick Wirt, 49–64. Lexington Books.

———. 1978. The effect of community leadership and the mass media on public behavior. *Theory Into Practice* 17 (April): 131–39.

———. 1995. The convergence of black and white attitudes on school desegregation issues during the four decade evolution of the plans. *The William and Mary Law Review* 36(2): 613–63.

Schuman, Howard, Charlotte Steeh, and Lawrence Bobo. 1985. *Racial Attitudes in America*. Harvard UP.

Sears, David O., Carl P. Hensler and Leslie K. Speer. 1979. Whites' opposition to busing': Self-interest or symbolic politics? *American Political Science Review* 73: 369–84.

Sears, David O., Richard R. Lau, Tom R. Tyler, and Harris M. Allen Jr. 1980. Self-interest vs. symbolic politics in policy attitudes and presidential votings. *American Political Science Review* 74: 670–84.

Serow, R.C. and D. Solomon. 1979. Parents' attitudes towards desegregation: The proximity hypothesis. *Phi Delta Kappan* 60: 752–53.

Taylor, D. Garth and Arthur Stinchcombe. 1977. The Boston school desegregation controversy. Chicago: National Opinion Research Center.

Watts, Robert. 1993. Shattered dreams and nagging doubts: The declining support among black parents for school desegregation. *Emory Law Journal*, 42.3 (Summer): 891–96.

Chapter 11

The Outlook for
School Desegregation

∞

*David J. Armor, Christine H. Rossell
and Herbert J. Walberg*

Any discussion of the future of school desegregation must begin with its past and present. There are many ways in which school desegregation and the civil rights agenda were successful. First, the civil rights movement literally transformed the hearts and minds of white Americans on issues of race. In 1942, the vast majority of white Americans, and virtually all white southerners thought that blacks and whites should go to separate schools. By the mid-1980s, all but a tiny minority of the white population supported the principle of integration, and there was virtually no difference between southerners and northerners. Almost everyone now believes that racism is immoral, that racial discrimination is wrong, and that racial isolation is a social problem that should be addressed in some fashion.

Second, public school officials are now conscious of the divisive effects of past discrimination and they seek unobtrusive ways in which they can ameliorate these effects. As documented in chapter 8, in many school systems black students are less likely to be suspended for the same offense as a white student. Moreover, the greater the discretion in suspensions, the fewer the black students suspended. Chapter 7 showed that in some desegregated school districts, black students are also much more likely to be enrolled in gifted programs than are white students of the same achievement level. Even in high school honors classes, where students have considerable choice in course and program enrollment, the worst outcome we observed is that black students are no less likely to be enrolled in honors classes than are whites of the same achievement level. In short, old-fashioned racial discrimination has largely disappeared and most school districts are now interested in promoting diversity.

School desegregation has had some important failures as well. Perhaps most significant is the failure to improve the academic achievement of black students, as shown in chapter 6. In this area, too much was expected of school desegregation, particularly since academic achievement depends so heavily on socioeconomic status, which is not addressed directly by most civil rights reforms. In a democratic society based on a free-market economy, it is very difficult to change a group's economic and social status. Past racial discrimination may have produced much of the current differences in socioeconomic status, but it did so over many generations, and it may take many additional generations before socioeconomic equality is achieved.

Where do we go from here? The answer must be approached with considerable circumspection. Not that predicting the future is easy for any social policy, but school desegregation presents such a complex intertwining of institutions and values, and it has such a convoluted history that anticipating its future course is fraught with contingencies and uncertainties. Doctrinal shifts by the Supreme Court, political changes in legislative bodies, advances in social science research and education policies, and evolution of values and attitudes in the general population can all have independent effects on the future of school desegregation.

This chapter will attempt to lay out some of the plausible directions that school desegregation policies may take, taking into account the findings presented in the previous chapters and with certain critical conditions specified. Especially important in this regard are future Supreme Court interpretations of the Fourteenth Amendment, demographic changes in urban areas, better understanding of the causes of the achievement gap, and public attitudes toward schooling and the issue of diversity.

FUTURE COURT DIRECTIONS

Perhaps the most important contingency affecting the future of school desegregation is the Supreme Court's doctrine regarding liability and remedy under the Fourteenth Amendment. Considering only more recent history, chapters 2 and 3 identified several stages in the evolution of court doctrines on school desegregation: from the *Brown* decision that state-enforced segregation is inherently unequal, to the *Green* and *Swann* rulings that transformed the remedy from prohibiting discrimination to forcing integration, to the *Dowell* and *Pitts* clarifications of unitary status, and finally to the current doctrine of "strict scrutiny" for any governmental policy that makes racial distinctions. These key decisions have been turning points in the law, departing from precedents (or at least perceived precedents) and often creating controversy and confusion about exactly where these judicial policies would lead.

Both liability and remedy issues seem fairly well resolved up through the unitary status rulings. There is still some doubt and even disagreement on the part of school boards about whether and how to pursue unitary status, but the uncertainties here arise more from ideological or practical considerations at the local level than from legal principles. Chapter 3 makes it clear that the legal basis for unitary status is well-established, and while the requirements for unitary status vary somewhat from one court to another, most school districts that have implemented comprehensive desegregation plans have been able to achieve a unitary status declaration, meaning they are dismissed from any further court oversight.

Many school boards with court-ordered plans, however, are reluctant to request unitary status and would prefer to operate their court-ordered desegregation plans indefinitely. There are two reasons for this: financial and educational. On the financial side, some school boards receive financial aid from state or federal agencies because they have a desegregation plan and terminating the plan would mean the loss of funds. Money was the major reason the St. Louis and Kansas City school boards[1] opposed a unitary status motion that was filed by the state of Missouri, which was funding the desegregation plans in both districts. State money was also the reason San Jose requested only partial unitary status in 1996 and why the plaintiffs were willing to settle with the district to return to neighborhood schools without being declared unitary. In all three school districts, the plaintiffs and the school boards had the common goal of keeping the desegregation money flowing into the district.

Indeed, the fact that states have been ordered by courts to fund desegregation in a number of school districts around the country has prompted the states themselves to petition for unitary status, not only in the Missouri cases, but also in such cases as Woodland Hills, Pennsylvania, and Benton Harbor, Michigan, or to intervene on behalf of unitary status for the district as occurred in Prince George's County, Maryland, after the court appointed a panel of experts to determine if the district was in fact unitary.

On the education side, some school boards want to maintain desegregation (racial balance) plans because they believe it enhances minority education, even though research has generally not supported this view (see chapter 6). This is the reason Charlotte-Mecklenburg opposed a unitary status motion initiated by parents.[2] It was also why San Jose voluntarily entered into a settlement agreement in 1994 that detracked the curriculum and expanded the school racial-balance requirements. A new superintendent believed in the educational benefits of desegregation and heterogeneous grouping, and the school board agreed.

For these and other reasons, we believe that many school districts that currently have court-ordered desegregation plans will refuse to file for unitary status in order to maintain their plans. As long as there is parental support for the plan (or at least no significant opposition) and it is not a major financial burden, these plans can continue under court order for an indefinite period. However, if a school board makes significant and controversial changes to a desegregation plan, such as increased mandatory busing, and it is not yet unitary, then it will only be a matter of time before some party (including the district court itself) will request a unitary status hearing. All it takes for a lawsuit is one parent who is angered about their child being denied admission to a magnet school because of their race. The lawsuit requests unitary status in order to prohibit the district from using race as a basis for assignment to schools. In fact, this was the reason for the motion for unitary status in Charlotte-Mecklenburg.

A much greater uncertainty involves the application of the Supreme Court's "strict scrutiny" doctrine to post-unitary school systems that maintain desegregation plans, or perhaps to school systems that want desegregation plans for the first time. There are two major reasons for the uncertainty: the Supreme Court itself has never applied the strict scrutiny test to a post-unitary school desegregation plan, and where the Court has applied the test to prohibit racial classifications, such as in minority contractor set-asides and employment, it has usually been decided by a divided court with a 5–4 vote.

Most school districts that have been declared unitary still maintain some type of desegregation plan, which is one reason there has been little change in the desegregation indices documented in chapter 4. Sometimes plans are modified so there is greater use of voluntary desegregation techniques, such as magnet schools or open enrollment, and greater reliance on neighborhood schools; in other cases, districts keep their original plans unchanged. Examples of modified plans include Norfolk, Virginia, and Savannah, Georgia, and examples of keeping original mandatory plans for many years are the districts in the Wilmington–New Castle County, Delaware, case. Indeed, the New Castle County school districts' failure to dismantle their mandatory reassignment plans after attaining unitary status in 1995 prompted the state legislature to pass a law in 2000 that required all school districts in Delaware not under court order to have neighborhood schools. This state law has obviated the need for further litigation so far, and therefore the strict scrutiny standard has not come up.

A number of post-unitary school districts that have maintained racial quotas in magnet schools, or in schools with academic entrance requirements, have been sued by white or Asian students under the Fourteenth Amendment (so-called "reverse discrimination" cases). In some of these cases, lower courts have applied the strict scrutiny test to eliminate the racial quotas (e.g., Boston and Montgomery County, Maryland), and in other cases the school boards have entered into settlement decrees that either eliminate the quotas or severely restrict them (e.g., Houston and San Francisco). If any case like these goes to the Supreme Court, and the court upholds the application of strict scrutiny to post-unitary school policies, then school boards will be severely limited in the ways they can use race in a desegregation plan. Unquestionably, comprehensive mandatory busing plans, controlled-choice plans with racial requirements for each school, and magnet schools or other specialized schools that establish strict racial quotas will almost certainly be ruled out.

In fact, the Delaware law might serve as an example and impetus for other states where local districts are maintaining race-based school assignments after being declared unitary or never having been declared liable by a court. Whether or not the Supreme Court itself applies strict scrutiny to a school desegregation case, passing a law that prohibits the use of race in assigning students to school could be defended on fourteenth amendment grounds, analogous to civil rights laws that prohibit racial discrimination on the same fourteenth amendment grounds.

Alternatively, magnet schools that desegregate by location or subject matter, but not by quotas, and purely voluntary transfers that encourage racial balance without racial quotas (e.g., free transportation for low-income students) would most likely pass constitutional muster. Of course, school boards can always assign students to schools on the basis of nonracial geographic and economic criteria, and these characteristics could form the basis of a plan to improve desegregation without racial prescriptions.

If the Supreme Court does not apply the principle of strict scrutiny to post-unitary school systems, either because of changes in legal doctrine or changes in the court's composition, then we can expect school desegregation to continue to be an important policy in the 21st century. Many educators, social scientists, and elected officials have joined civil rights advocates in embracing the concept of diversity in schools and in the workplace, and school desegregation plans are one means of ensuring racial diversity in schools.

Of course, since some desegregation techniques, such as mandatory busing, are still very unpopular among the majority of the population (as documented in chapter 10) and not very effective (as documented in chapter 4), school boards will encounter substantial public resistance if they try to use this technique. Considering the level of opposition to mandatory busing by both black and white citizens, it is unlikely that the massive busing remedies of the 1970s would have ever occurred without the intervention of the federal courts. Even if school districts are allowed to use race in school assignment, future desegregation plans are more likely to rely on incentives for voluntary transfers, such as magnet schools, than on mandatory reassignments.

FUTURE DEMOGRAPHIC TRENDS

It is clear from the discussion in chapters 4 and 5 that demography places severe constraints on the future of school desegregation. The nation's largest school districts, which contain a large fraction of African American and Hispanic student populations, are now predominately minority. For example, nine of the ten largest central-city school districts shown in table 11.1 have white enrollments ranging from only 5 to 19 percent as of 1997; the other large district, San Diego, has only 29 percent white enrollment. These ten districts enroll fully one-fourth of the total black and Hispanic students in public schools. Adding the next largest ten or twenty central-city districts does not change the racial composition of this group very much.

Clearly, meaningful desegregation is no longer possible for the black and Hispanic students who live within our larger cities. These trends in higher racial and ethnic concentrations in the public schools are likely to persist well into the 21st century. No large central-city school district has been able to reverse the trends in racial concentration. Unless some drastic (and un-foreseen) changes occur in public school attendance, a large fraction of black and Hispanic students will attend schools with very few white students for the foreseeable future.

Chapter 5 also indicated, however, that a growing number of minorities, especially black students, are migrating out to suburban school systems that have been predominately white. This has improved desegregation in many suburban communities, particularly where moderate-cost housing is available. Unfortunately, in some metropolitan areas, the proximal suburban districts have transitioned to become predominately minority. Some examples are Yonkers, New York; Long Beach, California; Prince George's County, Maryland; and DeKalb County, Georgia.

The growing racial isolation in cities has led some desegregation advocates (e.g., Gary Orfield) to call for more interdistrict or metropolitan desegregation plans (Orfield and Eaton 1996). But overcoming the legal and political barriers to metropolitan desegregation is a near impossible task. In

Table 11.1
Racial Composition of Largest Central City School Districts, 1997–1998

DISTRICT NAME	ENROLLMENT	% WHITE
NEW YORK CITY	1,070,307	16
LOS ANGELES	680,430	11
CHICAGO	428,184	10
PHILADELPHIA	212,865	19
HOUSTON	210,988	11
DETROIT	187,502	5
DALLAS	157,622	10
SAN DIEGO	136,283	29
MEMPHIS	111,750	15
BALTIMORE	107,416	13
Average	330,335	14

chapters 2 and 3, we learned that the *Milliken* decision ended the movement to create metropolitan desegregation plans through the federal courts. Although critics often blame this on the conservative courts, the *Milliken* doctrine stands squarely on the anti-discrimination principles of *Brown*. Many civil rights activists, including Orfield, continue to espouse the principle that all school segregation should be considered illegal, regardless of cause, in spite of the fact that no Supreme Court majority, nor any other federal court, has ever endorsed this concept. Moreover, it is highly unlikely that any Supreme Court in the near future is going to find de facto segregation unconstitutional under the Fourteenth Amendment.

EDUCATION, POLITICS, AND CHOICE

Not only are there legal barriers to finding de facto segregation unconstitutional, there are political barriers as well. As noted above, one of the more important changes in attitudes has taken place among educators and school boards. In the 1970s, school boards vigorously opposed busing. But by the time courts began returning local control to them in the 1980s and 1990s, many school boards and administrators were embracing desegregation under the broad umbrella of "diversity" goals. Promoting diversity has been a primary justification for keeping desegregation plans after unitary status (e.g., Boston and Houston) or refusing to seek unitary status (e.g., Charlotte-Mecklenburg and San Francisco).

The first major appearance of the diversity concept was in the *Bakke* decision, in a plurality opinion written by Justice Powell. By elevating diversity to a "compelling governmental purpose" when it came to graduate or professional schools, the *Bakke* decision led to decades of affirmative-action plans in higher education that are still being debated by courts, legislatures, and the public at large. Unfortunately for diversity advocates, a Supreme Court majority never agreed with Powell, and the current doctrine of strict scrutiny gives short shrift to governmental goals of diversity.

Nonetheless, diversity and affirmative-action goals are supported by the public at large, although majority support is generally found only for the broad goals of diversity and integration. When specific methods for attaining these goals are mentioned, such as busing for racial balance or racial preferences in hiring or admissions, public support declines dramatically. Support for racial balance and busing is usually found only among educators, a handful of intellectuals, and some elected officials, most of whom are Democrats.

Because metropolitan desegregation seems to have no future in the federal courts, some civil rights groups have filed suits in state courts in an attempt to further interdistrict integration. As discussed in chapter 3, some state constitutions have guarantees to equal educational opportunity, something not found in the U.S. Constitution. In addition, some state supreme courts (e.g., New Jersey and Connecticut) have interpreted their equal-protection clauses more broadly than the U.S. Supreme Court. In Hartford, Connecticut, the plaintiffs lost on the violation issue at the local superior court level, but won in the state supreme court. The state supreme court, however, gave the state legislature the job of devising a remedy. Not surprisingly, the elected state legislature did not devise the metropolitan racial-balance plan requested by the plaintiffs, but rather increased its funding of voluntary measures that included enhancements to a pre-existing interdistrict voluntary busing plan and funding for additional magnet schools located in the metropolitan areas of New Haven, Waterbury, and Hartford. A similar outcome occurred in a Minneapolis lawsuit, where Minnesota was sued for city–suburban segregation under the state constitution. The Minneapolis lawsuit was settled out of court, and once again the settlement does not include a comprehensive metropolitan racial-balance plan. It requires the state government to enhance an existing open-enrollment plan, so that suburban districts will accept more transfers from the city because of financial incentives. Interestingly, to avoid federal litigation under strict scrutiny, the state intentionally omitted racial quotas or guidelines from the expanded Minneapolis open-enrollment plan.

It is unlikely that either the Hartford or the Minneapolis plans will substantially increase integration in the suburbs, nor will they reduce racial isolation in the cities. Unlike federal courts and the U.S. Constitution, state courts and constitutions are more likely to be influenced by the normal political processes. Certainly state legislatures, when asked to devise a remedy, are not likely to embrace extensive, racial-balance, city–suburban desegregation plans (especially with mandatory busing) either because of the cost of such a plan or the extent of local suburban opposition. Even if a state court or legislature adopted a broad plan, it would undoubtedly be rejected by the public through a state constitutional amendment. For all of these reasons, it does not appear that litigation through state courts is going to have any major impact on city–suburban segregation.

Educators and civil rights advocates try to change public opinion with the argument that school desegregation has both educational and social benefits. As we saw in chapter 6, however, the black–white achievement gap has not changed much as a result of desegregation, and indeed it remains large even in highly balanced school systems that experienced only moderate levels of white flight, such as Charlotte-Mecklenburg, North Carolina, and Wilmington–New Castle County, Delaware. It is hard to convince the public, and especially African American parents who often bear the busing burden, that they should support city–suburban desegregation plans when there are no clear educational benefits for their children at the end of the bus ride.

The research on the social benefits from desegregation has not been that much more favorable, although chapter 9 does lay out a framework for enhancing intergroup relations as part of a desegregation plan. While there are undoubtedly many individuals, both minority and white, who receive social benefits from desegregation, it is unlikely that these social benefits, even if they could be enhanced, will outweigh the social and political costs of distance, parental access, political controversy, and lack of educational benefits associated with most comprehensive desegregation plans.

So what can be done, what should be done about the racial and ethnic isolation in our urban centers? Is this a social problem that needs remedy, and if so, are there policy options that are promising and that have a chance of winning broad public support? We believe that racial and ethnic isolation is a social problem worth addressing, but that the research shows that the policies of the past, such as racial quotas and massive busing, would be counterproductive. In short, their costs would outweigh their benefits. There are some other educational policy options that have received substantial public support and that are better tailored to the school quality problems that the public is concerned about.

First, there has been substantial public and legislative support for compensatory programs, such as preschool programs and Title 1, which are now well targeted to bring extra financial aid to high-poverty, low-achieving students and schools. A recent Gallup Poll surveyed a national sample of adults about the best way to help minority students. When asked to choose between integrating minority students with more white students or increasing funding for minority schools, 60 percent supported an increase in minority school funding and only 26 percent supported increasing integration efforts (Gillespie 1999).

Second, public opinion surveys suggest that most minority parents want what most white parents want—good education provided in their local schools. Compensatory programs are designed to do this. However, not all minority parents think their local school is up to par or many believe their child would do better in an integrated environment. Unlike middle-class white parents, who can move to another school system or use private schools when they are dissatisfied with their local school, minority parents often lack the resources to choose either of these options. We think these minority parents should be offered the same choices available to middle-class white parents, with government assistance if necessary.

School-choice programs such as interdistrict transfers (open enrollment), charter schools, or voucher programs, including vouchers for private and parochial schools, are ideally suited to solving this problem. Most of these programs enjoy broad popular support among white and minority families, unlike mandatory busing, controlled choice, or other policies that are based primarily on racial quotas.

Open-enrollment programs have been adopted by a number of states including Iowa, Massachusetts, Minnesota, Ohio, Washington, and many others (Armor and Peiser 1997). Open-enrollment programs can aid integration between cities and suburbs by offering transportation subsidies to low-income families, thus including many, if not most inner-city minority families. By basing assistance on income rather than race, open enrollment and other choice policies can avoid the problem of federal litigation under the strict scrutiny rule.

Charter schools are one of the fastest-growing choice options, with over 2,000 charter schools in 35 states and enrolling over 500,000 students (Center for Educational Reform 2000). Arizona, California, Michigan, and Texas now have hundreds of charter schools, and many other states have dozens. Although charter schools may or may not be fully desegregated, they do offer a meaningful alternative to minority parents who are not satisfied with their local school. As more states pass charter laws and expand the number of charter schools available, this may become the most popular choice program of all, at least in the near future.

State-funded voucher programs for private and parochial schools remain a more controversial option, although there have been some local successes in Milwaukee and Cleveland. Voucher programs are strongly opposed by teachers unions, particularly when proposed on statewide ballot initiatives, and they are often defeated when offered in that format. Some of the largest voucher programs are privately funded, as for example, the voucher programs targeted for low-income families in Dayton, New York City, and San Antonio. In spite of the controversy, the voucher concept still enjoys popular support, especially among minority families. There is no shortage of minority applicants, and most of these programs have long waiting lists.

None of these expanded choice programs are going to eliminate the racial and ethnic isolation in major urban school systems in the near future. As they expand, however, they will continue to offer meaningful alternatives to those minority families who are displeased with their local public school, without the disruptive and counterproductive consequences of large-scale desegregation plans.

We believe that those families who would choose an integrated or an alternative school should not only be able do so, but are the most likely to benefit from it. People who choose a course of action are more likely to be committed to making it work and more likely to be satisfied with the results of their action. They are also more likely to be accepted and to feel accepted. A major problem with the forced racial-balance plans of the last four decades was that they had a dual burden—racial integration and economic integration. To some degree, this was by design, because it was thought that greater educational benefits would flow from economic as well as racial integration, but it also made it more difficult to produce equal-status contact between the races. Schools of choice create new school communities where equal-status contact has a better chance of occurring and both black and white parents are committed to enhancing their child's educational experience.

The promise of *Brown* was that black students would have the same freedom and the same educational opportunities as white students. The policies we endorse here are slower and more indirect than the massive, mandatory reassignment plans of the last four decades, but by relying on the conscious decisions of all families, they are more likely to fulfill the promise of *Brown*.

ENDNOTES

1. Kansas City also collected a special tax to support school desegregation that was levied on individuals who worked in the city. They would lose that money if declared unitary.

2. *Capacchione at al. v. Charlotte-Mecklenburg Schools et al.*, 57 F. Supp. 2d 228: 9 September 1999.

REFERENCES

Armor, David J. and Brett M. Peiser. 1997, *Competition in Education: A Case Study of Interdistrict Choice*. Boston: Pioneer Institute.

Center for Educational Reform. 2000. Charter school ranks swell. 17 August. Washington, D.C.

Gillespie, M. 1999. Americans want integrated schools, but oppose school busing. Princeton: Gallup News Service. 27 September.

Orfield, Gary and Susan Eaton. 1996. *Dismantling Desegregation*. New York: New Press.

Subject Index

Index of Court Cases

About the Contributors

Christine H. Rossell is the Maxwell Professor of Political Science at Boston University. Her research interests include school desegregation, bilingual education, and educational policy. She has written five books—four on school desegregation and one on bilingual education, *Bilingual Education in Massachusetts: The Emperior Has No Clothes* (1996). She has published sixty articles and seventy reports on school desegregation, bilingual education, and other educational issues for scholarly journals and edited books, has been a consultant to parties and/or expert witness in almost fifty school desegregation and/or bilingual education cases, and has helped design and defend eleven voluntary "incentive" desegregation plans and numerous public opinion surveys.

David J. Armor is a professor of public policy in the School of Public Policy at George Mason University, Fairfax, Virginia. He teaches graduate courses in statistics and social policy and conducts research in the fields of education, race, and cognitive ability. His publications include *Forced Justice: School Desegregation and the Law* (1995). He has testified as an expert witness in more than forty school desegregation cases.

Herbert J. Walberg is University Scholar and Emeritus Research Professor of Education and Psychology at the University of Illinois at Chicago and Distinguished Visiting Fellow at the Stanford University Hoover Institution. Since 1962, he has investigated psychological conditions and educational policies and practices that foster learning and other human accomplishments. He has written or edited more than fifty books and written approximately 350 papers for educational and psychological journals. A fellow of five American, British, and international scholarly societies, Walberg often testifies before congressional and state legislative committees and federal and state courts. His latest edited book is *School Accountability*.

Charles M. Achilles is professor of education leadership at Eastern Michigan University, Ypsilanti, and Seton Hall University, South Orange, New Jersey (both on a part-time basis). Recent books include *Let's Put Kids First, Finally: Getting Class Size Right* (1999) and *Problem Analysis* (1997). He has conducted class-size studies since 1984. He has several areas of research interest including class size and student outcomes, preparation of education administrators, public confidence in schools, student behavior, and teacher/student classroom communications. Besides authored or co-authored books and chapters on the above topics, he has more than 300 contributions to the professional literature, including studies in the ERIC database.

William A.V. Clark is professor of geography at the University of California–Los Angeles. His research is focused on understanding and modeling population change in large U.S. cities, especially neighborhood demographic change. Two recent books are *Households and Housing: Choice and Outcomes in the Housing Market* (1996) and *The California Cauldron: Immigration and the Fortunes of Local Communities* (1998). He has an honorary doctorate from the University of Utrecht, a DSc from the University of Auckland, New Zealand, and in 1994–95 he held a John Simon Guggenheim Fellowship. In 1997 he was elected an Honorary Fellow of the Royal Society of New Zealand.

Alfred A. Lindseth is a partner with the law firm of Sutherland Asbill & Brennan leading the firm's education law practice. He is a frequent speaker and writer on education law issues and has more than twenty-five years of experience in representing states and school districts in major school desegregation and educational adequacy cases, including the states of New York, California, Florida, Connecticut, Minnesota, Michigan, and Missouri and large school districts in Maryland, Tennessee, Missouri, Florida, South Carolina, Washington, North Carolina, and Georgia. Mr. Lindseth is a graduate of the United States Military Academy and the Harvard Law School.

Jeffrey A. Raffel is the Charles P. Messick Professor of Public Administration and director of the School of Urban Affairs and Public Policy at the University of Delaware. Dr. Raffel's research interests include state and local management (e.g., privatization), and educational policy issues such as school desegregation and teacher recruitment and retention. His books include *Selling Cities: Attracting Homebuyers through Schools and Housing Programs, The Politics of School Desegregation: The Metropolitan Remedy in Delaware,* and *Historical Dictionary of School Segregation and Desegregation: The American Experience*. He has written more than thirty articles and book chapters and has served as a researcher, scholar, expert witness, practitioner, community leader, and parent in the school desegregation process.

Walter G. Stephan received his Ph.D. in psychology from the University of Minnesota in 1971. He has taught at the University of Texas at Austin and at New Mexico State University, where he holds the rank of professor. He has published more than one hundred articles on attribution processes, cognition and affect, intergroup relations, and intercultural relations. His most recent books include *Reducing Prejudice and Stereotyping in Schools* (1999), *Improving Intergroup Relations* (with Cookie White Stephan; 2001), and *Intergroup Relations Programs: Practice, Research, and Theory* (with Paul Vogt, forthcoming). In 1996 he won the Klineberg award for intercultural relations given by Division 9 of the American Psychological Association.